Using the IBM Personal Computer: WordStar™

IBM PERSONAL COMPUTER SERIES

Programming

N. Graham   PROGRAMMING THE IBM PERSONAL COMPUTER: BASIC

N. Graham   PROGRAMMING THE IBM PERSONAL COMPUTER: PASCAL

R. Rouse and T. Bugnitz   PROGRAMMING THE IBM PERSONAL COMPUTER: FORTRAN 77

S. V. Pollack   PROGRAMMING THE IBM PERSONAL COMPUTER: UCSD PASCAL

R. Rouse and T. Bugnitz   PROGRAMMING THE IBM PERSONAL COMPUTER: UCSD p-SYSTEM WITH FORTRAN 77

S. V. Pollack, R. Rouse, and T. Bugnitz   PROGRAMMING THE IBM PERSONAL COMPUTER: UCSD p-SYSTEM WITH UCSD PASCAL AND FORTRAN 77

Functions and Applications

D. Cortesi   YOUR IBM PERSONAL COMPUTER: USE, APPLICATIONS, AND BASIC

R. Crowley   USING THE IBM PERSONAL COMPUTER: VISICALC®

M. Franklin   USING THE IBM PERSONAL COMPUTER: MACRO-ASSEMBLER

CJ Puotinen   USING THE IBM PERSONAL COMPUTER: WORDSTAR™

J. Posdamer   USING THE IBM PERSONAL COMPUTER: GRAPHICS

Using the IBM Personal Computer: WORDSTAR™

CJ Puotinen

HOLT, RINEHART and WINSTON

New York Chicago San Francisco Philadelphia Montreal Toronto London Sydney Tokyo Mexico City Rio de Janeiro Madrid

This guide was written for WordStar version 3.2 (1982) and for the IBM Personal Computer Disk Operating System (IBM DOS) version 1.1 (1981, 1982).

It assumes that your IBM Personal Computer consists of an IBM Monochrome Display Monitor, an IBM Personal Computer System Unit incorporating Dual Disk Drives or a Single Disk Drive, an IBM Personal Computer Keyboard, and an IBM Matrix Printer or other compatible printer.

See Appendix D for information regarding WordStar version 3.3.

The cover illustration is The Additive Color Model from Miles Color Art, Tallahassee, Florida, prepared using the Digital Facsimiles process (patent pending), Center for Color Graphics, Florida State University, Tallahassee, Florida.

First distributed to the trade in 1983
by Holt, Rinehart and Winston General Book Division.

Address correspondence to:
383 Madison Avenue, New York, NY 10017

Library of Congress Cataloging in Publication Data

Puotinen, CJ
Using the IBM Personal Computer.

Includes index.
1. WordStar (Computer program) 2. IBM Personal Computer—Programming. I. Title.
HF5548.115.P86 1983 652 83-8410

ISBN 0-03-062857-1

Printed in the United States of America

Published simultaneously in Canada

4 5 6 039 4 3 2

CBS COLLEGE PUBLISHING
Holt, Rinehart and Winston
The Dryden Press
Saunders College Publishing

Acknowledgments

My husband, Dr. Joel Hollenberg, is a Professor of Mechanical Engineering at The Cooper Union School of Engineering in New York City, and it was for his laboratory students that I wrote the first version of what became this book.

I owe a debt of gratitude to Dr. Shunil Roy of Computer Systems International for recommending the manuscript's publication; to Dean Chor Weng Tan for his encouragement; and to a number of Cooper Union students for their suggestions.

In addition, Bill Usim and Jim Butcher improved the book's organization through their suggestions. Tony Estep of Idea Ware in New York City patiently answered my questions about the IBM PC and programming. Steve Goldschmidt and his ComputerLand staff in Totowa, New Jersey, provided information for the single-drive user. And Brete Harrison, my editor, made the project both possible and pleasant. To each, many thanks.

Last, let me acknowledge the important contributions of my office staff: the previously mentioned Dr. Hollenberg, who introduced me to computers, patiently taught me how to get along with them, and now delights in the consequences; and our teenaged cats, Hang Twelve and Kanga, experienced editorial assistants and therapists.

Contents

Introduction

If you are new to computers and if you are like most people, you may spend some frustrating moments adjusting your mind, eyes, and hands to the machine and system that await you. That often-heard advice from your childhood, "Be patient," applies now more than ever.

Computers change the way you think. The more you work with your computer, the more your thought processes will shift. You will no longer approach editing tasks with the same mental steps you use now. At first, some of the computer's demands may seem unnecessarily complicated and cumbersome, but with time (and not much of that), you'll be "thinking with" your electronic servant.

Of all the new concepts facing you, one of the most difficult to adjust to is this simple fact: The computer will do exactly what you tell it to do. But what you tell it to do may not be what you mean, and therein lies a problem. You must enter commands with care; you cannot make typographical errors and expect the computer to ignore them; and you must say exactly what you intend to when you issue instructions. All of this requires a shifting of mental gears.

As you become acquainted with the system, you may sympathize with the story reported about a police station and its local computer store. "Come get your computer," said the man at the desk. "It's dead." "We'll send a repairperson," offered the store manager. "No," came the reply. "Come get it, it's dead." And it was. Someone had shot the terminal screen with a revolver.

A Japanese bicycle company offered this philosophy in its do-it-yourself instruction booklet: "In order to assemble Japanese bicycle, it is necessary to have peace of mind." In order to work with WordStar, you will need some peace of mind, too. Don't work when you're tired or distracted. Telephones and visitors create frustrating interruptions, so try to short-circuit them. A well-placed "Do Not Disturb" sign, disconnected telephone, or pair of earplugs can improve your concentration.

At the same time, schedule frequent breaks from your new task. Computers are seductive. They generate "time warps" as they growl, hum, click, and blink. You may think 15 minutes have passed when the clock shows two hours, or you might forget appointments because you lose track of the time.

Memory experts report that the fastest way to learn something new is to interrupt yourself often and let your mind rest; then review before resuming. Physical breaks are as important as mental ones. Stand up and stretch, walk around your desk, look out the window, get some fresh air. Sitting at a terminal is hard on your eyes and shoulders, so don't plan marathon practice sessions. Do some exercises, let your eyes relax, review your work away from the computer, and take as much time as you need to understand a section before going on.

While it's true that WordStar is a "hands on" tool—experience at the terminal is what matters—it is also true that the more you study the system, the more productive your sessions at the terminal will be. WordStar is very logical, its commands are easy to remember and even easier to use, and in no time you'll be arranging and rearranging ambitious documents, technical reports, tables, business correspondence, and manuscripts. Soon you'll enjoy a new peace of mind, the kind your computer can provide, and it is appropriate to mention a few things that will keep your computer happy, too.

Computers don't like smoke, so keep cigarettes and cigars away from the monitor, disks, and disk drives. They don't like heat, so air-condition your room in warm weather. Computers don't like static electricity, so have a static-free mat installed over your carpet and use one of the widely available antistatic sprays to keep yourself and your equipment from generating electrical charges. It goes without saying that your computer doesn't like coffee in its disk drives, pastry crumbs in its keyboard, or cockroaches in the printer. Don't laugh. Computer repairpeople regularly complain about the unhappy results of poor computer housekeeping.

And respect your disks. Disks are fragile and sensitive. Handle them with care, keep them neatly filed in a disk holder, protect them from extremes of hot and cold, don't store them on top of the terminal, don't bend them, and keep them away from magnets. Disks have been erased because they spent a few hours under magnetized scissors, magnetic jewelry, memo magnets, or the magnet of a typist's copy holder. Pocket calculators and tape recorders are other potential sources of electromagnetic waves.

Your computer is a powerful tool. In a short time you'll think of it as a powerful friend as well. We hope this manual will speed and enhance your friendship.

Note

This book was designed to accompany, not replace, the WordStar manual and the IBM Personal Computer manuals. No installation instructions are provided here; it is assumed that your IBM Personal Computer includes a properly installed WordStar program. This manual describes word processing, not computer program writing and editing.

Note that throughout this guide, the following abbreviations are used:

^ represents the CONTROL KEY, marked Ctrl on your keyboard.

@ represents the RETURN KEY, marked with a downward left arrow ↵ on your keyboard.

This guide was written for WordStar version 3.2 (1982). For information describing WordStar version 3.3 (1983), see Appendix D.

WordStar is manufactured by MicroPro International Corporation, 1299 Fourth Street, San Rafael, California 94901. WordStar is a registered trademark.

This guide was written for the IBM Personal Computer Disk Operating System (IBM DOS) version 1.1 (1981, 1982), which uses single-sided or double-sided, double-density soft sector 5 1/4-inch disks.

IBM stands for International Business Machines Corporation, Boca Raton, Florida 33432.

This manual assumes that your IBM Personal Computer consists of an IBM Monochrome Display Monitor, an IBM Personal Computer System Unit incorporating Dual Disk Drives or a Single Disk Drive, an IBM Personal Computer Keyboard, and an IBM Matrix Printer or other compatible printer.

Throughout this guide, "IBM Personal Computer" will be abbreviated "IBM PC."

Although this book emphasizes the 64K IBM PC system, it includes information for WordStar users whose systems have additional memory. Commands and instructions for the IBM 80 CPS Printer are clearly labeled, as are commands and instructions for incremental (daisy wheel or thimble) printers.

Using the IBM Personal Computer: WordStar™

1

Meeting Your IBM Personal Computer

Your IBM Personal Computer system consists of several component parts, each with its own name. While you don't have to know the language of computers to work with WordStar, knowing the most basic terms will help you understand the system and its operation. As a fringe benefit, you'll have an easier time conversing with people who speak Computerbabble, a colorful tongue filled with strange and wonderful phrases.

HARDWARE refers to the physical parts of a computer system which enable it to perform computing functions. The integrated circuits or silicon chips that arrange electrical pulses into meaningful patterns are the heart (or brain) of the system. These circuits and their electrical and mechanical support systems make up the computer's hardware.

SOFTWARE refers to the programs that make your computer work. WordStar is a particular program designed to do word processing; it operates in conjunction with other software, such as the computer's operating system.

PERIPHERAL EQUIPMENT includes the other units that operate with the computer: its disk drives, printer, and monitor.

The SYSTEM UNIT contains your computer's circuit boards, which store and process information and control the computer's input and output. The IBM PC's disk drives are at the front of this unit.

DISK DRIVES are electromechanical devices that control disks so the computer has access to their encoded information and so the computer can enter new information or remove old material. If yours is a dual disk drive unit, the drives are arranged side by side, with the left drive labeled Drive A and the right drive Drive B. If yours is a single drive unit, Drive A is your only disk drive. Each disk drive has a door that locks or snaps shut and a red indicator light that comes on whenever the computer records material onto or retrieves information from a disk.

DISKS or DISKETTES are small plastic magnetic "records" measuring 5 1/4 inches or 8 inches in diameter. Disks are manufactured in various combinations of sectors, sides, and densities. Your IBM PC uses 5 1/4-inch single-sided or double-sided, double-density soft sector disks. When buying new disks, be sure to order the right kind for your system.

A FORMATTED DISK is one that has been prepared by the computer's operating system to receive information. Before you can use a new disk for file storage, it has to be formatted.

The LOGGED DISK DRIVE is the drive in use at the moment. Similarly, the LOGGED DISK is the disk in that drive. Both WordStar and DOS (the IBM Disk Operating System) have simple commands for changing the logged drive from A to B and vice versa, and to other drives in systems using more than two.

The MONITOR consists of a television-like video screen called a CRT, which stands for cathode ray tube. The computer displays your text and other information on the CRT. Your IBM PC monitor features green letters on a dark gray background. You can control the brightness of these letters, and you can also change the contrast between the screen's regular (bright) and highlighted (dim) letters with the control knobs at the screen's right.

Like most screens used for word processing, the IBM PC monitor screen displays 24 lines of 80 column/spaces. As two lines are taken up by WordStar's status and ruler (editorial reference) lines, this leaves 22 lines for text.

Your KEYBOARD is separate from the monitor and system unit. You'll be most comfortable using your IBM PC if you experiment with the keyboard's position and angle. In most cases, the system unit stands behind the keyboard, and the monitor sits on top of the system unit.

The computer's keyboard is similar to a typewriter keyboard except that it features a number of extra keys. As you study word processing, you should understand that WordStar software operates on a wide variety of computers, not all of which have the IBM PC's keyboard. When WordStar was adapted for use on the IBM PC, this computer's special keys were given specific command functions. However, WordStar's on-screen command reviews continue to list the "regular" WordStar command codes, not the IBM PC alternatives. Both command code systems are described in this book.

For a complete description of the IBM PC keyboard and its application to WordStar word processing, see Chapter 6, page 57–58.

The PRINTER is your computer's typing element. It looks like the top half of a typewriter, with its platen (paper roller) and carriage. Paper is fed through the carriage one page at a time or in a long, accordian-folded continuous sheet.

Your printer may be the IBM 80 CPS Matrix Printer. CPS stands for for "characters per second," which translates to about 960 words per minute. That's an impressive typing speed! Matrix printers work with a printing head consisting of several stiff rods positioned perpendicularly to the paper. Each rod or needle makes a tiny dot when it hits ribbon against paper, which is why this type is called a "dot matrix" printer. Individual dots combine to form letters, numbers, and other characters. This is called a NONINCREMENTAL PRINTER because it does not microjustify characters across the pages, shift the carriage a fraction of an inch for the printing of subscripts and superscripts, change character width, or change line height.

Daisy wheel and thimble printers work at a slower rate but produce a better or "letter quality" type. Characters are stored on replaceable typing elements shaped like a flat daisy or thimble-like cup, with letters on individual spokes. Daisy wheel and thimble printers are good for final copies, business correspondence, proposals, etc. These are INCREMENTAL PRINTERS because they support fractional adjustments of line height, character width, subscript and superscript position, and microjustification of characters across the page.

INPUT is anything you supply to the computer in the way of programs and entries. You'll see the word ENTER whenever commands are mentioned. To enter a command (part of your input), press the appropriate keys.

OUTPUT is what the computer produces with your entered material. HARD COPY is printed output, that is, the printed result or product.

RAM stands for random access memory, and it describes the amount of information storage space your system provides. A computer needs 64K RAM in order to run WordStar. 64K means 64×2^{10} "bytes," and each byte represents a "word" of a prescribed number of digits. Your IBM Personal Computer has at least a 64K memory. If you supplied additional memory when you purchased your system (128K, 192K, or 256K), you enjoy certain advantages over the IBM PC/WordStar user who has only 64K to work with. Some WordStar commands are easier to execute with additional memory, but nearly all WordStar procedures can be done on the 64K system.

The PROMPT is a screen signal (>) that appears when the logged drive first comes on and when you return to the computer's operating system. A> (A Prompt) means that A is the logged drive and that the computer is waiting for a program command, such as the code initiating WordStar. B> (B Prompt) means that Drive B is the logged disk drive, and the computer is waiting for an instruction. To initiate WordStar or any other program, the appropriate disk must be in the logged drive. Drive A is on the left and Drive B on the right.

The computer's OPERATING SYSTEM organizes the way in which information is entered onto or removed from the disks. WordStar is usually run with CP/M, which stands for Control Program for Microprocessors (CP/M is a trademark of Digital Research, Pacific Grove, California), but it was adapted for use with the IBM Personal Computer Disk Operating System. All of the disk operating system commands mentioned in this book describe the IBM PC Disk Operating System (DOS).

2

WordStar's Basic Features

What will WordStar do to make your life easier? Nearly everything you can think of — and some things you haven't yet imagined.

One advantage is the way WordStar rearranges documents at a keystroke. For the author, editor, or secretary who has to revise material, the editing commands mean hours of saved time.

Consider the evolution of a technical paper. Its first draft, some 30 pages with footnotes and bibliography, is typed into the computer, stored on disk and printed for proofreading. The author decides to replace one key word, which appears 53 times, with a better word. He wants to move a section from the middle to the front. He adds three bibliography entries and deletes a footnote. There are numerous typos to correct, and the author composes a lengthy addition to the introduction.

On a typewriter these corrections would take half a day's labor. In fact, the entire paper would have to be retyped. On the computer such revisions are simple — even the shifting of whole pages, the changing of footnotes, and the replacement of one word with another are easy. With the corrections made, the author has a new clean copy to consider. He makes a few minor adjustments and prints a perfect copy. But the story isn't over. The paper, once submitted to a technical journal, goes out for review. Several months pass and now the journal's editor requires these changes: replacing all round brackets with square brackets, revising the bibliography's format, deleting crossed-out phrases, incorporating penned-in corrections, and typing the final camera-ready report on special paper mats. Someone working "by hand" would be typing the paper a fourth time, each edition an opportunity for new errors and omissions. But the word processing typist enters only specified corrections and new material. Most of the document remains unchanged, despite dramatic differences in its final appearance.

As you work with WordStar, you'll encounter a whole new vocabulary. Some of its words are common to the computer industry and others are unique to WordStar. Here is an introduction.

MENUS

Menus are lists of features, rather like the list of dishes in a restaurant. WordStar's Main Menu shows the system's basic cursor-moving and editing commands, but there are other menus to chose from. The Quick Menu lists commands that rapidly move you to specified parts of the document. The program's Block Menu displays text-manipulating codes, called "block" commands because they mark and then move or change sections (blocks) of text. WordStar's On-screen Menu describes format revisions, such as changing the line spacing, margins, and tab stops. Its Print Menu reviews special effects created by the printer, such as underlining, boldface print, subscripts, superscripts, and overprinting. The Help Menu lists a wide assortment of on-screen explanations and reviews.

WordStar's menus are optional. The Main Menu appears "by default" or automatically; other menus are called for when needed. All are easy to remove for maximum screen space.

FILES

If you think of disks as miniature file cabinets, the concept of "files" is easy to understand. Like the files in a drawer, disk files carry names or labels. Each file can contain anything from a single line of information to a long document. And again like the files in your cabinet, they're easy to rearrange. You can delete, add, and reorganize material within a file. The disk is a file "drawer" whose space is limited; a single disk can hold dozens of short files or one very long one.

As mentioned, files have names. Only your imagination and the requirements of WordStar limit your selection of file names. When you start a file, the screen will remind you that a file name consists of one to eight letters and/or digits, followed by (optional) a period and (optional) up to three additional characters.

A file name can be one letter or number or symbol long (for example, A or % or 3), or it can be as long as DOMINOES.7B&, or any other combination of eight characters followed by a period and three more characters.

It makes sense to name your files so they will be easy to recognize. When you're working with just a few files you'll remember them all, but let several months go by and you'll wonder over every cryptic notation.

When you call up WordStar and obtain the No-File Menu, a directory of the logged disk's contents will appear on the screen. Each disk has a label you can use to note file names (be sure to use a felt tip marker and not a pencil or ball point pen when writing on a label attached to a disk); most disk holders and jackets have space for recording file contents as well.

WordStar offers two kinds of files. The Document File is the one you'll use in word processing. When you work in WordStar's document file mode, the computer sets the right margin, separates your text into pages and creates a regular "document," hence the name. A Non-Document File doesn't recognize pages or right margins. This format is convenient for the person writing computer programs or creating other long lists of statements.

COMMANDS

Commands are coded keystrokes that instruct the computer to execute certain maneuvers. WordStar commands are simple to enter and most involve the CONTROL (CTRL) key in combination with one or two letter keys. Because the IBM PC provides two additional keyboards (the F-Function keys at left and the numeric keyboard at right), some WordStar commands are entered directly, without using the CONTROL key.

There are commands for moving within a document, for deleting and changing material, for rearranging the text, for storing or saving material, for printing, and so forth. The list of WordStar commands may seem formidable, but after a few weeks on the system you'll remember most of them. That's because nearly every command is named for its relation to the keyboard (up, down, right, left) or for letters in its name.

Editing commands are those dealing with the cursor and its motion, the entering and changing of text, and the saving or storing of text.

THE CURSOR

You'll notice a flashing underline dash (_) on the screen. It's illustrated here and in the WordStar manual as ■. (Because we can't make the _ symbol flash and blink on paper, the ■ stands out more.) This is the cursor. It moves across the screen at your direction and points to where you are in the document. If you're about to insert a new character or make a change, the cursor's position shows where the next character will go.

As you work with WordStar you will notice that cursor-moving commands operate only within a file, not outside of it. When you start a new file you'll have to enter material into that file before the commands for moving the cursor left, right, up, or down will work. When you reach the end of a file, the cursor will not move farther.

ON-SCREEN FORMATTING

This is the phrase WordStar uses for its physical arrangement of a document, features that are displayed on the screen: the setting of margins and paragraph tabs, the centering of lines, resetting of type, and similar adjustments. Not all word processing programs display such format changes on the computer's screen; with many, you have to wait until a file is printed to see what it looks like. Most of WordStar's text-formatting commands consist of the CONTROL key (Ctrl) entered with two letter keys.

HELP SYSTEM

WordStar provides a comprehensive system of visual cues in abbreviated form at the top of the screen. The new user may find these memory jogs convenient because they explain various commands without reference to an instruction manual; however, because the on-screen summaries don't describe the special IBM PC keys you can use with WordStar, you may want to refer instead to the Condensed Command Index printed inside the back cover of this manual.

WordStar offers different degrees of "help." The maximum amount of information (help level 3) appears automatically and covers the upper screen. A person who wants to see more of his or her own material will find it easy to remove help notations from the screen. They can be recalled with a simple command.

HIGHLIGHTING

Highlighting calls attention to words, sections of text, special hyphens, and other screen notation by displaying characters in faint light. A highlighted section of text is ready to be moved somewhere or copied or deleted. A highlighted hyphen will not print if it appears in the middle of a line; it has to be at the end of a line to show on the printed page. Certain screen notations, like markers and information lines, appear highlighted as well. Highlighting calls attention to an unusual or special word, section, or hyphen.

You can increase or decrease the contrast between highlighted and nonhighlighted screen characters by turning the upper knob to the right of the screen. The lower knob increases or reduces the brightness of screen characters. At night you will probably want to reduce the brightness of screen letters, while during the daytime you will want to increase it.

DEFAULT

WordStar offers an overwhelming number of choices regarding page length, character width, line spacing, margin justification, and other specifics. To simplify matters, WordStar uses "default values" that preset the system. You can enter whatever changes you like, but until you do so, WordStar reverts to a standard format "by default." Unless your work involves special forms, legal-sized paper, or other variations from the norm, you'll find default values convenient as they are preset for the standard 8 1/2 × 11-inch page.

WORD WRAP

Word wrap is WordStar's term for the way the computer carries a word from the end of a line to the beginning of the next line, automatically setting the right margin. On a regular typewriter you do this manually by using the carriage return to reposition the paper or typing element. Word wrap causes the words themselves to move.

PARAGRAPH REFORM AND HYPHEN-HELP

Another convenient WordStar feature is its paragraph reform command. You can edit a document by changing text, removing words, adding new material, and altering the line spacing or margin width, and then use a single command to arrange the paragraphs correctly, realigning the margins and line spacing. When this command is executing, the cursor may stop at the end of a line within a multisyllable word, asking whether you want to hyphenate the word at that point. If so, press - and the word is hyphenated. This automatic feature is called hyphen-help.

SOFT AND HARD SPACES, HYPHENS, AND RETURNS

In WordStar's vernacular, "soft" spaces are arranged by the computer to spread words across a line as its sets the right margin. These are not permanent spaces; during editing or paragraph reforming, they can be widened or removed. A "hard" space is created by the space bar, which enters one hard space at a time, or by the TAB key, which enters hard spaces from the cursor to the next tab stop. The computer remembers and preserves every hard space no matter how the document may be edited.

A "hard" hyphen is entered by pressing the - key when operating WordStar in its regular mode. This hyphen appears in bright light, matching other letters on the screen. It will always print. A "soft" hyphen is entered by hyphen-help, or entered by you while using a special command. Soft hyphens are highlighted and they print only if positioned at the end of a line. Soft hyphens in the middle of a line will not print, even though they appear on-screen.

You enter "hard" line breaks when you press RETURN, just as you do with the carriage return key or lever on a regular typewriter. The computer remembers and preserves all hard returns. They are not affected by editing or paragraph reforming. "Soft" returns are set by word wrap as it adjusts the right margin and brings a word down to the beginning of the next line. Soft returns will be rearranged during editing and paragraph reforming. They are not permanent.

JUSTIFIED RIGHT MARGIN

A justified margin is straight, giving a typeset appearance. WordStar offers straight (justified) and ragged (unjustified) right margins. The justified margin is an advantage in report and proposal writing while the uneven margin is preferred for business correspondence.

STATUS LINE

At the top of your screen you'll see two highlighted lines. The first is your status line, which lists the logged drive, current file, cursor location (page, line, and column), and other information as appropriate. Whenever you enter a command code, it will display at the status line's left edge. When you change the line spacing or release the margin, notations will appear at right. The status line also shows whether WordStar's insertion feature is on or off.

RULER LINE

The ruler line appears just below the status line, also in highlighted form. It illustrates, quite graphically, the location of margins and tab stops now in use. As you change the position of margins and tab stops, the ruler line changes.

Neither the status line nor the ruler line print. They appear on the screen for your reference.

MESSAGE LINE

Several WordStar commands involve messages from the computer, usually requests for additional information or descriptions of errors you've made. Messages appear in highlighted letters at the top of the screen. Once you enter the appropriate information or response, a message line disappears.

TOGGLE COMMANDS

Toggle commands are "on/off" entries. To turn the function on, enter the command; to turn it off, enter the command again. A few examples are the commands that turn margin justification, hyphen-help, word wrap, and insertion on and off.

FLAGS

As you enter text in a file, different symbols will appear at the screen's right edge. These "flags" note hard and soft line returns, mark unused file lines, and signal other information as appropriate. WordStar's flags include these symbols: < . + ? – and a blank space.

SAVING AND STORING

You can type 25 pages of material without stopping, but unless you use one of WordStar's save commands, the computer won't retain a word of it for printing or future editing. WordStar's storing codes are simple to use and you should employ them frequently. Computer lore abounds with complicated entries that were lost forever when a system "crashed." Unless you store it first, your on-screen material will be lost in the event of a power outage or voltage interruption, if your disk fills up without your realizing it, or if for some mysterious reason the system stops working. "Store often" is sound advice and an insurance bargain.

3

Working with DOS

Before you begin your first word processing file, you'll have to boot up the system and call up WordStar.

Need a translation?

"Booting up" means starting your computer, going from a "cold start" to an operating condition. "Calling up" WordStar means activating the WordStar program. This is sometimes called "invoking WordStar" or using the WordStar "invocation."

You'll learn how to boot up the system in this chapter; the next chapter shows how to call up WordStar.

One bit of advice you'll hear again and again is: Protect yourself by copying everything. Make copies of your important disks so you will have a backup should anything happen to the originals. In fact, computer experts recommend that you make two copies of each new program disk as soon as you receive it, then store the original and one copy in separate, safe places. The second copy becomes your working disk.

A red indicator light on your disk drive will glow whenever the computer records or receives information on or from a disk. Always wait until this light is off before changing or removing a disk. Never remove a disk during printing or storing. The safest time to change disks when you're working with WordStar is when WordStar's No-File Menu appears on-screen. As you work with different DOS commands, on-screen instructions will tell you when to change disks.

Be meticulous as you handle disks. Insert each disk carefully, holding it straight and not at an angle. Never try to jam or force a disk into the disk drive; push it gently. Hold the disk so its long, exposed oval (which you should never touch) points away from you and the notched edge faces left. After inserting your disk, close the door of your disk drive. The door will snap or lock shut.

When you're not using a disk, keep it in its protective jacket or in a specially designed disk holder. Most disks come in boxes that make perfect storage compartments, and commercial stationery stores can show you a variety of disk storage carrousels, notebook pages, and miniature file cabinets. Protect your disks from extremes of hot and cold, from sources of magnetism, from dust and smoke, from electrical charges, from anything that might bend or break them, and from other damaging conditions. Because disk drives must be kept clean, computer stores sell disk-cleaning kits. How often you have to clean the drives will depend on your immediate environment, the amount of use your computer receives, the care you take with disks, and the quality of disk you use. Frequent reading errors may mean your disk drives need cleaning.

Keep original system and program disks and their copies in separate cool, safe places, and make a note of those places. A small box or cushioned envelope in a file cabinet or bookshelf may be a good storage depot. If you have a fireproof storage place, so much the better.

USING THE IBM PC DISK OPERATING SYSTEM

You may already be familiar with the IBM Personal Computer Disk Operating System (DOS) disk and its programs' commands. If so, make backup copies of your WordStar disk (you may want to store WordStar's file's and certain DOS disk files on the same disk for convenience), and turn to Chapter 4's section on calling up WordStar.

If you are new to the IBM PC, this chapter will help you understand the DOS commands you will use most often as you work with WordStar. The IBM DOS disk offers additional commands, but they are not included here because you won't need them to operate WordStar. In several cases there are WordStar commands and DOS disk commands for performing the same function, and even though you will probably use the WordStar commands more often, you should know how to perform several tasks in both modes.

Note

The symbol @, used throughout this book, represents use of the RETURN key. This gray key is on the right side of your regular letter keyboard; it's longer than most of the other keys and is labeled with an arrow pointing down and to the left: ↵. The IBM PC user manuals call this the ENTER key. WordStar calls this the RETURN key because it serves as your CARRIAGE RETURN key when you type and edit. Wherever you see the symbol @, which stands for RETURN or ENTER, press this key.

Don't confuse the two uses of "enter." In this book, "enter" means the same as "type." You enter or type text, instructions, commands, and information. Your IBM Personal Computer Software Library references use the word differently, because command codes are not really "entered" into the computer's memory until you press the RETURN (ENTER) key.

Where the IBM instructions say, "Type format a:/s and press the Enter key," this book says, "Enter FORMAT A:/S@," which means the same thing.

Commands can be typed in upper- or lowercase letters. Most of the IBM PC manual instructions show lowercase entries, and IBM PC screen messages appear in lowercase letters, but WordStar and this book use uppercase letters for command codes.

"BOOTING UP" OR STARTING YOUR COMPUTER

Before turning on the power switch on the system unit's right side, insert your DOS disk in Drive A. Close the drive's door. Now turn the power switch on.

A beep will sound, the disk drives will growl, and a screen message will request today's date. Use this format: month-day-year. To complete your entry and signal the computer, press RETURN. If today is April 5, 1984, enter: 4/5/84, 4-5-84, 4-05-84, 4/05/84, 04-5-84, 04/5/84, 04-05-84, or 04/05/84. So long as you follow the month-day-year format and use dashes or slashes between numbers, the computer will accept your entry.

If you enter an unacceptable date (4-31-84, for example, or 13-22-84, or a year prior to 1980), the screen message repeats or an error message ("Invalid date") appears.

As soon as you enter a valid date, a second screen message appears, this one requesting the current time. Enter the time of day as an even hour (11, for example), followed by the RETURN key, or use 24-hour time (11 a.m. is 11:00 and 11 p.m. is 23:00.) The computer will accept time entries that include a tenth of a second: 02:45:16.7, for example.

If you don't know (or care) what day or time it is, take a shortcut by pressing RETURN. Using the RETURN key sets a default date and time, such as as January 1, 1980, and midnight.

As soon as the computer accepts your responses, a copyright notice and the screen prompt A> appear. Whenever you see the message A>, it means that the disk operating system (DOS) is in use, A is the logged disk drive, and the computer is waiting for you to enter a program command.

To activate any program, that program's file(s) must be on the logged disk. If you enter a program command incorrectly, or if you enter the command correctly but the appropriate program is not in the logged disk drive, an error message will appear: "Bad command or file name." Should this happen, check your entry carefully and be sure the appropriate disk is in the logged drive. (If the needed disk is in the unlogged drive, simply change the logged drive.)

If you make a mistake typing a file name or command code, use the BACKSPACE key to erase one letter at a time from right to left. The BACKSPACE key is in the top row of keys at right; it's gray and labeled with a left arrow ←.

RESTARTING THE SYSTEM

If your computer is already turned on, you can start or restart the system by pressing these three keys simultaneously: CONTROL, ALTERNATE, and DELETE. The CONTROL key (abbreviated Ctrl) is just left of the "A" letter key; the ALTERNATE key (abbreviated Alt) is to the left of the space bar; and the DELETE key (abbreviated Del) is in the keyboard's lower-right corner.

Pressing these three keys causes the initial date request to appear, unless Drive A doesn't contain the appropriate DOS files. Should that happen, an error message will appear:

```
Non-System disk or disk error
Replace and strike any key when ready
```

Your DOS disk, or a disk containing the DOS files, must be in Drive A for the system to reboot.

However, the DOS disk doesn't have to be in either drive for the system to crash when you press these three keys, which is why you should stay away from this command as you edit your WordStar files. The computer will never assume that you entered a command by accident, or that you didn't really mean what you typed. Don't absent-mindedly press the reboot command (CONTROL/ALTERNATE/DELETE) in the middle of your great American novel's longest chapter, or all your unsaved editing changes will vanish into space.

As a general rule, use this command to start the computer if the power is already on (insert the DOS disk in Drive A before pressing the command code) or to restart the system when you aren't editing a file.

CHANGING LOGGED DISK DRIVE

If yours is a dual disk drive unit, the drive at left is DRIVE A and the drive at right is DRIVE B. When A is the logged disk drive and you have returned to the operating system, A> is the screen prompt. B> means that B is the logged disk drive.

To change the logged drive from A to B, enter B, a colon, and RETURN:

```
A>   B:@
```

To change the logged drive from B to A, enter:

```
B>   A:@
```

A NOTE ON COMMAND ENTRY

From time to time you will use the prefix A: or B: in front of a file's name or to designate a disk, and you should understand how the computer "thinks" when it encounters these notations.

If you are using a dual disk drive system, the prefixes are easy to understand because they represent Drive A and Drive B; and if you are using a single drive system, you will use these codes to represent File A and File B or Disk A and Disk B.

Here is how the prefixes work with DOS commands and file names.

You will enter the command code first, and then the file name. If you are using two different file names, the first file name is the source file (the one holding information that is being copied or used as a reference), and the second file name is the destination or target file (the one receiving the information being copied, or the one being compared against the original).

If you put a prefix (A: or B:) in front of a file name, you signal the computer that the file will be found (or should be placed) on the disk in that drive. If you do not use a prefix, the computer looks for (or records) the file on the logged disk.

These distinctions will be more apparent as you study and work with the commands described here.

INTERNAL AND EXTERNAL COMMANDS

The procedures described in this chapter are "internal" or "external," depending on whether the basic DOS program supports their commands or whether an additional program file must be on the logged disk for the command to work.

To understand the DOS program, read the formatting section carefully. There are many programs on your DOS disk, but only one is the essential disk operating sytem program.

As long as this one program is on a disk, you can use that disk for booting up or restarting the system, copying a file, listing a disk's directory of files, erasing a file, and renaming a file. These are "internal" commands; they do not require additional program files.

When you enter the command for an internal program, the DOS disk does not have to be in either disk drive. All that's necessary is that your system prompt (A> or B>) be on the screen.

To copy an entire disk, compare one disk to another, compare one file to another, check a disk's condition, or format a disk, you will need the appropriate program file on your logged disk. These are "external" program functions. The appropriate program must be in the logged disk drive when you enter the command.

WRITE-PROTECTION

With every new box of disks you acquire, you should receive a set of small metallic stickers. These are called "write-protect" stickers, and when you cover the notch on a disk, you prevent it from being erased or written on by the computer.

As soon as you copy your original DOS disk, and as soon as you copy your original WordStar disk, you should place write-protection labels over the disks' notches. That way you won't accidentally erase their contents.

MAKING A BACKUP COPY OF YOUR DOS DISK

As mentioned, backup disks are very important and the first thing you should do when you receive a new program disk is make at least two backup copies. Store the original and one copy for safekeeping; use the second copy as your working file. It's a good idea to make backup copies of that copy, too.

The IBM PC user handbooks recommend a specific and sensible procedure for copying your original DOS disk — something you should do before anything else.

Two separate DOS disk commands will be used in the procedure outlined here. You will find more detailed descriptions of these two commands (disk copy and disk check) later in this chapter.

You will need two disks in this procedure: your original DOS disk and a backup disk. The backup disk can be a new, unused disk or it can be a disk which contains material you don't need any more. The disk copying procedure, which automatically formats the destination or copy disk, erases that disk's previous comments. (You will read more about disk formatting on page 22.)

Label your backup disk with a felt tip pen. Call it DOS COPY or something similar. Remember that your disk should go back into its paper jacket the moment it comes out of the disk drive.

COPYING DOS (SINGLE DRIVE UNIT): DOS BACKUP DISK

If your computer system has only one disk drive, you will exchange the disks back and forth in the disk drive several times during this operation. It's important to keep the disk jackets handy and to verify the labels as you go along.

With the DOS disk in your disk drive, boot up the system. When the prompt message A> appears, enter this command:

```
DISKCOPY@
```

The following screen message appears:

```
Insert source diskette in drive A
Strike any key when ready
```

Because the DOS disk, already installed in Drive A, is what you want to copy, press any key. A bit later, this message appears:

```
Insert target diskette in drive A
Strike any key when ready
```

Be careful not to touch the keyboard as you change disks. Remove the DOS disk to its paper envelope and place the backup disk in your disk drive. Now press any key on the keyboard. This message will display when it's time to change disks again:

```
Insert source diskette in drive A
Strike any key when ready
```

Because the computer can copy only a segment of the disk at a time, you will have to change disks several times. Check your disk labels to be sure you're inserting the original (source) and backup (target) disks as instructed. You'll know when the backup copy is ready by the following message:

```
Copy complete
Copy another? (Y/N)
```

Answer Y for Yes or N for No. It's a good idea to make more than one copy, but you can copy the copy after retiring the original.

To be sure the two disks match exactly, enter this last command:

```
DISKCOMP@
```

The screen displays this message:

```
Insert first diskette in drive A
Strike any key when ready
```

Press any key. Either the original or the backup disk can be in the drive when you do so. As in the disk copy command, the screen tells you when it's time to change disks. Continue to switch disks as the screen instructs until the comparison has been completed. At that point, you should see this friendly message:

```
Diskettes compare ok
Compare more diskettes? (Y/N)
```

Again, answer Y for Yes or N for No.

If the two disks aren't identical, start over. If your DOS disk isn't working right, you have a problem. Go through the steps carefully to be sure you're inserting each disk at its proper time. If the DOS disk is defective, call your computer dealer.

COPYING DOS (DUAL DRIVE SYSTEM): DOS BACKUP DISK

With the DOS disk in Drive A, boot up the system as instructed earlier. Insert your backup disk in Drive B before or after you enter the copy command:

```
DISKCOPY A: B:@
```

This screen message appears:

```
Insert source diskette in drive A
Insert target diskette in drive B
Strike any key when ready
```

With your disks correctly positioned, the original (source) DOS disk in Drive A and the destination (backup copy) disk in Drive B, press any key.

As the computer copies information from Drive A onto the disk in Drive B, you'll see the red disk drive lights flash on and off, and the drives will hum, growl, and click. A screen message informs you when the procedure has finished:

```
Copy complete
Copy another? (Y/N)
```

Answer this question Y for Yes or N for No, depending on whether you plan to make another copy directly from the original DOS disk.

Now compare the two disks to be sure your backup copy matches the original by entering this command:

```
DISKCOMP A: B:@
```

The following message will display:

```
Insert first diskette in drive A
Insert second diskette in drive B
Strike any key when ready
```

Press any key to signal the computer. As soon as the disks have been compared, this message should appear:

```
Diskettes compare ok
Compare more diskettes? (Y/N)
```

Again, answer Y for Yes or N for No.

Should the disks not compare, go through the copying procedure again. If your original DOS disk is defective, call your computer dealer.

STORE DOS ORIGINAL AND BACKUP COPY

At this point, assuming all has gone well, tuck your original DOS disk in its folder and have a safe place ready for its permanent storage. With your backup copy you can make additional copies, one of which will become your working disk.

And with your working disk in hand (or in Drive A), you can go on to a host of DOS disk commands — and WordStar.

DISPLAY FILE DIRECTORY

The directory display command is internal. Because it does not require a separate program file to operate, your DOS disk does not have to be in either disk drive when you type the command. All you need is the screen prompt A> or B>.

To see what files are in the logged disk drive, enter this simple command:

```
DIR@
```

That disk's contents will be listed by name, file length (bytes), and the date/time at which the file was stored — based on the date/time you entered as you started the system.

Note that file names can have what the IBM handbooks call "extensions." An extension comes after the file name and consists of a period (.) plus one, two, or three characters (letters, numbers, or symbols).

When you display the file directory in WordStar mode, you will see each file name printed as a single word. But the DOS file directory displays names without any periods, and it separates names from their extensions. For example, what the file directory shows as COMMAND COM is really COMMAND.COM, and what the screen shows as FORMAT COM is really FORMAT.COM.

If any IBM DOS disk files are in your directory, they show their copyright date(s). Programs copied from another source file, such as your WordStar program files, do not show a date. Files you create yourself show the date/time at which they were stored on the disk, based on the date/time you used when you started the system.

To display the contents of a disk in the other disk drive, add the appropriate prefix. If B is the logged drive and you want to see what's on the disk in Drive A, enter:

```
B>  DIR A:@
```

If A is the logged drive and you want to see what's on the disk in Drive B, enter:

```
A>  DIR B:@
```

DISPLAY A LONG DIRECTORY

There are two options you can use to make long file directories easier to read.

To slow the display of a long directory, enter the command like this:

```
A>  DIR/P@
```

The P stands for *P*ause, which is what the computer does after showing the first screenful of files. Press any key to display the second screenful, etc.

If you did not use the /P option, you can stop the display manually by pressing the CONTROL key and the NUM LOCK key simultaneously. This action suspends system operation until you press the space bar or any other key, causing operation to resume. Press Ctrl/NumLock and the screen "freezes" so that you can read a long directory one segment at a time.

To list only file names, removing the file bytes, dates, and times from your directory, enter the command like this:

```
A>  DIR/W@
```

The W stands for *W*ide display. Now all of the disk's file names can appear on the screen at one time.

CHECK AVAILABLE AND USED DISK SPACE

Check disk is an external function supported by the CHKDSK.COM program. This program must be on the logged drive's disk when you enter the command.

If you have a dual drive system, insert the disk to be checked before entering the command. If using a single drive unit, use the designation B: to inform the computer that the disk to be checked is other than the currently logged disk.

This command gives a status report showing the number of files on the disk, bytes on the disk, bytes available, bytes of total memory, and memory bytes available.

If the disk to be checked is in Drive A, enter:

```
A>  CHKDSK@
```

If the disk to be checked is in Drive B, or if yours is a single drive unit and you want to change disks, enter:

```
A>  CHKDSK B:@
```

The screen will display a message like this one:

```
     4 disk files
160256 bytes total disk space
145408 bytes remain available
 65536 bytes total memory
533392 bytes free
```

Your screen message will vary according to the size of your system, the number of files on a disk, and the kind of disk you are using. This screen message appeared on a 64K IBM Personal Computer using single-sided disks.

CHKDSK is an external command. For it to work, the program file CHKDSK.COM must be on the logged disk.

FORMAT A BLANK DISK

Formatting means preparing a disk to receive information. While you don't have to format a disk if you plan to copy an already-formatted disk's contents onto it, you will have to format every disk intended for file storage before it can be used by DOS. And because your WordStar use will generate files-only storage disks and disks which are not copied directly from other disks, formatting is a good habit.

When a disk is being formatted, every sector of the disk is "written on," a directory is established for future file records, and any bad sectors are found and allocated to a file called BADTRACK. You will never see the BADTRACK file in your disk directory, but this "invisible" file performs an important function: it keeps the defective area separate from your data file.

In addition, although this is an optional consideration, you can format your disks so they contain DOS. Note that DOS does not include all the programs found on the DOS disk; DOS really consists of these four parts: the boot record, the IBMBIO.COM program, the IBMDOS.COM program, and the COMMAND.COM program. Three of these, like BADTRACK, are "invisible"; you never see them on the screen.

In brief, the DOS programs perform the following functions: The boot record always goes at the beginning of your disk, and it's automatically loaded into memory every time you start DOS. This program loads the rest of the DOS programs. IBMBIO.COM reads data from and writes data to the computer's memory and to its peripheral equipment. IBMDOS.COM contains a file manager and service functions used by any program designed to run with DOS. COMMAND.COM is a command processor which accepts the commands you enter and runs the appropriate programs. If you format using the option that copies these four programs onto your otherwise blank disk, only one will appear on your file directory: COMMAND.COM. The other three programs, though present, are "invisible."

If you are formatting disks that will be "document-only" or "document storage" disks, the simple FORMAT@ command will save disk space.

The FORMAT command is external; the program file FORMAT.COM must be on the logged disk for this command to operate.

FORMAT A DISK (SINGLE DRIVE UNIT)

With DOS in the disk drive, answer A> with this command:

```
FORMAT@
```

Or, to use the option described above to copy the DOS programs, enter:

```
FORMAT/S@
```

The /S option stands for Operating *S*ystem files. This screen message appears:

```
Insert new diskette for drive B:
and strike any key when ready
```

Remove the DOS disk from the drive and replace it with your new disk. (The new disk can be literally new, or it can be an old disk you are "renewing" for use with the IBM PC and WordStar. Remember that the format command erases anything previously stored on the disk.)

Watch for this message:

```
Formatting...Formatting complete
System transferred
Format another? (Y/N)
```

If you used the simple FORMAT@ command without the /S option, the screen message does not include "System transferred."

You may want to format several disks at a time, such as a box of 10. Answer Y for Yes or N for No. A Y answer repeats the process; N returns the A> screen prompt.

FORMAT A DISK (DUAL DRIVE UNIT)

With the DOS disk in Drive A, answer the A> screen prompt with this command:

```
FORMAT B:@
```

or, to bring the system commands with you, enter:

```
FORMAT B:/S@
```

The screen message says:

```
Insert new diskette for drive B:
and strike any key when ready
```

While formatting takes place, you will see the disk drive lights blink on and off, and the drives growl and hum. After formatting, the screen shows this message:

```
Formatting...Format complete
System transferred
Format another? (Y/N)
```

The screen message does not include "System transferred" if you used the simple FORMAT B:@ command without the /S option.

If you answer Y for Yes, the screen instructions repeat and you can replace the disk in Drive B with a disk waiting to be formatted. It's usually convenient to format several disks at a time, such as a box of ten. If you answer N for No, the A> screen prompt reappears.

COPY A DISK (SINGLE DRIVE UNIT)

This command allows you to copy all of the files on one (source) disk onto another (target or destination) disk, erasing all previous contents of the destination disk. The two disks will then be identical.

As this is an external command, the program file DISKCOPY.COM must be on your logged disk for the procedure to work.

With the program file in Drive A and the A> message on the screen, enter this command:

```
DISKCOPY@
```

The screen message gives this instruction when it's time to insert the original disk:

```
Insert source diskette in drive A
Strike any key when ready
```

And it offers this when it's time to insert the duplicate disk:

```
Insert target diskette in drive A
Strike any key when ready
```

Because the computer copies the disk's contents in segments, you may have to switch disks several times. Be sure to follow the screen's instructions exactly. Do not switch disks until the appropriate message appears, and do not touch the keyboard until the correct disk is installed in the drive. Check the labels on your disks as you make each change to be sure you're inserting the right disk at the right time.

At the end of this procedure, the screen will announce:

```
Copy complete
Copy another? (Y/N)
```

A Y for Yes response repeats the initial instruction message; N for No returns the A> screen prompt. The two disks should be identical.

To copy all of the files from one disk onto a second disk without erasing the second disk's previously entered files, a procedure that does not generate identical disks, use the file copy command described on page 27.

COPY A DISK (DUAL DRIVE UNIT)

This command will copy all of the files of a source (original) disk onto a target (destination) disk, erasing all of the target disk's previous contents so that the two disks match in every way.

Because this is an external program command, the file DISKCOPY.COM must be on your logged disk.

Answer the A> screen prompt with this command:

```
DISKCOPY A: B:@
```

This means, copy everything from Drive A onto Drive B. The command generates this screen message:

```
Insert source diskette in drive A
Insert target diskette in drive B
Strike any key when ready
```

At this point, remove the program disk from Drive A and replace it with your original (source) disk. Insert the target disk in Drive B. Press any key.

Depending on the amount of material being transferred, you will see the disk drive lights flash back and forth a few or several times. Accompanying noises come from the disk drives. When the copy has been made, this screen message appears:

```
Copy complete
Copy another? (Y/N)
```

To copy the same disk again or another disk, enter Y for Yes. N for No brings the A> screen prompt.

COMPARE TWO DISKS (SINGLE DRIVE UNIT)

To compare two disks to determine whether they are identical, the disk in your logged drive must contain the DISKCOMP.COM program file. This is an external command. Answer the A> message with:

```
DISKCOMP@
```

The screen says:

```
Insert first diskette in drive A
Strike any key when ready
```

After you do so, the screen lets you know when to insert the duplicate disk:

```
Insert second diskette in drive A
Strike any key when ready
```

Because the computer can compare only one segment at a time, you will have to repeat the procedure until all the contents have been compared.

If the disks match, this screen message appears:

```
Diskettes compare ok
Compare more diskettes? (Y/N)
```

If the disks don't match, notations like the following will appear:

```
Compare error(s) on track 29
Compare error(s) on track 30
```

Interrupt the command's execution at any time by pressing the CONTROL and BREAK keys simultaneously. (The BREAK key is also labeled Scroll Lock.)

Note that two disks may contain the same files but they may not be identical. If you have copied individual files one at a time from one disk to the other, the files may be arranged in a different order on the second disk.

COMPARE TWO DISKS (DUAL DRIVE UNIT)

The following command compares the contents of a disk in Drive A with the contents of a disk in Drive B. It is usually used right after the DISKCOPY command, as you saw in the DOS backup copy instructions, but you may want to use it at other times as well.

Your logged disk must contain the DISKCOMP.COM program file as this is an external program.

Enter the command like this:

```
DISKCOMP A: B:@
```

The screen instructs:

```
Insert first diskette in drive A
Insert second diskette in drive B
Strike any key when ready
```

After comparing all of the tracks on a track-by-track basis, the computer tells you that the disks are identical:

```
Diskettes compare ok
Compare more diskettes? (Y/N)
```

or that they aren't:

```
Compare error(s) on track 36
Compare error(s) on track 37
Compare error(s) on track 38
```

The screen will lists those tracks that don't match.

If two disks don't match at all, the list will be quite long and you can interrupt it by pressing the CONTROL key and the BREAK key (also labeled Scroll Lock) at the same time.

Remember that two disks can contain identical files that match in every way without being identical disks. If files were copied onto the duplicate disk one at a time rather than in a single DISKCOPY procedure, their arrangement on the disk may be different from their arrangement on the original disk. See page 29 for instructions on comparing individual files.

COPY A FILE (SINGLE DRIVE UNIT)

You can copy a single file onto the same disk or onto a separate disk using a simple internal command.

For the single disk drive user, the procedure is identical to that described for the dual drive user. Screen messages like those you have already met tell you when to change disks if you are copying from one disk to another.

Even though the commands look as though they require two disk drives, think of your original file as positioned on Disk A and your *B*ackup file as positioned on Disk B when you use these command codes.

COPY A FILE (DUAL DRIVE UNIT)

To duplicate a file and record its copy on the same disk, you will need a new name for the second (copied) version. The command is simple:

```
COPY [NAME] [REPLACEMENT NAME]@
```

If your original file is called Photos and your duplicate file called Pictures, enter the command like this:

```
COPY PHOTOS PICTURES@
```

You have instructed the computer to find the file named Photos on the logged disk, make an exact copy of it, store that copy on the same disk, and label that copy Pictures.

When copying a file from one disk to another, you can keep the original file name. The command is:

```
COPY [NAME] B:@
```

For example, to copy the original Photo file from the disk in Drive A and to store that copy, still named Photo, on the disk in Drive B, you would enter:

```
COPY PHOTO B:@
```

To copy a file from one disk to another and change the copy's name, use this command:

```
COPY [NAME] B:[REPLACEMENT NAME]@
```

In our example, your command

```
COPY PHOTO B:PICTURE@
```

tells the computer to make a copy of the Disk A Photo file, store that copy on Drive B, and label the Drive B copy Pictures.

To copy a file from the disk in Drive B onto the logged disk in Drive A, enter the command like this:

```
COPY B:[NAME]@
```

This instructs the computer to find the source file on Disk B, make a copy of it, store the copy on Disk A, and keep the original name.

The command:

```
COPY B:[NAME] [REPLACEMENT NAME]
```

tells the computer to find the source file in Drive B, make a copy of it, store the copy on the logged disk in Drive A, and change the name.

When the computer finishes making your copy, the screen says:

```
1 File(s) copied
```

To compare two files, the original and its copy, use the "compare file" command described on page 29.

COPY SOURCE DISK FILES WITHOUT ERASING DESTINATION DISK FILES

To duplicate all of the files on the source disk without erasing files having different names from the destination disk, use this command:

```
COPY *.* B:@
```

The asterisk (*) is one of the IBM PC's "global characters." It signals that any character (letter/number/symbol) or characters can occupy the asterisk's place in a file name. File names can have extensions (the period with additional letters) after them, so the file name is entered as *.* rather than * by itself. Even though the period is a symbol and would otherwise be represented by the asterisk, it has a special meaning in file names — every period in a file name, in both DOS and WordStar use, separates the file name from its extension.

You have instructed the computer to make copies of all files in Drive A, storing them in Drive B without changing their names, and without erasing the previous contents of Drive B. However, remember this exception: If the same file name appears on both disks, the Disk A version will replace the Disk B version on Disk B.

To copy all the files on Disk B onto Disk A, enter the command like this:

```
COPY B:*.*@
```

Does this seem confusing? Think back to the earlier discussion of prefixes and how they work. Once you give the computer a command, it carries out that command by turning first to the source of whatever is to be done and then to the destination or target.

Remember that in all of this chapter's commands and descriptions, Drive A is the logged drive, and the commands are entered in response to the A> screen prompt.

The command COPY *.* B:@ tells the computer to copy everything labeled [any characters].[any characters] — which describes or includes all the files — on the source disk. Because you have not used a prefix, the source disk is in the logged drive, or Drive A. Where is the material going to be stored once copied? Onto the disk in Drive B, according to your B: command. The copy command requires a "from" disk and a "to" disk; here A is the "from" disk and B is the "to" disk.

The command COPY B:*.* @ says that the "from" or source disk is Disk B and, because you have not used another prefix, the computer knows that your "to" or destination disk is the logged disk, Disk A. What do you copy from Disk B? All of its files. Where do they go? Onto the disk in the logged drive.

A Note on Disk Space

Should you not have sufficient disk space on the destination disk when executing the COPY *.* B:@ or COPY B:*.* @ command, an error message will appear, such as the one below:

```
Insufficient disk space
7 File(s) copied
```

If that happens, you may want to try again, erasing any non-essential files already on the disk. You need not erase the files that were successfully copied in the command's partial execution because they will be recopied when you use the command again. The source disk version of any file having the same name as a file on the destination disk will replace the destination disk's version of that file.

When copying a single file at a time, insufficient disk space will generate the same error message.

COMPARE TWO FILES (SINGLE DRIVE UNIT)

Use the commands given below for the dual drive unit and follow screen directions if it's necessary to change disks.

COMPARE TWO FILES (DUAL DRIVE UNIT)

The comparison program is external; your logged disk must contain the file COMP.COM for this procedure to work.

To compare two files which appear on the same disk, respond to the A> screen prompt with this DOS disk command:

```
COMP [NAME1] [NAME2]@
```

You have instructed the computer to find the first named file and compare it to the second named file, both of which it will find on the disk in Drive A. However, you won't insert the source disk in Drive A until completing your command entry.

The screen will say:

```
Mount diskette(s) and strike any key
```

If the two files match, you'll see this screen message:

```
Files compare ok
Enter primary file name
Or strike the ENTER key to end
```

The screen is inviting you to compare two more files. To do so, enter the next source (original or primary) file name and press RETURN; the screen will ask for the comparison file's name.

To stop at this point without comparing more files, press RETURN.

To compare two files on different disks, enter the command like this:

```
COMP [DRIVE A NAME] B:[DRIVE B NAME]@
```

or, if the files have identical names, use fewer keystrokes:

```
COMP [NAME] B:@
```

The screen will reply with this message:

```
Mount diskette(s) and strike any key
```

The "compare disks" command compares two disks on a track-by-track basis. The "compare files" command compares two files on a byte-for-byte basis. If the files don't match, a screen message tells you they are of unequal sizes.

ERASE A FILE

Before using the erase command, understand that this is an internal function. If the prompt signal A> or B> is on-screen, the computer doesn't need additional files to interpret your command. Also, the computer will not give a screen message telling you to change disks or to press a key when ready; it assumes that the file to be erased is in the drive when you press the RETURN key.

The command is simple:

```
ERASE [FILENAME]@
```

If the file is in the unlogged disk drive, preface the name accordingly.

If the disk's directory already appears on-screen because you called it up with the DIR command, the erased file's name will continue to appear. (This is different from the file directory you will work with in WordStar mode, which is continually updated.) Enter DIR again and the name will be gone.

To erase all of the files on a disk, insert the disk to be erased before entering this command:

```
ERASE *.*@
```

or, if a drive prefix is necessary:

```
ERASE B:*.*@
```

You met the IBM PC "global character" (*) in the dual drive unit diskcopy command.

RENAME A FILE

Like the erase file, this DOS command is straightforward. An internal command, it does not require an additional program; as long as the screen prompt A> or B> appears, the system is ready to rename a file.

First enter the current file name, then its replacement name:

```
RENAME [CURRENT NAME] [REVISED NAME]@
```

If the file is in the unlogged drive, preface the current name accordingly.

Because this command does nothing but change a file's name, you can't enter something like RENAME A:JOURNAL B:DIARY (which tells the computer to find a file on Disk A called Journal and change it to a file on Disk B called Diary) and expect the command to work. However, you can use the file copy command to change a file's location and rename it at the same time.

DOS ERROR MESSAGES AND SCREEN MESSAGES

You will find a complete list of DOS messages in Appendix A of your DOS manual, but here are the error and information lines you're likely to meet as you use the commands described in this chapter.

Attempted write-protect violation

This message occurs during formatting if the disk being formatted is protected by a special label on its notched side. Your original program disks should come with such protection, and you can protect any backup disk by using one of the write-protect stickers supplied with your box of disks on the notch. Any disk whose notch is covered cannot be written on or erased by the computer.

Bad command or file name

The command you just entered is not supported by any file on the logged disk. Change disks and try again.

[Number] bytes disk space freed

When using the CHKDSK command, you may see this screen message. It means that the number of bytes shown was marked as allocated when it really wasn't in use. This command's execution freed the space so it is now available.

Cannot compare file to itself

In a compare file (COMP) command, this message appears if you use the same file name without indicating different disks.

Compare error at offset [number] or
Compare error(s) on track [number]

These messages may appear after a compare files (first message) or compare disks (second message) command. As indicated, the files or disks being compared are not identical.

Data error reading drive A
Abort, Retry, Ignore?

This message and its close cousins. **Disk error reading Drive A,** or **Disk error writing Drive A,** or **Data error writing Drive A,** or **Drive B** in any of the above, indicate a problem in receiving information from or recording information on a disk or file.

The message will not appear until the computer has tried the command three times. Now the system waits for your entry of the letter A, R, or I:

- R — Retry: The error may not occur if you repeat the command.
- A — Abort: This option aborts or abandons the program and returns you to the disk operating system (A>).
- I — Ignore: Disregard the error condition and continue the program. The IBM DOS handbook does not recommend this option because you may lose data.

Disk unsuitable for system disk

While formatting with the /S option (entered FORMAT/S), a defective track was detected in the area reserved for the DOS system files. You can format the disk with the simple FORMAT command instead and use it for file storage.

Diskette not initialized

This message appears during CHKDSK if the directory or file allocation table of the disk being checked cannot be located. This disk should not be used again without being reformatted. If it contains files you want to save, you may be able to copy them onto another disk first.

Duplicate filename or file not found

Using the rename command, you tried to rename a file with a name already on the disk, or you are trying to rename a file which is not on the disk.

EOF mark not found

When comparing two files, the end of valid data (end of file) could not be found. This message usually appears when comparing program files; it should not occur when comparing text files.

File cannot be copied onto itself

When copying a file, your destination file must be different from the source file; it must have a different name if on the same disk, or the file name must be preceded by the appropriate disk drive if using a different disk for the copy.

File [name] empty or
File [name] not found

When comparing two files, both must have valid contents for the procedure to continue. Both must be on the disk(s) described in the command.

File size error for file [name]

Using CHKDSK, a discrepancy was found between the file size shown in the disk's directory and the file's actual size. The directory size is corrected.

Files are different sizes

This message appears in a file comparison command if the files don't match.

File [name] not found

If you use an incorrect name in the COMP command, the computer will not be able to locate that file.

Files cross-linked: [name] and [name]

Using CHKDSK, two different files are found to share the same disk area. The computer takes no corrective action. You should make copies of both files with the copy command, then erase the originals and inspect the copied files, editing if necessary.

Format failure

The disk, because of an error found during formatting, is not usable.

Missing filename

The rename command requires two file names, the original and the replacement. If you do not include the second name in your command, this message appears.

If you type a prefix and leave a space after it, the computer interprets the blank space as a missing name.

Not ready error reading drive A or
Not ready error writing drive A or
Sector not found error reading drive A or
Sector not found error writing drive A
Abort, Retry, Ignore?

See the Section on Disk Errors.

Target diskette unusable

When copying a disk, this message follows an unrecoverable read, write, or verify error message.

Target diskette write protected
Correct, then strike any key

Your destination disk in a disk copy command has its notch covered by a special label or sticker. This is probably an original program disk or its copy. Replace the disk (and store it in a safe place), then press any key.

Track 0 bad — disk unusable

During formatting the disk's first track is found defective. The disk's boot record, file allocation table, and directory must reside on track 0.

Unrecoverable read error on drive or source A or
Unrecoverable verify error on target or
Unrecoverable write error on target

These are DISKCOPY error messages. In each case, six attempts were made to complete the command: reading data from the source/original disk or recording data onto the target/duplicate disk.

Write error

In formatting, a write error occurred while DOS copied the boot record or system files. Try again. If you entered FORMAT/S, try FORMAT without the /S option.

10 Mismatches — aborting compare

In comparing two files, 10 mismatched locations were found. As the files are too different to match, the command cancels.

COPYING WORDSTAR

Now that you know how to copy the files from one disk onto another, you should make backup copies of your WordStar disk. Retire the original to a safe, cool, dry place and work with your backup disks.

CREATING AN IBM DOS/WORDSTAR MASTER DISK

Because you'll probably want to use several DOS disk programs as well as your WordStar programs as you work with WordStar, here is an easy procedure to follow.

1. Make a copy (using DISKCOPY) of your DOS disk.
2. Using the DIR command, display the contents of your DOS disk copy, which we will call your "master" disk. There are so many files on this disk that unless you use the /P or /W options described earlier, you won't be able to see them all.
3. There are many nonessential programs on the DOS disk, and they are easy to erase. The first group you can eliminate includes every file whose extension (suffix) is BAS. The list includes ART.BAS, COLORBAR.BAS, MUSIC.BAS, etc.

   Though the list looks formidable, it's easy to erase using *, the global file character you met earlier. An asterisk represents any character or characters, so to remove all the .BAS files, enter:

   ```
   ERASE *.BAS@
   ```

   This means, erase any file containing the extension .BAS. Now redisplay the file directory and you'll see a much shorter list.

   A number of .COM files may be expendable, too: MODE.COM, SYS.COM, EDLIN.COM, DEBUG.COM, BASIC.COM, and BASICA-.COM. You won't need the LINK.EXE program, either. If desired, erase these files individually.

   Here are the program files you may want to preserve on your master disk: CHKDSK.COM, COMMAND.COM, COMP.COM. DISKCOMP.COM, DISKCOPY.COM and FORMAT.COM. This set of files supports all the commands described earlier.
4. Leave your master disk in Drive A and place a copy of your WordStar disk in Drive B. There are three program files on your WordStar disk, all of them essential: WS.COM, WSMSGS.OVR, and WSOVLY1.OVR. Copy these programs onto your master disk with this single command (which preserves the files already on that disk):

   ```
   COPY B:*.*@
   ```

   This command instructs the computer to copy everything on the Drive B disk onto the logged (Drive A) disk, retaining the logged disk's previous content.

   Alternately, copy the files individually, using the COPY [FILENAME] command.

   Your master disk should now contain the three WordStar files and the DOS disk files mentioned above.

5. Make a few backup copies of your master disk. Keep them with the backup copies of WordStar by itself (disks that contain only the three WordStar files), especially if your system has 64K. A number of storage and text-moving maneuvers will be easier to execute if you have two kinds of "master" disks.

Here is an alternate way of setting up a "self-sufficient" WordStar disk. Format a blank disk with the FORMAT/S option, so that the operating system files are on that disk. Now transfer the three WordStar files.

Although this master disk will not support the Check Disk, Compare Files, Compare Disks, Disk Copy, and Format commands, it will boot the system up and you will be able to copy a file, erase a file, rename a file, and list a disk's file directory.

Having made these preparations, and armed with a box of blank, formatted disks, you're well equipped for your introduction to WordStar.

USING WORDSTAR WITH A SINGLE DISK DRIVE UNIT

If your IBM Personal Computer has a single disk drive, you will be able to use WordStar but you will have to use certain procedures, such as copying files from one disk to another, more often than your counterpart whose system has dual disk drives.

You will conserve disk space by keeping DOS files and WordStar files on separate disks. Learn to work on one file at a time. Then, after storing its contents, copy that file onto a storage disk. When ready to edit the file again, copy it back onto your WordStar disk, having erased everything on your master disk except the WordStar files: WS.COM, WSMSGS.OVR, and WSOVLY1.OVR. These three files occupy over 9,000 bytes of your disk's space. If you retain unnecessary editing files on the same disk, you'll soon run out of space.

Of course, as you work with WordStar you will develop several editing tricks that will work around the limitations of a single drive, just as all users of the 64K system will learn how to work around the computer's memory limitations. But fancy footwork comes with experience, so take your time.

Throughout this book you'll find special hints for the single drive user, for the 64K system user, and for the IBM Matrix Printer user. Mark the appropriate sections as you read them and, as your experience increases, refer back to them. Soon you'll be inventing your own editing procedures.

INDEX OF DOS COMMANDS

In the following command index, A> is the logged disk drive, Disk A is the disk in that drive, and Disk B is the disk in drive B. For single disk drive units, Disk B is the disk to be exchanged for the disk in Drive A.

1. Check a disk.
(The CHKDSK.COM file must be in Drive A.)

a. Check the disk in the default drive:

```
A> CHKDSK@
```

b. Check disk B:

```
A>CHKDSK B:@
```

(No screen message appears regarding insertion of disk.)

2. Compare two disks.
(The DISKCOMP.COM file must be in Drive A.)
a. Compare any two disks:

```
A> DISKCOMP A: B:@
```

(Screen message: Insert disks, strike key when ready. Interrupt listing of non-matching tracks, if necessary, by cancelling command with Ctrl/Break.)

3. Compare two files.
(The COMP.COM file must be in Drive A.)
a. Compare two files on Disk A:

```
A> COMP [filename 1] [filename 2]@
```

b. Compare two files having separate names on separate disks:

```
A> COMP [filename A] B:[filename B]@
```

c. Compare two files having the same name on separate disks:

```
A> COMP [filename] B:@
```

d. Compare two files on disk B:

```
A> COMP B:[filename 1] [filename 2]@
```

(Screen message: Mount disks, strike key when ready.)

4. Copy a disk.
(DISKCOPY.COM file must be in drive A.)
a. Command:

```
A> DISKCOPY A: B:@
```

(Screen message: Insert disks, press key when ready.)

5. Copy a file.
(Internal command; no external file necessary. Insert appropriate disk(s) before entering command.)
a. Copy a file from Disk A, write copy on Disk A, renaming the copy:

```
A> COPY [filename] [new name]@
```

b. Copy a file from Disk A, write copy on Disk B, retaining original file name:

```
A> COPY [filename] B:@
```

c. Copy a file from Disk A, write copy on Disk B, renaming file:

```
A> COPY [filename] B:[new name]@
```

d. Copy a file from Disk B, write copy on Disk A, retaining original file name:

```
A> COPY B:[filename]@
```

e. Copy a file from Disk B, write copy on Disk A, renaming file:

```
A> COPY B:[filename] [new name]@
```

f. Copy all files on Disk A, write copies on Disk B, keep names, and retain Disk B's original contents, except files having Disk A file names:

```
A> COPY *.* B:@
```

g. Copy all files on Disk B, write copies on Disk A, keep names, and retain Disk A's original contents except files having disk B file names:

```
A> COPY B:*.* @
```

6. Display disk directory.
(Internal command; no external file necessary. Insert appropriate disk before entering command.)

a. Display directory of Disk A:

```
A> DIR@
```

b. Display directory of Disk A, pausing to show each screenful separately:

```
A> DIR/P@
```

c. Display directory on Disk A in a single screenful of file names only (wide display):

```
A> DIR/W@
```

d. Display directory of disk B:

```
A> DIR B:@
```

e. Display directory of Disk B, pausing to show each screenful separately:

```
A> DIR B:/P@
```

f. Display directory of Disk B in a single screenful of file names only (wide display):

```
A: DIR B:/W@
```

g. Suspend screen display, if necessary, while directory scrolls: Ctrl/Num-Lock. Press any key to resume.

7. Erase a disk.
(Internal command; no external file necessary. Insert disk to be erased before entering command.)

a. Erase disk in Drive A:

```
A> ERASE *.*@
```

b. Erase disk in Drive B:

```
A> ERASE B:*.*@
```

8. Erase a file.
(Internal command; no external file necessary. Insert disk containing file to be erased before entering command.)

a. Erase file in Drive A:

```
A> ERASE [filename]@
```

b. Erase file in Drive B:

```
A> ERASE B:[filename]@
```

9. Format a disk.
(File FORMAT.COM must be in Drive A when entering command.)
a. Format Disk A:

```
A> FORMAT@
```

b. Format Disk A, copying system files:

```
A> FORMAT/S@
```

c. Format Disk B:

```
A> FORMAT B:@
```

d. Format Disk B, copying system files:

```
A> FORMAT B:/S@
```

(Screen message: Insert disk, press key when ready.)

10. Rename a file
(Internal command; no external file necessary. Insert file's disk before entering.)
a. Rename a file on Disk A:

```
A> RENAME [original name] [replacement name]@
```

b. Rename a file on Disk B:

```
A> RENAME B:[original name] [replacement name]@
```

4

Welcome to WordStar

You're armed with an IBM DOS disk and a copy of your WordStar disk, or you have a single master disk combining the two.

Now you're ready to start a word processing file.

First, boot up the system.

After you respond to the date/time requests, either by entering numbers or by pressing RETURN, the A> screen prompt appears. This tells you that A is the logged disk drive and that the computer is ready to receive a program command.

If your WordStar files are on a separate disk, remove the IBM DOS disk at this time and replace it with the WordStar file disk. If you have both programs on a single master disk, leave the disk where it is.

CALLING UP WORDSTAR

The command that "calls up" or "invokes" WordStar is WS, followed by the RETURN key. The W and S may be entered in upper- or lowercase letters.

Thus, your first command is:

```
A>       WS@
```

Now the first WordStar "menu" appears. This is the "No-File" Menu, so named because you are operating outside of, rather than within, a file.

```
                    < < < N O - F I L E   M E N U > > >

--Preliminatry Commands--      |  --File Commands--  | --System Commands--
L Change logged disk drive     |                     |    R Run a program
F File directory off (ON)      |  P  Print a file    |    X EXIT to system
H Set help level               |                     |
--Commands to open a file--    |  E RENAME a file    | -WordStar Options-
 D Open a document file        |  O COPY a file      |    M Run MailMerge
 N Open a non-document file    |  Y DELETE a file    |    S Run SpellStar

DIRECTORY of disk A:
  PRACTICE    PRACTICE.BAK  STORAGE    STORAGE.BAK  TEMP.A    TEMP.B
  TEMP.BAK
```

Beneath the No-File Menu you will see a directory of the logged disk's contents. Unlike the DOS file directory which you met earlier, the WordStar directory lists files without separating their names and extensions. File names appear next to one another rather than in separate columns. No new file name will appear on the directory until its contents have been stored on that disk with a save/store command.

The WordStar file directory is continually updated. As soon as you erase a file with the proper command (which you will meet in the next chapter), that file's name disappears from the screen. As soon as you copy a file from another disk (another command you'll meet in Chapter 5), its name is placed in the file directory.

OPENING A DOCUMENT FILE

To open or enter a file, you must enter a command code. For word processing, you will want to create a "document file," and the command for doing so is D. This letter can be typed in upper- or lowercase.

Further instructions appear on the screen, explaining that a file name is one to eight letters or digits, followed by (optional) a period and one to three additional characters. The optional part of the file name is its "extension."

Don't use an asterisk (*), colon (:), or question mark(?) in your file name, and don't begin the file's name with a period (.). Even though the * and ? are global file name characters in IBM DOS commands, they are not acceptable WordStar file names.

Don't use .BAK or .$$$ in your file name, as these are extensions used only by WordStar, and do not name your file CON, AUX, COM1, LPT1, PRN or NUL, as these have special meanings for the IBM disk operating system.

Enter your file's name by typing it in upper- or lowercase letters. When you have finished typing the name, press the RETURN key, which signals the completion of your entry. For example, the first file we will use in this guide is named PRACTICE, entered as follows: PRACTICE@.

THE FILES-ONLY DISK

An alternate way to open a file is to insert your WordStar disk in Drive A and a formatted disk in Drive B. Now you can instruct the computer to store your projects on the disk in Drive B. As no space is taken up by WordStar and/or the IBM DOS disk programs, you can enter more material before running out of room. The files-only disk is recommended for all editing tasks on the 64K IBM Personal Computer because of memory limitations and for anyone using single-sided disks because of disk space limitations.

If yours is a single disk drive unit, do your editing on the WordStar disk and then, after storing, copy the file onto your files-only disk. The following directions apply to dual disk drive systems.

When the message A> appears, type WS@. To begin your new file, enter B: before the file's name. Using our previous example, your entry is B:PRACTICE@.

Alternately, enter WS@ and when WordStar's No-File Menu appears, press L to change the logged disk to Drive B. Follow the screen's instructions. Now you can enter D to open a new file and not have to preface the file name with B: as described above.

The WordStar manual notes that for WordStar to operate, you must have a disk in Drive A at all times, as well as in the logged drive if other than A.

WHAT IF YOU MAKE A MISTAKE?

If you make a typographical error in your file name (the keyboard responds differently from a regular typewriter), use the DELETE key (abbreviated DEL) or ^S to remove one letter at a time, right to left, or use ^Y to delete the entire entry and start over. The ^S and ^Y commands are entered by holding the CONTROL key (abbreviated CTRL on the keyboard) while pressing the appropriate letter. The screen carries additional instructions for removing and restoring entries, and these same commands can be used whenever WordStar asks for a file name as part of a command. Note that these are file-name-only delete commands; the same entries have different meanings when you edit text. ^S deletes letters from right to left and ^Y erases a single entry only when WordStar's message line asks for a file name or other information.

There are other ways to erase one letter at a time from right to left. As you learned when you entered DOS disk commands in response to the A> screen prompt, the BACKSPACE key will delete one character at a time. Your IBM PC numeric pad keyboard, to the right of the regular keyboard, has another left arrow key (4) which does the same when you enter a file name or other information in response to a WordStar screen message. And though you haven't yet met this command, and probably won't use it much, ^H does the same.

If you press the wrong command key, you won't necessarily have a problem. WordStar will respond only to the letter codes listed on the No-File Menu. But if you accidentally press one of the No-File Menu commands (such as E when you meant to press D), correct your mistake by pressing ^U. ^U is the "cancel command" code; it cancels any command before or after its execution begins. When the No-File Menu reappears, try again.

If you forget to enter the D command and absent-mindedly type the file's name, thinking that the program is ready to receive this information, WordStar will not respond until you type one of the letter codes of the No-File Menu. For example, you forget to press D and, thinking WordStar is ready for a document file name, you type CHAIN, the name of your file. WordStar will respond to the H in this name, interpreting it as the "set help level" command. If your file's name were BEND, it would obey the E (rename file) code. If your file's name were PHLOX, an entry that includes five separate commands (print a file, set help level, change logged disk drive, copy a file, and exit to system), the computer would record all five commands. As soon as the first command was executed or cancelled, the second would appear on-screen, etc. Interrupt any erroneously entered command with ^U and start over.

THINGS YOU WILL NOTICE

As soon as you enter the command D followed by a file name and the RETURN key, the screen will display page 1 of your new file, with the file's name and cursor location on the status line, the margins and tab stops on the ruler line, and several lines of the Main Menu.

WordStar's Main Menu is a list of basic cursor-moving commands. While learning WordStar, you may find this listing helpful, although many of its commands can be replaced with special IBM PC function key shortcuts.

If, like most typists, you would rather use the entire screen for your document, take this opportunity to press F1, the F-function key in the upper-left corner of your keyboard unit. F1 sets the help level by asking whether you want to use help level 3, 2, 1, or 0. (The regular or standard WordStar command for doing this same resetting within a document file is ^JH. You will see ^JH mentioned on the screen menu that reviews WordStar's help commands. F1 is a specially programmed key on the IBM PC keyboard, and your computer will interpret either the F1 key or the command ^JH in the same way.)

Help level 3, which previously occupied eight lines, can be replaced by help level 0, which removes all notation. Press the zero key and you will have an empty screen to work with. To restore the help levels, you can use F1 followed by 1, 2, or 3, depending on how much screen notation you desire. F1 3 provides the most cues. Help level 2 may become your favorite; it keeps command lists off the screen during regular text entry but offers timely messages during editing.

Alternately, you can set the help level while WordStar's No-File Menu is on the screen. One of the No-File options is H, just as another is D for editing a file. From the No-File Menu, press H. An explanation of WordStar's help levels (0, 1, 2, and 3) appears, and you can enter the desired level. The F1 key operates outside a document file, too, so you can use this special key at any time. F1 does exactly what H does at the No-File Menu and what ^JH does within a file.

Here is the screen message that appears whenever you enter F1 from within a file or from WordStar's No-File Menu:

```
HELP LEVELS
  3  all menus and explanations displayed
  2  main editing menu (1-control-char commands) suppressed
  1  prefix menus (2-character commands) also suppressed
  0  command explanations (including this) also suppressed

CURRENT HELP LEVEL IS 3

ENTER Space OR NEW HELP LEVEL (0, 1, 2 OR 3)
```

As you edit a file, you can display information about aspecific WordStar functions. Whenever you want information about a WordStar function, use ^JI to review the help command *I*ndex, and enter the prefix ^J by itself (at help levels 2 or 3) to review the list of command menus. Then enter the letter code for the function you would like to review. From time to time, as you work with WordStar, review the different help menus. They will make more sense as the system becomes familiar.

Here is what the screen displays when you enter the command ^JI:

```
COMMANDS TO --                     ARE --
move cursor                        on main and ^Q menus
scroll file up or down             on main menu; also find (^QF)
delete text                        on main and ^Q menus; also ^KY
move or copy text                  on ^K menu
end edit / save file               ^KD; see ^K menu
print (while editing)              ^KP
set tabs and margins               on ^O menu
reformat text                      ^B; ^JB gives info
find a string; replace             ^QF; ^QA; ^L repeats last
                      space bar for "entering text":
```

Don't be concerned if this menu looks confusing at first. Some of the right column entries are commands and some are screen messages where commands are explained. The index will be more helpful after you meet more of WordStar's commands.

This is a two-part screen message. Pressing the space bar reveals this second portion:

```
                  ***** ENTERING TEXT *****
To enter text at cursor position, just type the text.
Use RETURN key for paragraph end or other fixed line break;
    let word wrap form lines within paragraph.
Type ^V to turn insertion off (to overtype) or back on.
^N may be used to create blank lines ahead of cursor,
    as before inserting a paragraph.
Use ^B to realign margins after corrections.
^JM shows info on margins, tabs, table entry, outline entry.
                         press space bar after reading:
```

Again, some of this information is cryptic, but it will make sense shortly.

When you enter the prefix ^J by itself at help level 2 or 3, this index of Help Menus appears:

```
                        < < <      H E L P     M E N U       > > >
                                             :                       :   -- Other Menus --
H  Display & set the help level      :  S Status line       :  (from Main only)
B  Paragraph reform (CONTROL-B)      :  R Ruler line        :  ^J Help   ^K Block
F  Flags in right-most column        :  M Margins & Tabs :  ^Q Quick  ^P Print
D  Dot commands, print controls      :  P Place markers     :  ^O Onscreen
I  Index of commands                 :  V Moving text       :  Space Bar returns
                                             :                       :   you to Main Menu.
```

This menu presumes that you understand its commands are entered after the ^J prefix. Set the help level with ^JH, display the paragraph reform summary with ^JB, explain the right-most column flags with ^JF, etc. Notice that none of the special IBM PC keys are described in WordStar's on-screen review. F1, which you have already met, works the same as ^JH, but only ^JH is mentioned on the menu above.

MEETING A HELP AID

This is an appropriate time to meet a help aid, so enter ^JR. WordStar will tell you about the ruler line. This on-screen explanation will appear even if you have removed all help commands with F1 0. When you finish reading the explanation, press the space bar and it will disappear.

Your screen will display the following:

```
                    ****  RULER LINE  ****

L----!----!----!----!----!----!----!----!---------R

L    Left margin (set with ^OL)
R    Right margin (set with ^OR)
!    regular tab stop (set with ^OI, clear with ^ON)
#    decimal tab stop (set with ^OI, clear with ^ON)
-    other positions between margins

                              press space bar after reading:
```

Now enter ^JS, which explains the status line. This is a two-part description; press the space bar when you're ready for part 2 and again when you finish reading.

```
            ***** STATUS LINE (top line of screen) *****
^JS              at left end of line is command now executing
A:NAME.TYP       is name of file you are now editing
PAGE n           is page number of cursor (disregards .PN's)
LINE n           is printout line on page of cursor position
COL n            is printout column of line of cursor position
INSERT ON        shows if character insertion is on (^V command)
MAR REL          shows if margins are released (^OX command)
decimal          shows during decimal tabbing
LINE SPACING n     shows if line spacing is not 1 (^OS command)
when WAIT appears, stop typing.               Press space bar:
```

When you press the space bar, part 2 of this message displays:

```
      If page break display is OFF (^OP command) or edit
      was started with N command, then Status Line shows
      FC = nnnn FL = nnnn    in place of    PAGE n  LINE n.

FC=nnnn   cursor position in characters (bytes) from
          beginning of file
FL=nnnn   cursor position in file lines from beginning
          of file, including dot command lines

                                            space bar:
```

STATUS AND RULER LINES

Here's a partial translation of what you just read.

After opening a file, you will see your document file's STATUS LINE at the top of the screen. The status line lists your disk drive, file name, page number, cursor position (line and column), and other information as applicable.

For example, if your first file's name is PRACTICE and you have just entered a five-line paragraph on its first page, the status line will look something like this:

```
A:PRACTICE    PAGE 1 LINE 5 COL 20                INSERT ON
```

This means that the cursor appears 20 spaces from the screen's left margin (space or column 20) on the fifth line (line 5) of the first page (page 1) of the file titled Practice, located on a disk in Drive A. "Insert On" is a screen notation you will meet on page 105. In normal use, INSERT ON appears just as you see here. If your status line doesn't say INSERT ON, press the key labeled Ins, just to the right of the Caps Lock key. Later on, you'll turn insertion on and off for editing reasons, but in the beginning of your WordStar use, keep the function turned on. Other information is displayed on the status line from time to time, depending on what command you are entering or what conditions are in effect.

You will soon meet other status line cues, but a notation to keep in mind this early in your WordStar use is the WAIT command. WAIT means just what it says. WordStar is reading from or writing onto the disk and unless you stop typing or type very slowly, you may lose characters. As soon as WordStar catches up, this warning disappears.

If you leave WordStar's help commands on the screen, they will appear below the status line.

Below the status line and the Main Menu or other menu of help commands, if any, you'll see a highlighted RULER LINE. The standard ruler line, preset by WordStar, looks like this:

```
L----!----!----!----!----!----!----!----!----!----!----!--------R
```

L stands for the *L*eft margin, positioned here in column (space) 1. R stands for the *R*ight margin, positioned here in column (space) 65. Each exclamation mark (!) is a tab stop; these appear at five-space intervals, beginning at column 6.

You will learn in later chapters how to alter the margins and tab stops. For now, to keep things simple, we'll leave everything as WordStar preset it. These preset conditions are called "default values." You can set your own line spacing, margins, hyphens, and other factors, but if you don't, the computer sets them for you "by default."

WORDSTAR'S PRESET PAGE

The page you see on the screen is, for the most part, the page you will see on paper. However, there are differences between the on-screen page and the printed page, and certain conditions have been simplified in the description that follows. Though this is not a comprehensive explanation of the default page, it defines the screen page you'll be working with so you can understand how text and page break lines are arranged as you type.

You will meet the default page again in later chapters, and you will be able to make almost infinite changes in a page's dimensions and other conditions with format control codes and dot commands.

On the standard page, which you see on the screen as you type and which is set automatically or by default:

- The left margin is set for space/column 1.
- The right margin is set for space/column 65.
- Tab stops appear every five spaces, beginning at space/column 6 and ending at space/column 56.
- The page is set for single spacing.
- The character width of printed letters is set for 10 cpi (characters per inch), which corresponds to a 10-pitch typewriter, or the letter size on most pica machines.
- The line spacing is set at six lines per inch, something to keep in mind when you leave room for figures or illustrations.
- The standard page is 55 lines of text in length.

When you type past the 55th line of your page, you will see a PAGE BREAK LINE. It looks like this:

```
---------------------------------------------------------------P
```

During printout, when your document appears on paper (called "hard copy" in the computer business), your pages will begin and end where page break lines indicate. Like the status and ruler lines, the page break line appears only on the screen. It will not print.

Other on-screen notations appear at the far right of the screen. More of these symbols (or "flags," as they are called) will be discussed later and are reviewed on the demonstration disk and on page 307. For now, you should know about the following three flags:

- A blank space at the far right means that your text was "wrapped" as you typed and the line ends in a "soft" carriage return. During later editing and revision, this "soft" or flexible line ending may be rearranged. If you remove or add words and then reform the paragraph, word wrap will review the line breaks automatically.
- A < represents a "hard" carriage return. This symbol appears when you press RETURN, and it shows that the line break indicated on the screen is permanent. Adding new material or revising the text will not disturb this configuration.
- A period (.) marks every line below or after the end of your document. If you are on line 5 and haven't reached line 6, you'll see a dot at the end of line 6, another at the end of line 7, and so on. Your file's size is defined by the characters you insert; WordStar will respond to cursor-moving commands within your file, but it will not move the cursor outside of your file. You cannot move the cursor any higher than line 1, and it will not move into any line marked by the dot described here. The only way to move the cursor into a line marked by a dot is to use the RETURN key (entering a "hard" return, replacing the dot with a < symbol), or keep typing and words will wrap automatically, replacing the dot with a blank space.

THINGS YOU WILL NOTICE

As you use the TAB key, you'll notice a difference between the way it works here and what you're used to on a typewriter. Each ! on the ruler line is a tab stop, and pressing TAB sends the cursor to the next stop. However, the TAB key doesn't stop at the end of a line (column 65). Once you reach the last !, pressing TAB will send the cursor down to the next line and the next ! stop. The fastest way to reach the end of a new line (the right margin) is to use the space bar after you reach the last ! stop.

Tab stops can be rearranged or eliminated with simple commands, as you'll see in Chapter 11.

When you open a document file, WordStar will check through the disk to see if the file already exists. If so, its first page will appear on-screen and you will be "in" the file. That way you can add new material, make revisions, and correct errors. If the computer cannot find the file, it will begin a new one and the first (blank) page of the new file will appear on the screen.

About a third of the page will appear; you can see 22 lines of your file's text on the screen if you set the help level to 0 or 1. WordStar's Main Menu, which appears at help level 3, and the five prefix menus (^J, ^K, ^O, ^P, and ^Q), which appear at help levels 2 and 3, take up as much as eight lines of screen space, or 36 percent of your viewing area.

REVIEW: CALLING UP WORDSTAR

You may work with separate DOS and WordStar disks, or you may combine the two on a master DOS/WordStar disk. Single drive system users should use separate disks to conserve disk space.

- Insert the IBM PC DOS disk in Drive A and turn on the power switch, or insert the DOS disk and restart the system by pressing the CONTROL, ALTERNATE, and DELETE keys simultaneously. Answer the screen messages.
- When the prompt A> appears, remove the DOS disk from Drive A and insert the WordStar files disk (if necessary) and enter WS@ (W, S, and RETURN).
- WordStar's No-File Menu appears on the screen.
- If desired, press H or F1 at this point to remove help notations from the file screen (enter 0), or change to help level 1 or 2. Help level 3 is the preset or default level.
- To open a document file on the disk already in Drive A, press D.
- Enter the file's name and press RETURN.
- A document file's name can consist of one to eight letters and/or digits followed by (optional) a period and (optional) up to three additional characters.
- Do not use an asterisk (*), question mark (?), or colon (:) in your file name; do not begin the file name with a period (.). Do not use the extensions .BAK or .$$$, and do not use the file names CON, AUX, COM1, LPT1, PEN, or NUL.

To set up a files-only disk, a procedure recommended for those using the 64K system and/or single sided disks, follow this procedure (dual disk drive system):

- Call up WordStar.
- Insert a formatted blank disk in Drive B.
- With WordStar's No-File Menu on the screen, press L to change the logged disk to Drive B. Enter B:@ .
- If desired, remove or change help notations at this time with H or F1 followed by 0 (zero), 1, or 2.
- Press D to open a document file and enter an appropriate file name as described above.

If you don't press L to change the logged disk drive, you can leave A as the logged drive and enter your command like this:

- Press D to open a document file.
- Enter B: followed by the file's name, then press RETURN.
- Remember to preface your file name with B: whenever your master disk is in Drive A and Drive A is the logged disk drive.

If yours is a single disk drive unit, edit your file on the WordStar disk, then store your file and, finally, copy it onto a formatted files-only disk. Check to be sure the files match exactly. Now you can erase the original version from the WordStar disk, freeing this disk space for your next editing project. Make a backup copy for safekeeping. To re-edit a file, copy it back onto the WordStar disk.

To correct mistakes in the file name, use ^S, ^H, the BACKSPACE key, the numeric pad's ← (4) key, or the DELETE key to remove one letter at a time, right to left, or ^Y to erase the entire entry. The commands ^S, ^H, BACKSPACE, ← (4), and ^Y have different meanings in text editing; they operate as described here only when you enter a file name or other information in response to a screen message.

A disk must be in Drive A, as well as in the logged drive if other than A, for WordStar to run successfully.

REVIEW: ENTERING TEXT

- WordStar defines your file's size by the number of characters you have entered and by the position of those characters.
- WordStar defines the length of a line by the letters, numbers, symbols, and hard spaces you have typed. The line begins (usually in column 1) with the cursor's leftmost position during text entry. It ends with the rightmost character or hard space.
- Hard spaces are created by the space bar and TAB key.
- Hard returns are entered by the RETURN key.
- The cursor will not respond to any cursor-moving command that would take it outside the file (above line 1, below the last line, to the right of a line's rightmost entry, or to the left of a line's leftmost entry).

QUIZ

1. What does "booting up" mean, and how do you do it?
2. How do you "call up" WordStar?
3. What is the No-File Menu?
4. What command opens or re-enters a word processing file?
5. How can you change the logged disk drive?
6. What are Help Menus, and how can you remove them from your screen?
7. What does A> mean?
8. What is the correct way to hold a disk when inserting it into the drive?
9. How should you store a disk after using it?
10. What do the following "flags" mean, and where do they appear?
    a. [blank space]
    b. <
    c. .
11. What is the status line, and what information does it contain?
12. What is the ruler line and what does it reflect?
13. What is the page break line? On a normal page, where will this line appear?

QUIZ ANSWERS

1. Booting up means turning the computer on and going into an operating condition. To boot up the IBM PC, insert the DOS disk in Drive A and turn on the power, or restart the system (with DOS in Drive A) by pressing CONTROL/ALTERNATE/DELETE simultaneously. Respond to the screen's request for date and time with month-day-year and current time or by pressing RETURN twice. This action generates the screen prompt A>.
2. Enter WS and the RETURN key.
3. Calling up WordStar displays the program's No-File Menu. This is a list of commands you can enter at this point, such as changing the logged disk drive, renaming a file, printing a file, turning the file directory on and off, opening a document file, opening a non-document file, etc.
4. To open (create or re-enter) a word processing file, press D. D stands for Document file.
5. Press L and answer screen message.
6. Help Menus are lists of editing commands in abbreviated form. Their purpose is to instruct or remind you of the commands to use for different editing tasks, but they occupy several lines of screen space. To prevent the Help Menus from appearing on your screen, enter H or F1 while the No-File Menu is on-screen, then enter 0 (zero) or 1. Alternately, wait until you have entered a document file and enter F10 or F11. Level 1 is convenient while editing because it suppresses the command menus but offers occasional instructions.
7. A> is a screen prompt informing you that the logged disk drive is Drive A and that it's ready to receive a command.
8. Hold the disk with the exposed oval pointing away from you and the notched edge facing left.

9. Keep disks in their paper folders and store in the original disk box or a special disk holder.

10. a. The line has been set by word wrap with a soft return.
b. The typist has entered a hard return.
c. The document doesn't extend this far yet.

11. An information line at the top of the screen, it lists your disk drive, current file name, cursor location, and other information as appropriate.

12. The ruler line illustrates line width (margins) and tab stops.

13. Page break lines show where one page ends and the next begins. This line usually appears after line 55.

5

Notes on the No-File Menu

The No-File Menu appears when you call up WordStar, and it will reappear often. This introduction should remove the mystery from its notations.

PRELIMINARY COMMANDS

L Change logged disk drive
F File directory off (ON)
H Set help level

Two of these commands you've encountered already: L for changing the logged disk and H for setting the help level. To activate either command, simply press the appropriate letter.

F turns the file's directory on and off. Its current status or condition is shown on-screen capitalized and in parentheses, (OFF) or (ON). In our example above, the directory is on, which is its normal status.

When you change the disk in a logged drive, the screen will continue to show the old directory. To see what files are on the replacement disk, press F twice — once to turn the directory off (which won't change the screen data) and again to list the new disk's contents.

If you turn the file directory off and leave it off, subsequent visits to WordStar's No-File Menu will not show file names. It's a good idea to leave this directory on-screen.

WordStar calls F the "file directory toggle" because it's an on/off command. Enter the command once and you turn the directory off; enter the same command again and it turns back on.

COMMANDS TO OPEN A FILE

D Open a document file
N Open a non-document file

You have already met D, the command for opening a document file. This command creates or re-enters a file containing pages, margins, and word wrap's automatic carriage return feature. The document file is used for word processing.

A non-document file has no right margin, pagination or word wrap. It uses different tab stops from those of the document file, and tabulation operates differently. This is a convenient file to use if you're writing a computer program or creating other long lists of short statements or numbers.

FILE COMMANDS

P Print a file
E Rename a file
O Copy a file
Y Delete a file

You haven't met these self-explanatory commands yet but they will be introduced in subsequent chapters.

After you have saved or stored a file, you can print it using P, the print command.

You can rename a file using E, which brings an appropriate message to the screen.

O will copy a file onto the same or a separate disk. This command duplicates only one file at a time; to copy an entire disk of files, use the DOS disk copy command described on page 24. Using O from the No-File Menu, you can copy one file into an already-existing file (erasing that file's previous contents), or you can copy a file from one disk onto another.

In the latter case, answer the screen questions with your source file's name (assuming your source file is on your logged disk) and your destination file's name preceded by its drive letter. Example: B is the the logged disk and your file named "January" is on the disk in Drive B. You want to copy "January" onto the disk in Drive A. Do this by pressing O, then answer the first screen question with: JANUARY@ . Answer the second screen question with: A:JANUARY@.

If the source file is in an unlogged drive, prefix its name with the disk drive; if you're copying the file onto the disk in the logged drive, the destination file name does not need a prefix.

You can erase any file on your disk with Y. The letter Y doesn't appear in its function's name the way the codes for *P*rint, c*O*py and r*E*name do, but you'll soon associate Y with deleting and erasing. Nearly every WordStar command that contains the letter Y removes something. Because files take up room on the disk, you'll want to delete those you no longer need. As you edit a file, WordStar creates a backup copy, usually labeled with the file's name and .BAK . When you no longer need a file, erase its backup file, too.

SYSTEM COMMANDS

R Run a program
X Exit to system

The R command allows you to run a different computer program without leaving WordStar. If your primary interest is word processing, you won't use this command often, if at all. X leaves WordStar altogether and returns you to the operating system.

WORDSTAR OPTIONS

M Run MailMerge
S Run SpellStar

MailMerge and SpellStar are optional programs sold by MicroPro, the manufacturer of WordStar. The first of these programs creates mailing lists, form letters, and other convenient business tools; the second is a proofreading program. Although listed on your screen, the commands have no meaning unless their corresponding programs are installed on your system. Otherwise, entering M or S will generate an error message.

This manual is concerned only with WordStar and does not describe MailMerge or SpellStar.

If you don't have these optional programs, try entering their commands from the No-File Menu to generate an error message. Error messages can be unnerving, especially when you don't expect them and when the business of word processing is still new and unfamiliar. Error messages describe mistakes and tell you how to correct them; they're really helpful rather than terrifying. By inviting an error message, you can become acquainted with this constructive feature under relaxed circumstances.

A NOTE ON WORDSTAR'S SCREEN QUESTIONS

When entering a file name as part of the No-File Menu's D, N, P, E, O, or Y commands, or when WordStar requests a file name or other information before it executes a command, the following codes have special meanings:

^S = Delete character at left
^Y = Delete entry
^D = Restore character
^R = Restore entry
^F = Display file directory if not already on-screen
^U = Cancel command

The preceding codes operate as shown when you enter a file name or other information in response to a screen message. In text editing, all but ^U work differently. At help levels 2 and 3, these codes are displayed at the top of the screen whenever WordStar calls for a file name. They operate as described regardless of the help level in use.

^S is not the only command to use for erasing a single letter. The BACKSPACE key, the ← (4) key, and ^H also remove one letter at a time from right to left. Within a file, where the commands operate differently, each of these entry codes moves the cursor one space to the left *without* erasing a letter.

When WordStar asks a question, replacing your status line with a question, these same codes operate. When you enter a find, find-and-replace, block write, read file, or other command generating a screen message, ^D and^R restore the last-entered response to that particular command; ^Y and ^H erase your response; ^F displays the disk's file directory; and ^U interrupts the command.

6

Moving the Cursor

If you are an experienced typist, you have a head start on the WordStar system because you know the keyboard's letter and number key positions. As you type material, you will use the basic keyboard the same way you use a typewriter keyboard.

In addition to the standard letters and numbers, your computer provides special function keys.

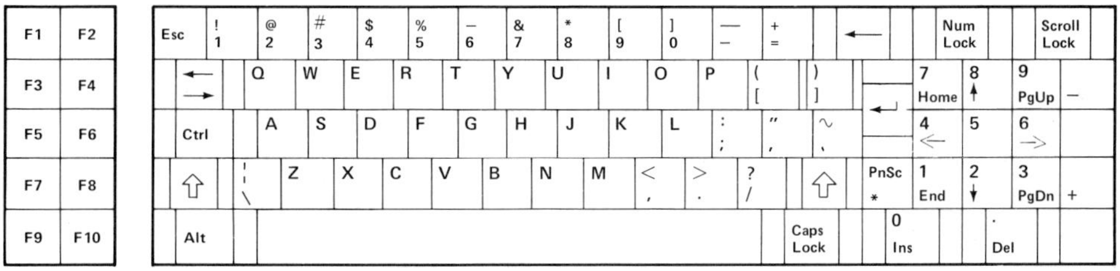

USING THE IBM PC KEYBOARD

Note that:

- Ctrl stands for CONTROL. This key is used like a shift key when WordStar commands are entered. In this manual and in the WordStar instruction book, the use of this key is abbreviated with a caret mark (^). To enter CONTROL A, press the CONTROL or Ctrl key and at the same time, press the letter A. This entry is abbreviated ^A.
- Your DELETE key is labeled Del. The DELETE key removes letters from the screen, one at a time, from right to left.
- The ESCAPE key is abbreviated Esc. It is positioned at the left side of the regular keyboard's row of numbers. You will use the ESCAPE key after interrupting a command, and it will save keystrokes in several commands providing options.
- You will use the ESCAPE, CONTROL and DELETE keys often as you work with WordStar. No WordStar commands use the ALTERNATE key, positioned to the left of the space bar.
- Your RETURN key is twice as long as the letter keys, and it's labeled with a downward arrow: ↵ . You will use the RETURN key for two purposes: (1) to signal the end of a paragraph or to skip a line (the way you use the carriage return of a regular typewriter), and (2) to signal the completion of an entry.
- At the right side of the number row is the BACKSPACE key. This is labeled with a left arrow (←). The BACKSPACE key moves the cursor from right to left one character at a time, but it does not remove characters as the DELETE key does.
- Your TAB key is labeled ⇆ . Even though the arrows point in both direction, the TAB key will move the cursor one tab stop to the right (never to the left) in WordStar use.
- The shift keys on your keyboard are labeled with upward arrows (↑). To capitalize a letter, or to obtain the uppercase symbol on a number or symbol key located on

the regular letter keyboard, you will have to press the shift key. There are two shift keys, one to the left and one to the right of the space bar.

- To the right of the space bar and just below the right shift key is a Caps Lock key. This key provides the "locked shift" function — with important variations. When this key is on, you can type any letter in capital form, but numbers will print as numbers and not as their capitalized symbols. This means that with the lock key on, you can type ABCD1234EFGH567 without interruption. Like the numbers, these keys are not affected by Caps Lock: - = []; ' ' \, ./. If you type something in all caps and need a colon (:), you'll have to use the regular shift key or you will obtain a semicolon (;) even though the lock key is turned on.

Also, the Caps Lock key can surprise you if you leave it depressed and then use the regular shift key. This Is Typed With The Caps Lock Key Off, bUT tHIS iS tYPED wITH tHE cAPS lOCK kEY oN. To remove the Caps Lock feature, simply press this key again.

THE NUMERIC PAD AND F-FUNCTION KEYBOARDS

At the right of your regular keyboard is the numeric pad keyboard. Its keys, showing numbers and symbols, are arranged in regular adding machine or calculator order.

However, you will not use these keys to generate numbers in your WordStar use. If you should press one of the keys and see a number on the screen, it's because the keyboard's lock key, labeled Num Lock (a gray key in the top row at right) is depressed. Press the Num Lock key again and the number keys will behave as described later in this chapter. Note, however, that these keys will not operate as described if you press the regular shift key when using them.

To the left of your regular keyboard is the F-key board. Ten keys are arranged in two columns, numbered F1 through F10. Each of these keys has been given a special WordStar definition. You will meet them all in subsequent chapters, and they are reviewed inside the back cover.

You should know about one last key, the PrtSc key, which stands for Print Screen. This is just below the RETURN key. Because it has nothing to do with WordStar's commands, it will not be described again in this book. However, it can be a real convenience because it causes whatever is on the screen to print on paper without your having to go through the usual storage and print command procedures. If you press the PrtSc key by itself, it will create an asterisk (*) on the screen. But if you press it while holding the shift key, and if your printer is turned on, it will transfer everything on the screen to the printer.

Throughout this book, these abbreviations are used for the keys on the numeric pad at the regular keyboard's right:

End(1)	The 1 key, also labeled End
↓(2)	The 2 key, also labeled ↓
PgDn(3)	The 3 key, also labeled PgDn
←(4)	The 4 key, also labeled ←

(The numeric pad's 5 key is not used in WordStar)

→(6)	The 6 key, also labeled →
Home(7)	The 7 key, also labeled Home
↑ (8)	The 8 key, also labeled ↑
PgUp(9)	The 9 key, also labeled PgUp
Ins	The Ins key, also labeled 0
DELETE	The Del key, also labeled .

The + and - keys at the board's far right are not used in WordStar; neither is the Scroll Lock/Break key at its top.

The Num Lock key, once correctly positioned, will not be changed. (In one position, the Num Lock key produces numbers from the numeric pad keyboard; if pressed again, it causes the cursor to move, as described in this chapter.)

The F-function keyboard is arranged in two columns at the regular keyboard's left:

F1	F2
F3	F4
F5	F6
F7	F8
F9	F10

MEETING THE CURSOR

On a typewriter, you position paper by using the carriage return or paper roller and the space bar or tab key. These tools allow you to move to any line and space on the page so that you can correct an error, cross something out, or pick up where you left off.

Typing on the computer with WordStar is rather different. To move to a certain line or a certain part of a line, you have to control the cursor.

The cursor is represented here and in the WordStar manual as a solid bar ■, but on your screen it displays as a flashing underline dash (_). Its position marks the place that will be taken by whatever letter or number or space you enter next. As you type and edit, you will want to move the cursor in different directions; this chapter introduces cursor-moving commands. They have been summarized on pages 69–70 and in Appendix A, listed in the index, and reviewed in the Condensed Command Index inside the back cover.

As you become familiar with these command codes, you will see how logical they are. Even if your time at the terminal is limited, you can make sense of cursor commands by reading this chapter while you visualize the keyboard.

A Note on WordStar's Command Codes

Although the IBM PC's keyboard simplifies a number of WordStar commands, you will be meeting both the regular WordStar command codes and the IBM keyboard's shortcuts in this book. You don't have to use the codes that have IBM keyboard alternatives, but because these command codes appear on your screen menus, because they are used in the WordStar manual, and because so many commands you will use are based on or closely related to these simple codes, they are introduced here.

Remember that the numeric pad keys won't work as described here if you hold the shift key while pressing them. (In that case, they'll generate the numbers shown on the keys.) They won't work if you press the CONTROL key while typing them, either. (If you do that, nothing happens. The cursor doesn't move and nothing is added to the screen.)

MOVING THE CURSOR

A mnemonic device is anything that helps or aids the memory. Your mnemonic device for WordStar's cursor-moving commands is the terminal keyboard. Letters in the top row point up; those in the bottom row point down. In the middle row, letters to the left point left and those to the right point right. The center keys in this mnemonic configuration form a diamond.

The "key" keys are usually typed with the left hand, and the "key diamond" is in the middle of this group:

```
    W   E   R
       / \
  A   S   D   F
       \ /
    Z   X   C
```

You will meet other mnemonic devices or memory aids in later sections, but the direction commands you learn here are those you will use most often.

Another memory aid, this one appearing at the top of your screen, is WordStar's Main Menu. You will find the Main Menu most helpful as you begin to work with WordStar, for it reviews the basic cursor-move commands. However, this menu will not appear on your screen unless the help level remains level 3, the default value, and it does not display the IBM keyboard's alternate commands. As mentioned before, most typists prefer to see as much of their own work on the screen as possible. In a short time, if not from the beginning of your WordStar practice, you will want to remove the Main Menu.

Here's what it looks like:

```
                    < < <     M A I N   M E N U     > > >
  --Cursor Movement --      | -Delete-   |  -Miscellaneous-     |  -Other  Menus-
^S char left ^D char right |^G char     | ^I Tab     ^B Reform | (from Main only)
^A word left ^F word right |DEL chr lf  | ^V INSERT ON/OFF     |^J Help   ^K Block
^E line up   ^X line down  |^T word rt  |^L Find/Replce again|^Q Quick ^P Print
   --Scrolling--            |^Y line     |RETURN End paragraph|^O Onscreen
^Z line up   ^W line down  |            | ^N Insert a RETURN |
^C screen up ^R screen down|            | ^U Stop a command  |
```

The Main Menu lists more commands than you will meet in this chapter, so don't worry if some of its notations look confusing. The cursor movement codes listed at top left are those you'll work with in a moment. Scroll commands and delete commands follow in Chapters 8 and 9. The remaining Main Menu commands will become familiar shortly.

Remember that the Main Menu appears by default, or whenever the help level is set at level 3. The Main Menu does not appear at any other help level.

It's time to meet the cursor.

To experiment with this feature, set up a file as instructed in the last chapter and type any short paragraph you like. Don't worry about mistakes or typographical errors; just get a paragraph of words on the screen. As you type you will notice that the computer automatically justifies the right margin. DO NOT use the RETURN key when you reach the end of a line unless you have completed a paragraph and want to begin a new one, or unless you want to skip a line. The carriage return habit may be hard to break if you are used to an electric typewriter.

After you have entered your first practice paragraph, try the following commands. Watch the cursor on the screen as you press the keys.

Word at Left, Letter at Left

^A moves the cursor to the beginning of the word at the cursor's left. Assuming there are words at the cursor's left, try this command. The cursor stops at the first letter of the word at left. In the key diamond, A points to the left.

^S moves the cursor one character to the left. Repeat this command until you reach the beginning of the word at the left. In WordStar's key diamond, S points to the left—but not so far as A does. A points a whole word to the left; S points a letter to the left.

The numeric pad key ←(4) does the same thing as ^S. Try this command. WordStar has still more ways of reaching the letter at left: the BACKSPACE key and ^H work the same way, too. Although you will probably use the ←(4) key more than any of the others, try all four commands and watch the screen.

Things You Will Notice

If you are already at the far left of the page when you enter ←(4), the cursor will move up a line and continue going from right to left, beginning at the end of the preceding line. In other words, the cursor moves from one space to the space preceding it or from one word to the word preceding it regardless of position on the page. When it moves from a lower line to an upper line in response to your "move left" command, the cursor will pause at the end of that line. Enter the command again to move left.

Word at Right, Letter at Right

^F moves the cursor to the beginning of the word at the cursor's right. This makes sense because F is the rightmost key in the diamond's middle row. Try this command.

^D moves the cursor one character to the right. D is also on the right side of the diamond, but not quite so far right as the F. It moves the cursor one space, rather than one word, to the right. Repeat this command until you reach the end of the word.

The IBM numeric pad keyboard has an alternate command for moving one space to the right: →(6). Try this command a few times, too.

Neither ^F, ^D, nor →(6) disturbs the screen's text. They simply move the cursor one word or one space to the right.

Down One Line, Up One Line

On the numeric pad keyboard you will see ↑(8) and ↓(2). These keys move the cursor up one line or down one line without disturbing text already on the screen.

The Main Menu shows WordStar's regular commands for these line moves, ^X (down one line) and ^E (up one line).

Try ↓ (2). This moves the cursor down one line, unless you are already on the file's last line.

Enter ↑ (8). This moves the cursor up one line, unless you are already on the file's top line.

Note that WordStar won't move your cursor straight up or straight down the way you expect at first. This is because the cursor will not move any farther right on a line than it has already been. If the cursor has been as far right as column 5, and you are a line below it but over at column 15, your command to move up one line will move the cursor up and left at the same time.

Therefore, whenever you want to position the cursor at a certain line and column, move up or down first. Then move left or right. You'll waste time if you painstakingly move to the proper column and then use an up or down command, because the cursor probably won't maintain its column position.

For example, here is the cursor in three consecutive "down one line" moves.

```
     New  York  City covers 300  square
miles at the mouth of the Hudson River,
and  it  includes five  boroughs:  Man-■
hattan,  The Bronx,  Brooklyn,  Queens,■
and Staten Island.■
■
```

The cursor begins at the paragraph's right edge, and the first ↓ (2) command moves it down one line, retaining the column position. This is because the cursor had previously moved to the far right of the line below. It did so when that line's text was entered.

However, the cursor never reached the end of the next line down, so another ↓ (2) command moves it down and to the left. How far left depends on how far right the cursor went on its previous paths through that line.

The last ↓ (2) command moves the cursor all the way over to column 1. No text was entered on this line, so the cursor never moved beyond column 1.

In a double-spaced document, this cursor response can be especially distracting. If there's no text on the line, the cursor will scoot back to column 1.

Always move up or down first; then move right or left. Position the cursor on the proper line; then move to the proper column.

THE KEYBOARD MEMORY AID

The left side of the keyboard makes the WordStar regular (Main Menu) commands more obvious. Remember your mnemonic device?

↑
E
up one line

←- A	←- S	D -→	F -→
left one word	left one letter	right one letter	right one word

down one line
X
↓

The numeric pad keys are even easier to remember because of their labels:

↑(8)

←- (4) -→(6)

↓(2)

THINGS YOU WILL NOTICE

Nearly every key on the IBM PC keyboard is an "automatic repeat" key. What typewriter companies advertise as exotic options can be, in such abundance, almost an inconvenience. Lean too hard on the space bar and you'll generate a line of blank spaces; press the tab key with a heavy hand and you'll scoot past two or three stops. It's common for new computer users, regardless of their typing expertise, to produce double letters when they don't intend to. Combining a letter key with the control key doesn't slow it down, so don't be surprised if ^A moves you several words to the left instead of just one, or if ^F moves you three or four words to the right.

You can prolong a command to take advantage of its repeating nature. Enter a long ↓ (2) and watch the cursor jump down one line after another, or press ←(4) and move left. Use this method for short distances and the cursor's motion will stop as soon as you release the command. If your entry is extended, the cursor will continue to move while it catches up with the computer's commands. Experiment with your screen and keyboard, and keep an eye on the status line. If a WAIT message appears, release the command. There are more efficient ways to reach a point several lines or spaces away, but from time to time the repeating keys will come in handy.

REVIEW: CURSOR-MOVING COMMANDS

↑ ^E moves the cursor up one line
↑ ↑ (8) moves the cursor up one line
↓ ^X moves the cursor down one line

↓ ↓(2) moves the cursor down one line
← ^A moves the cursor one word to the left
← ^S moves the cursor one letter to the left
← ←(4) moves the cursor one letter to the left
← BACKSPACE moves the cursor one letter to the left
← ^H moves the cursor one letter to the left
→ ^F moves the cursor one word to the right
→ ^D moves the cursor one letter to the right
→ →(6) moves the cursor one letter to the right

Note that ^F and ^A move the cursor to the beginning (first letter) of the word at right or word at left.

The commands ^E, ^(8), ^X, and ↓(2) operate in single spacing, moving one line at a time, regardless of the line spacing in use.

QUIZ

Match the commands to the cursor's motion.

1. (8) A. Right one letter
2. (2) B. Up one line
3. (4) C. Down one line
4. (6) D. Left one letter
5. ^F E. Right one word
6. ^A F. Left one word
7. What are three alternate commands for moving one character left?

QUIZ ANSWERS

1. B
2. C
3. D
4. A
5. E
6. F
7. ^H, ^S, or the BACKSPACE key.

7

Expanded Cursor-Moving Commands

THE TWO-LETTER CODE

You can combine directional cursor-moving commands with ^Q to move the cursor farther and faster. ^Q is the Quick prefix; it accelerates or expands the command it precedes. Several commands that have the ^Q prefix in regular WordStar use have been replaced by special keys on the IBM PC.

MOVE TO TOP OF SCREEN, MOVE TO BOTTOM OF SCREEN

On the numeric pad keyboard you'll see a key labeled Home(7) and another labeled End(1).

The Home(7) key always returns the cursor to the screen's upper-left corner: column 1, line 1.

The End(1) key moves the cursor to the "end" of the screen, its lowest line. That is, it moves to the lowest line the cursor can enter — you will be able to read another screen line below that, but the cursor cannot move into that line without another command from you.

The regular WordStar commands for these moves are ^QE and ^QX.

^QE is slightly different from Home(7) because while both take you to the screen's top line, Home(7) moves left to column 1 every time. ^QE will often do so, but if your screen has text on every line, it may move the cursor straight up to the middle or right side of the top line.

^QX and the End(1) key operate identically.

MOVE TO BEGINNING OF LINE, MOVE TO END OF LINE

^QS moves the cursor to the screen's left edge (the beginning of a line), extending the ^S command, which moves the cursor to the left one letter at a time.

You may wonder whether ^Q entered before the other left-one-space commands does the same thing. It doesn't. ^QH moves the cursor to the left a space at a time, and if you let the command run, the cursor will eventually reach the beginning of the line. (If you try this command, you can interrupt it by pressing the space bar.) ^Q←(4) doesn't move the cursor at all. And ^Q BACKSPACE is something to approach with caution: it moves the cursor to the beginning of the line, all right, but it erases everything along the way.

^QD moves the cursor to the far right edge (end of a line), continuing the function of ^D, which moves right one letter at a time. ^Q→(6) will do the same, but because the Q and D keys are so close together on the keyboard, you can enter ^QD faster.

DIRECTIONAL COMMANDS

As you can see, there are several ways to get the cursor from where it is to where you want it to be. To go from the far left of a line to the far right of that same line, you can move:

- One letter at a time by using →(6),

- One letter at a time by using ^D,
- One word at a time by using ^F, or
- In a single step by using ^QD or ^Q→(6).

You can go back to the beginning of a line by moving:

- One letter at a time with ←(4),
- One letter at a time with ^S, ^H, or the BACKSPACE key,
- One word at a time with ^A, or
- In a single step with ^QS.

You can move up by going:

- One line at a time with ↑ (8),
- One line at a time with ^E, or
- To the top of the screen with Home(7) or ^QE.

You can move down by going:

- One line at a time with ↓ (2),
- One line at a time with ^X, or
- To the bottom of the screen with End(1) or ^QX.

THINGS YOU WILL NOTICE

^QD moves the cursor to the end of a line, but if that line is very short, the cursor won't go far. Similarly, ^QX moves to the bottom of the screen, but if your document ends halfway down, the cursor can't move farther.

It takes some time to grow used to the computer's logic, especially when you can't see the conditions that determine its action. For example, if you move onto a new, unused line and press the space bar 20 times, that line is now 20 columns or spaces wide. Every hard space is an entered character. Move back to the beginning of the line with ^QS, then enter ^QD. The cursor will stop at space 20, the "end" of that line. Until the cursor actually reaches space 65, either because you type that far or because you use the tab key or space bar, WordStar will define the ruler line's right margin and the end of a line as two different and unrelated places.

MOVE TO END OF FILE, MOVE TO BEGINNING OF FILE

Once you have entered several pages of material, you will appreciate the next commands.

To return to the beginning of your file in a single step, enter F10. To reach the end of a file, use F9.

While these commands are executing, your status line will show the signals ^Q^R (when you enter F10) and ^Q^C (when you use F9). This is because ^QR and ^QC are the regular WordStar commands for reaching the beginning and end of a file.

You can use two numeric pad keys to reach the end of a file and the beginning of a file, though this isn't a very efficient shortcut: ^Q(9) will take you to the beginning of your file and ^Q(3) will take you to the end. You will work with the PgUp(9) and PgDn(3) keys in Chapter 8. Their abbreviations stand for "page up" and "page down."

Try to think of a clever way of associating F9 with the file's end and F10 with its beginning. Or tape a label beside the keys. These commands appear in the Condensed Command Index inside the back cover.

MOVE TO PREVIOUS CURSOR POSITION

If you are editing a document and want to return the cursor to its previous position (the point it occupied before you entered the last command), you can move it back by entering ^QP. Remember this command by thinking: *Q*uickly return to *P*revious position.

WHAT IF YOU MAKE A MISTAKE?

If you enter the wrong cursor command, you may find yourself quite a distance from where you wanted to go. Use ^QP to move the cursor back to where it was before you entered the erroneous command, or move the cursor in the right direction a space, a line, a word, or a section at a time with the commands introduced here.

INTERRUPTING A TWO-LETTER COMMAND

When you type the prefix of a two-letter code, such as ^Q, and then change your mind about using it before entering the second letter, you can interrupt the command in any of these ways:

- Press the space bar, or
- Press RETURN, or
- Press ^U, the INTERRUPT code, or
- Press ESCAPE.

Note

When you enter a two-letter code, it's a good idea to hold the CONTROL key as you enter both letters. This isn't always necessary; in most cases, as long as you enter a command's first letter with the CONTROL key depressed, the second letter can be typed separately. In a few situations, though, entering the second letter without depressing Ctrl may leave you with an invalid entry and an extra letter on the screen. This doesn't happen with the ^Q Quick commands, but holding the CONTROL key for both letters is a good habit. Whenever a *number* is part of a command, enter the number by itself; do not press the CONTROL key simultaneously.

REVIEW: EXPANDED CURSOR-MOVING COMMANDS ON-SCREEN

When you enter ^Q, that prefix will appear on the status line at the upper-left corner. This notation disappears when you complete the entry.

If you are using help level 2 or 3 (F1 2 or F1 3), ^Q by itself produces the Quick Menu, a review of all the ^Q commands. This menu disappears when you complete your entry by adding a second letter, or you can press the ESCAPE key, the space bar, RETURN, or ^U to cancel the command. WordStar's Main Menu, listing the basic cursor-moving codes, returns to the screen. F1 0 and F1 1 remove the menu.

Here is the Quick Menu as it appears on-screen:

```
                          < < <    Q U I C K    M E N U    > > >
  ---Cursor Movement---     : -Delete- : --Miscellaneous-- : --Other Menus--
S left side   D right side :Y line rt :F Find text in file: (from Main only)
E top scrn    X bottom scrn:DEL lin lf:A Find & Replace    :^J Help   ^K Block
R top file    C end file              :L find Misspelling  :^Q Quick  ^P Print
B top block   K end block             :Q Repeat command or :^O Onscreen
0-9 marker    Z up     W down         :  key until space   :Space Bar returns
P previous    V last Find or Block    :  bar or other key  :you to Main Menu.
```

The Quick Menu lists all commands beginning with the prefix ^Q. You will not meet many of these commands until much later in the book. To avoid future confusion, you should know that it contains one command (^QL) which will not operate correctly without the SpellStar proofreading program. If you enter ^QL and do not have SpellStar, appropriate (but meaningless) screen questions will appear.

REVIEW: CURSOR-MOVING COMMANDS

These commands move the cursor to the right:

→ →(6) moves right one character (so does ^D).
→ ^F moves right one word.
→ ^QD moves to the end of the line.

These commands move the cursor to the left:

← ←(4) moves left one character (so do ^H, ^S, and the BACKSPACE key).
← ^A moves left one word.
← ^QS moves to the beginning of the line.

These commands move the cursor up:

↑ ↑(8) moves up one line (so does ^E).
↑ Home(7) moves to top left corner of screen.
↑ ^QE moves to the top of the screen (not necessarily its left corner).
↑ F10 moves to the beginning of the file (so does ^QR).

These commands move the cursor down:

↓ ↓(2) moves down one line (so does ^X).
↓ End(1) moves to the bottom of the screen (so does ^QX).
↓ F9 moves to the end of the file (so does ^QC).

Additional command:

- ^QP moves to the cursor's previous position.

The directional commands you will use most often are these IBM key shortcuts:

- Up one line with ↑ (8)
- Down one line with ↓ (2)
- Left one character with ←(4)
- Right one character with →(6)
- To beginning of file with F10
- To end of file with F9
- To top left of screen with Home(7)
- To bottom of screen with End(1)

You will continue to use the standard WordStar letter codes for these commands:

- Right one word with ^F
- Left one word with ^A
- To beginning of line with ^QS
- To end of line with ^QD

And occasionally you may move:

- To top of screen with ^QE
- To bottom of screen with ^QX

EXERCISE: MOVING THE CURSOR WITH EXPANDED COMMANDS

So that you can practice the different cursor-move commands, type several lines of text on the screen. They can be lines of nonsense; just create a number of lines of different length, and make the document file longer than a single screen in length.

If you already have a document file in which to practice, enter that file now.

You may want a friend to read these instructions out loud so that you can watch the screen as you work.

1. Move the cursor to the end of your file with F9.
2. Now move the cursor back to the beginning of your file with F10.

   Watch the screen while these commands execute. Whatever command is in progress is shown on the status line at far left. The screen will always display the standard or regular WordStar command codes, even when you use IBM PC alternate keys, so the screen should show ^Q^R when you use F10 and ^Q^C when you use F9.

3. Now return to the end of your file. Once you have reached the end of the file, check the status line and note your cursor position. You will know how long the file is because the status line reports your position by PAGE and LINE number.
4. While you are at the end of your file, press ↓ (2). Because you are already on the file's last line, WordStar will disregard the command. ↓ (2) normally moves the cursor down one line.

5. Enter F10 again. The cursor will move to the top or beginning of your file, positioning itself at page 1, line 1, column 1. Check the status line; it should reflect this position. While you are here, enter ↑ (8), which normally moves the cursor up one line. Because you are already in the file's first line, the cursor cannot move up, so WordStar will disregard the entry.
6. Now enter End(1). The screen text will not move, but the cursor will disappear from the top of your screen and reappear at the bottom. Even though you will be able to see one line beneath the cursor, the cursor is in the last line you can work on. To reach the next line down, using the ↓ (2) key, you will cause the screen's text to shift. Press ↓ (2) and watch this happen.
7. Enter Home(7). This moves you to the top of the screen without shifting the on-screen text.
8. Now enter ^QP. The cursor will return to the place it occupied before you entered the last command, so it should return you to the bottom of the screen, which is where you were before you entered Home(7). ^QP returns the cursor to its previous position.
9. Enter ^QD. The cursor moves to the end (far right) of its line.
10. Enter ^QS. The cursor returns to the beginning (far left) of the line.
11. To understand more about ^QD and ^QS, move back to the end of the file with F9 and use the RETURN key to skip a line or two. Now press the space bar 25 times. WordStar considers this line 25 columns long; it begins at column 1 and ends at column 26. ^QS will take you to the beginning of the line (column 1), and ^QD will take you to the end of the line (column 26). Enter these codes and watch the screen. Even though the line is invisible, WordStar remembers the cursor's path across it and defines the line accordingly.
12. While your text is still on your screen, review the cursor-moving codes you met in Chapter 6.

    - ↑ (8) moves up one line
    - ^A moves left one word
    - ← (4) moves left one letter
    - BACKSPACE moves left one letter
    - ^F moves right one word
    - → (6) moves right one letter
    - ↓ (2) moves down one line

Press each of these commands several times. Now review the expanded cursor-move commands, which you met in this chapter:

Home(7) moves to the top left corner of the screen.
End(1) moves to the bottom of the screen.
^QD moves to the end of a line.
^QS moves to the beginning of a line.
F10 moves to the beginning of the file.
F9 moves to the end of the file.

Review the commands until they become familiar.

QUIZ

1. List the commands for moving the cursor:
   a. up one line.
   b. down one line.
   c. one letter to the left.
   d. one letter to the right.
   e. one word to the left.
   f. one word to the right.
2. What is the fastest way to move the cursor:
   a. to the top of the screen?
   b. to the bottom of the screen?
   c. to the beginning of a file?
   d. to the end of a file?
   e. to the right of the screen?
   f. to the left of the screen?
3. What is the code for moving the cursor back to the place it occupied before the last command was entered?

QUIZ ANSWERS

1. a. ↑ (8) b. ↓ (2) c.←(4) d.→(6) e. ^A f. ^F
2. a. Home(7) b. End(1) c. F10 d. F9 e. ^QD, unless the cursor has not yet been to the screen's far right, in which case the TAB key and space bar will move you. f. ^QS
3. ^QP

   You can also use any of WordStar's regular commands: ^E moves up one line, ^X down one line, ^S (or ^H or the BACKSPACE) moves left one character, ^D moves right one character, ^QE moves to the top of the screen, ^QX moves to the bottom of the screen, ^QR moves to the beginning of a file, and ^QC moves to the end of a file.

8

Scrolling

SCROLLING DEFINED

When typing on regular paper, it's easy to scan through what you have already prepared. Just look through the pages.

When your material is stored on a disk, looking through it requires a different approach.

Scroll commands move the screen across your text so that you can look through several pages quickly or very slowly.

However, the terms usually used to describe scrolling create more confusion than comprehension. It's worth spending a moment defining the business of scrolling.

Think of your file as inscribed on one long sheet of paper or parchment. Depending on the length of your file, it may be a short or very long sheet. Regardless of its overall length, only a few lines (usually 22) can be viewed at one time on the screen.

You can think of the parchment itself being pulled up or down past a stationary viewing area, or you can think of the viewing screen being moved up or down (like a magnifying glass, for example) over the stationary parchment. These different definitions of "up" and "down" create most of scrolling's misunderstandings.

The WordStar manual and the screen's Main Menu complicate this matter by using a mnemonic device based on one definition and a two-word description based on the other. To avoid confusion, and to be consistent, think of the screen as your portable magnifying glass and the parchment on which your document is inscribed as a stationary, motionless sheet. The file doesn't move; instead, your special viewer moves up, down, left, and right over the file. Once you imagine your file and the screen in this relationship, you'll find it easy to understand scrolling and easy to remember WordStar's scroll commands. In the section that follows, and whenever you think of scrolling, disregard what the WordStar manual and the screen menus say about scrolling up and down.

REVEAL LOWER LINE

You can make one additional lower line visible by pressing ^Z. Z is in the bottom row of keys, so it points down. Every time you enter ^Z, a new line moves into view at the bottom and the top line of text disappears.

Remember this command by thinking of new lower lines and the position of Z on the keyboard, pointing down to where the new line of text will appear.

REVEAL UPPER LINE

Make additional upper lines visible by using ^W. Every time you enter ^W, a new line arrives at the top of the screen and the bottom line of text disappears.

W is in the top row of letter keys, so it points up. Your eyes move up to the top of the screen as new material moves into view, making the correlation between W and "up" easy to remember. In the same way, you move our hypothetical magnifying glass up from its previous viewing position. ^W, at the top of your keyboard, points to the top of your screen.

CONTINUOUS SCROLL

Just as ^Q extended the function of earlier codes, it makes W and Z "continuous scroll" commands.

If you are at the beginning of a page and want to see the whole thing a line at a time, press ^QZ for continuous scrolling. This command reveals text, a line at a time, with the new lines appearing at the bottom of the screen. Scrolling continues until you reach the end of the file, or until you interrupt by pressing the space bar or any other key.

^QW scrolls in the opposite direction, bringing new lines of text into view at the top of the page until the cursor reaches the beginning of the file or until you interrupt with the space bar or a letter key.

The directions "up" and "down" correspond with W and Z on the keyboard. W points up, symbolizing the display of new text at the top of your screen; Z points down, representing new lines of text at the bottom.

CHANGE SPEEDS IN CONTINUOUS SCROLLING

^QZ and ^QW offer different speeds. Enter any number between 1 and 9 after the command (the default speed is 3) to speed up or slow down the scrolling action. The fastest speed is 1, the slowest 9. ^QW9 moves very slowly in sporadic jumps from a file's end to its beginning. ^QZ1 moves rapidly from beginning to end.

WordStar allows you to change speeds at any time during scrolling. If you begin with the default speed by entering ^QZ, you can let several lines go by and then speed up by typing the number 1. This number is entered alone; the CONTROL key isn't pressed with it. After a few lines go by, you can slow back to the default speed by typing the number 3, or you can slow scrolling further by pressing 5.

SCREENFUL-AT-A-TIME SCROLL

WordStar offers two additional vertical scroll commands.

^C scrolls an entire screenful, bringing the next section of text into view. Each section that appears with the ^C command comes after, or below, material already on the screen.

On the numeric pad keyboard, PgDn(3) does the same thing. Think of this key having a downward arrow on it, just like ↓ (2) beside it. You are moving your viewing screen "down the page," so PgDn (page down) is appropriately labeled.

To scroll in the opposite direction a screenful at a time, press ^R. R is on the top row of keys, so it points up.

PgUp(9) does the same thing. Think of this key as having the same upward arrow as the ↑ (8) key beside it. You are moving your viewing screen "up the page," so PgUp (page up) is appropriately labeled.

CONTINUOUS SCREENFUL SCROLL

^QQ is a special code. It means, "Repeat next command until interrupted," and it can turn a cursor-moving entry into a "continuous" command.

For example, ^C normally causes a full-screen scrolling action. By entering ^QQC, you get a rapid screenful-at-a-time scroll that ends when you interrupt by pressing the space bar (or any other key) or when you reach the end of your file.

Similarly, ^QQR moves in the opposite direction, causing one screenful after another to appear in a backward motion. Scrolling continues until you interrupt with the space bar or until you reach the beginning of the file.

Enter these commands by depressing the CONTROL key the whole time (^Q^Q^C and ^Q^Q^R). ^QQ means REPEAT NEXT COMMAND, and it can be placed before any cursor-moving instruction. In addition, it will create a string of letters if you don't hold the CONTROL key with the final letter, producing a series like this: ccccccccccccccccccc. With most two-letter commands WordStar is flexible; so long as you use the CONTROL key with its prefix, the command is likely to work. With ^QQ, hold the CONTROL key with the final entry: ^Q^Q^C, ^Q^Q^R, etc.

You can obtain the same results by pressing the CONTROL key with the first ^Q, releasing it before typing the second Q, and depressing it again with the final entry: ^QQ^R and ^QQ^C. But it's faster to keep the key depressed with your left hand during the entire command entry.

As with ^QW and ^QZ, you can control the speed of ^QQR and ^QQC with the numbers 1 to 9. ^QQC followed by the number 1 creates the fastest scroll of lower screenfuls; ^QQR followed by 9 brings the slowest continuous scroll of upper screenfuls. You can change the speed at any time by entering a new number. Any key other than a number key will stop the scrolling action.

Remembering the numeric pad keyboard, you can enter the commands like this: ^QQPgUp(9) and ^QQPgDn(3). However, this is one case where the numeric key doesn't offer a shortcut. Like the previously mentioned commands ^QPgUp(9) and ^QPgDn(3), which move you to the beginning and end of your file, respectively, these codes are rather awkward. You'll probably find ^QQC and ^QQR faster to type, and because ^Q^Q^C and ^Q^Q^R appear on the status line even when you use the numeric pad keys, the standard WordStar command codes are easy to remember.

HORIZONTAL SCROLLING

Horizontal scrolling scans the text from left to right, a necessity in wide documents. You can set the right margin far beyond column 65, but because the screen cannot display much beyond the standard line, it's impossible to see the whole entry.

You will study horizontal scrolling in more detail on page 153 in the section on wide documents, but the commands are already familiar.

^QD moves the cursor to the end of a line, and when the line is longer than the screen is wide, WordStar shifts the viewing area so you can see "off-screen" text. By using ^QD, ^D, or ^F, you can scroll from left to right.

By using ^S, ^A, or ^QS, you can scroll back to the originally displayed section. ^QS, which moves the cursor to the beginning of a line, is the fastest command to use for this purpose; it returns the cursor to column 1 in a single motion.

REVIEW: SCROLL COMMANDS

Note that in this review, as in the preceding discussion, the directions up, down, right, and left, and the adjectives upper and lower, refer to the direction followed by your eyes as you view newly revealed text. This is the same direction your imaginary, movable viewing screen follows as you reposition it over the file's stationary text.

These scroll commands reveal upper lines of text:

- ^W reveals one upper line.
- ^QW reveals upper lines continuously.
- ^R reveals an upper screenful.
- PgUp(9) reveals an upper screenful.
- ^QQR reveals upper screenfuls continuously.
- ^QQPgUp(9) reveals upper screenfuls continuously.

These scroll commands reveal lower lines of text:

- ^Z reveals one lower line.
- ^QZ reveals lower lines continuously.
- ^C reveals a lower screenful.
- PgDn(3) reveals a lower screenful.
- ^QQC reveals lower screenfuls continuously.
- ^QQPgDn(3) reveals a lower screenful.

The continuous scroll commands ^QZ, ^QW, ^QQC, and ^QQR offer different scroll speeds, 1 to 9. The fastest speed is 1, the slowest is 9, and 3 is the default speed. Numbers can be entered to change the continuous scroll speed at any time. Interrupt continuous scrolling with the space bar or any key other than a number key.

Depress the CONTROL key with the R and C in ^QQR and ^QQC commands. Don't press the CONTROL key with the numeric pad keys if you use ^QQPgUp(9) and ^QQPgDn(3).

Horizontal scroll commands for wide documents:

- ^QD scrolls to the right in shifts or segments. In a very wide document, it will be necessary to enter this command several times before reaching the end of the line.
- ^D and ^F scroll right when the cursor is already positioned at far right, revealing 10 or 11 additional spaces.
- ^QS returns the cursor to the beginning of a line, shifting the screen area left if entered with the cursor to the right of space/column 80 on most screens. While ^QD moves to the end of a wide line in segments, ^QS returns to the beginning of that line in a single step.
- ^A and ^S scroll left a short segment at a time when near the screen's left edge in a wide line.

QUIZ

1. If you want to scan, one at a time, several lines of text that come after or below the cursor's position, what continuous scroll command would you use? How can you speed it up?
2. What scroll command can you use to scan, a screenful at a time, several paragraphs of material appearing before or above the cursor's present position? How can you make this a continuous scroll command?
3. What scroll command moves everything on the screen up one line so that the top line of text disappears and a new bottom line is revealed? What command scrolls one line at a time in the opposite direction?
4. What is horizontal scrolling? What commands can you use to scroll to the right? To the left?
5. List the commands for scrolling as follows:
   a. Bring lower lines of text into view, one line at a time, at slowest possible speed.
   b. Bring upper lines of text into view, one line at a time, at fastest speed.
   c. Bring one lower line of text into view, making top line disappear.
   d. Bring one upper line of text into view, making bottom line disappear.
   e. Bring one screenful of lower text into view.
   f. Bring one screenful of upper text into view.
   g. Scan through entire document, a screenful at a time, from beginning to end.
   h. Scan through entire document, a screenful at a time, from end to beginning.
6. How can you stop a continuous scroll command?

QUIZ ANSWERS

1. ^QZ reveals lower lines one at a time, continuously. Because the default speed is 3, the numbers 1 and 2 speed scrolling; 4 to 9 slow it down.
2. ^R and PgUp(9) scroll a screenful at a time from the cursor point toward the beginning of the file. Enter ^QQR (^Q^Q^R) or ^QQPgUp(9) to make this a continuous scroll command.
3. ^Z. ^W.
4. Horizontal scrolling displays portions of wide documents that appear beyond the screen's right edge. To scroll right (moving the screen in that direction) in order to see the rest of a wide line, use ^QD or any other command that moves the cursor to the right. The screen's display will shift accordingly. To scroll left (moving the screen in that direction), use ^QS or any other left-moving cursor command.
5. a. ^QZ9 b. ^QW1 c. ^Z d. ^W e. ^C or PgDn(3) f. ^R or PgUp(9) g. ^QQC or ^QQPgDn(3) h. ^QQR or ^QQPgUp(9).
6. Press the space bar or any letter key. With the commands ^QZ and ^QW, pressing a number key during scrolling will only change the speed.

9

Correcting Mistakes

Open a new file and call it ERASE.

Remove the help commands by entering F1 and then 0 or 1.

When ready, type this sentence:

```
Once upon a time there were four bears.
```

Obviously, we have made a mistake. We want to delete the word "four" and replace it with "three."

Move the cursor back to the beginning of the word "four" by using ^A twice. As you recall, ^A moves the cursor to the beginning of the word at left.

Now you are at the beginning of the word you want to replace.

REMOVE LETTER AT RIGHT

^G will remove one letter at a time from left to right. Although the ^G command is usually translated as "removes character at right," it really removes whatever is directly above (in the same space with) the cursor while moving everything at the cursor's right one space left. If pressed again, it removes the next letter, and so forth, from left to right. Press this key until you have removed the word "four." Now type "three." Be sure there is a space between "three" and "bears."

REMOVE WORD AT RIGHT

^T will remove the word at right. Because there is a space between the cursor and the word "bears," you will have to press ^T twice, once to remove the empty space at right and once to remove the word "bears." ^T will remove any blank space to the right of the cursor, no matter how wide, in one move. Now replace the word by retyping it.

As far as ^T is concerned, a word consists of a blank space beginning at the cursor point and ending at a character, or it consists of a string of one or more characters (letters and/or numbers and/or symbols) beginning at the cursor position and ending with a space or a punctuation mark. A word, from ^T's view, includes one punctuation mark.

Move down a line and experiment with ^T to see how this works. Obviously, "the" is a word. WordStar interprets "the." as a word, too. However, "the.." is considered or treated as two words. One ^T will remove the letters and first period; you'll need another ^T command to remove the second period. Symbols such as @, #, $, %, &, *, (,), +, =,{,}, [,], ', ", ',~, <, and > are not interpreted as word-ending punctuation marks. Neither is the dash or hyphen -. Every comma, period, colon, semicolon, question mark, and exclamation mark, even if appearing in the middle of a string of letters, will be interpreted as the end of a word.

^T removes the punctuation mark attached to the word it deletes. In addition, ^T will remove the empty space between words, treating each gap as a separate word, and letters over and to the right of the cursor from the middle of a word.

For example, if the cursor is positioned at the underline (_) in the following examples, ^T will remove words and spaces as follows:

1. `Remove this _          space.`

The command ^T removes the empty area between the cursor and the "s" in "space." Now the sentence looks like this:

```
Remove thissPace.
```

2. `Remove this word.`

^T removes the entire word "word" and the period following it. Now the screen looks like this:

```
Remove this
```

3. `Remove the "lined" in underlined.`

^T erases the letter above (in the same space with) the cursor and everything to its right, up to and including the punctuation mark. Now the sentence looks like this:

```
Remove the "lined" in under
```

Type each of these example sentences; place the cursor as shown, and enter ^T. Your results should match those given here.

REMOVE LINE

Return the cursor to the three bears.

^Y will remove an entire line. Press this command and you'll see everything in the cursor's line disappear, and everything beneath that point will move up to compensate. Now retype the line.

^Y will remove blank or empty lines as well. Every ^Y causes the current line and its hard return (if any) to disappear while everything following the erasure moves up a line.

REMOVE LETTER AT LEFT

The DELETE key, abbreviated Del, removes one letter at a time from right to left. Remove the word "bears" by using this key. Now restore the word.

If ^QD (move to end of line) moves you farther right than you anticipated, it's because you've been pushing blank spaces ahead of the cursor. Use the DELETE key to move from this point left (until you reach the line's last word) to remove or erase those blank spaces.

DELETE FROM CURSOR TO END/BEGINNING OF LINE

If you have erased the sentence, "Once upon a time there were three bears," restore it before going on.

Move the cursor to the beginning of the word "time." Press ^QY. This command deletes everything from and including the letter occupying the cursor's space to the end of the line. Go back and restore the whole line.

Now position the cursor at the end of the word "were." Press ^Q DEL, using ^Q and the DELETE key. This command removes everything between the cursor and the beginning of the line. Note that unlike ^QY, described above, ^Q DEL does not erase the character occupying the cursor's position.

You may remember from Chapter 6 that ^Q BACKSPACE will also erase everything between the cursor and the beginning of the line.

THINGS YOU WILL NOTICE

When you remove a single word or letter, WordStar shifts everything at the cursor's right to the left, moving letters to fill the potentially empty space. Words on lower lines do not move.

REMOVE EMPTY SPACES AND LINES

^T and ^G, the commands for deleting the word (^T) and character (^G) at right, erase blank spaces and blank lines. To remove an empty gap at right, use either command, although ^T works faster (^G removes one column/space at a time). To remove blank columns from right to left, use DEL, the delete key. If you inadvertently run two words together in the process, move the cursor to the second word's first letter and press the space bar.

^G, ^T, and ^Y remove blank lines. All three commands cause lower lines to move up a line at a time, filling the empty section, but ^Y works fastest. ^G and ^T must remove any hard spaces to the right of the cursor before erasing the hard return.

When a space is left at the end of a line, eliminate the unwanted gap by using ^G or ^T, with the cursor positioned to the left of the empty zone. The next word of text will be shifted up from the line below, along with the rest of its line, so that the combined line "overflows" the right margin. ^T usually works faster.

When a space is left at the end of a line and the cursor is positioned to the right of that space (in the normally off-screen area at far right), remove the unwanted hard spaces with the delete key. This action erases the gap while returning the cursor to your text.

REALIGNING THE RIGHT MARGIN

You will meet the ^B paragraph reform command in more detail on page 134, but you should know that this simple command code can repair the most ragged right margin, and ragged right margins are what you create with WordStar's delete commands.

Experiment by putting two lines of text on the screen. Now remove the right half of the top line with ^QY. With the cursor one space to the right of that line's last remaining word, bring the lower line up by pressing ^T. Your single line now extends beyond the right margin, so press ^B to reform the paragraph — and the margin correction will be made automatically. (If the cursor stops in the middle of a word at the end of the first line, press ^B again.)

REMOVING A LINE WHILE RETAINING ITS SPACE

You can remove all the words on a line with ^Y, but doing so also removes the line — that is, everything coming after that line will be pulled up to compensate. If you want to remove all its words but retain an empty line, place the cursor in column 1 and enter ^QY. Like ^QY, the delete commands ^T and ^Q DEL remove words without removing the line itself. Of course, ^G and the delete key will do the same, but at a snail's pace.

UNWANTED BLANK PAGES

If you print your file and a neatly numbered empty page emerges at the end, it's because you have several hard carriage returns (marked < at the screen's right) on empty lines following the end of your text. You can prevent the printing of empty pages by removing these hard returns with ^Y. When the end of your file is marked with dot flags in the far right column rather than < signals, you'll know all hard returns have been removed.

EXERCISE: DELETE COMMANDS

If you're like most new users, you'll have plenty of typographical errors to correct in your own files, many of them due to the computer's unfamiliar keyboard. Rather than work an ambitious exercise, such as an error-filled business letter, take advantage of the keyboard's "repeating key" feature to enter the following lines (or a close approximation). Press each key for a second or two and it will repeat automatically. Press RETURN at the end of each line.

```
aaaaaaaaaaaaaaa   bbbbbbbbbbbbbbbb
cccccccccccccc   ddddddddddddddddd
eeeeeeeeeeeeee   fffffffffffffffff
gggggggggggggg   hhhhhhhhhhhhhhhhh
```

1. The cursor should be at the end of this series, following the final h. Use DEL to remove all of the h's, one at a time, from right to left.
2. Use ^QS to move the cursor to the screen's far left. The cursor should now be at the first g. So far as WordStar is concerned, gggggggggggggg is a word, so ^T should remove it. Enter ^T, which removes the word at right.
3. Use ^E to move the cursor up into the next line. ^Y will erase this line in one stroke.
4. With ^E, move up another line and position the cursor at the first c. Use ^G to remove the row of c's, one letter at a time, from left to right.
5. The letters dddddddddddddd remain on this line. Use ^QY, which removes everything between the cursor and the end of the line, to remove this series.
6. Move up to the remaining line with ^E. Position the cursor between the a's and b's. Enter ^Q DEL. This command removes everything between the cursor and the beginning of the line, so the a's should disappear. Use the command(s) of your choice to make the last set, the b series, disappear. Now this part of your screen should be empty.

REVIEW: DELETE COMMANDS

^G→	Removes the character over or in the same space as the cursor; removes letters left to right
←DEL	Removes the character at left; it removes letters right to left
^T→	Deletes the word at right
←^Y→	Removes the entire line
^QY→	Deletes from and including cursor position to the end of the line
←^Q DEL	Deletes from one space left of cursor to the beginning of the line
←^Q BKSP	Deletes from one space left of cursor to the beginning of the line
^G or ^T→	Removes empty space or gap at right
←DEL	Removes empty space or gap at left
^G, ^T or ^Y	Removes empty lines

QUIZ

1. Here is a spaceship from Mars. ■

List three ways to remove the entire sentence, starting with the cursor at the far right. What is the simplest command for erasing the sentence?

2. ■ There go the little green men.

List four ways to remove this sentence, moving from left to right.

3. Perhaps we'll go ■ for a ride.

If you enter ^Q DEL with the cursor positioned as shown, what will happen? What if you enter ^QY?

4. Here are the electrodynamometers, graphs and supplies

What will happen if the cursor is positioned at the underline and you enter ^T once? Twice?

5. What does ^G do?

6. How do you delete everything between the cursor and the end of the line?

7. List the commands for deleting:

a. one letter at a time, left to right.
b. one letter at a time, right to left.
c. one word at a time, left to right.
d. the entire line.
e. everything between the cursor and the beginning of the line.
f. everything between the cursor and the end of the line.

8. What does ^T remove?

QUIZ ANSWERS

1. The delete key (DEL) will remove one letter at a time, right to left. ^Q DEL will remove everything between the cursor and the beginning of the line. ^Y, the simplest command to use here, removes the entire line.
2. ^G removes one letter at a time, left to right. ^T removes one word at a time, left to right. ^QY removes everything between the cursor and the end of the line. ^Y removes the entire line.
3. ^Q DEL will remove "Perhaps we'll go" because it erases everything between the cursor and the beginning of the line. ^QY removes "for a ride," everything from the cursor to the end of the line.
4. One ^T: `Here are the electro graphs and supplies.`

   ^T^T: `Here are the electrographs and supplies.`

5. ^G removes the letter over the cursor and shifts the letters following the cursor (on the same line) to the left one space. In this manner, ^G removes one letter at a time, left to right.
6. ^QY.
7. a. ^G b. DEL c. ^T d.^Y e. ^Q DEL f. ^QY
8. ^T removes the word or space at right. If removing a space, it pulls the first letter of the next word to the cursor position. If removing a word, it stops at the first hard space or punctuation mark, removing the punctuation mark (. , ! ? ; :) as well.

10

Formatting Your Document

Format commands arrange your text by setting line spacing, changing tab stops, rearranging margins, and making other revisions. WordStar's format commands share the prefix ^O, which stands for *O*n-screen formatting.

Note

Format conditions remain in effect (unless you change them) through an entire editing session, moving to different files and disks. This means that if you remove all the tab stops before saving a file and opening a new one, the no-tab-stops ruler line will go with you when you enter a new file. To bring back all of WordStar's default values in a single step, you have to exit from WordStar, return to the disk operating system (DOS), and start over.

CENTER A LINE

It's easy to center a line of type. Just type the line and then position the cursor anywhere within the line before entering ^OC. (The C is for *C*enter). Your line will move to the center of the screen. For example:

```
This line is centered. ^OC
```

You'll see the sentence move to the center of the screen.

The "center" of a line depends on its margins. If you change the line width, be sure to re-center titles and headlines.

CHANGE LINE SPACING

^OS is the line space entry command. You can insert any number between 1 and 9 to set new line spacing.

To cancel this (or any other) two-letter command after entering the first letter, press the space bar, ESCAPE key, RETURN key, or ^U. The revised line spacing remains in effect throughout an editing session or until you change it with another ^OS command. Associate the code ^OS with the S in *S*pacing.

SETTING THE MARGINS

Tired of your old margins? WordStar can set text in narrow columns or wide, wide lines. The commands are ^OL (for *L*eft margin) and ^OR (for *R*ight margin). In each case the message line will ask where you want the new margin to appear.

For example, set the left margin at 10 and the right margin at 55. To do this, enter ^OL and then (note the message line) 10 and press the RETURN key. Now enter ^OR, the number 55, and press the RETURN key. In our system of abbreviations, these commands are ^OL 10 @ and ^OR 55 @.

The computer gives an additional option, that of setting the margin at the cursor's column. Place the cursor where you want a margin to be and enter ^OL ESC or ^OR

ESC. Be sure to position the cursor ahead of time because it will disappear from the text and flash in the upper-right corner until you complete the entry.

An even faster way to set the margins is with the F-function keys.

F3 sets the left margin at the cursor position, and F4 sets the right margin at the cursor position. The arrangement of these keys will help you remember what they do because the two are side by side with F3 on the left (it sets the left margin) and F4 on the right (it sets the right margin).

WHAT IF YOU MAKE A MISTAKE?

If you change your mind after typing ^OL or ^OR, don't press ESC or RETURN. Instead, enter ^U (interrupt command). A screen message tells you when to press the ESCAPE key, which returns you to the text.

If you press F3 or F4 without meaning to, reset the margin with ^OL or ^OR, unless you can still move the cursor to the desired column. If you can position the cursor at the correct column, do so and then press F3 or F4 again.

SETTING MARGINS FROM ALREADY-ENTERED TEXT

Your document may contain sections of various widths and margin settings. When you move the cursor into a line of already-entered text, the fastest way to match the line's margins and tab stops is with ^OF. ^OF sets right and left margins to match those of the cursor's line, and it includes every tab stop that previously appeared between the new margins. Remember this command by thinking of the new margins being set *F*rom a line of already-entered text.

Try typing three lines of text, beginning and ending each at a different column. Move the cursor to the top row, enter ^OF, and watch your ruler line change. Move down a row and try the command again; the margins will change to match the second row, and so on.

Note

Exclamation marks already on the screen will set new tab stops if they appear in the cursor's line when you enter ^OF. For example, type this line:

```
Help! Oh! It was awful! Terrible!
```

Now enter ^OF. Your new ruler line will look something like this:

```
!---!!--!-!----!----!-!--!----!-!
```

This is because WordStar retained the original every-five-line tab stops while inserting new ones at each exclamation mark.

SETTING MARGINS FROM YOUR OWN MID-TEXT RULER LINE

WordStar allows you to create your own ruler line on the screen, using dashes (- - -) and exclamation marks (!) to denote column spaces and tab stops, then using ^OF to set those conditions for text entry. See page 158 for a complete description of this procedure.

TO REVIEW FORMAT COMMANDS ON-SCREEN

WordStar's On-Screen Menu appears at help levels 2 and 3 whenever you enter the ^O prefix by itself. All of WordStar's on-screen format command codes appear in the menu.

```
                  < < <       O N S C R E E N   M E N U        > > >
 -Margins & Tabs-  | -Line Functions- |  --More Toggles--   | -Other Menus-
L Set left margin  |C Center text     |J Justify   off (ON)|(from Main only)
R Set right margin |S Set line spacing|V Vari-Tabs off (ON)|^J Help   ^K Block
X Release margins  |                  |H Hyph-Help off (ON)|^Q Quick  ^P Print
I Set  N Clear tab |  -- Toggles--    |E Soft hyph on (OFF)|^O Onscreen
G Paragraph tab    |W Wrd wrap off(ON)|D Prnt disp off (ON)|Space Bar returns
F Ruler from line  |T Rlr line off(ON)|P Pge break off (ON)| to Main Menu.
```

Shown here are the format commands described earlier and a number of format command codes you will meet in later chapters.

REVIEW: FORMAT COMMANDS

- ^OC is the line centering command. Enter this code after typing text to be centered. The cursor must be in the featured line. A line's center is defined by the ruler line's current margins.
- Change line spacing with ^OS and any number from 1 (for single spacing) to 9 (for every-nine-line spacing).
- Set a new left margin with ^OL, the new column number, and RETURN. Alternately, set the new left margin at the cursor's column with ^OL ESC or F3.
- Set a new right margin with ^OR, the new column number, and RETURN. Alternately, set the new margin at the cursor's column with ^OR ESC or F4.
- Set margins matching those of an already-entered line of text by entering ^OF after positioning the cursor in that line.

11

Using Tab Stops

PRESET TAB STOPS

Not every keyboard is equipped with a TAB key, so WordStar uses ^I as an alternate TAB entry command. ^I and the TAB key operate identically. Even though you will not use ^I to indent to the next tab stop, you will set new stops with a command using this letter. Associating ^I with tabbing will help you remember the command.

At the top of your screen, the ruler line shows preset tab stops:

```
L----!----!----!----!----!----!----!----!----!----!----!--------R
```

Each exclamation mark is a tab stop. Hit the TAB key and the cursor moves five spaces to the right; continue and it moves across the line in five-space increments. The TAB key enters hard, not soft, spaces. When you reach the last tab stop (column 56), another TAB entry moves the cursor down to the next line, where it stops at the first ! setting (column 6). The cursor won't stop at the end of the line the way the carriage of a typewriter stops when you reach the end of the line.

ERASE TAB STOP

In much of your typing, the preset stops will prove adequate. However, you may want to remove or revise stops for certain projects, such as tables or special reports. Remove any tab stop by pressing ^ON. (Think of the N in *N*ullify.)

The message line will ask which tab stop you want removed; enter the column number and the RETURN key. If you want all the tab stops removed, press A (for *A*ll) and the RETURN key. If you want a stop removed at the cursor's position, use ESC. Be sure to note the cursor's position before entering this last command because it will disappear from your text; you'll see it flashing in the upper-right corner.

SET TAB STOP

To set a new tab stop, enter ^OI. (Think of the I in *I*nsert, and remember that ^I is an alternate TAB command.) The message line will ask for the column number desired, or you can select the ESC key option for a tab stop at the cursor's position. Note the cursor's position (or deliberately place the cursor) before entering this command because the cursor will disappear from your text until you complete the command.

The first preset tab stop appears in column (space) 6; default stops are located in columns 6, 11, 16, 21, 26, 31, 36, 41, 46, 51, and 56.

Here is a simple exercise. Set the cursor at the first stop by pressing the TAB key. Press ^ON and the ESC key, then move two spaces to the right and press ^OI and ESC again. You'll see the exclamation mark disappear from column 6 and reappear in column 8. To confirm the cursor's position, check the status line at the top of the screen.

WHAT IF YOU MAKE A MISTAKE?

As soon as you enter ^ON or ^OI, the cursor disappears. If you can't remember where you want the tab stop set or erased, don't press ESC. Use ^U, the interrupt command code.

If you set a tab stop at the wrong place, remove it with ^ON; if you erase one accidentally, replace it with ^OI.

If you enter the ^O prefix and then change your mind about entering the command, interrupt with the space bar, RETURN key, ESCAPE key, or ^U.

REVIEW: TAB-RELATED COMMANDS ON-SCREEN

One of the help commands is ^JM, which generates a five-part review of WordStar's margin and tab stop formatting procedures. Several commands and options listed by ^JM are explained in later sections of this guide.

Here are the first three screen messages provided by ^JM:

```
                  *****   MARGINS *****
To set left margin: Type ^OL.   WordStar will ask for column.
     Type desired column number 1-240 and press RETURN.
     Or, to use column of cursor in file, just press ESCAPE.
To set right margin: type ^OR, proceed as above.
To set both margins to match text in a line already entered:
     place cursor in that line, type ^OF.
To temporarily set left margin to next tab stop: type ^OG.
Margins apply to text subsequently entered.   To remarginate
     text already entered: set margins and use ^B.
                                    press space bar after reading:
```

```
          *****   LINE SPACING AND JUSTIFICATION   *****

To set line spacing: type ^OS.   WordStar will ask for line
     spacing.   Enter a digit 1 thru 9.
To turn justification off (for ragged right format),
     or to turn justification back on: type ^OJ.
Line spacing and justification settings apply to text
     subsequently entered; they may be applied to previously
     entered text with the paragraph reform command (^B).
                               press space bar for "Tab Stops":
```

```
                  *****   TAB STOPS   *****

To set a tab: type ^OI.   WordStar will ask for column number.
     Type column number and press RETURN.   Or, to use cursor
     column press the ESCAPE key.   To set a decimal tab stop,
     type "#" before typing column number or pressing ESCAPE.
To clear a tab stop or all tab stops: type ^ON.
To tab: type ^I or press TAB key if present.   Tabbing
     inserts spaces to next tab stop if insertion (^V) is on.
     Tabbing advances cursor over text if insertion is off.
                                        press space bar:
```

EXERCISE: TAB STOPS

Set the left margin at 15 (^OL 15@) and the right margin at 50 (^OR 50@). Remove the tab stop at column 16 (^ON 16@) and set a new one at column 20 (^OI 20@). Enter this paragraph:

```
     Punctuation    clarifies    the
meaning of a written  sentence.   In
spoken conversation, punctuation is
made obvious by pauses,  stops   and
vocal variations.
```

Now move the cursor to a lower line and set the margins back to 1 and 65 (^OL 1@, ^OR 65@). Type this sentence:

```
Commas, periods, exclamation points, question marks, dashes
and semicolons indicate tone of voice in print.
```

Move the cursor back to any sentence in the first paragraph using ↑ (8). Enter ^OF. The ruler line will change to match the margins of that sentence. ^OF in the indented first line produces a narrower ruler than ^OF in the second line. ^OF in the first paragraph's last line produces the narrowest ruler.

Using ^X, move down to any sentence in the second paragraph. Enter ^OF again. The margins will change accordingly, but neither will be 65 columns wide. That's because neither line in the second paragraph extends across the screen.

Although WordStar usually defines the length of a line by the cursor's path through that line, treating hard spaces as characters, ^OF sets its left margin at the first letter/digit/symbol on a line and its right margin at the last letter/digit/symbol.

Tab stops appearing on the new ruler line are those of the ruler already in use. If you erase all tab stops and use ^OF to reset the margins, your new ruler line will be empty, too. If you enter 10 new tab stops and use ^OF, the resulting ruler line will contain whatever stops appear within its revised margins.

Move the cursor to a new line and indent to space or column 11 (second tab stop on the normal ruler line). Enter F3, which sets the left margin at the cursor's position. Use the TAB key to move to space 56 (final tab stop on the normal ruler line) and enter F4, which positions the right margin at the cursor's place.

Your ruler line will look like this:

```
!--------!!----!----!----!----!----!----!----!----!
```

The second and third stops were positioned in our previous exercise; you removed the stop at column 16 and set a new stop at column 20. Because a default tab stop was already at column 21, you have two in adjacent columns.

Remove all the stops with ^ON A@. Now set a single stop at column 18 (^OI 18@). Move the cursor five spaces to the right (column 23) and enter ^OI ESC. A second stop should now appear at space 23.

Remove the first stop by entering ^ON 18@. Press RETURN to move down a line.

Hit the TAB key to position the cursor at space 23. Enter ^ON ESC to remove this stop.

Practice WordStar's tab-setting and tab-removing commands before going on. Try different variations.

REVIEW: PARAGRAPH TABBING

- The TAB key indents to the ruler line's next stop. Tab stops are marked by exclamation marks on the ruler line.
- ^ON removes a single tab stop (enter ^ON, column number, and RETURN), a single stop at the cursor's position (enter ^ON ESC), or all preset tab stops (enter ^ON A@).

- ^OI sets a new tab stop (enter ^OI, column number, and RETURN) or a new stop at the cursor's place (enter ^OI ESC).
- Use ^U to interrupt/abandon ^ON or ^OI.

QUIZ

1. List the keystrokes to use in setting the left margin at 25 and the right margin at 50.
2. Describe two other ways to set these same margins.
3. What does ^ON do?
4. What options does the ^ON command have?
5. What does the command ^OF do?
6. What does ^OI do?
7. What option does the ^OI command have?
8. What will your ruler line look like after you enter these commands?

```
^OL 5@  ^OR 35@  ^ON A@  ^OI 12@  ^OI 17@
```

QUIZ ANSWERS

1. ^OL 25@ ^OR 50@. Alternately, move the cursor to column 25 and press F3; move to column 50 and press F4. (^OL ESC is the same as F3; ^OR ESC is the same as F4.)
2. (1) Place the cursor in column 25 and enter F3 or ^OL ESC; place the cursor in column 50 and enter F4 or ^OR ESC. (2) Move to a new line and place any character in column 25; place another character in column 50; enter ^OF.
3. ^ON removes one or more tab stops.
4. (1) Enter ^ON, a column number, and the RETURN key. (2) Enter ^ON and the ESC key to remove tab stop at the cursor's position. (3) Enter ^ON, A, and the RETURN key to remove all tab stops.
5. ^OF sets new margins to match those of the cursor's present line.
6. ^OI sets a tab stop.
7. (1) Enter ^OI, column number, and RETURN key. (2) Enter ^OI ESC to set tab stop at cursor's position.
8. Your ruler line will look like this:

```
L------!----!----------------R
```

Left margin begins at space (column) 5; tab stops appear in column 12 and 17; right margin appears at column 35.

12

Saving and Storing

WORDSTAR'S SAVE COMMANDS

Your document is a valuable item, one that deserves to be locked in a safe place. Think of the terrible things that can happen if your carefully entered text isn't saved. An electrical surge or a blackout, even one lasting a fraction of a second, can destroy the whole file. Systems "crash" or stop working for a number of reasons, all of them fatal to unstored material. You can even lose an entry because the disk fills up and you run out of storage space.

For these reasons the WordStar manual cautions you to "Save early and save often!" Get in the habit of storing your material every few pages. If you type a complicated table, you may want to enter more than one "store" command before it's finished. If you later decide that something you stored wasn't worth saving, it's easy to erase — and erasing is easier than retyping.

During saving or storing, your computer transfers the contents of a file from its memory to the magnetic disk. The disk drive's red indicator light comes on during this process.

WordStar gives you three storage choices.

SIMPLE SAVE

The ^KS command is the one you'll use most often in word processing or typing projects. It prevents the loss of your editing efforts without erasing block markers or place markers, should you be using them. ^KS stores everything you have just entered or altered, and then it returns you to the beginning of the file. You have not left the file you're working on, but you have safely stored its contents. This is the SAVE AND RE-EDIT command. Associate the letter S with the word *S*ave. During this and other save procedures, a screen message notes that the computer is saving the file.

DONE-EDITING SAVE

Once you have completed all the changes you want to make and it's time to go on to another file or to print your file, use the ^KD command. It means DONE EDITING THIS FILE. Remember the code by thinking of *D*one. After the computer stores your material it will put WordStar's No-File Menu back on the screen. You have left the file but you remain in WordStar mode.

SAVE AND EXIT FROM WORDSTAR

^KX (X for e*X*it) saves the document and exits from WordStar to the computer's operating system, DOS. The logged disk drive's screen prompt will appear, A> or B>. This is another DONE EDITING command but unlike ^KD, ^KX leaves WordStar entirely. You will use ^KS and ^KD most often as you prepare reports and other documents.

ABANDON EDIT

What if you don't want to keep the changes you have made? Use ^KQ, the ABANDON EDIT command. "*Q*uit" is your mnemonic device as you memorize this command. Here's what happens. A message appears on the status line verifying your decision to abandon your current file, listing its name and giving you a Y/N (Yes/No) option. To abandon the edit, press Y for Yes and WordStar will erase all changes and entries made since the last save command. Your previously saved material will not be lost, only recently entered (and unsaved) material. WordStar returns you to the No-File Menu.

If you go into a file and decide not to make any changes, ^KQ proceeds without further verification. The status line notes that you're abandoning an unchanged file and you return to the No-File Menu.

EXERCISE: SAVING AND STORING

In order to practice saving, you need something to save. If your practice file is empty, type a few paragraphs. Once you have some material to work with, press the ^KS command. This stores the material and returns you to the beginning of the file. ^KS saves any place markers you may be using.

Now enter ^KD. This is your "done editing" command, and the screen shows a corresponding message at the top of the screen. After the computer transfers your material to the disk for permanent storage, WordStar's No-File Menu appears on the screen.

Press D to return to your practice file, and enter the file's name. WordStar returns you to the beginning of the file you just left. Now enter a row of x's like this xxxxxxxxxx anywhere in the document, preferably between two words. To see how the ^KQ (abandon or Quit edit) command operates, enter this code: ^KQ. WordStar will verify your intentions on the message line with a Yes/No query. Press Y for Yes. Now WordStar will abandon the editing project, remove the row of x's, restore the file to its previous condition, and return you to WordStar's No-File Menu. Once again enter D and your file's name. Now you can see that the xxxxxxxxxx entry was indeed removed and the file's original contents have been preserved.

Try ^KX. This eXits you from the WordStar program and the logged disk's prompt A> or B> will appear. Assuming your WordStar disk is in the logged drive, press WS@ to bring back the No-File Menu. If B is the logged drive and yourWordStar disk is in Drive A, change the logged drive by entering A; and the RETURN key, or enter A:WS@.

REVIEW: SAVING AND STORING

- ^KS saves newly entered material, returning the cursor to the file's beginning. Block markers and place markers survive this store command.
- ^KD saves material, leaves the file, and returns you to WordStar's No-File Menu. It erases block and place markers.
- ^KX saves material and leaves WordStar altogether, returning you to the computer's operating system.

- ^KQ abandons the current edit, erasing all material entered since the last save command. It also erases block and place markers. ^KQ returns you to WordStar's No-File Menu.

QUIZ

1. What is "saving" or "storing?"
2. What save command should you use if you're working on a long document and want to save every page as you enter it? Why is this the best save command for such a project?
3. What save command can you use if you finish work on one file and plan to work on another?
4. What save command should you use if you have finished editing a file and want to print it?
5. What save command stores your material and then exits from the WordStar system?
6. Give the command for abandoning an editing project.
7. What appears on the screen after storing with the ^KS command? What appears on the screen after using the ^KD or ^KQ command? What appears after using ^KX?

QUIZ ANSWERS

1. Saving or storing encodes newly entered material on magnetic disk permanently.
2. ^KS. This command saves your material, returns you to the beginning of your current file, and preserves block and place markers.
3. ^KD
4. ^KD
5. ^KX
6. ^KQ
7. After storing with ^KS, the first lines of your current file appear on the screen. After using ^KD or ^KQ, WordStar's No-File Menu appears. After using ^KX, a control system prompt (usually A>) appears.

13

Printing Your File

INTRODUCTION TO PRINTING

You will find a more comprehensive description of WordStar's print function in Chapter 36, but this introduction will show how to print your first files, giving you the satisfaction of seeing your words on paper as well as on-screen.

You have already met ^KD, the "done editing" command, and once it has been entered you can print your file. The No-File Menu reappears automatically and offers the P (for *P*rint) function.

To print a file, be sure paper has been inserted correctly and that the printer is on. If you are using the IBM Matrix Printer, the On-Line key must be turned on, too. Now press P on the keyboard.

The screen will ask, "Name of file to print?" Answer with the name of your stored file. Be sure to spell it correctly because the computer does not accommodate typographical errors; if you make a mistake, use the DELETE key, BACKSPACE, or ^S to remove incorrect letters, or ^Y to remove the entire entry. These are the same delete commands you met while opening your document file.

After typing the correct file name, press RETURN to signal the computer.

If your file is only a page long (or less), or if your computer paper comes in a long perforated sheet, you can use a shortcut. This shortcut is the ESCAPE key, entered instead of the RETURN key at the end of your file's name. ESC initiates printing at once and the whole file prints without stopping.

Alternately, you can enter your file name the standard way (Name@), using the RETURN key. A list of questions will appear. At any time, regardless of how many questions you have answered, you can press ESC to eliminate the remaining questions and printing will begin.

WORDSTAR'S PRINTING OPTIONS

Here are WordStar's print option questions with appropriate new-user responses. For more detailed explanations, see Chapter 36. Press RETURN for each default answer.

- DISK FILE OUTPUT (Y/N) — Press RETURN key.
- START AT PAGE NUMBER (RETURN for beginning) — Press the RETURN key if you want to begin with page 1. Otherwise, type the page you want to begin with. Press RETURN after the number.
- STOP AFTER PAGE NUMBER (RETURN for end) — Press the RETURN key if you want to end with the file's last page; otherwise, give the page you want to end with. Press RETURN after typing the number.
- USE FORM FEEDS (Y/N) — Press RETURN key.
- SUPPRESS PAGE FORMATTING (Y/N) — Press RETURN key.
- PAUSE FOR PAPER CHANGE BETWEEN PAGES (Y/N) — Press the RETURN key if you don't have to stop to change the paper. If you're using single sheets of paper or stationery, press Y for Yes. Then the printer will stop at the end of each printed page and wait for you to insert a new sheet of paper. When you're ready with the next sheet, resume printing (a page at a time) by pressing the letter P.

Although the IBM Matrix Printer stops printing and beeps unless the continuous paper form is depressing a metal tab, you can use single sheets of paper by first inserting a 3 × 5 card, which keeps the tab depressed.

- READY PRINTER, PRESS RETURN — This means just what it says. If you're ready to print, press the return key and printing will begin.

WHAT IF YOU MAKE A MISTAKE?

If you enter the file name incorrectly, an error message will appear. To remove the error message, press the ESCAPE key and try again. The file name must be spelled exactly as it appears on-screen in the disk's directory.

If you notice a typographical error in the file name, don't press RETURN or ESC. Instead, use the DELETE key, BACKSPACE, ^S, or ^Y to remove incorrect letters, then make the appropriate correction.

While the printer is running, you can stop print by pressing the letter P. It doesn't have to be capitalized, and you don't have to use the control key.

After printing stops you can abandon the printing entirely, or you can return to editing and later resume printing where you left off, or you can resume printing right away. The screen will list the three options and their codes.

Y is the ABANDON PRINT option. Use this after entering P to stop print. Now the No-File Menu will appear.

^U returns you to the No-File Menu. When you next enter the P print command, printing resumes where it was interrupted. This option allows you to edit another file (but not the same file you are printing) before finishing the print function. Not all systems have the necessary disk space and RAM for editing before printing has completed; the 64K IBM PC, for example, does not support this option. An error message will appear after you enter ^U or when you enter D from the No-File Menu if this is your situation. Be sure to hold the control key while entering this option; U by itself causes printing to resume at once.

N is the RESUME PRINT option. Printing will continue where it was interrupted.

If you have paused between pages to insert paper and then realize you should make editing changes before resuming, press P twice. This interrupts before printing begins. After the screen's option message appears, type Y, which abandons print and returns the No-File Menu, or ^U, which allows you to edit before resuming.

Remember that WordStar never allows you to edit the same file you are printing. If your system supports the ^U option, it will allow you to suspend printing and then edit another file before resuming, and (as you will see in Chapters 36 and 37) you will also be able to edit one file while printing another. But you cannot simultaneously edit the same file you are printing, or print the same file you are editing, efficiently.

Warning or error messages will appear on the screen if your system does not support the ^U option, or if you cannot print one file while simultaneously editing another, or if you try to print and edit the same file simultaneously.

PRINTING WITH A SINGLE DISK DRIVE

If the file you want to print is on the same disk as your WordStar files, enter P and proceed as described above.

If the file you want to print is on a separate disk, such as a document-files-only disk, remove the WordStar disk and replace it with the appropriate file disk before entering that file's name in response to the print command's screen message. Proceed as above.

THINGS YOU WILL NOTICE

The printer's response to your "interrupt print" command may be fast or slow. When something horrible happens (you forgot to enter the "stop underlining" command and now the whole page is being underlined, or your complicated table is crooked, or the printer is typing on the platen instead of the paper), it's human to panic and press buttons right and left in an attempt to stop the printer and abandon print. Stay calm. Enter P, which is the STOP PRINT command, and then watch the screen. The printer may strike a few keys before the monitor asks for your option. As soon as it does, enter Y or ^U.

Before printing any file, and before resuming any interrupted printing:

- Be sure the printer is turned on.
- If you are using the IBM Matrix Printer, be sure the On-Line key is turned on as well.
- Be sure the paper is positioned correctly.
- If you are using the IBM Matrix Printer, you can use single sheets of paper after suppressing the metal sensor tab that triggers the "no paper" alarm by inserting a 3 × 5 card.

Additional information about WordStar's print function appears in Chapter 36, Printing Options. Chapter 37, More About Disks and Files, reviews the "print while editing" function. This option is supported by IBM Personal Computers having more than 64K.

EXERCISE: PRINTING

Using any file you have stored, preferably one that is several pages long, try the different print commands. You may want to print one of the files on your demonstration disk. Printing can be an intimidating process, especially when something happens that you don't expect, so take notes as you try different procedures. Getting acquainted with your printer one step at a time is far more pleasant than waiting until you have a deadline.

QUIZ

1. What menu should be on the screen when you enter the print command?
2. What is the print command?
3. After you enter the print command, several questions appear on the screen. If you already know that you can eliminate the individual questions by using default values, what shortcut command can you use?
4. Before initiating the print command, what should you check on the terminal screen and the printer?

5. How can you interrupt printing?
6. What are the three options you have after printing has been interrupted?
7. List the commands you would enter to print the following file. The file's name is LIBRARY and you want to print pages 4 through 7 using separate sheets of paper. List every command, starting with the print command. Use @ to abbreviate the RETURN key.

QUIZ ANSWERS

1. WordStar's No-File Menu.
2. P
3. Enter the file name and press ESC.
4. Check the printer to be sure paper is positioned correctly and the printer is turned on; check the terminal screen to be sure the No-File Menu appears and that the file you want to print is listed on the disk's directory.
5. Press P while printer is running.
6. The letter Y abandons print; ^U interrupts printing, allows you to edit a different file, then resumes printing where it left off in the original file; N resumes interrupted printing without delay.
7. P LIBRARY@ @ 4@ 7@ @ @ Y @ . This sequence begins with WordStar's No-File Menu. P initiates the print function. Name of file to print: LIBRARY@. The RETURN key (@) gives a default answer to the DISK FILE OUTPUT question. The next two questions are START AT PAGE NUMBER and STOP AFTER PAGE NUMBER, so 4@ and 7@ were entered. @ and @ give the default response to USE FORM FEEDS and SUPPRESS PAGE FORMATTING. The answer Y for Yes was entered for the PAUSE FOR PAPER CHANGE BETWEEN PAGES question. The last entry, a hard return (@), cues the printer to begin.

   Alternately, use this sequence: LIBRARY@ @ 4@ 7@ @ @ Y ESC. Pressing ESC after the final non-default response saves a keystroke.

14

Insertion

WordStar's insertion mode allows you to add new material to already-entered text without erasing anything already on the screen. New material is "inserted" and old material remains.

The notation INSERT ON appears at the top of your screen in the upper-right corner whenever you call up WordStar and enter a document file. Insertion is on by default; it will stay on until you turn it off. To do so, you can use the insertion key, labeled Ins (0), to the left of the DELETE key, or the standard WordStar command for turning insertion on and off.

Because of the insertion key's proximity to the right shift and Caps Lock keys, you may press it by accident from time to time. If the cursor isn't acting the way you expect it to, check the status line. If insertion is off, no screen message appears at upper right; if insertion is on, the screen says INSERT ON.

The standard WordStar command for insertion on/off is ^V. Press this command code and you'll generate the same response. If insertion is on, you'll turn it off with ^V; if it's off, ^V turns it back on. You can use either ^V or the insertion key, but you'll find the latter more convenient.

INSERTION ON

When insertion is on, any letters or numbers that you insert in front of a word already on the screen will bump that word toward the right. In other words, the new word is *inserted* and it doesn't remove or replace anything already in the text.

INSERTION OFF

When insertion is turned off, the "insert on" message disappears and any letters you enter in a line of text will actually replace characters by "overprinting" them on the screen.

DEMONSTRATING THE DIFFERENCE

Experiment with a short sentence. Leave insertion on (its default condition). Place the cursor in front of any word in the sentence and add a new word. Everything to the cursor's left remains undisturbed; everything to the cursor's right is bumped to the right; and everything you insert takes its place on the screen without eliminating or erasing the already-entered text.

Now turn insertion off by pressing ^V. The INSERT ON message disappears from your status line, indicating that this feature or mode is no longer operating. Position the cursor at the beginning of your sentence and type any new word. You'll see the new word replace the old, while the old word vanishes from the screen and nothing is bumped to the right.

THE RETURN KEY WITH INSERTION ON

In normal (insert on) use, the RETURN key adds blank lines to already-entered text. Each new line is marked with the < hard return flag at right.

Put the cursor at the end of any line that's in the middle of a paragraph and press RETURN. An empty line will separate that line from the one following. Position the cursor in the middle of a word and press RETURN. Everything under and to the right of the cursor will be bumped down.

THE RETURN KEY WITH INSERTION OFF

But with insertion turned off, the RETURN key moves the cursor down-screen without relocating or disturbing any text.

Try this command by placing the cursor at the beginning of a paragraph or screenful of text. Turn insertion off. Now press the RETURN key several times while you watch the screen.

With insertion turned off, the RETURN key simply moves the cursor. It does not reposition any on-screen text.

However, if you are in a line marked by a soft return flag, the RETURN key will change the soft return to a hard return, even though it does not reposition text. This feature may interfere with future editing and reforming (^B) of that line.

THE TAB KEY WITH INSERTION ON

Similarly, in normal use (insertion on) the TAB key moves everything at the cursor's right a corresponding tab stop distance (usually five spaces) to the right.

If the cursor is in column 1, it indents the text; if in the middle of a line, it creates an empty space between words.

Try this command by turning insertion back on and positioning the cursor at the beginning of a line of text. Press the TAB bar. Everything on the cursor's line moves right a corresponding number of spaces, and the cursor stops at the first ! tab stop it comes to.

Position the cursor in the middle of a line of text and press the TAB key two or three times while watching the screen. Again, everything to the cursor's left remains as it was; everything to the cursor's right is bumped to the right. The cursor stops at the appropriate ! tab stop.

THE TAB KEY WITH INSERTION OFF

With insertion turned off, the TAB key moves the cursor "through" or "over" words without disturbing or repositioning them.

Try this command by turning insertion off and placing the cursor at the beginning of a line. Now press the TAB key while watching the screen. Press it again; repeat the command until the cursor reaches the rightmost tab stop.

This is an easy way to move the cursor across the screen without disturbing already-entered text. If you are making corrections on a table, for example, for which you have set special tab stops, you can use insertion off to reach specific entries very quickly.

THE SPACE BAR WITH INSERTION ON

When insertion is turned on, the space bar generates hard spaces which it inserts at the cursor position. If you place the cursor in the middle of a line of text and press the space bar several times, you will generate a corresponding number of hard spaces at the cursor position.

Text to the left of the cursor remains as it was; text to the cursor's right is bumped right.

THE SPACE BAR WITH INSERTION OFF

Insertion off creates a different condition. When you press the space bar in this mode, you literally replace or "overtype" already-entered text with blank spaces. This is a convenient feature because you may want to delete letters or words without disturbing the rest of a paragraph or sentence. With insertion turned off, you can replace any letter with a blank space by pressing the space bar.

Try this, working from left to right on your screen. Place the cursor at the beginning of any line of text and, with insertion turned off, press the space bar. Whatever letter occupies the cursor's column will disappear; a blank space will replace it.

THE INSERTION KEY IS A TOGGLE KEY

Remember that the insertion key is a "toggle" or "on/off" command key. Press it to turn insertion off; then press it again to turn it back on. The status line carries no notation when insertion is turned off. The INSERT ON message appears whenever insertion is on. "Insertion on" or "insertion mode" is the default position.

THINGS YOU WILL NOTICE

With insertion off, the space bar deletes letters and numbers without disturbing already-entered text to the cursor's right. However, WordStar's regular delete commands (^G, for example, or the DELETE key) will behave in their normal manner, shifting text to the left as each letter is erased.

To remove any letter or word at the cursor's left without shifting the position of other text, move the cursor left, to the beginning of the target, and then use the space bar to go from left to right, replacing letters with blank spaces.

EXERCISE: USING INSERTION ON AND OFF

Using single spacing, create this five-line block. Each line contains 10 x's.

```
xxxxxxxxxx
xxxxxxxxxx
xxxxxxxxxx
xxxxxxxxxx
xxxxxxxxxx
```

1. With insertion turned off, place the cursor at the first x and enter ooooo.
2. Leaving insertion off, hit the RETURN key. The cursor will move down to the second row.
3. Turn insertion back on and enter ooooo again. Instead of replacing an x with each o, you're now bumping already-entered letters to the right.
4. Use ^QD to move to the end of the line and press the RETURN key. This creates a blank line between the second and third rows of letters.

5. With ^X move down one line so that the cursor is again positioned at the beginning of a row of letters. Press the TAB key. Again, because insertion is on, letters already on-screen are bumped to the right to accommodate the indentation.
6. Move down another line. Turn insertion off. Now press the TAB key. The cursor "jumps" or "skips" over already-entered text. Enter ooooo. New letters replace old without shifting text to the right.

REVIEW: INSERTION ON/OFF

- Insertion is on by default.
- The insertion key (Ins) turns insertion on and off. ^V is the standard WordStar command for doing the same.
- Characters or spaces entered when insertion is on bump subsequent material on that line a corresponding distance to the right.
- Characters or spaces entered when insertion is off replace already-entered characters one at a time by "typing over" the on-screen characters. Subsequent letters in the line do not move.
- When insertion is on, use of the RETURN KEY bumps following material a corresponding number of lines down, creating a blank or empty area marked with hard return flags (<). When insertion is on, use of the TAB KEY bumps material a corresponding number of spaces to the right, creating an indentation.
- When insertion is off, use of the RETURN KEY moves the cursor down through previously entered text without moving or disturbing the text. Use of the TAB KEY moves the cursor to the right, moving over already-entered text without disturbing letters.
- When insertion is on, INSERT ON appears at the right of the status line.
- When insertion is off, no message appears.

QUIZ

1. What is the insertion on/off toggle command?
2. What is the difference between insertion on and insertion off?
3. If you have entered a complex table of numbers, why would insertion off be an advantage in correcting an error?
4. What happens in a section of already-entered text if you start at the top of the screen and hit the RETURN key five times with insertion on? What happens with insertion off? What happens when you hit the TAB key five times with insertion on? With insertion off?
5. What will happen in the following sentence if you enter five spaces with insertion off?

   ```
   ■123456789
   ```

   What would happen with insertion on?
6. You can tell when insertion is off by looking at the status line because:
   a. INSERT OFF appears at right.
   b. the status line disappears.
   c. the INSERT ON message disappears.

7. Pressing the RETURN key when insertion is off causes the cursor to:
   a. move across the screen a tab stop at a time without disturbing already-entered text.
   b. move to the end of the file.
   c. move down the screen creating blank or empty lines with each entry.
   d. move down the screen without disturbing already-entered text.
8. Pressing the space bar with insertion off causes any letter at the cursor's position to ______.
9. Pressing the TAB key (or ^I) with insertion on causes words to the right of the cursor to ______.
10. `The quick brown fox jumps over the lazy ■dog.`
    With insertion on, type the word "cat; with insertion off, type the word "cat." what happens in each case?

QUIZ ANSWERS

1. The insertion key (Ins) to the right of the space bar, or ^V, the standard WordStar command.
2. "Insertion" refers to the insertion of letters and words into already-entered text. When insertion is on, new characters and spaces are entered and everything to the right is moved a corresponding number of spaces in order to accommodate the new entry. When insertion is off, new material literally replaces the old, a character at a time.
3. With insertion off, you can move quickly to any line using the RETURN key and TAB bar, then enter correct figures directly over incorrect numbers without disturbing the table.
4. With insertion on, five carriage returns will create an empty zone that many lines deep. With insertion off, the cursor will move down through five lines of text without disturbing the document. With insertion on, the TAB key entries will create a corresponding empty area, bumping any text located to the right of the cursor a corresponding number of spaces to the right. With insertion off, the TAB key relocates the cursor a corresponding number of spaces to the right without disturbing text.
5. With insertion off, the entry of five hard spaces will erase the digits 12345. With insertion on, entering five spaces will move the whole number (123456789) five spaces to the right without erasing anything.
6. c
7. d
8. Disappear.
9. Move right one tab stop (5 spaces).
10. With insertion on, the result is:

    `The quick brown fox jumps over the lazy cat dog.`

    With insertion off, the result is:

    `The quick brown fox jumps over the lazy cat.`

15

WordStar's Print Controls

INTRODUCTION TO PRINT CONTROLS

Fancy footwork like **boldface type,** underlining, subscripts$_1$, superscripts^2, ~~crossing out~~.

centering a heading

in the middle

of a page,

typing in narrow columns

with nicely justified

right and left margins

like those shown here,

single spacing, double spacing, triple spacing, and even nine-line spacing, reforming paragraphs, and

shifting the left margin a tab stop to the right for the tabular formatting of bibliographies, outlines, charts, and other technical references

are all easy to arrange with WordStar.

Some of these special effects are created by format commands, which you'll meet in later chapters. Others depend on print controls, introduced here and in the next chapter.

Print controls instruct the printer to create unusual conditions, such as boldface type, underlining, subscripts and superscripts, crossing out, overprinting, the changing of ribbon color and type size, and the setting of special unexpandable spaces. Most print control commands begin with the prefix ^P. Although holding the CONTROL key (^) with the second code in a two-letter command is recommended, the computer will recognize print controls so long as P and the CONTROL key are entered simultaneously.

BOLDFACE AND DOUBLESTRIKE

WordStar offers a choice of darker-than-normal type.

The first, called "doublestrike," is created as the printwheel or printing head strikes each letter twice. Doublestrike is useful in the preparation of stencils and ditto masters, and it makes the output of a matrix or non-daisy wheel printer easier to read.

The second, called "boldface," is heavier because characters are slightly offset in the second striking, making a dark and dramatic contrast. Its letters are excellent for chapter headings and other emphasis.

To use doublestrike or boldface, remind yourself that the appropriate code must be given both before and after the word/line/sentence to be emphasized.

Doublestrike

The command for doublestrike is ^PD (D for *D*oublestrike). ^P is the standard print control prefix. Print controls determine the printer's action, so their results won't be obvious until you print a file, but you will see appropriate notations on-screen.

The printer initiates doublestrike print when it reaches your first ^PD signal, and the featured type continues until a second ^PD signal (the cancelling code) appears. There is no limit to the size of a doublestrike entry; it can be a single letter in length or it can last a 100 pages. The same is true for all print control commands that have to be entered both before and after the text involved.

This is an on/off toggle commands: Enter the code once to start the condition, then enter it again to stop.

Type this sentence:

Here is a word in ^PD doublestrike ^PD type.

The screen notation is:

```
Here is a word in ^Ddoublestrike^D type.
```

When printed, this message will be:

Here is a word in doublestrike type.

Boldface

Boldface type creates a darker, wider printing of characters. In standard or regular WordStar use, ^PB is the boldface command. This code (the B is for ***B*oldface**) goes before and after the text to be emphasized.

However, ^PB does not operate with the IBM Personal Computer and the IBM Matrix Printer the way it does with most other systems. As your introductory material from MicroPro points out, if you try to use the boldface ^PB command, you may create triple-striking instead.

The F-function keyboard supplies your boldface entry command. F6 is the boldface key. However, when you use F6, your screen will show the same ^B boldface print control character that the use of ^PB normally generates.

Type this sentence:

Here is a word in F6 boldface F6 type.

The screen will show this message:

```
Here is a word in ^Bboldface^B type.
```

When it is time to print, the ^B signals will not appear but the word between them will be set in boldface characters. Your printed result will be:

Here is a word in **boldface** type.

REMOVING PRINT CONTROL CHARACTERS FROM THE SCREEN

As you practice entering print controls, you'll see how confusing the screen can look with a few notations on a line. When paragraphs look unjustified it is because the computer has provided extra spaces to compensate for those taken up by the on-screen control characters. The status line will reflect your actual column number. If you enter six print controls on a line, they will take up 12 spaces. The cursor may be at the right margin (column 65) but the status line will show column 53, your actual printing position.

WordStar allows you to remove print control characters from the screen to check margins and inspect text. ^OD is the print control display toggle, a format command you'll meet again in Chapter 19. Use the same command code to turn this function on and off. While you work the exercises and examples that follow, enter ^OD to see how an entry will look. The screen won't show the actual boldface type, etc., but it will reflect the text's appearance more accurately. Get in the habit of turning ^OD back on as soon as you inspect the text. Print control characters are important reminders of special conditions, and you don't want to forget which ones you've entered.

WHAT IF YOU MAKE A MISTAKE?

Print control characters offer some of the most colorful and frustrating mistakes you can make with WordStar, and that's because in most cases you have to enter the command twice: first when you want the special condition to start and again when you want it to end. In the F6 (boldface) example, F6 goes before and then again after the word you want printed in boldface letters. But what if you forget to enter that second F6? Then everything coming after the first one will print in boldface — until a second F6 appears, at which point normal type resumes. In a document filled with boldface commands, a single error creates the negative image of what you want: normal type prints as boldface and what should be boldface prints as normal type. The same reversal can happen with underlining, crossing out, subscripts, superscripts, and doublestrike.

If you enter the wrong print control character command (^PD when you wanted ^PT), remove the control character with DEL, ^G, or ^T. Print controls behave like normal letters when you use delete commands.

If you enter the ^P prefix and decide not to enter a print control command, use the space bar *only* to cancel the command. In other two-letter codes, you can interrupt with ^U, the ESCAPE key, or RETURN, but these keys entered after ^P produce the on-screen character ^U, the on-screen character ^[(although your system may generate a different notation), and the line-overprint command, respectively. Of course, if you forget this rule and try to cancel the command with ^U, ESC, or RETURN after entering the ^P prefix, it's easy to remove the unwanted screen character with any delete command.

ENTERING PRINT CONTROLS WITH INSERTION OFF

When you add print controls to already-entered text with insertion on, the print controls bump everything at the cursor's right farther right to make room. But these control characters are "invisible": You can remove them from the screen with ^OD and they don't appear on the printed page.

But if you enter print control commands in already-entered text with insertion turned off, they won't behave the same way.

For example:

```
Here is a sentence on the screen.
```

Add ^PD with insertion on and it becomes:

```
Here is a ^Dsentence^D on the screen.
```

The ^D control characters show where doublestrike will begin and end, and the sentence's text remains exactly what it was.

But add ^PD with insertion turned off and the screen shows:

```
Here is a ^Dentence^Don the screen.
```

And if you print the sentence, it will read:

Here is a **entence**on the screen.

WordStar considered the ^D control character a single unit. This single character "wrote over" or replaced whatever occupied the cursor's column when it was entered.

Therefore, whenever you plan to enter print controls to already-entered text, be sure insertion is turned on.

UNDERLINING

In regular WordStar use, you underline by typing ^PS before and after whatever you want to feature.

For example, enter this sentence:

Here is an ^PSunderlined^PS word.

The screen will show:

```
Here is an ^Sunderlined^S word.
```

The printer will print:

Here is an <u>underlined</u> word.

The F-function key F5 is also defined as an underline command. You can repeat the above example using only one keystroke:

Here is an F5 underlined F5 word.

The screen will show:

```
Here is an ^Sunderlined^S word.
```

The printer will print:

Here is an <u>underlined</u> word.

OVERPRINT NEXT CHARACTER

^PH is the overprint or strikeover command. The entry code ^H by itself moves the cursor one space to the left; adding ^P moves the cursor one space left and overprints the second character over the first.

This command goes between the characters that will occupy the same space. For example:

apple pie a ^PH` la mode

The screen shows:

```
apple pie a^H` la mode
```

The printer prints:

apple pie à la mode

Or try this one:

pin ^PH ~ ata

The screen shows:

```
pin^H~ata
```

The printer prints:

piñata

The symbol for cents (¢) doesn't appear on the terminal keyboard, but you can create your own like this:

50¢^PH/

which appears on screen as:

```
50c^H/
```

and prints as:

50¢

To overprint three letters or characters, enter two ^PH commands. For example, the command / PH \ ^PH—will show on the screen as /^H \^H —and print as ⋇ .

OVERPRINT NEXT LINE

Use ^PH to overprint a single character at a time. To overprint an entire line, you have two choices: ^PM and ^P (that is, ^P followed by the RETURN key).

Type the first line, then enter ^PM or ^P@. The cursor moves down a line and a - flag appears at the screen's far right. Now enter your second line. Notice that the status line indicates the same line number when you position the cursor in either of these two lines.

Example:

```
Here are two overprinted lines ^PM
These two lines are overprinted.
```

When you print this combination, your hard copy will show:

```
Hheeeeatwotwonesearpeintedrprinted.
```

Unless you're in the hidden messages business, you won't often overprint lines of text. But if you have a section to cross out with slashes instead of the dashes WordStar's strikeout control provides, you could enter a command like this:

```
let us remove this ^PM
//////////////////
```

The two lines will overprint like this:

```
l̸e̸t̸/u̸s̸/r̸e̸m̸o̸v̸e̸/t̸h̸i̸s̸
```

You will also use the line-overprint command when working with certain kinds of tables, as illustrated in Chapter 21.

STRIKEOUT

^PX is the strikeout command. Like the underline and boldface print controls, this command code goes before and after the word, phrase, or character you want to cross out.

Example:

^PX$110^PX marked down to $85.95

The screen shows:

```
^X$110^X marked down to $85.95
```

And the printer prints:

~~$110~~ marked down to $85.95

As mentioned, if you prefer to cross something out with slashes, use the line-overprint command. You can use the same procedure to cross out with other letters: xxxxxxx, \\\\\\\\, etc.

SUBSCRIPTS AND SUPERSCRIPTS

Footnotes, coefficients, equations, and exponents are easy with WordStar's subscript and superscript features—assuming your printer is equipped to accept the commands.

A superscript prints slightly above the line of print, as in mathematical notation (x^2) or footnotes. A subscript prints slightly below the line of print, as in chemical equations (H_2O) or coefficients of a series (A_1, A_2, A_3 ...).

The "slightly above" and "slightly below" descriptions are true for incremental printers, such as daisy or thimble printers. A nonincremental printer (like the IBM Matrix

Printer) places the subscript a full line down and the superscript a full line up, requiring the double or triple spacing of text. In fact, subscripts and superscripts entered with single spacing on a nonincremental printer will print as regular text on the same line. In that case, you *must* doublespace the text or subscripts and superscripts won't work. If you are using the IBM Matrix Printer, use the double-space command, ^OS 2, or the triplespace command, ^OS 3, before entering subscripts and superscripts.

Note that not all printers support the ^PT and ^PV superscript/subscript commands. If your printer doesn't, the commands will have no effect and the emphasized text will print on the regular text line.

The keyboard will help you remember the subscript and superscript commands. T appears in the top row of letters, pointing up, so it's appropriate that ^PT be the superscript command. V is in the bottom row, pointing down, and ^PV is the subscript command.

To type x^2, enter:

x^PT2^PT

The screen will show:

```
x^T2^T
```

This will print:

x^2

Try 180° × 2 = 360°, which is simple with ^PT and a lowercase "o" for the degree symbol.

Now enter

H^PV2^PV0.

The screen will show:

```
H^V2^V0
```

The printout will read:

H_2O

EQUATIONS

Ready for an ambitious equation? Indent to column 16, the third tab stop, and try this hyperbolic identity:

$$\sinh^2 z_1 - \sinh^2 z_2 = \sinh(z_1+z_2)\sinh(z_1-z_2)$$

Enter a space before and after the = sign.

If you enter this equation correctly, here's what your screen will look like:

```
sinh^T2^Tz^V1^V-sinh^T2^Tz^V2^V = sinh(z^V1^V+z^V2^V)sinh(z^V1^V-z^V2^V)
```

Each ^T is the print control for a superscript (which prints above the line) and each ^V the print control for a subscript (which prints below the line). The entry commands are ^PT and ^PV, respectively.

When you enter this equation, keep typing as though all of the equation fits on one line — it does, even though the print controls take up almost as much space as the equation! The screen window will shift or scroll to the right so that you can see your text as it's entered; a + flag at the screen's far right indicates that the line continues off-screen.

Return to the beginning of the line by scrolling left with ^QS. Now use ^QD, the scroll right command, to examine the off-screen portion of your line. Enter as many ^QD commands as you need to reach the last symbol with the cursor. (^QD scrolls to the right in shifts; the wider your line, the more ^QD commands you will need to reach the end of it.)

Take a look at the status line when you reach the end of this equation. Having indented three tab stops before beginning the equation, you should end several spaces to the right of the R, the ruler's right margin. Yet the status line claims you're at column 52. The status line reflects the printing position of characters on the line, not their apparent position on the screen.

This is a good time to try ^OD. ^OD removes the on-screen print controls so that you can see the whole equation and check for typographical errors without having to wade through ^T and ^V notations. Be sure to reinstate the print controls by entering ^OD again.

REVIEW: PRINT CONTROL COMMANDS

Print controls give special instructions to the printer regarding the positioning of characters on the line and special effects such as underlining and boldface type.

The following commands are entered before and after the featured word or section. In this sense they are "toggle commands" because the same code turns them on and off.

- F6 Boldface
- ^PD Doublestrike
- F5 Underline or ^PS Underline
- ^PX Strikeout
- ^PT Superscript
- ^PV Subscript

These commands are entered once, directly before the character or line to be overprinted:

- ^PH Overstrike or Overprint Next Character
- ^PM or ^P@ Overstrike or Overprint Next Line

16

Additional Print Controls

In addition to the print control codes introduced in Chapter 15, WordStar offers the following.

CHANGE RIBBON COLOR

Your printer may be equipped with a two-color ribbon (usually red and black). To change ribbon color and print a word in the optional color, enter ^PY before and after the special word. You could enter, for example:

> This is a ^PYred^PY word.

The printer will change the ribbon from black to red, print the word "red", then shift back to the normal black ribbon.

This command is not supported by the IBM Matrix Printer.

STOP PRINT

If your printer uses a daisy wheel, you probably know what a wide selection of type styles you can choose from. You may want to shift from regular type to italics, or from larger to smaller characters. To stop the printer at a prearranged location in order to change the print wheel or ribbon, use ^PC. Enter this command only once, at the desired place. The printer will stop as soon as it reaches ^PC (which appears on-screen as ^C). A screen message will tell you how to resume printing when ready. In normal printing, P is the "resume print" command.

If you are using the IBM Matrix Printer, ^PC will cause your printer to stop before printing anything on the line containing your ^PC command. Printing will resume after you press P again.

ALTERNATE CHARACTER PITCH

Daisy wheel printers, as mentioned before, can use different type sizes. The most common or standard are 10-pitch (10 characters per inch) and 12-pitch (12 characters per inch). WordStar is preset for 10 characters per inch. In order to use a 12-pitch daisy wheel, you should adjust the character width accordingly. You can use a dot command, as you'll learn in Chapter 30, or you can enter ^PA. (Associate A with *A*lternate pitch.)

You may set an entire file for 12-pitch print by using ^PA at the beginning. To change from regular to smaller letters in the middle of a document, enter both ^PA and ^PC so you can change the daisy wheel before continuing.

^PN is the command for returning to normal 10-pitch mode. (Associate the N with *N*ormal pitch.) Again, if you want to shift from 12-pitch to 10-pitch characters in the middle of a document, enter ^PN and ^PC at the same time so that you can change daisy wheels.

^PA and ^PN have no effect on most non-daisy printers, including the IBM Matrix Printer.

NON-BREAK SPACE

It's frustrating to type a chart, bibliography, or other document, with hard spaces carefully positioned, and then have the computer add additional spaces where you don't want them.

For example, here is a short table entered without any special provisions for the preservation of spaces as typed:

```
                PUNCTUATION


1.  Use a period to end a declarative or
imperative sentence.
2.   Use   a   period to end   an   indirect
question  or a polite request phrased as
a question.
3.   Use   a   period to   end   a   sentence
fragment.
4.      Use     a     period     after     most
abbreviations,   such as Mr.   Mrs.,   Ms.,
Dr., etc.
5.  Use a period as a decimal point when
writing numbers.
6.  Use a period to separate the dollars
from cents in writing monetary figures.
```

In order to justify the right margin, the computer has added several "soft" or extra spaces between words that were entered with only one space between them. Note how the capital U in the word "Use" at the beginning of each line jogs right and left as you scan down the column. In every case, the number was typed, then the period, then two hard spaces, and the word "Use." Yet the computer has positioned that word as few as two and as many as six spaces from the period preceding it.

In a rough draft or informal report, this lack of alignment hardly matters. But in a formal proposal or similar document, the ragged arrangement you just saw looks unprofessional.

To prevent the addition of soft spaces, use ^PO, the non-break space entry command.

Try this example:

I.^PO^POText begins here and will not move right.

The screen will show:

```
I.^O^OText begins here and will not move right.
```

This will print:

I. Text begins here and will not move right.

No matter how you edit or rearrange the document, two spaces and only two spaces will appear between I. and the word "Text." Of course, in a short line like this it isn't necessary to enter ^PO; just press the space bar twice and enter the heading. Your hard return, creating a < flag at the end of the line, prevents the addition of spaces or the spreading of words to justify the right margin.

But when you have long lines of type, or narrow margins, the non-break space will prevent the shifting of carefully positioned text.

PHANTOM RUBOUT AND PHANTOM SPACE

These exotic names apply to two special characters found on different typing elements, such as daisy wheels and print thimbles. You may find £, the symbol for English pounds, or ¢, the symbol for cents. It's a good idea to check every printwheel in your inventory and run through your whole keyboard, capitalized and lowercase, because even the regular number keys may not print what they indicate.

Some daisy wheels, for example, feature the copyright symbol ©instead of the carat mark ^ above the number 6. When you print your sample keyboard, enter each line systematically in both capitalized and lowercase form, and don't neglect the phantom rubout and phantom space characters.

^PF = Phantom Space
^PG = Phantom Rubout

On most non-daisy printers, including the IBM Matrix Printer, these commands have no meaning.

REVIEW: ADDITIONAL PRINT CONTROLS

- To change ribbon color when using a two-color ribbon (and to resume regular color after featured text), enter:

  ^PY

- To stop print at a specific place in order to change the ribbon or daisy wheel, enter:

  ^PC

After printing stops, resume by pressing P again, as the screen reminds you.

- If you have daisy wheels in two sizes, 10-pitch and 12-pitch, you can alternate between them. For best printing effects, change the character width with these commands:

  ^PA Alternate Pitch (shifts to 12 characters per inch)
  ^PN Resume Normal Pitch (10 characters per inch)

- To prevent the addition of soft spaces in a line of text, especially after the setting of a numbered sentence or paragraph, use:

  ^PO Non-Break Space

This command inserts a hard space which will not be expanded during word wrap or paragraph reform.

- Phantom Rubout and Phantom Space refer to extra characters on daisy wheels which are printed by the commands:

  ^PF and
  ^PG

  The easiest way to check a daisy wheel for its contents is to print the whole keyboard, including phantom keys.

- The IBM Matrix Printer does not support the commands ^PY, ^PC, ^PA, ^PN, ^PF, or ^PG as they are described here.

PRINT CONTROL CHARACTERS IN SCREEN TEXT

When print control characters appear on the screen, they do not retain their ^P prefix. To proofread print control characters on the screen, make these associations:

• ^B	Boldface	^D	Doublestrike
• ^S	Underline	^H	Overprint Character
• ^X	Cross Out	^Y	Change Ribbon Color
• ^T	Superscript	^V	Subscript
• ^C	Stop Print Here	^O	Non-Break Space
• ^A	Alternate Pitch	^N	Resume Normal Pitch
• ^F	Phantom Space	^G	Phantom Rubout

The screen notation for a line-overprint command (^PM or ^P@) is a - flag at the right edge of the screen. This flag indicates that the following line will overprint the line on which the flag appears.

On-screen print controls can be removed with ^OD. ^OD is an on/off toggle command.

REVIEW: PRINT CONTROL CHARACTERS ON-SCREEN

When you enter the ^P prefix, that notation appears at left on the status line. If you have set the help level to 0 or 1, that's all that happens until you complete or interrupt the command. But if you have restored help level 3 (F1 3) or 2 (F1 2), pressing ^P by itself brings the Print Menu on-screen. This menu reviews all of WordStar's standard print controls. It will be replaced by WordStar's Main Menu (at help level 3) when you complete the command or interrupt with the space bar. Do not interrupt a print control command after entering the ^P prefix with ^U, the ESCAPE key, or the RETURN key.

```
                   < < <      P R I N T    M E N U      > > >
------ Special  Effects  ------  ¦ -Printing Changes-  ¦  -Other Menus-
(begin and end) ¦  (one time each) ¦ A Alternate pitch   ¦ (from Main only)
B Bold D Double ¦ H Overprint char ¦ N Standard pitch    ¦ ^J Help   ^K Block
  S Underscore  ¦ O Non-break space¦ C Printing pause    ¦ ^Q Quick  ^P Print
  X Strikeout   ¦ F Phantom space  ¦ Y Other ribbon color¦ ^O Onscreen
  V Subscript   ¦ G Phantom rubout ¦ --User Patches--    ¦ Space Bar returns
  T Superscript ¦ RET Overprint line¦ Q(1) W(2) E(3) R(4) ¦ you to Main Menu.
```

You have met all of the special effects and printing changes described in the Print Menu, above. The only category not detailed here is that of "user patches".

During installation of WordStar, each of these controls may be defined as a specific function. Until a definition is installed, the four command codes (^PQ, ^PW, ^PE, and ^PR) do nothing. Refer to the WordStar Installation Manual for information on installing your own definitions or using definitions already activated by your printer.

QUIZ

1. List the print control commands for these conditions:
   a. Underlining
   b. Boldface Type
   c. Doublestrike
   d. Subscripts
   e. Superscripts
   f. Crossing Out
   g. Changing Ribbon Color

2. What happens to the ^P prefix when you enter these commands?

3. What do the commands above have in common?

4. How will this screen notation print?

```
O^HX
```

5. How can you cause the printer to stop so that you can change daisy wheel printing elements at a specific place in the document?

6. What is the non-break space and how does it work?

7. How can you remove and reinstate the on-screen print control characters?

8. What are the commands ^PG and ^PF? What effect may they have on a non-daisy wheel or matrix printer?

9. What happens when you enter ^PM?

10. What do the commands ^PA and ^PN mean?

11. Describe what the following line will look like when printed.

^PY^PDGrown in limited quantities^PD at an altitude of 7,000 feet, ^PBJamaican Blue Mountain coffee^PB is unusually ^PSsoft, mellow, aromatic, and delightfully sweet-tasting.^PS^PY

12. What does this screen notation say?

```
a^V3^V^T2^T = a^V1^V^T2^T + a^V2^V^T2^T
```

You get extra points for knowing what it means.

13. Which of the print control commands offered by WordStar are not supported by the IBM Matrix Printer?

14. How should you interrupt a ^P command if you change your mind after entering the ^P prefix?

QUIZ ANSWERS

1. a. ^PS or F5 b. F6 c. ^PD d. ^PV e. ^PT f. ^PX g. ^PY
2. The ^P disappears and the command's second letter shows on-screen as ^S, ^B, ^D, ^V, ^T, ^X or ^Y.
3. These are on/off commands which must be entered before and after the featured text.
4. ⊗
5. Enter ^PC at the change point.
6. ^PO enters a hard space (^O) which will not be expanded or changed.
7. ^OD
8. Phantom space and phantom rubout produce two additional characters on daisy wheel printers. The characters vary from one daisy wheel to another.
9. ^PM is the line-overprint command. A - appears at far right, the cursor moves down one line, and the two lines so created overprint. Alternate entry: ^P@ (^P and RETURN).
10. ^PA changes to 12-pitch character width (closer letter spacing). ^PN resumes normal character width.
11. Ribbon color will be the alternate color for the entire entry (^PY appears at beginning and end); the first heavy or emphasized type is doublestrike.

    Grown in limited quantities at an altitude of 7000 feet, **Jamaican Blue Mountain coffee** is unusually soft, mellow, aromatic, and delightfully sweet-tasting.
12. $a_3^2 = a_1^2 + a_2^2$. This is the Pythagorean theorem, in which a_1 and a_2 are the sides of a right triangle and a_3 is its hypoteneuse.
13. The IBM Matrix Printer does not support the commands ^PC (stop print at command entry location), ^PY (change ribbon color), ^PA (shift to alternate character size), ^PN (resume normal character size), ^PF (phantom rubout), or ^PG (phantom space).
14. Press the space bar. Do not press RETURN, ESCAPE, or ^U as these entries will insert characters on the screen or complete the line overprint command.

17

Advanced Tabular Formatting

Manuscripts and technical papers often require the use of outlines, charts, or tables prepared in a specific format.

This chapter describes the preparation of such documents using WordStar's paragraph tab and non-break space commands.

THE PARAGRAPH TAB COMMAND

^OG is WordStar's regular paragraph tab command. Your IBM PC offers a one-key shortcut on its F-function keyboard: F2 indents text to the next tab stop.

The paragraph tab command will come in handy as you prepare a bibliography in indented form, type an outline, or arrange any document whose left margin shifts to the right.

Enter the first line as usual, but press F2 before reaching the end of the line. WordStar will set following lines one tab stop to the right. This automatic indentation continues until you enter a hard return, at which time the normal left margin resumes.

Here is an example to try. Start at the far left of the page and enter the keystrokes exactly as shown.

Hollenberg, Joel W., and Potter, J. H., "An Investigation F2of Regenerative Blowers and Pumps," F5Journal of Engineering for IndustryF5, Vol. 101, No. 2, May 1979.

This was an exercise in tabular formatting and underlining. You will see the automatic indentation on-screen, and if you print this example, here's what it will look like:

Hollenberg, Joel W., and Potter, J. H., "An Investigation of Regenerative Blowers and
Pumps," <u>Journal of Engineering for Industry</u>, Vol. 101, No. 2, May 1979.

Enter F2 two (or three) times in a single line to generate the automatic indentation of two (or three) corresponding tab stops.

Watch the ruler line as you press F2. With each entry, a corresponding section of the ruler is displayed in bright light. These ruler lines reflect one, two, and three successive F2 entries:

```
L-----!----!----!----!----!----!----------R     (F2)
L-----!----!----!----!----!----!----------R     (F2  F2)
L-----!----!----!----!----!----!----------R     (F2  F2  F2)
```

By watching the ruler line, you can verify the revised left margin before typing to the end of the line.

EXERCISE: BIBLIOGRAPHIES

Create a new ruler line with these commands: ^OL 1@ ^OR 65@ ^ON A@ ^OI 6@ ^OI 11@. The result should be 65 columns wide with tab stops at columns 6 and 11.

While typing bibliographic references, enter F2 with the cursor positioned after the first word but before the end of the first line.

It's important to punctuate bibliographies correctly, and standard academic guidelines appear below. Note the positions of commas, periods, quotation marks, and underlining as you type the following citations.

To prevent the underlining of punctuation marks which are not part of a book's title, be sure to enter the closing F5 command before the period, as: F5TitleF5.

Book title:

Finney, Jack. Time and Again. New York: Simon and Schuster, 1970.

Translated Book:

Maimonides, Moses. The Guide for the Perplexed. Translated from the Arabic by M. Friedlaender, Ph.D. New York: Dover Publications, 1956.

Two Authors:

De Santillana, Giorgio, and Herta von Dechend. Hamlet's Mill: An Essay on Myth and the Frame of Time. Boston: Gambit, Inc., 1969.

Edited Work:

Stonehouse, Bernard, editor. The Biology of Penguins. London: University Park Press, 1975.

Author and Editor:

Breuer, Josef, and Sigmund Freud. Studies on Hysteria. Translated from the German and edited by James Strachey. New York: Basic Books, Inc., 1957.

Gibbon, Edward. The Decline and Fall of the Roman Empire. Edited by Dero A. Saunders. New York: Viking Press, 1952.

(The bibliography examples above show, first, a work whose editor is also its translator, and a more common author-editor notation.)

Book Without Author:

Beekeeping in the United States. Washington, D.C.: United States Department of Agriculture, Agriculture Handbook No. 335, 1971.

Magazine and Newspapers:

Waring, Richard H. "Land of the Giant Conifers," Natural History, Vol. 91, No. 10, October 1982, 54–63.

Article Without Author:

"Excerpts From Interview With Chancellor Kohl," The New York Times, November 11, 1982, p. A10.

Same Author Listed Again:

Peterson, Roger Tory. A Field Guide to the Birds East of the Rockies. Fourth Edition. Boston: Houghton Mifflin Company, 1980.

———. "My Favorite Bird (King Penguin)." International Wildlife, Vol. 12, No. 2, March–April, 1982, 4–11.
———. Penguins. Boston: Houghton Mifflin Company, 1979.

Bibliography notations are listed in a single section, alphabetized according to each entry's first word, whether it be an author's last name, editor's last name, or title's first word.

If using a daisy wheel equipped with matching italic type, use ^PC to stop the printer and change wheels.

The Roger Tory Peterson entries above print like this on a daisy wheel printer using 12-pitch Courier and Courier Italic type:

Peterson, Roger Tory. *A Field Guide to the Birds East of the Rockies.* Fourth Edition. Boston: Houghton Mifflin Company, 1980.

----------------------. "My Favorite Bird (King Penguin)," *International Wildlife,* Vol. 12, No. 2, March-April 1982, 4-11.

----------------------. *Penguins.* Boston: Houghton Mifflin Company, 1979.

Before going on to the next exercise, reinstate the default ruler line. The fastest way to do this is to leave WordStar with the ^KX save command, or with X from the No-File Menu. Then call up WordStar with WS@ and use D to set up a document file. Alternately, remove and add tab stops as necessary (using ^ON and ^OI) so that the ruler line, which begins at column 1 and ends at column 65, has tab stops at these columns: 6, 11, 16, 21, 26, 31, 36, 41, 46, 51, and 56.

HANGING INDENTATION

I. This paragraph was typed using one F2 command in the first line. Its text can be any length, and automatic indentation continues until the entry ends in a hard < return.

   A. This paragraph was created by pressing the tab bar before entering "A.", and two F2 commands were placed in the first line. Alternately, you could enter F2 before typing the first letter, then add a second F2 command later. Entering F2 before typing the first letter indents text one tab stop.

      1. Similarly, this paragraph contains three F2 commands. Indent twice with the tab bar before typing "1." and enter three F2 commands later, or press F2 twice before typing the number, then insert a third F2 before reaching the end of the line. This paragraph's left margin is 16 spaces from the normal left margin; it appears at the third tab stop of the normal ruler line.

Once you reach the end of a tabulated paragraph, the left margin returns to its L position on the ruler. To create another tabulated section, enter the appropriate number of F2 commands in the appropriate places.

Should any text in a paragraph's first line move out of alignment do to word wrap's addition of soft spaces, use the ^PO non-break space command to enter hard spaces that will not be expanded. Although this procedure is not usually necessary when using the F2 paragraph tab command, readjustments sometimes happen.

OUTLINES

Outlines usually follow this format:

- I. Roman Numeral, Capitalized
  - A. Capital Letter
    - 1. Number
      - a. Lowercase Letter
        - (1) Number in Parentheses
- I. Major Heading
  - A. Subheading of the First Degree
    - 1. Subheading of the Second Degree
      - a. Subheading of the Third Degree
        - (1) Subheading of the Fourth Degree

It's unusual to need more than the first three subordinations.

EXERCISE: HANGING INDENTATION

In typing any chart in outline form, such as the one that follows, remove all tab stops with ^ON A@ and set new ones according to the number of columns you'll need as you indent. Because Roman numerals expand from left to right, your first section heading may be as wide as VIII (8) or XVIII (18). In this exercise, the largest Roman numeral is III (3).

Here is how tab stops were generated for this table. First, the numeral III was typed with a period and two spaces. This brought the cursor to the column that will be occupied by the first capital letter, setting the first indented margin. ^OI ESC set the first tab stop at this location. The subheading A was typed in this space, followed by a period and two more spaces. Again, ^OI ESC set the tab stop. After entering the number "1.", two hard spaces brought the cursor to its final indentation at column 15. Because this table was indented only as far as the numbers 1, 2, 3, etc., no further tabs were required. Here is the reference line generated by the tab setting procedure, with x marking the final indentation:

	III.	A.	1.	x
	↑	↑	↑	↑
column	1	7	11	15
	[tab stop column numbers]			

To set the correct tab stops for any chart or outline, use this same procedure, starting with the longest Roman numeral you will use. Allow at least four spaces for each new column (one for the letter or number, one for the period following, and two blank spaces to separate the notation from text). You can allow more space between settings if using two-digit numbers or if you so prefer; just be sure that the spacing is uniform.

"The Chart of the Genus Iris" appears in full in The Wise Garden Encyclopedia (New York: Grosset & Dunlap, 1970), pages 693–697. Our typing exercise is a condensed version.

Prepare this table, indenting (F2) and underlining (F5) where necessary. Read to the end of the exercise, including the "Things You Will Notice" section on page 132, before beginning.

CHART OF THE GENUS IRIS

I. RHIZOMATOUS. Irises growing from rhizomes, which are thickened stems or root-stocks, belong in this major category. Rhizomatous irises creep horizontally below or partly above the soil line. Clusters or fans of leaves grow from them.

  A. BEARDED OR PAGONIRIS. Flowers have three lower divisions and bear a strip of fuzzy growth of varying colors at the base.

    1. Bearded or Pagoniris include tall bearded, intermediate and dwarf plants.

    2. Oncocyclus are strangely marked irises from western Asia, featuring large blooms, beards and patches.

    3. Regelia irises resemble the above but are taller, measuring 12 to 30 inches.

    4. Pseudoregelia is a small class related to the above but not in cultivation.

  B. CRESTED OR EVANSIA irises feature a toothed ridge instead of a beard.

  C. BEARDLESS OR APOGON irises make up the largest and most widely distributed category. These are "wet" or aquatic flowers, requiring heavier soil and more moisture.

    1. Sibirica is the most widely known of this category. Flowers bloom in May and June.

    2. Spuria irises are important for their lovely flowers and decorative foliage.

    3. California types are low growing and well adapted to the Pacific coast.

    4. Longipetala are a small division resembling the sibiricas.

    5. Hexagona irises are named for their six-ridged seed pods.

    6. Japanese types are descended from the most magnificent irises, originating in Japan.

    7. Miscellaneous: This category includes the wild flag and swamp iris and others of assorted heights and seasons.

  D. PARDANTHOPSIS contains one species, the vesper iris, which features numerous buds and has a long growing season.

II. BULBOUS DIVISION plants grow from bulbs, not rhizomes. The foliage of these plants is different from that of the previous section.

  A. XIPHIUM irises have sparse, slender foliage.

    1. Spanish iris is a good cut flower but waning in popularity. Colors range from white and yellow to blue and bronze.

    2. Dutch iris has become the staple of flourists because of its robust, large blooms.

    3. English iris is heaviest in growth of these three types and resemble miniature Japanese irises.

  B. JUNO is the least typical iris, with foliage resembling cornstalks and blossoms growing from the leaf axils. This variety's bulbs are easily damaged.

C. RETICULATA or netted iris has a network pattern on the bulb. This iris has an early season (March–April) and a height of only 2 to 4 inches.

III. CORMOUS. This category has only one species, growing from a small bulb or corm. Botanists have not agreed that this is a true iris.

THINGS YOU WILL NOTICE

Demanding though it is, the preceding exercise is a crash course in paragraph tabbing. You have to enter a new paragraph tab command (F2 or F2 F2 or F2 F2 F2) in the first line of each new paragraph. In addition, unless you use ^PO to enter hard spaces after the letter or number headings, soft spaces may disturb your neat alignment of text.

If you forget to enter F2 and type a paragraph without indentation, finish the section. Then move back to its first line, position the cursor toward the middle of the line, enter the appropriate number of F2 commands, and enter ^B. Your paragraph will be reset with correct margins.

To enter the numeral I., skip the first two spaces; to enter II., skip one space. The entry III. begins at column 1.

To see what your text looks like without the distracting ^S print control characters, enter ^OD.

Another way to set a table filled with print control characters is to first enter the text without them, align the paragraphs correctly, check for typos, save the table with ^KS, then add each print control command where needed. Be sure insertion is turned on when you add print controls to already-entered text.

18

Paragraph Reform and Hyphen-Help

REFORMING PARAGRAPHS

Once you set a page of text, it doesn't have to stay that way. You can rearrange it, moving from single spacing to double spacing, from a justified right margin to a ragged right margin, from narrow columns to wide lines, and from a spread-out version to its condensed counterpart without retyping a single sentence. WordStar does all the work.

To appreciate WordStar's paragraph reform command, watch it in action.

Type this paragraph:

```
     From  now  until August 1,  the Orange  County  Agricultural
Society is conducting its 142nd county fair.  Beef, dairy cattle,
goats,  sheep,  arts  and crafts,  fresh fruits  and  vegetables,
flowers, baked goods, needlecraft and pickles will compete for
blue ribbons and prize money.
```

First, reform this paragraph by changing its width. Instead of using the normal 65-character-wide page, substitute a narrow column. Your first task is to reset the margins. Leave the left margin where it is for now and reset the right margin at column 35 (^OR 35@).

Now position the cursor at the top of the paragraph, anywhere in its first line. The command for paragraph reforming is ^B.

Before entering this command, you should know that when WordStar reforms a paragraph, it will stop at the end of a line whenever it finds a word that might be hyphenated and continued on the next line. In this first exercise, the cursor will stop in the word "pickles." Instead of hyphenating anything during the first part of this exercise, press ^B again to resume paragraph reforming. ^B says "No" to the "Shall we hyphenate this word?" question.

After you've reformed the example paragraph, it should look like this:

```
     From now until August  1,   the
Orange  County Agricultural Society
is  conducting  its  142nd   county
fair.  Beef,  dairy cattle, goats,
sheep,  arts  and  crafts,   fresh
fruits  and  vegetables,  flowers,
baked  goods,    needlecraft   and
pickles  will  compete  for   blue
ribbons and prize money.
```

HYPHEN-HELP

Return the cursor to the first line. Now press ^B again, only this time put a hyphen where hyphen-help suggests. When the cursor stops at the end of the line and flashes, it's asking whether you want to hyphenate the word at that location. To hyphenate, press the - key. Now your example paragraph looks like this:

```
     From now until August  1,  the
Orange  County Agricultural Society
is  conducting  its  142nd   county
fair.   Beef,  dairy cattle, goats,
sheep,   arts  and  crafts,   fresh
fruits  and  vegetables,   flowers,
baked  goods,  needlecraft and pic-
kles will compete for blue  ribbons
prize money.
```

The problem, as you can see, is that hyphen-help didn't put the hyphen in the right place. Look in a dictionary and you'll see that pickles should be hyphenated pick-les, not pic-kles. Don't assume that because the computer offers a hyphen, it is neces arily correct. Always check the dictionary for proper syllabication.

How can you correct the hyphenation of pickles? Move the cursor back to the "soft" or highlighted hyphen and remove it with ^G. Use ^T to bring the last letters of pickles back together with the first letters. ^G or ^T will eliminate unwanted space between words or letters, but ^T works faster. Leave the line extending to the right of the right margin and put the cursor into one of the paragraph's upper lines.

Enter ^B again. Once more the cursor will stop, offering a hyphen between the "c" and "k" in pickles. Use ^D to move the cursor one space to the right, so it's under the "l." This is the correct hyphening position, so press the - key and a soft hyphen should appear. Your screen will look like this:

```
     From now until August  1,   the
Orange  County Agricultural Society
is  conducting  its  142nd   county
fair.   Beef,  dairy cattle, goats,
sheep,   arts  and  crafts,   fresh
fruits  and  vegetables,   flowers,
baked goods,  needlecraft and pick-
les  will compete for blue  ribbons
and prize money.
```

If hyphen-help separates a word at the wrong place, you can correct its position by using ←(4) or the BACKSPACE key to move left, or →(6) to move right. Be careful when moving right. If you move beyond the right margin, you'll make the pre-hyphen part of a word too long. In that case the entire word, including a hard hyphen, will appear on the next line. Hard hyphens print regardless of position. Remove any unwanted hyphen, hard or soft, with ^G or the DELETE key.

You can reform a paragraph without resetting the margins in order to take advantage of hyphen-help. Try this example, leaving the right margin set at 35. Type the following paragraph:

```
     The  Senate  tax  bill    would
write   into   law  a  variety   of
```

```
compliances      and      enforcement
mechanisms   aimed   chiefly   at   the
self-employed.     In   addition,   it
would modify or repeal some of   the
tax    relief   previously   given   to
businesses.
```

The arrangement of text is uneven because words were separated to fill space across the line during word wrap. To condense this or any other already-entered text through hyphenation, use ^B. Try this, placing the cursor in the top line before entering the command code. If you press the hyphen key whenever the cursor stops at the end of a line in this example paragraph, it will occupy seven lines instead of the original eight.

```
     The      Senate   tax   bill   would
write   into law a variety   of   com-
pliances and enforcement mechanisms
aimed chiefly at the self-employed.
In   addition,   it   would modify   or
repeal some of the tax relief   pre-
viously given to businesses.
```

The hyphen in "self-employed" is a hard hyphen, entered as part of the initial text. It will always print, no matter how the paragraph might be rearranged. The hyphens in "com-pliance" and "pre-viously" are soft hyphens, appearing in faint light (highlighted) and printing only if they appear at the end of a line.

Reset the right margin at 65 (^OR 65@), and use ^B to reform this paragraph once more. Now you'll see one soft hyphen at the end of a line (com-pliance), one hard hyphen at the end of a line (self-employed), and one soft hyphen in the middle of a line (pre-viously). Your screen will look like this:

```
     The    Senate tax bill would write into law a variety of   com
pliances   and   enforcement mechanisms aimed chiefly at the   self
employed.   In addition, it would modify or repeal some of the ta
relief pre-viously given to businesses.
```

Which hyphens will print? The hyphen in "compliance" will print, even though it's a soft hyphen, because it appears at the end of a line. The hyphen in "self-employed" will print because it's a hard hyphen, which prints regardless of position. The hyphen in "previously" will not print, nor will it use any space in the printed document.

If you are reforming several pages of material and already know that you will not want hyphenated words to appear (or hyphenations other than those you have preset), it's easy to remove the hyphen-help feature by pressing ^OH. (Associate the H with *H*yphen-*H*elp.) Turning hyphen-help off does away with any delay at the end of a line during reforming. ^OH is another toggle or on/off command. To turn it back on, enter ^OH again.

SOFT HYPHEN ENTRY

You can hyphenate as you type, entering both hard and soft hyphens. ^OE is the "soft hyphen *E*ntry" command. This is a toggle or on/off command code; WordStar's soft hyphen entry mode is off by default, but you can turn it on and then off again with ^OE. Move the cursor down to an empty line and use the ^OE command before typing the following line:

```
This dis-play il-lus-trates which func-tions are work-ing.
```

All the hyphens are highlighted, and none will print unless at the end of a line. This is of course an extreme example, but you have no way of knowing how words will appear in your final document, especially if it goes through several revisions. If your text contains some complicated terms, you may want to enter soft hyphens when you first type them so that no matter what editing steps are taken, proper hyphenation will take place.

If you're entering soft hyphens with ^OE and need a hyphen that will print regardless of its position, enter ^P-. This enters a hard hyphen without leaving soft hyphen mode.

As you revise text to accommodate a figure, diagram, graph, technical illustration, or other material, you may use some very narrow margins. In narrow columns, hyphens are often avoided as a matter of aesthetics, but whenever an unhyphenated line contains more blank space than letters, hyphenate to balance the line.

A GUIDE TO HYPHENATION

John C. Hodges and Mary E. Whitten offer these guidelines for hyphenation in the *Harbrace College Handbook* (New York: Harcourt, Brace & World, Inc., 1967):

- Do not divide a word so that a single letter remains at the end of a line. Examples: a-larm, o-pen.
- Do not confuse your reader by separating the final letters in a past tense verb when they're pronounced as part of the preceding syllable. Examples: remain-ed, align-ed.
- In a word already containing a hyphen, don't add additional hyphens. Examples: low-spirit-ed, full-blood-ed.
- Avoid strings of broken words; try to type several lines of uninterrupted text between hyphenated words. Hyphens always distract the reader. Example:

```
     Of all the mammals, marsu-
pials may be the most interest-
ing. The female marsupial car-
ries her young in a pouch. Wom-
bats, bandicoots, numbats, wal-
labies, koalas, phalangers, kan-
garoos and certain moles belong
to the category.
```

RESETTING TEXT WITH THE REFORM COMMAND

As you add, remove, and rearrange text, a formerly well-groomed paragraph can grow alarmingly untidy. But so long as there are no hard returns (<) between its first and last words, ^B will set the text perfectly. To realign any paragraph after editing, place the cursor in its first line, or above the first out-of-alignment line, and press ^B. If the indentation is not correct, change it first. The cursor should be in a line of text (rather than a blank line) to keep line spacing uniform.

To alter the margins of an already-entered paragraph, set new margins and enter ^B with the cursor in its first line.

To condense a paragraph, use ^B in conjunction with hyphen-help.

To change a paragraph from regular margins to hanging indentation, pull the first word left to column 1 (if appropriate), move to the right of the first word, type F2, then enter ^B. This will leave the first line flush left and indent subsequent lines one tab stop. To indent two tab stops, enter F2 F2. These indentations are measured from the ruler line's left margin, which may not be the on-screen text's margin or column 1. Your ruler line should illuminate the corresponding indentation when you enter F2.

^B uses whatever margins and tab stops appear in the ruler line.

^B repositions everything from the cursor's line to the first < hard return it encounters.

If you move from single spacing to double spacing, ^B will not add a line between paragraphs. Enter extra lines with the RETURN key or ^N (see page 141). Once the cursor reaches a hard return ^B will stop. It will not add lines between consecutive hard returns and it will not remove blank lines ending in <.

REVIEW: PARAGRAPH REFORM COMMANDS ON-SCREEN

^JB is the paragraph reform help command. To see WordStar's three-part review of ^B and its uses, enter this code. The message appears regardless of help level.

```
                 ***** PARAGRAPH REFORM (^B) *****
To realign margins of a paragraph after corrections, place
     cursor at beginning of paragraph and type ^B.
To change margins of paragraph already entered, set margins
     (^OL, ^OR), place cursor at paragraph beginning, type ^B.
To change between justified and ragged right, or change line
     spacing, set desired justification (^OJ) & line spacing
     (^OS), place cursor at paragraph beginning, and type ^B.
To obtain WordStar's help in hyphenating long words, place cursor
     at beginning of paragraph and type ^B.
                                 press space bar for more:

 ^B reforms lines to end of paragraph as indicated by "hard"
     carriage return (< in rightmost column).
 Thus, it is important not to use RETURN between lines within a
     paragraph when entering text.
 ^B may be used to form hanging indents, change margins in mid-
     paragraph, etc.  The exact rule is:
     "^B starts on the cursor line, at the left margin col-
     umn, or at the cursor position, whichever is farther
     left, and proceeds to the next 'hard' carriage return".
                                          press space bar:

                  ***** Hyphen-Help *****
  ^B will occasionally stop before the end of the paragraph
      and ask you whether you wish a word hyphenated.
  Following the instructions that appear on the screen, move
      the cursor if desired to adjust the hyphen position,
      then press "-" to hyphenate, or ^B to not hyphenate.
  To turn off "hyphen'help", type ^OH.
                                          press space bar:
```

ENTERING THE HARD RETURN

As mentioned before, the RETURN key enters a "hard" return, one that will not be rearranged during future editing and paragraph reformation.

A second hard return entry is ^M. You met ^M in the line-overprint command (^PM) on page 115. ^M is identical to the RETURN key in its operation.

There is still another way to enter hard returns with WordStar, and that is with ^N. What's the difference?

- ^N inserts a return whether insertion is ON or OFF. When insertion is turned OFF, pressing the RETURN key moves the cursor down through text without disturbing or rearranging it. If you're editing a document with insertion turned OFF and want to create extra blank lines, use ^N to do so. The RETURN key will not create the extra space you need.
- ^N always leaves the cursor before the inserted return, while the RETURN key leaves the cursor positioned after the carriage return. If you are dividing what was a single paragraph into two paragraphs, you can choose whether to leave the cursor in the first section (^N) or send it down with the second part (RETURN key).
- ^N always creates single spacing while the RETURN key follows whatever line spacing is in use.

EXERCISE: PARAGRAPH REFORM, HYPHEN-HELP, HARD RETURNS

Set double spacing with ^OS 2. Enter ^OE to turn soft hyphen entry on. Margins should be set at columns 1 and 65 with the first tab stop at column 6. (Reset these conditions if necessary.)

Type the following text exactly as it appears here:

I
THE PERIOD

It was the best of times, it was the worst of times, it was the age of wisdom, it was the age of foolishness, it was the epoch of belief, it was the epoch of incredulity, it was the season of Light, it was the season of Darkness, it was the spring of hope, it was the winter of despair, we had everything before us, we had nothing before us, we were all going direct to Heaven, we were all going direct the other way—in short, the period was so far like the present period, that some of its noisiest authorities insisted on its being received, for good or for evil, in the superlative degree of comparison only. In both countries it was clearer than crystal to the lords of the State preserves of loave and fishes, that things in general were settled for ever.

1. Enter soft hyphens by moving the cursor to these locations and typing - : incre-dulity, every-thing, author-ities, super- lative, compar-ison.

2. Return to the end of the first sentence ("...degree of comparison only.") and place the cursor to the right of the period. Enter ^N twice. Subsequent text ("In both countries it") moves down while the cursor stays with the first sentence.
3. Use ^T to reunite the two sentences.
4. Press RETURN and notice how its action differs from ^N's. Two < flags will appear at right while the cursor moves down two lines with the second sentence. Indent to the first tab stop and insert the following sentence. Text will move right to accommodate. Add two spaces at the end of your insertion.

   There were a King with a large jaw and a queen with a plain face, on the throne of England; there were a King with a large jaw and a queen with a fair face, on the throne of France.
5. Turn soft hyphen entry off with ^OE. Reset the right margin at space/column 35 (^OR 35@). Set single spacing (^OS 1). Return to the first line with F10 (return to beginning of file). Use ^OC to center the two headings. Use ^B to reform both paragraphs, leaving a blank line between the two. Enter a - when hyphen-help stops at the end of a line.
6. Turn print control characters off with ^OD.
7. Use the scroll commands PgUp(9) or ^R and PgDn(3) or ^C to inspect your file. Your excerpt from *A Tale of Two Cities* by Charles Dickens should look like this:

```
                I.

            THE PERIOD

     It   was the best of times,   it
was the worst of times,   it was the
age   of wisdom,   it was the age   of
foolishness,   it   was the epoch   of
belief,   it was the epoch of incre-
dulity, it was the season of Light,
it was the season of   Darkness,   it
was the spring of hope,   it was the
winter   of despair,   we had   every-
thing   before us,   we   had   nothing
before us, we were all going direct
to Heaven, we were all going direct
the   other way -- in short the   pe-
riod   was   so far like the   present
period,   that some of its   noisiest
authorities   insisted on its   being
received,   for good or for evil, in
the   superlative degree of   compar-
ison only.

     There were a king with a large
jaw   and a queen with a plain face,
on   the throne   of   England;   there
were   a king with a large jaw and a
queen   with   a fair   face,   on   the
throne   of France.   In both   coun-
tries   it was clearer than   crystal
to the lords of the State preserves
of loaves and fishes,   that   things
in general were settled for ever.
```

REVIEW: PARAGRAPH REFORMING

- ^B is the paragraph reform command.

- To reform any paragraph, place the cursor in its first line before entering ^B. Margins will be set according to the ruler line.
- To reform a paragraph using F2 (paragraph tab) indentation, place the cursor toward the middle of the top line, enter F2 as many times as appropriate (once for each tab stop indentation), then ^B. Margins and tabs are set from the ruler line.
- ^B reforms paragraphs in accordance with your format conditions: line spacing, margins, tabs, and justification.
- ^B stops at the first hard return (<) it encounters.

REVIEW: HYPHEN-HELP

- In normal use, hyphen-help works automatically with the ^B command.
- Hyphen-help offers a Yes/No choice at each potential hyphenation. To hyphenate (Yes), press -. To continue without hyphenating (No), press ^B again.
- Hyphen-help enters soft hyphens which appear highlighted and which do not print unless at the end of a line.
- Hyphen-help does not always syllabicate correctly. To shift the position of a hyphen, use ^D or ^S to move one letter at a time, then enter - at the correct break. Do not move right of the right margin when changing the hyphen's position.
- ^OH is the hyphen-help on/off (toggle) command. Hyphen-help is on in normal use.
- ^B can be used at any time, without resetting margins, to condense text with hyphen-help.

REVIEW: HYPHENS

- Hard hyphens are entered with regular text using the - key. Hard hyphens appear on the screen in bright light and always print.
- Soft hyphens appear in faint light (highlighted) and are entered by hyphen-help or by hand when using the soft hyphen entry command (^OE). Soft hyphens print only when positioned at the end of a line.
- To enter a hard hyphen when soft hyphen entry is on, enter ^P and the hyphen key -.
- ^OE is an on/off or toggle command. In normal (default) use, the soft hyphen entry is turned off.

REVIEW: HARD AND SOFT RETURNS

- A hard return is entered with ^N, ^M, or the RETURN key. Every hard return generates a < flag at far right. Hard returns are permanent; they are not rearranged by paragraph reforming or editing.
- A soft return is generated by word wrap; its flag is a blank space at far right. Soft returns are temporary line breaks; editing and paragraph reform may rearrange them.
- ^M and the RETURN key operate identically.
- ^N inserts a hard return always. RETURN inserts a hard return only if insertion is on.

- ^N leaves the cursor above the return it creates; RETURN sends the cursor down to the next line.
- ^N always uses single spacing. The RETURN key uses whatever line spacing is in effect.

QUIZ

1. What is the paragraph reform command?
2. Where should you position the cursor when reforming a paragraph?
3. What line spacing, margins, and tab stops will the paragraph reform command utilize?
4. What does a flashing cursor at the end of a line mean during reforming?
5. What is ^OH?
6. What is ^OE?
7. What does ^P- do when ^OE is on?
8. Describe the three ways of entering a hard return.

QUIZ ANSWERS

1. ^B
2. Position the cursor anywhere in the top line of the paragraph being reformed.
3. ^B will use whatever margin settings, tab stops, and line spacing are shown on the status and ruler lines.
4. Hyphen-help offers a hyphen at the cursor's position.
5. ^OH is the hyphen-help on/off toggle command.
6. ^OE is the soft hyphen entry on/off toggle command.
7. ^P- enters a hard hyphen when ^OE is turned on.
8. ^M and RETURN operate identically. When insertion is on, they generate hard returns according to the line spacing in effect, and they move the cursor down the screen with each line break. When insertion is off, ^M and the RETURN key do not generate hard returns; they send the cursor down-screen through lines of text without disturbing or rearranging that text.

   ^N generates hard returns whether insertion is on or off. ^N always uses single spacing. This command leaves the cursor above the new line break instead of below it.

19

Format Toggle Commands

A toggle command is an ON/OFF switch. You enter the same code to turn the function on as you do to turn it off; each entry reverses the previous condition.

In earlier chapters you met toggle commands for insertion, soft hyphen entry, hyphen-help, the No-File Menu's file directory and the print control display. Print control commands are themselves toggle codes. This chapter reviews format toggles you've already met while introducing a number of new ones: the margin release, word wrap, margin justification, ruler line display, and page break display.

THE MARGIN RELEASE

^OX is the margin release ON/OFF toggle. However, the RETURN key is also a "margin release off" command, so you won't usually enter this command a second time to turn it off. Here's how it works.

Whenever you want to enter text to the right of the preset margin, type ^OX before you reach the end of the line. Now you can keep typing and the line will continue until you press RETURN.

When the margin release is on, you'll see a notation to that effect on the status line (MAR REL). When off (normal use) there is no notation. If you have set a narrow line, the ruler will reflect your margin release by illuminating tab signals left and right of the ruler line's margins.

EXERCISE: MARGIN RELEASE

Set the left margin at 15 and the right margin at 50. Enter this paragraph, turning the margin release on ^OX and pressing the return key @ where indicated.

```
                L!-----!-----!-----!-----!-----!-----!---R
                With the margin release turned on,
                you can go beyond ^OX the normal right margin @
                as shown. When you press the RETURN
                key and the cursor moves back inside
                the ruler line, MAR REL disappears
                from the status line and margin
                release is turned off. You can move
                left of the left margin if you have
                room by @
^OX pressing the RETURN key and entering the margin release code @
                before typing any text. This
                releases both left and right
                margins.
```

WORD WRAP

Word wrap sets the right margin and carries words from the end of one line to the beginning of the next. In normal (default) use, word wrap is turned on. Turning word wrap off is like releasing the right margin except that ^OX turns off when you press the RETURN key. With word wrap off you can press RETURN, come back into the ruler line's territory, and continue typing beyond the right margin.

The on/off toggle command for word wrap is ^OW. Remember this code by thinking of the W in *W*ord *W*rap.

JUSTIFICATION ON/OFF

In normal (default) use, WordStar justifies your right margin, making it straight by spreading letters and spaces across the line. You will want to turn justification off for business correspondence and anything that shouldn't have a "set by computer" look. The command is ^OJ. (Remember this code by thinking of the J in *J*ustification.) Enter it once to turn justification off; enter it again to turn justification back on.

You can type a document with justification turned off, then revise it by turning justification on and using ^B to reform the paragraphs, or vice versa.

"Ragged" is the term used to describe the uneven margin created by a regular typewriter, or by WordStar when justification is turned off. As mentioned, a ragged right margin is preferred in business correspondence.

You may want to turn justification off when entering tables or any text in which you don't want soft spaces entered.

RULER LINE ON/OFF

In normal use, the ruler line appears at the top of your screen, illustrating margin settings and tab stops. You can remove the ruler line by pressing ^OT. To reinstate the ruler, enter ^OT again. Removing the ruler line reveals one additional line of text.

PAGE BREAK DISPLAY ON/OFF

The normal or default page is set for 55 lines of text. After the 55th line, a page break line appears:

```
-------------------------------------------------------------------P
```

In addition, the page break function controls page and line location information on the status line. When you enter ^OP, the *P*age break on/off toggle command, page breaks disappear from your text and the status line shows your cursor location in this form: FC=(number)   FL=(number) COL (number). FC and FL are measured from the file's beginning; the column number is measured from the screen's left edge.

FC stands for file characters (bytes) preceding or above the cursor, FL gives the file line number, and COL stands for column number. On the fifth page of a double-spaced document, your ^OP OFF status line would read something like this:

```
FC=5734     FL=227     COL 28
```

PRINT CONTROL DISPLAY ON/OFF

When you enter a number of print control commands, such as those for boldface type, subscripts, superscripts, doublestrike, underlining, etc., the print control characters occupy screen space and distort the appearance of your document. To inspect text without the distraction of control characters and ^ signals, turn their display off with ^OD. (Remember this command by thinking of the D in *D*isplay.) Leave this command on (its default position) while editing; after you turn it off to inspect text, turn it back on before continuing.

^OD removes soft hyphens not positioned at the end of a line. In addition the "non-break space" (^PO) displays as a space rather than ^O.

HYPHEN-HELP AND SOFT HYPHEN ENTRY ON/OFF TOGGLES

When left on (its default position), hyphen-help condenses text through hyphenation when you use ^B. When hyphen-help is turned off (^OH), ^B reconfigures paragraphs without interruption. Turn the function back on again with ^OH.

Soft hyphen entry inserts highlighted hyphens that will print only if positioned at the end of a line. To enter a hard hyphen when ^OE is ON, type ^P-. This function is turned off by default. To turn it on, enter ^OE; this same command turns it back off again.

DEFAULT TOGGLES

In a regular document file, these are the preset or default conditions:

- Word Wrap is ON.
- Justification is ON.
- Ruler Display is ON.
- Page Break Display is ON.
- Print Control Display is ON.
- Soft Hyphen Entry is OFF.
- Margin Release is OFF.
- Hyphen-Help is ON.

In a non-document file, created by using N instead of D when you open the file, nearly all these conditions are reversed. Word wrap, justification, ruler display, page break display, and hyphen-help are all turned off. The page break display cannot be activated in this mode. In addition, tab stops are arranged and operate differently. In the WordStar instruction manual you'll see references to ^OV, the variable tabbing on/off toggle. In normal word processing use, variable tabbing mode is left on and you won't enter ^OV. If you plan to use non-document mode, see page 301. Should the TAB key not behave properly in a document file, you may have entered ^OV by mistake. Check the On-screen Menu for this toggle's status and, if off, turn it back on.

CHECKING THE STATUS OF FORMAT TOGGLES

When deep in an editing project and making numerous format changes, you may forget whether justification or the print display is on, or the status of other toggles. The status line notes whether insertion is on, if your line spacing is other than 1, and if the margin release is on, but you have no status line reminders of the toggle keys' status.

To check, reinstate help level 2 or 3 (F1 2 or F1 3) and enter ^O by itself. The ^O prefix produces an On-screen Menu display. Each toggle command appears with (ON) or (OFF) at its right, indicating its present status. After checking individual toggles, reverse the status of any by completing the command (enter its second letter code), or interrupt with ^U, ESC, RETURN, or the space bar. Remove WordStar's Main Menu with F1 1 or F1 0.

Here is the On-screen Menu as it appears when you enter ^O by itself at help level 2 or 3:

```
                <<<      O N S C R E E N   M E N U       >>>
 -Margins & Tabs-  | -Line Functions- |  --More Toggles--   | -Other Menus-
L Set left margin  |C Center text     |J Justify    off (ON)|(from Main only)
R Set right margin |S Set line spacing|V Vari-Tabs  off (ON)|^J Help   ^K Block
X Release margins  |                  |H Hyph-Help  off (ON)|^Q Quick  ^P Print
I Set  N Clear tab |  -- Toggles--    |E Soft hyph  on (OFF)|^O Onscreen
G Paragraph tab    |W Wrd wrap off(ON)|D Prnt disp  off (ON)|Space Bar returns
F Ruler from line  |T Rlr line off(ON)|P Pge break  off (ON)| to Main Menu.
```

In the menu shown above, all toggles except the soft hyphen entry mode are turned on. Every toggle's current status appears in the right column, in capital letters, in bright light, and in parentheses.

EXERCISE: FORMAT TOGGLES

Start a new file named MYTH, and type the following, centering the title (^OC) and using the underline (^PS), superscript (^PT), and boldface (^PB) commands.

```
           Introduction ^BThe Age of Fable^B, Continued
                  From ^SBulfinch's Mythology^S

    Jupiter,  or Jove (Zeus^T1^T),  though called the father of gods
and  men,  had  himself  a beginning.  Saturn (Cronos)  was  his
father,  and Rhea (Ops) his mother.  Saturn and Rhea were of the
race of Titans,  who were the children of Earth and Heaven, which
sprang  from Chaos,  of which we shall give a further account  in
our next chapter.
    There  is another cosmogony,  or account of  the  creation,
according to which Earth,  Erebus, and Love were the first of the
beings.  Love (Eros) issued from the egg of Night, which floated
on  Chaos.   By his arrows and torch he pierced and vivified all
things, producing life and joy.
---------
^T1^T  The names included in parentheses are the  Greek,  the  others
being the Roman or Latin names.
```

The ^S print control stands for underlining; ^B stands for boldface; and ^T represents a superscript. These print control characters were entered with the commands F5, F6, and ^PT, respectively.

1. Turn hyphen-help off (^OH). Use double spacing (^OS 2). Set the help level at 2 (F1 key). Reset margins at ^OL 10 and ^OR 50. Remove stops all tab with ^ON A@. Set a new tab stop at ^OI 15@.

2. Press ^OD. This turns the print control display off, so print control characters ^B, ^S, and ^T disappear. Watch the screen and scroll to see all 16 lines. Press ^OD again to reinstate the print control display.
3. Enter ^OJ to turn justification off. Move the cursor to the top (title) line. Enter ^OC to re-center this line.
4. Move down to the next line and press ^OC to re-center its text.
5. With the cursor in the first line of the first paragraph, enter ^B.
6. Position the cursor in the first row of the second paragraph; enter ^B.
7. Press ^OE, the soft hyphen entry command.
8. Move to the end of the second paragraph and press RETURN. Insert the following text as a new paragraph, pressing the - key where shown. Remember that ^P- is the hard hyphen entry when in you are in soft hyphen mode.

   Saturn and Rhea were not the only Ti-tans. There were others, whose names were Ocean-us, Hy-perion, Ia-petus, and Ophi-on, males; and The-mis, Mne-mo-syne, Eury-nome, females. They are spoken of as the elder gods, whose domin-ion was after-wards trans-ferred to others. Saturn yielded to Ju-piter, Ocean-us to Nep-tune, Hy-perion to Apol-lo. Hyper-ion was the father of the Sun, Moon and Dawn. He is therefore the original sun^P-god, and is painted with the splendour and beauty which were after-wards bestowed on Apollo.

9. Now enter ^O. Check the screen display to affirm that soft hyphen entry is on, justification is off, word wrap is on, print control display is on, and hyphen-help is off. If any of these conditions are not as indicated here, press its command's second letter code. If your toggle display agrees with the conditions above, press the return key.
10. Turn the print control display off with ^OD. What happens to your soft hyphens? What happens to the hard hyphen you entered with ^P- ?
11. Enter ^OJ to reinstate right margin justification, ^OE to turn soft hyphen entry off, and ^OT to turn the ruler line off. Now enter ^OL 1@ and ^OR 60@. Reinstate the ruler line with ^OT.
12. Enter ^OP to turn the page break display off. Your status line will list the cursor position in characters or bytes (FC=) and the file line (FL=). Column position is shown following COL.
13. Return the cursor to the first line of your file (F10). Re- center the headings. Your ^O menu should show hyphen-help off, soft hyphen entry off, justification off and page break display off. Enter ^O to confirm this. Now type P, which completes the ^OP command and turns the page break display back on.
14. Because this is a short file and because everything in it should conform to the new margin setting and other format conditions, enter the prefix ^QQ before the ^B reform command. ^QQ causes the next-entered command to repeat continuously. Therefore, ^QQB (entered as ^Q^Q^B or ^QQ^B) causes WordStar's paragraph reform command to repeat automatically.

15. Watch the screen as ^B reforms the entire document. You will not have to enter another command. When it reaches the end of your file, the cursor will stop.

    Print the MYTH file.

If you have a daisy wheel printer, your hard copy should look like this:

Introduction:The Age of Fable, Continued

From **Bulfinch's Mythology**

Jupiter, or Jove (Zeus[1]), though called the father of gods and men, had himself a beginning. Saturn (Cronos) was his father and Rhea (Ops) his mother. Saturn and Rhea were of the race of Titans, who were the children of Earth and Heaven, which sprang from Chaos, of which we shall give a further account in our next chapter.

There is another cosmogony, or account of the creation, according to which Earth, Erebus, and Love were the first of the beings. Love (Eros) issued from the egg of Night, which floated on Chaos. By his arrows and torch he pierced and vivified all things, producing love and joy.

Saturn and Rhea were not the only Titans. There were others, whose names were Oceanus, Hyperion, Iapetus, and Ophion, males; and Themis, Mnemosyne, Eurynome, females. They are spoken of as the elder gods, whose dominion was afterwards transferred to others. Saturn yielded to Jupiter, Oceanus to Neptune, Hyperion to Apollo. Hyperion was the father of the Sun, Moon and Dawn. He is therefore the original sun-god, and is painted with the splendour and beauty which were afterwards bestowed on Apollo.

----

[1] The names included in parentheses are the Greek, the others being the Roman or Latin names.

REVIEW: TOGGLE ON/OFF COMMANDS

Command Code	Function	Default Position
^OW	Word Wrap	(ON)
^OJ	Right Margin Justification	(ON)
^OT	Ruler Line	(ON)
^OP	Page Break Display	(ON)
^OD	Print Control Display	(ON)
^OX	Margin Release	(OFF)
^OH	Hyphen-Help	(ON)
^OE	Soft Hyphen Entry	(OFF)

- To verify the current status of any ^O toggle, enter that prefix with the help level set at 2 or 3 (F1 2 or F1 3). Each command will show its present status capitalized, in bright light and in parentheses.
- Format toggles survive both ^KS and ^KD save commands. When you move from one file to another in a single editing session, the previous file's configuration goes with you.

QUIZ

1. What is a toggle command?
2. Translate these toggles:
   a. ^OW
   b. ^OJ
   c. ^OT
   d. ^OP
   e. ^OD
   f. ^OX
   g. ^OH
   h. ^OE
3. Which of these commands usually turns off automatically?
4. What toggle commands can you recall from previous chapters?
5. What happens to soft hyphens when you turn ^OD off?
6. Which of the toggles listed in question 2 are off by default?

QUIZ ANSWERS

1. An on/off command for which the same command code is entered to turn the function on and off.
2. a. Word wrap on/off.
   b. Right margin justification on/off.
   c. Ruler line display on/off.
   d. Page break display on/off.
   e. Print control display on/off.

    f. Margin release on/off.
    g. Hyphen-help on/off.
    h. Soft hyphen entry on/off.

3. ^OX, the margin release, turns off after the cursor moves outside of the margin area and then back inside.

4. Toggles from previous chapters include ^V (insertion on/off), F (file directory on/off, from the No-File Menu), and print controls for boldface, doublestrike, subscript, superscript, cross out, and ribbon color change.

5. They are removed, except for those appearing at the end of a line.

6. ^OX and ^OE (margin release and soft hyphen entry).

20

Wide Documents and Illustrations

WIDE MARGINS

Your screen displays 79 columns of text at a time, but your printer may handle paper (and printed lines) as wide as 130, 250 or more characters.

Note that the IBM Matrix Printer cannot print lines wider than 80 columns, and you will need a special dot command (see page 237) if the line is wider than 72 or 75 columns.

The widest right margin WordStar accepts with word wrap turned on is set at column 255. But with word wrap turned off you can type to column number 32,000!

Whenever you enter a line wider than the screen can show, a + appears at right. The same + flag appeared when you set print controls that bumped text beyond the right margin.

Experiment by setting your right margin at 80 and typing the following sentence. Notice the ruler line, where a + replaces the right margin R.

The principal conquests of the Romans were achieved under the republic; and the emperors, for the most part, were satisfied with preserving those dominions which had been acquired by the policy of the senate, the active emulation of the consuls, and the martial enthusiasm of the people.

This sentence, from Edward Gibbon's *The Decline and Fall* of *the Roman Empire,* activates WordStar's horizontal scroll feature. As you typed, text should have shifted on-screen to display the final entry of each line. After typing, position the cursor in any of the top three lines of the sentence and enter ^QD. Use ^QS to return to column 1. Your screen should look like these two illustrations in the process:

```
     The principal conquests of the Romans were achieved under the  republic; an+

the emperors,  for the most part, were satisfied with preserving those dominion+

which had been acquired by the policy of the senate, the active emulation of th+

consuls, and the martial enthusiasm of the people.
```

```
quests of the Romans were achieved under the  republic; and

e most part, were satisfied with preserving those dominions

ed by the policy of the senate, the active emulation of the

ial enthusiasm of the people.
```

Horizontal scrolling can be hard to follow, so it's sometimes easier to enter a wide document with regular margins, reforming it later with ^B and a revised margin setting.

ACCOMMODATING ILLUSTRATIONS

You can use margin setting commands to accommodate illustrations and figures that will appear in your final copy by first measuring the illustration, then determining how many spaces you must allow horizontally and vertically. On the standard page, six lines of text equal one inch. Note that this means from the base of one line to the base of the line six lines above or below it.

The standard character width is 10 characters per inch (cpi). This means that one horizontal inch equals 10 columns or spaces.

Let's say you have a figure whose actual measurements are 2 × 2 inches and which will appear on the right side of a page. The illustration itself will occupy the space taken up by 12 vertical lines and 20 horizontal spaces. To leave a narrow margin above, below and to the left of the figure, let's make it 14 vertical lines and 22 horizontal spaces. Now we'll borrow a paragraph from the preface of Noah Webster's 1806 edition of *A Compendious Dictionary of the English Language* to leave space for such an illustration. Three lines use the 65-wide margin, then the right margin shifts to column 43 (22 spaces from column 65) for a total of 14 lines. After 14 lines, it returns to column 65.

You would set the paragraph's format conditions by beginning with ^OL 1 and ^OR 65 (left margin at column 1, right margin at column 65). On the fourth line, change the right margin to ^OR 43. On line 17 of this paragraph, return the right margin to column 65 with the command ^OR 65.

Here's how the text appears on-screen:

```
     On   the   first publication of my Institutes of   the   English
Language,   more   than twenty years ago,   that   eminent   classical
scholar and divine,   the late Dr. Goodrich of Durham, recommended
to   me   to complete a system of   elementary
principles, for the instruction of youth in
the  English language,   by   compliling   and
publishing a dictionary.    Whatever respect
I   was inclined to pay to that  gentleman's
opinion, I could not, at that time, believe
myself  qualified for such an  undertaking;
and     various     private     considerations
afterwards     interposed     to     retard     its
execution.     My     studies     however     have
occasionally   had reference to an   ultimate
accomplishment   of such a work;   and for   a
few   years   past,   they have been   directed
immediately    to   that  object.    As   I   have   advanced   in   my
investigations,   I   have   been,   at every  step,   more   and   more
impressed  with the importance of this work;  and an acquaintance
with the Saxon language,  the mother tongue of the  English,  has
convinced  me that a careful revision of our present dictionaries
is absolutely necessary to a correct knowledge of the language.
```

Be sure to measure the space you need against an actual page of your document's printed text before entering the appropriate commands, especially when using an unusual character width or line spacing.

Remember that on the standard page:

- 1 inch equals 6 lines down.
- 1 inch equals 10 spaces across.

If your printer uses 12-pitch type, or if you change from standard to 12-pitch letters, multiply the inches you need by 12 to determine the number of columns to indent.

REVIEW: WIDE MARGINS

The normal screen can display up to 79 characters in a line, but many printers print much wider lines. With word wrap off, WordStar will format lines up to 32,000 characters in width; with word wrap on, the limit is 240 columns.

- To set the right margin at any width, use ^OR and the desired column number.
- As you enter wide text, the screen will scroll right to display words as you type.
- To inspect a wide document, use the horizontal scroll feature by moving right with ^QD (or another right-moving cursor command) and left with ^QS (or another left-moving cursor command).
- A + at right means the line continues off screen. A + on the ruler line (replacing the usual R) means the right margin is set beyond column 79.

REVIEW: LEAVING SPACE FOR ILLUSTRATIONS

You can leave space for illustrations, tables, graphs, and other material by adjusting the margins accordingly.

- On the normal page:
  10 characters = 1 horizontal inch
  6 lines = 1 vertical inch
- "Pitch" refers to characters per inch, so a 10-pitch daisy wheel prints 10 characters per inch (cpi). A 12-pitch wheel prints 12 cpi.
- Many printers offer a choice between the standard 10 cpi type size and 12 cpi. These sizes correspond with the normal pica (10 cpi) and elite (12 cpi) typewriter type sizes. See ^PA and ^PN, page 120.
- To leave space for an illustration, measure its length and width. Convert inches to columns (horizontal) and lines (vertical). Add additional columns and lines to allow a margin between figure and text. At the desired location, change the left or right margin accordingly, using the new setting for an appropriate number of lines. Then return to the original margin setting and resume.

QUIZ

1. How do you set the margins for a document 85 spaces wide?

2. How does the ruler line reflect this wide document?
3. When the cursor is in column 1, what screen notation informs you that text is continued off-screen?
4. How can you scroll horizontally to inspect a wide line?
5. How many characters and lines would you normally indent/skip to accommodate an illustration measuring 1 inch square?

QUIZ ANSWERS

1. With the left margin set at 1, enter ^OR 85@.
2. A + replaces the R on the ruler line at top of screen.
3. A + appears at far right.
4. Use ^QD to scroll right and ^QS to scroll left. Alternately, use any right-moving or left-moving cursor command (^F, ^A, etc.).
5. One horizontal inch equals 10 characters in normal (default) use; 1 vertical inch equals 6 lines. The illustration itself will occupy this much space; to allow an additional margin around the illustration, you can reduce the right or left margin by 12 to 15 spaces for 8 to 10 lines.

21

Creating Tables

A table is an organized array of information arranged in rows and columns. Its information may consist of numbers or text or both.

This chapter introduces a simple approach to tables, using your ruler line's tab stops. Any text arrangement employing these ! stops to create columns, indented margins, and special effects is called tabular formatting.

EXERCISE: SIMPLE COLUMNS

To become acquainted with tabular formatting, remove the preset tab stops by entering ^ON A@.

Set new stops using ^OI and these column numbers: 25, 45, and 55. The entry is ^OI 25@ ^OI 45@ ^OI 55@. Your resulting ruler looks like this:

```
L-----------------------!-------------------!---------!--------R
```

Set the spacing command (^OS) for double spacing.

Enter and center the top line of the table below; then press RETURN and enter the headings as shown. (The command for centering a title is ^OC.) Press RETURN twice before typing the text.

Wives of the First Five United States Presidents

Name	State	Married	Lived
Martha Washington	Virginia	1759	1732–1802
Abigail Adams	Massachusetts	1764	1744–1818
Martha Jefferson	Virginia	1772	1748–1782
Dorthea Madison	North Carolina	1784	1768–1849
Elizabeth Monroe	New York	1786	1768–1830

USING A MID-TEXT RULER

WordStar makes it possible to create new tabular rulers in the middle of your document. For example, use the space key to move in to column 10. With the cursor at space 10, press the hyphen key 20 times, enter a !, add another 10 hyphens, another !, and another 10 spaces. Your line looks like this:

```
---------------------!-----------!----------
```

With the cursor at any position in this line, enter ^OF, the command you met on page 88. ^OF resets the margins and tab stops to conform with the ruler you have typed.

Using this ruler you can enter the following table. Move the cursor down from the ruler line and enter the title, centering lines with the ^OC command. Do not press the TAB key before entering names; even though the cursor is in column 1, WordStar will indent to column 10 before displaying text.

Nobel Prize Winners in Chemistry, 1910–1920

Winner	Year	Country
O. Wallach	1910	Germany
M. Curie	1911	France
F. Gringard	1912	France
P. Sabatier	1912	France
A. Werner	1913	Switzerland
T. Richard	1914	United States
R. Willstaetter	1915	Germany
F. Haber	1918	Germany
W. Nernst	1920	Germany

An alternate way to enter the table is with a tab stop in the far left column:

```
!------------------!----------!----------
```

When you reach the end of a line, hit the TAB key and the cursor will move down a line to the next tab stop. This technique eliminates use of the RETURN key altogether.

CREATING A NONPRINTING MID-TEXT RULER

The only problem with the ruler line you have just used is that the printer will print it exactly as it appears.

After preparing a table while using an on-screen ruler line, you can remove it with a delete command (^Y), or you can instruct the computer not to print the ruler.

Leaving the ruler line on-screen simplifies future editing. To instruct the printer not to print it, you can use a dot command. Dot commands are explained in detail in later chapters. The dot command to use here is two periods (..), which instructs the printer not to print what follows.

Move the cursor up one line from the ruler line and be sure it's in column 1 at the far left of the screen. Also, be sure insertion is on. Now enter the two periods, followed by ^PM, which is the command to overprint a line. (^P and the RETURN key will also work; this is an alternate "overprint line" command.)

A hyphen flag appears at right.

After entering this dot command with a mid-text ruler, your screen will look something like this:

```
..                                                              -
    L------------------!----------!----------R                 <
```

The upper line is empty except for two dots at the far left and a hyphen at the far right. Your ruler occupies the next line and a <, showing hard return, is at right.

Why does this procedure work?

The dot command (..) instructs the computer, Do not print this line. ^PM (^P@) in the nonprinting line causes the next line (the ruler) to overprint. The computer regards these two lines as one nonprinting entity, connected by the - flag at right. Therefore, the entire entry remains on-screen but does not print.

DECIMAL TABS

Move down two lines and create a new ruler line, using # instead of ! to mark the tab stops. This is going to be a table of decimal numbers. With # in the ruler line, the computer aligns the decimals.

Enter this ruler line:

```
--------------------#----------#----------
  (20 hyphens)             (10)        (10)
```

Leave the cursor in the ruler line and press ^OF. Now move the cursor up one line and enter two periods at the far left. Press ^PM. Move the cursor two lines below the ruler, by using ↓ (2), ^QD, and the RETURN key. Type the following table.

```
..                                                   -
L------------------#----------#---------R           <
A.                21.438       26.9                 <
B.            349872.4       1269.4938              <
C.                 0.3529       0.34                <
D.             43989.4         28.3829              <
```

You don't have to worry about how the decimals will line up. As soon as you press the TAB key and begin typing a number, the computer shifts digits to the left until a decimal appears. Whenever the cursor stops at a decimal tab stop, the word "decimal" displays on the status line.

You can set ruler lines with both regular ! and decimal # tab stops. To set decimal tab stops (#) in the regular ruler line at the top of your screen, use ^OI and type a # before the desired column number, or position the cursor where you want a decimal tab and enter ^OI # ESC. A message at the top of the screen reminds you of your options here.

Enter #43@. The decimal tab (#) appears at column 43. Move the cursor two spaces to the right and enter ^OI # ESC. Another decimal tab (#) appears at column 45.

Be careful when using a ruler line that includes a decimal tab where you indent for paragraphs. To understand why, put a decimal tab stop in column 6 by entering ^OI #6@. Now indent as you normally would to this first tab stop and type a word that's several letters long. See what happens? The computer is waiting for a decimal point or period, so it keeps shifting letters to the left until they reach the left margin. If you enter a one-letter word, such as "a" or "I," the line won't shift at all; if you enter a two-letter word, it will shift only one letter to the left. That's because the space you enter after the word stops the computer's search for a decimal point.

Before going further, replace the # stop in space 6 with a regular tab stop by entering ^OI 6@.

To revise or correct columns of numbers like the decimal tab example you just worked, turn insertion off so the decimal alignment is not disturbed. Insertion off allows you to replace one number with another by entering one directly over the other, or to remove numbers by using the space bar. Spaces "overprint" or replace numbers when insertion is off.

For more on the creation and manipulation of columns, see Chapter 27.

REVIEW: TABULAR FORMATTING

Tab stops appear on the normal ruler line at five-space intervals, beginning at column 6. Regular tab stops are indicated by the ! symbol, decimal stops by the #. On the normal (default) ruler line, regular stops appear at columns 6, 11, 16, 21, 26, 31, 36, 41, 46, 51, and 56.

When you press TAB, the cursor moves to the next tab stop. When you reach the final stop on a line, the cursor moves down to the next line, entering a hard return while doing so, and stops at the first ! or # on that line.

The command ^ON removes tab stops.

- To remove a single stop, enter ^ON, the column number, and the RETURN key.
- Alternately, position the cursor at the stop you wish to remove and enter ^ON and the ESCAPE key (ESC).
- To remove all tab stops, enter ^ON A@ .

Tab stops can be set from a ruler line typed within a document. To do this, type a new ruler using the hyphen key (- - - - -) and exclamation marks (!) to indicate line width and tab stops.

- ^OF entered with the cursor in the typed ruler line sets this ruler at the top of the screen.
- To prevent a typed ruler line from printing in your document, place the dot command .. (two periods) in columns 1 and 2 in the line directly above the typed ruler. Enter ^PM or ^P@ anywhere in the dot command's line. Now the typed ruler line will not print.
- ! is the symbol for regular paragraph tabs used in text entry; # is the symbol for decimal tabs. To enter a decimal tab in the regular ruler line, enter ^OI, #, the desired column number, and the RETURN key. To enter a decimal tab at the cursor column, enter ^OI # ESC.
- When editing a column or table of decimal numbers, turn insertion off to retain correct decimal positions.
- The fastest way to enter a table of names, short phrases, or numbers is to set the margins wider than the table will be, clear all tab stops, and set column tabs, including one at the table's left margin, using ! for text and # for decimal numbers. Use the TAB key to move from one tab stop to the next and from one line to the next; do not use the RETURN key when you reach the end of a line.

REVIEW: TABULAR FORMAT COMMANDS ON-SCREEN

Paragraph tabs, decimal tabs, and mid-text ruler lines are explained by ^JM, the Help Menu listing margins and tabs. Enter ^JM at any help level.

Here is the text of WordStar's ^JM tab message:

```
                  *****  TAB STOPS  *****

To set a tab: type ^OI.  WordStar will ask for column number.
     Type column number and press RETURN.  Or, to use cursor
     column press the ESCAPE key.  To set a decimal tab stop,
     type "#" before typing column number or pressing ESCAPE.
To clear a tab stop or all tab stops: type ^ON.
To tab: type ^I or press TAB key if present.  Tabbing
     inserts spaces to next tab stop if insertion (^V) is on.
     Tabbing advances cursor over text if insertion is off.
                                  press space bar:


     ENTERING A COLUMNAR TABLE -- We Suggest:

Set a tab stop for each column of table.
Clear all other tab stops.
If not at end of file, turn on insertion (^V),
     or use ^N to make blank lines.
Tab (^I) after entering each table item.  After last column
     on a line, tabbing will move to first item on next line.
                                        space bar:

     OUTLINE FORMAT TEXT ENTRY -- We Suggest:
Set tab stops at desired indentations.
Set right margin as desired.
For each item:
          Type ^OG's as required for item number indentation.
          Type item number.
          Type ^OG.
          Type text of item, without using RETURN.
          At end of item, press RETURN.  Left margin resets.
          Press RETURN again if blank line desired.
                                       press space bar:
```

QUIZ

1. What will your ruler line look like after these commands are entered?

   `^ON A@   ^OI 15@   ^OI #25@`

2. What is the difference between ! and # on a ruler line?
3. How can you enter a ruler line in the text? How can you prevent it from printing?
4. Why is it a good idea to turn insertion off when editing a table of decimal numbers?
5. Define each of these codes:
   a. ^OI
   b. ^ON
   c. ^OF

QUIZ ANSWERS

1. Assuming the margins remain at 1 and 65, the ruler line will show dashes all across the line except for a ! in column 15 and a # in column 25.
2. The ! is a regular tab stop for use in text entry; the # aligns decimal numbers so every decimal appears directly below the # stop.
3. Type a ruler line the way you want it to appear at the top of the screen, then enter ^OF with the cursor anywhere within that line. To prevent the typed ruler line from printing, enter the dot command .. (two periods) one row above the typed

line at the far left (columns 1 and 2), then enter ^PM or ^P@ anywhere in that same line.

4. With insertion off you will not disturb the alignment of decimals and numbers while making corrections.

5. a. Set tab stop.
b. Erase tab stop.
c. Set margins and tabs from text line.

22

Place Markers

When working on a long document, you will want to mark certain sections for later additions or editing commands. WordStar has the computerized equivalent of paperclips and red pencils in its place markers.

SET A PLACE MARKER

Place markers are set by typing ^K and any number between 0 and 9: ^K0, ^K1, ^K2, ^K3, etc. Here your mnemonic device is the word mar*K*er. Do not hold the CONTROL key while entering the marker's number.

Your screen will show the highlighted marker like this: <0>, <1>, <2>, <3>, etc. Even though markers take up room on the screen, they don't print and they don't take up space in the actual document.

FIND A PLACE MARKER

Once a marker is set, you can find it quickly by using ^Q and the appropriate number. ^Q1 moves the cursor to place marker <1>, ^Q2 moves it to place marker <2>, etc.

Place markers are not permanent. You can't come back a week later to find them still in place. Place markers can be set so that they last through a single file's editing session, or you can replace and remove them while working on a document.

PLACE MARKERS ARE MOVABLE

Even though you can set only 10 place markers (0 to 9) at a time, you can move those you don't need any more. Set place marker <1> by entering ^K1. Now move down a few lines and watch the marker as you enter ^K1 again. The <1> notation disappears from its original place and reappears at the cursor location.

HIDE A PLACE MARKER

What happens if you enter ^K1 again, only without moving the cursor? It disappears. However, it hasn't been erased; it's been "hidden."

Try this by entering the command ^K1 with the cursor positioned just to the right of the <1> marker. As you see, it vanishes from the screen. Text that has been bumped to the right moves left to its original position.

Redisplay marker <1> by entering ^K1 again.

FIND A HIDDEN PLACE MARKER

If you enter ^Q with the number of a hidden marker, the cursor will find that marker and redisplay it. For example, enter ^K6 and watch the <6> appear. Enter ^K6 again and it vanishes. Move several lines away and enter ^Q6. The cursor returns to your previous position and <6> redisplays.

KEEP TRACK OF PLACE MARKERS

As you mark various sections for reference, keep track of the numbers and their locations. Then if you need an additional marker, you can refer to your list and decide which is expendable. Enter its command and it will move to the cursor's place.

PLACE MARKERS ARE TEMPORARY

Place markers make it easy to relocate blocks or sections of text, but remember that place markers are temporary; storing with ^KD or ^KX erases them. However, markers survive the ^KS save command, which makes them convenient for editing. When you plan to move blocks of text from one place to another you can mark the sections involved and relocate them quickly.

REVIEW: PLACE MARKERS

- Place markers can be set with the command ^K and any number between 0 and 9 (^K1, ^K2, ^K3, etc.).
- Place markers take up room on the screen but they do not print or alter the final document.
- Place markers are located with the command ^Q and the corresponding number (^Q1, ^Q2, ^Q3, etc.).
- Hide a marker by entering its command with the cursor at the marker's right. The appropriate ^Q command will find a marker whether hidden or displayed.
- Place markers are erased by the ^KD and ^KX store commands, but they survive the ^KS save command.
- Reposition a marker by entering its command from a new location.

REVIEW: PLACE MARKERS ON-SCREEN

^JP is the place marker help entry. When you want to review place markers on-screen, enter this command.

Here is the text of WordStar's ^JP help command:

```
                    *****  PLACE MARKERS  *****

Up to 10 place markers, identified by numbers (n) 0-9,
     may be set in a file while the file is being edited.
To set place marker n at the cursor position: type ^Kn.
     <n> will display to indicate the marker position.
To return the cursor to place marker n: type ^Qn any
     time during the same edit.
To remove the <n> from the display: type ^Kn when the
     cursor is already at the marker position.
                                          press space bar:

          ****  OTHER MARKER & RELATED COMMANDS  ****

The block beginning marker, <B>, and the block end marker,
     <K>, are set and moved to in a similar manner; the
     text between these markers can be moved (^KV), copied
     (^KC), deleted (^KY), or written to a file (^KW).

^QP moves cursor to its position before preceding command.

^QV moves cursor to start of last find/replace, or to
          source of text for last block move or copy.
                                          press space bar:
```

EXERCISE: SETTING, HIDING, AND FINDING PLACE MARKERS

If your margins are not already set at columns 1 and 65, enter ^OL 1@ and ^OR 65@. Be sure the first tab stop appears on your ruler line at column 6.

Where you see (^K1) and (^K2) in the exercise, enter place markers 1 and 2 by pressing the CONTROL key and K at the same time; then type the number by itself.

Type these four paragraphs:

The urban gardener can grow a surprising variety of vegetables despite a lack of yard space by planting in containers. Everything from barrels to tubs, hanging baskets and clay flowerpots can make for a bountiful harvest.

(^K1)Cucumbers, potatoes, cherry tomatoes, herbs, carrots, lettuce, peas and peppers do nicely on patios and balconies, providing they get plenty of moisture and regular fertilizing.

(^K2)At only four weeks from planting to harvest, radishes and spinach make perfect crops for the impatient. Eggplants and peppers take much longer, requiring ten weeks or more to mature.

To meet the needs of limited-space gardeners, most seed companies offer "miniature" hybrids. Thanks to the efforts of today's plant breeders, many container plants require a fraction of the space needed by their "normal" cousins. Dwarf citrus trees bear full-sized oranges, limes and lemons; the portable orchard can boast apple, pear and peach trees; and a balcony garden may host compact tomatoes, cucumbers, carrots, melons and squash.

When you reach the end, your screen should look like this:

```
          A:PRACTICE        PAGE 1 LINE 20   COL 8             INSERT ON
L----!----!----!----!----!----!----!----!----!----!----!--------R

          The   urban  gardener  can  grow  a  surprising  variety  of
vegetables   despite  a  lack  of  yard  space  by  planting   in
containers.  Everything from barrels to tubs, hanging baskets and
clay flowerpots can make for a bountiful harvest.                     <
     <1>Cucumbers,   potatoes,   cherry  tomatoes,  herbs,  carrots,
lettuce,  peas  and  peppers do nicely on patios  and  balconies,
providing they get plenty of moisture and regular fertilizing.        <
     <2>At  only four weeks from planting to harvest,  radishes  and
spinach  make  perfect crops for the  impatient.  Eggplants  and
peppers take much longer, requiring ten weeks or more to mature.      <
     To  meet  the needs of limited-space  gardeners,  most  seed
companies  offer "miniature" hybrids.  Thanks to the efforts  of
today's plant breeders,  many container plants require a fraction
of  the  space needed by their "normal"  cousins.  Dwarf  citrus
trees  bear full-sized oranges,  limes and lemons;  the portable
orchard  can boast apple,  pear and peach trees;  and  a  balcony
garden may host compact tomatoes,  cucumbers, carrots, melons and
squash.█
```

The place markers <1> and <2> have bumped text to the right so that the lines on which they appear do not look justified. As you know, markers do not print, so the text shifts left accordingly, and the right margin is really straight. Three < flags, showing hard returns, appear to the right of your text and show where you pressed the RETURN key. Lines not marked by the < flags were set by word wrap.

1. Use ^Q1 to move the cursor to place marker <1>. You will be back in the gardening paragraph and the cursor should stop at the word "Cucumbers."
2. Press ^Q2. Now the cursor should be at place marker <2> at the beginning of the third paragraph.
3. Leave the cursor next to the <2> marker and enter ^K2. This causes the <2> to disappear or "hide."
4. Enter ^Q1 again to return to the <1> marker.
5. Even though marker number 2 does not appear on the screen, ^Q2, the command to find it, will locate this marker and cause it to redisplay. Enter ^Q2 and watch the screen. The cursor should now be positioned at the right of the <2> marker.
6. Move the cursor to the beginning of the exercise's last paragraph. Enter ^K1 while watching the screen. The <1> marker will disappear from its original location and reappear at the cursor's position.

QUIZ

1. What is a place marker?
2. How do you set place marker 1? How does it appear on the screen?
3. How do you find place marker 1?
4. How many place markers can you set in a single document file?
5. Are place markers permanent?
6. How can you hide a place marker?
7. Must a marker be displayed for its find command to work?
8. How can you move a place marker from one position to another?

QUIZ ANSWERS

1. Place markers are highlighted numbers set to mark your place within the text.
2. Enter ^K1. It appears as <1> in highlighted characters.
3. Enter ^Q1.
4. Ten (<0> through <9>).
5. Place markers are erased by the save commands ^KD and ^KX but they survive ^KS. They are not permanent.
6. Hide a marker by positioning the cursor one space to the right of the displayed marker and typing its entry command (^K and the number) again.
7. No. ^Q and the marker's number will locate and redisplay the hidden marker.
8. Move the cursor to the new location and type the entry command again.

23

Find Commands

FINDING WORDS IN TEXT

When you want to find something in a hurry, scrolling through page after page is not only a slow procedure, it's one conducive to errors and eyestrain.

Instead, WordStar offers two convenient "find" functions. One will locate any word in the file; the other replaces one word with another.

WORDSTAR'S FIND COMMAND

Here's what happens when you enter the simple "find" command, whose entry code is ^QF. (Think of the F in *F*ind as you memorize this command.)

The screen will ask what word you want the computer to locate (the message line says: FIND?), and you enter your desired word.

WordStar will accommodate entries up to 30 characters in length, and they can be any combination of letters, spaces, numbers, and symbols. However, the command works best with very short strings, such as a single word or a pair of words.

Press the RETURN key after your entry to signal the computer.

Another question will appear on the message line: (OPTIONS?). WordStar's find command options are described on the next page. If you want to use one or more of the available options, you will enter the appropriate code(s) and press RETURN to signal completion of your entry.

You can eliminate the options question by pressing RETURN twice or the ESCAPE key once. This means that if you won't be using an option, you can enter a find command in either of these two ways:

- ^QF Target Word @@ or
- ^QF Target Word ESC

Try this by selecting a target word from your screen. Choose a word that comes after the cursor's position and a few lines away.

Press ^QF. The message line asks what to search for. Enter your target word. Be sure to spell it correctly, then press the RETURN key twice or the ESC key once. The cursor will stop at the first example it can find of your target word.

REVIEWING FIND OPTIONS ON-SCREEN

The message line carries another notation which appears when you hit the return key: (? FOR INFO). If you want the screen to review WordStar's different find options, which you will meet in a moment, enter a question mark (?), then the return key. A review of the find options will appear at the top of the screen.

This is the text of WordStar's options message:

```
    Normally press RETURN only, or enter one or more of:
number=repeat count, B=search Backwards, W=whole Words only,
U=ignore case, N=replace w/o asking, G=replace in entire file.
```

Not all of these options work with the simple find command; two operate only with WordStar's find-and-replace command, and you will meet them in the next chapter.

FIND (^QF) OPTIONS

Here are the options that work with a ^QF find command. Options can be entered in upper- or lowercase letters.

Number

Any number up to 65,535 can be entered instructing the computer to search for the nth location of the word desired. If you want the computer to stop at the fourth appearance of "almanac," enter ^QF almanac@ 4@. The computer searches forward, beginning at the cursor's location, unless you use the next option.

B — Search Backward

Search the file, beginning at the cursor's position. To locate the word "almanac" in a paragraph above or before the cursor, enter ^QF almanac@ b@. To find the fourth example of "almanac" before the cursor's place, enter ^QF almanac@ 4b@. Remember this option by associating B with Backward.

W — Match Whole Words Only

Without this notation, the find command will locate any string of letters or numbers even if it is found within another word. The command to find "man" will stop in "almanac" unless you use the option W. The command to find "sing" will normally stop at "single," "singe," and "dousing," should those words appear in your file. Associate the W with *W*hole *W*ords.

U — Ignore Upper/Lowercase Letters

This allows "Almanac" to match "ALMANAC" to match "almanac," etc. Experiment by entering the same word with variations, as illustrated above. Without U, the computer will ignore any word not capitalized exactly as your target entry. Think of the U in *U*ppercase and remember that this option ignores the distinction between upper- and lowercase letters. Don't press ^U or you'll cancel the command.

ADDITIONAL COMMANDS

^L

^L is not really an option; it's a separate command that can be entered at any time. It means, REPEAT THE LAST FIND INSTRUCTION.

Let's say you used ^QF to find the word "heritage" and you made some editing changes. Now you want to find the next appearance of the same word. Instead of entering ^QF again, press ^L and the cursor will stop at the next "heritage." If you're looking for a specific appearance of a word and you aren't sure where it is, use ^L to find successive entries until you reach the one you're seeking.

^L can be entered at any time, even after the ^KS save command. In fact, it survives ^KD, too, so ^L can be entered in an altogether different file.

^L re-enters the preceding find command, complete with all its options. If you find a word using ^QF and B, and then enter ^L with the cursor in line 1, it will generate an error message. That's because the cursor, already positioned in your file's first row, will attempt to search backward.

^R

^R isn't an option, either, but it can be used to save keystrokes in your find or find-and-replace command. This is the "restore entry" code you met in the No-File Menu commands.

If you enter ^QF hexagon and the option B, and then decide to search forward for the same word, you won't want to use ^L. ^L re-enters the entire command, complete with all its options.

Instead, enter ^QF ^R. The screen will show hexagon as the target word, and you can press ESC to accelerate the search or press RETURN to use a different set of options.

RETURN CURSOR TO PREVIOUS POSITION

^QV, entered after any find command, will return the cursor to the position it occupied before that command was executed. You will meet ^QV again in the find-and-replace chapter and in the chapter on block commands. This is because ^QV has more than one meaning, depending on whether a find/replace command or block move was most recent. When you receive an error message explaining that a word wasn't found, you will probably be at the beginning or the end of your file. ^QV can return you to the cursor's pre-search position, so you won't have lost your place. ^QP (return to previous position) will do the same, but not if you enter another command code or two along the way. ^QV can be entered at any time, even after several editing commands.

WHAT IF YOU MAKE A MISTAKE?

If the computer can't find the word you requested, the message line says:

```
*** NOT FOUND: [target word] *** PRESS ESC KEY
```

Press the ESCAPE key and try again. If the computer was searching forward in the file, you'll be at the end of your document; if you used B to search backward, you'll be at the beginning of the file.

If you use an unrecognized option, the screen will respond with three question marks, suspending the command until you enter a correct option.

For example, enter ^QF experiment@ V@.

The screen shows: V??? and waits for another option code. To interrupt the command, use ^U.

THINGS YOU WILL NOTICE

In theory, the find command will work on whole sentences; the screen accepts entries up to 30 characters long. In practice, ^QF doesn't like long entries and it works more efficiently with a single word or single number.

This is because word wrap adds soft spaces between words as it spreads text across the screen when you use a justified margin. Unfortunately, WordStar cannot distinguish between hard spaces (entered by you) and soft spaces (entered by the computer) as it searches for a matching pair or series of words in a find command entry.

For example, if you want to find "wind generator" in your text, you would normally enter

^QF wind*space*generator@

However, if word wrap has added a soft space between these two words, the cursor will not find the phrase. You may have to enter

^QF wind*space space*generator@

in order to find this pair of words. And, although this happens less often, word wrap will occasionally add two soft spaces between a pair of words, generating three separating spaces altogether.

Similarly, if the words are on two different lines, separated by a soft return (set by word wrap), the cursor will not locate your target word. In that case, you may want to try the special character described on page 175 in your find command response.

Experiment with ^QF by entering a short sentence or series of words as your target string. If an error messages appears, try targeting a single word instead. Look for a word that's unusual in its spelling, capitalization, or punctuation if your target word appears frequently.

When you edit hard copy and put the document on-screen to make corrections, you'll wish the computer could take you to page 9, paragraph 4, automatically.

It can — it's just that you'll have to rephrase your request. Look for an unusual word or a word that includes a punctuation mark or which is capitalized — or all three — close to or in the paragraph you want to edit. ^QF should move you to the right section without delay. If your target word (exactly as entered) is used more than once, the cursor will stop at its first appearance. Use ^L to repeat the command.

REVIEW: FIND COMMANDS

WordStar can locate any page and line in your document through its word-matching function.

- ^QF is the find command.
- When the screen asks FIND?, enter your target word. Signal the entry's end with the return key.
- When the screen asks OPTIONS?, enter:
- [number] to find the nth appearance of your target word,

- U to ignore upper/lowercase,
- B to search backward, and/or
- W to match whole words only.
- To eliminate the options questions, press ESC instead of RETURN at the end of your target word.
- ^L repeats the previous find command.
- ^R repeats last-entered target word.
- ^QV returns to the cursor position at your last find command's entry.
- To review find options on-screen, enter a question mark [?] at the options question.

QUIZ

1. What is the "find" command?
2. What message appears at the top of the screen when you enter this command?
3. How would you enter a command to find the word "Albuquerque," eliminating all of the find options?
4. What do these options do in combination with a find command?
   a. 23
   b. B
   c. U
   d. W
5. What does this entry instruct the computer to do?

   ^QF Hazard@ 5BW@

   Will the cursor stop in the word Hazardous? Will it match the target word if it isn't capitalized?
6. List the keystrokes you would use to locate the third appearance of the word "Zenith," spelled and capitalized as shown, with the cursor positioned at the top of the document.
7. How can you review the different find options on the screen?
8. What happens if the computer can't find the word you entered?
9. What is the difference between ^L and ^R?
10. What does ^QV do if entered immediately after a find search?

QUIZ ANSWERS

1. ^QF
2. FIND?
3. ^QF Albuquerque ESC
4. a. Find the 23rd appearance of the target word.
   b. Search backward from the cursor's point.
   c. Ignore upper/lowercase distinctions.
   d. Match whole words only.

5. Find the fifth appearance of "Hazard," measuring backward from the cursor's position, matching whole words only. The cursor will not stop at "Hazardous" because of the W option (whole words only). It will not match an uncapitalized "hazard" because the U option was not used.
6. ^QF Zenith 3W@
7. Enter ? (a question mark) at the options question: ?@.
8. An error message will appear. Press ESC to resume editing.
9. ^L repeats the previous find command, including all its options. ^R repeats the previously entered ^QF target word. Both can be entered at any time, including after the ^KS and ^KD save commands.
10. ^QV returns the cursor to the position it occupied before the most recent search was executed.

SPECIAL FIND CHARACTERS

WordStar offers four special codes that can be entered with your find command. All four may be convenient for computer programmers, but the average individual will find one or perhaps two of interest. The special characters are not options; they are entered with or instead of the target word.

Special Find Character: ^PA

^PA matches any single character appearing with the letters or characters you include with this entry. ^PA appears on-screen as ^A. The WordStar manual offers the example X^A^AX, which means: a word or string which is four characters long, beginning and ending with X. Remember that a space counts as a character. If the following notations appear in your file, the cursor will stop at the first one it reaches: XABX, X1.X, or X+ X. Each of these expressions consists of an X, two additional spaces or characters, and a final X. This control character is entered by pressing ^P first: X ^PA^PA X. The ^P notations do not appear on-screen, so the message line shows X^A^AX.

How would you enter the find command for a six-letter word beginning with "a" and ending with "r"?

Enter ^QF (find) a ^PA^PA^PA^PA r. Think of the word "blank" each time you enter ^PA: a- - - -r. The message line shows a^A^A^A^Ar. In our hypothetical example, the cursor could stop at the word "appear."

As this is a regular find command entry, you can include options. Entering W (whole word match) prevents the cursor from stopping in "appearance." Entering U (ignore upper/lowercase distinctions) allows it to stop at "Appear" and "APPEAR."

Special Find Character: ^PN

^N is a hard return command (carriage return plus line feed), as you know from page 141. The special character ^PN can be entered to find line breaks. In this procedure, WordStar will not distinguish between hard and soft returns. Hard returns are marked at the right edge of your screen with <; soft returns are marked with blank spaces in the flag column. ^PN appears on-screen as ^N.

To find a target word only if it's located at the beginning of a line, enter ^PN before the word. Example: ^PNHardwood appears on the message line as ^NHardwood. The cursor will stop at the word "Hardwood" only if it appears at the beginning of a line. (Any word at the beginning of a line is obviously preceded by a hard or soft line return.)

To find hardwood at the end of a paragraph, enter hardwood.^PN. Include the period, which ends a paragraph. To find it at the end of an unpunctuated line, such as in a table, enter hardwood^PN without a period. Remember that the computer has no imagination. You have to say exactly what you mean.

To move the cursor 25 lines from its present position, enter this find command: ^QF ^PN@ 25@. In other words, enter the find command (^QF), the special return character (^PN), and the number option, 25. The cursor moves 25 lines down.

To find the next blank line, enter ^PN^PN, which is two adjacent returns. To find a blank section consisting of four or more empty lines, enter ^PN four times. (In this case you would not use the number 4 as an option because the cursor would simply stop at the fourth return it located, measured from the cursor position.)

Page 173 mentioned the problem you face when your target string is a pair of words that have been positioned by word wrap on consecutive lines with a soft return between them. In our previously entered example (wind generator), let's assume that "wind" appears at the end of one line and "generator" at the beginning of the next line, with a soft return between them.

If the document is single spaced, you would use this entry sequence:

^QF wind*space* ^PNgenerator@

Type a single hard space after the first word, then the ^PN entry (which appears on the screen as ^N) and, without adding another space, type the second word. This target string will appear on the screen as follows:

```
wind ^Ngenerator
```

If the document were double spaced, this would be the correct entry sequence:

^QF wind*space* ^PN^PNgenerator@

If you know exactly how your target is positioned in the document, you should be able to locate it, even if your first find command entry proves unsuccessful.

Special Find Characters: ^PS and ^Ox

WordStar's other special character codes are ^PS and ^Ox. As mentioned, these entries may be of limited interest to the average WordStar user.

The WordStar manual defines ^Ox and ^PS as follows:

^Ox matches any character other than x, where x is any character entered immediately after the ^O. ^PS matches any character not a letter or digit.

Note that each of these codes has a different meaning in normal text editing, as do the special characters ^PN and ^PA.

24

Find - and - Replace Commands

If your hard copy contains a misspelling that you want to correct, or if you want to replace one technical word with a better choice, or if you want to make any substitution of one word with another, ^QA makes it simple.

USING ^QA

^QA is WordStar's find-and-replace command.

When you enter ^QA, the computer asks what word you want to find and then what word you want to replace it with. What could be simpler?

In an engineering paper prepared (fortunately) on a WordStar-equipped computer, the word "rotor" appeared 53 times. After the paper was typed, the author decided to substitute "impeller" for "rotor" in each of its 53 appearances. You can appreciate what a chore this could be on a regular typewriter. Because the word being substituted is several letters longer than the original word, every section containing "rotor" would have to be retyped. Avoiding all that work, WordStar solved the problem in less than a minute.

Try the replacement yourself by typing this sentence in a new file. (As you'll soon test an option that causes the computer to search through the entire file, you'll find a new — and short — file most convenient for this exercise.)

```
The rotor tip speed and the rotor blade make two fine  rotor
terms for us to use in this example.
```

Position the cursor in or above the first line. Enter ^QA. Our object is to replace the word "rotor" with the word "impeller." The computer asks FIND? and you reply: rotor@. The computer asks REPLACE WITH? and you reply: impeller@.

REPLACEMENT-ONLY OPTIONS

Now the screen asks OPTIONS? Let's jump ahead and enter the two options you haven't met yet so you can see them in action. Enter G and N. They needn't be capitalized; enter gn@ or GN@. G instructs the computer to search the entire file; N means the substitution will be made without stopping for verification. Wasn't that easy?

Because "impeller" takes up more room than the word it replaces, the revised sentence now extends beyond the right margin. Use ^B, the reform command, to reconfigure the text.

Try reversing the substitution. Put the cursor back in the first line of the sentence or above it, then enter: ^QA impeller@ rotor ESC. The ESCAPE key eliminates the options question, so now the substitutions will be made one at a time.

The cursor will stop at the first "impeller" and ask whether you want to make this particular substitution. The message line will say: REPLACE (Y/N): ■, with the cursor blinking in the upper-right corner of the screen. You can answer Y for Yes or any other key for No, depending on whether you want the replacement made here. The computer recognizes Y, y, ^Y, and ^y as Yes responses. For this exercise, press the Y key so that "rotor" replaces "impeller" in the first appearance of the word.

REPEAT FIND-AND-REPLACE ENTRY

To complete the replacement, enter ^L. You met this command a few pages ago; it repeats the last find (or find-and-replace) command. Once again, the cursor will stop at "impeller," and after you press Y, "rotor" will appear on the screen.

As you edit a document and use ^L, it will move the cursor according to the find or find-and-replace command most recently entered. The computer remembers not only the last word match or replacement; it remembers all the options entered, too. If you used the option B for searching backward, don't enter ^L with the cursor in line 1.

You can use ^L throughout an editing session because, like place markers, its conditions last through the ^KS storage command. In addition, it survives ^KD so you can enter the same command in another file without having to retype the entry. The computer's memory of your last find or find-and-replace command will be erased by ^KX.

The special command ^R works in ^QA commands as it does in ^QF commands, restoring the last-entered target word. You can use ^R to restore the target word only, or, if you're using ^QA again, it will restore the replacement word as well. In addition, ^R will answer the options question with your last-entered options; however, you're not likely to use it this way because the command (^R) is most convenient when retaining an entry but changing its options.

RETURN CURSOR TO PRE-SEARCH POSITION

^QV is another cursor-moving command. It means RESTORE THE CURSOR to its previous position. Entered after any find, find-and-replace, or ^L command, it moves to whatever position the cursor held before that command was executed. If the option G or a number was used, ^QV returns the cursor to the position it occupied before the final or last replacement.

However, if a block has been moved, copied, or erased since the last find or find-and-replace command, ^QV has another meaning. You will meet block commands in the next chapter. ^QV's destination depends on which command was most recently entered. It is especially convenient in find or find-and-replace commands when the screen shows a NOT FOUND error message and the cursor waits at the end of your file. In that situation, ^QV returns you to your pre-search location very quickly.

FIND-AND-REPLACE OPTIONS

The options already described for a simple find command work for find-and-replace situations, too.

Number

When you enter a number after ^QA, you instruct the computer to make the replacement that many times. Note that this is different from the effect of a number entered after ^QF.

With ^QF, the cursor stops at the nth appearance of a word; with ^QA, the substitution is made n times.

ACCELERATE THE NUMBER-OPTION REPLACEMENT

The screen normally displays each substitution, but you can accelerate a replacement by pressing any additional key while the command is executing. The WordStar manual recommends a "harmless" entry, such as "cursor up" (^E). This simple action suppresses the normal display of each substitution as it takes place and the screen will remain "frozen" until the replacement has been made n times. At that point, the screen shifts to the cursor's position at the final replacement.

Accelerating the execution of ^QA in this fashion naturally prevents you from seeing each replacement as it takes place. You can interrupt at any time with ^U.

ADDITIONAL OPTIONS

The options B, U, and W operate in a ^QA entry exactly as in the ^QF command you have already studied:

B Search backward in the file.
U Ignore the distinction between upper- and lowercase characters.
W Match on whole words only.

REPLACEMENT-ONLY OPTIONS

In addition to the find options, these options apply only to find-and-replace commands:

G — The *G*lobal Replace

The computer checks through the entire file by first moving the cursor to the file's first line, then doing the replacement repeatedly, stopping to ask Yes or No at each replacement.

If you have a long document, the G option lets you move rapidly while verifying the accuracy of each substitution. The difference between G and ^L, which repeats the previous find command, is that G operates more quickly. However, G does not allow you to stop and make editorial corrections in the middle of your search through the document. G takes you from beginning to end, and all it allows you to do is answer Yes or No to each substitution. If you press N, or any other key but Y, the cursor moves to the next appearance of your target word without making the change. If you press Y, the word is replaced and the cursor moves on.

When editing a long document, use ^KS (the save command) before entering ^QA and G. This is because the cursor has to move back to the beginning of the file before executing the search, and when relocated by the G option, it uses so much memory that you may get a DISK FULL warning. The advantage to ^KS is that it saves all recent editing changes while returning the cursor to line 1.

N — *N*o Delays

Replace without asking. If you know there will be no unwanted matches, this is the fastest replacement method.

Use N in combination with G to check the entire file from beginning to end.

Use with B to run the automatic replacement in the portion of the file before or above the cursor.

Use with any number (50, for example, or whatever will be an overestimate) to move from the cursor point forward to the end of the file, making the replacement each time. This is one way to reach the end of the file quickly while making all appropriate substitutions. When the cursor reaches the end of a file without having found 50 substitutions, an error message appears on the screen. In this case it's a desired one. By deliberately overestimating the number of replacements, you can be sure the entire file (following the cursor's position) will be checked. You can also use a small number, such as 5, to make the substitution that many times without stopping.

ACCELERATE GLOBAL REPLACEMENT

You may accelerate a global replace command even when N is in effect by preventing the screen from displaying each substitution as it is made. Press any key while the command is executing (the WordStar manual recommends a "harmless" key, such as ^E). This suppresses the normal updating of the screen, which is the most time-consuming factor in a global replace. The replacement continues even though the screen remains "frozen" until the cursor has reached the end of the file and all replacements have been made.

If you decide to interrupt the execution of this command, enter ^U at any time.

WHAT IF YOU MAKE A MISTAKE?

What if you enter a substitution on the screen and then realize you misspelled your entry? Or that you hit the wrong option key?

If you notice the mistake before pressing RETURN, use the DELETE or BACKSPACE key to remove letters one at a time, or erase the entry with ^Y. Don't press ESC. That will only accelerate the command's execution.

Before or after a search is in motion, you can interrupt by typing ^U, the INTERRUPT COMMAND instruction. If the command is already executing, you won't know your location until text appears on-screen, but you can return to the cursor's former position with ^QP or ^QV.

To interrupt any ^Q command after entering the first letter, press the RETURN key, ESCAPE key, space bar, or ^U.

USING ^QA TO REMOVE WORDS

To erase a word, string, or short sentence, use ^QA and enter RETURN (@) as the replacement word. The computer will find the target word, remove it, then replace it with nothing. Use ^L to repeat the command, or use a replacement option when you enter ^QA.

REVIEW: FIND-AND-REPLACE COMMANDS

As you use the ^QA or "find-and-replace" command, you can use these options:

- NUMBER (any number, up to 65535, to make the replacement that many times)
- B (to search backward from the cursor's position)
- W (to match whole words only before making the replacement)
- U (to ignore the distinction between upper- and lowercase letters)
- G (to check the entire file, from beginning to end, offering the Y/N choice at each appearance of the target word)
- N(to make the replacement automatically, without stopping for verification)

The ESC key eliminates the ^QF and ^QA options question.

^L can be entered at any time to repeat the most recently entered ^QA or ^QF command, complete with all options used.

^R will restore the last-entered target word and/or replacement word.

^U will interrupt the computer's search for your target word in any ^QA or ^QF command.

QUIZ

1. What is the find-and-replace command?
2. What keystrokes would you use to replace the word "Rotor" with the word "Impeller" without using any of the options available?
3. What happens when the cursor stops at the first appearance of your target word in such an instance?
4. What options can you use with the find-and-replace command? What do they do?
5. How can you interrupt a find-and-replace search?
6. If you interrupt your search, how can you quickly return to your previous place in the document?
7. What does this string of commands instruct the computer to do?

   ^QA blue@ red 2bw@

QUIZ ANSWERS

1. ^QA
2. ^QA Rotor@ Impeller ESC.
3. The cursor flashes and waits for you to enter Y (Yes) or N (No) for the substitution.
4. Any number between 1 and 65535; G; B; N; W; U. A number means to make the replacement that many times. G stands for global search, checking the whole document from beginning to end. B means search backward. N means no delay; substitutions are made automatically, without stopping for verification. W matches on whole words only. U ignores the difference between upper- and lowercase letters.

5. Enter ^U.
6. Enter ^QP or ^QV.
7. Find "blue" and replace it with "red" twice, going backward from the cursor's position and matching whole words only.

USING ^QA AND SPECIAL FIND CHARACTERS

See page 175 for a description of ^PA and ^PN, two special characters that can be entered with any find or find-and-replace command.

If you want to create a border around a table or form, you should know that WordStar can draw vertical lines. Your keyboard has a | key, which draws a long straight line or two vertical dashes, one above the other.

The fastest way to draw a border is with ^QA, the find-and-replace command. You can replace each line return with the | symbol, both at the beginning and at the end of the line. Enter the command like this:

FIND ^PN@ REPLACE WITH |^PN|@ OPTIONS n N @

Using the number option, enter one more line than the border should be in length, and use N (No delay) so the replacements will be made automatically, without stopping for individual verification.

By entering |^N|, as it will appear on the screen, you have instructed the computer to enter the | symbol before and after every line return. As mentioned earlier, WordStar does not distinguish between hard and soft returns in this procedure. The computer won't set a border around an empty (unentered) area, but it will set a border around hard spaces.

Try this special effect. Clear all the tab stops with ^ON A@. Now set a single tab stop at column 50 (^OI 50@). Use single spacing for this exercise.

Press the TAB key and RETURN key 10 times in succession. This action sends the cursor across to column 50, down a line to column 1, across to column 50, down to column 1, etc., until it has moved 50 spaces across each of 10 lines. The computer doesn't consider these lines empty any more. Even if they already contained text, you could turn insertion off and not disturb it.

Move one line up from the first of your special effect lines and enter this command:

^QA ^PN@ |^PN|@ 11 N @

There's your border. Put a row of dashes across the top, remove the two extra | lines, type another row across the bottom, and you've got a box.

The left border will always appear in column 1. To move a completed table to the right, use the space bar or TAB key with insertion turned on. To center the table, use ^OC on each line. To move the table using a column block command, see Chapter 27.

When you complete a table or column and place a border around it, turn insertion off before making corrections. That way the entry of new letters will not disturb the border.

You can use other symbols, too. The replacement command *[^PN]* will draw a border with asterisks; x ^PN x will draw one with x's.

USING ^QA AND THE SOFT HYPHEN ENTRY

After typing a document, you may want to ensure that certain words are hyphenated at specific syllables during editing and paragraph reforming. Instead of entering soft hyphens throughout the original entry, you can save time by combining ^OE with the ^QA replacement command. ^OE is the soft hyphen entry toggle.

Let's pretend you've written a paper about hagiography, the critical study of the lives of saints. Your text includes the words "hagiographic" and "hagiographical" at regular intervals, and you want these words separated at their major accent syllables: "hag-iograph-ic" and "hag-iograph-ical."

Finish typing the paper, then turn on ^OE, the soft hyphen entry, and enter this command: ^QA hagiographic@ hag-iograph-ic@ GN @.

The cursor will find each appearance of "hagiographic" and make this softly hyphenated substitution.

Similarly, go through replacing "hagiographical" with "hag-iograph-ical," "Hagiographic" with "Hag-iograph-ic," and "Hagiographical" with "Hag-iograph-ical."

During later editing and paragraph reforming, these key words will be hyphenated, if at all, on their accent syllables — and you'll have been spared the task of entering soft hyphens separately or checking each selection of hyphen-help.

25

Block Commands

Of all WordStar procedures, block commands may be the tool you'll appreciate most as you edit long documents.

A block is any section of text marked by you for a special purpose. Once marked, a block can be erased, copied, moved to another part of the document, moved into another file, or entered from another file into your text.

Here is a list of basic block commands. All begin with the prefix ^K, which comes from the word blocK. In addition, the second letter code is easy to associate with the function it performs.

WORDSTAR'S BLOCK COMMANDS

^KB	marks the *B*eginning of a *B*lock
F7	marks the beginning of a block (alternate entry)
^KK	marks the end of a bloc*K*
F8	marks the end of a block (alternate entry)
^KH	*H*ides and redisplays a block
^KC	*C*opies a block
^KV	mo*V*es a block
^KW	*W*rites a block from one file into another
^KR	*R*eads a block from one file into your text
^KY	erases the block (^Y is a regular erase command)

Let's take a look at each command.

MARKING A BLOCK

First, so you can get used to the business of marking blocks, take any paragraph of text and position the cursor at its beginning. The IBM PC key for the procedure's first command is F7, the F-function key at left. WordStar's regular "mark block beginning" code is ^KB, derived from the word *B*loc*K*, which begins with B and ends with K.

Appropriately, the regular WordStar command for marking the end of a block is ^KK. Your IBM PC shortcut key is F8. Position the cursor at the end of your paragraph and enter the ^KK command or F8.

Mark the beginning of your block with F7. Mark the end of your block with F8. The block begins with the first character after your F7 keystroke and ends with the last character before F8.

THINGS YOU WILL NOTICE

A highlighted <B> appears when you enter F8. As soon as you enter F8, the entire block dims on the screen in highlighted letters. If you enter the block end command first (F8), <K> will appear until you enter F7, at which time the <K> disappears and the words change to highlighted form. This is a "marked" block.

This is a practice block. It is very short.

Note the cursor under the T. Press F7 with the cursor positioned as above.

<B> This is a practice block. It is very short.

The <B> marker bumps the sentence three spaces to the right and the cursor remains under the T. Screen letters remain bright but the <B> marker is highlighted and appears in faint light.

<B> This is a practice block. _ It is very short.

Now you have moved the cursor to the end of the sentence.
Press F8 with the cursor positioned as above.

This is a practice block. **It is very short.**

The <B> mark disappears, text shifts back to its original position, and the marked block is highlighted. Screen text that is not part of the marked block continues to display in regular, bright light.

Here is another block.

```
xxxxxxxxxx
xxxxxxxxxx
xxxxxxxxxx
xxxxxxxxxx
```

Mark it first with F7 marker, with the cursor positioned as above

```
xxxx<B>xxxxxx
xxxxxxxxxx
xxxxxxxxxx
xxxxxxxxxx
```

Now move the cursor into the third line

```
xxxx<B>xxxxxx
xxxxxxxxxx
xxxxxxxxxx
xxxxxxxxxx
```

and press F8. The o's below represent the highlighted block:

```
xxxxoooooo
oooooooooo
ooooooooxx
xxxxxxxxxx
```

The marked block displays in faint (highlighted) characters.

If you enter F8 rather than F7 first, the marker will look like this:

```
xxxxxxxxxx
xxxxxxxxxx
xxxxxxxx<K>xx
xxxxxxxxxx
```

As soon as you position the cursor and enter F7 as in the first illustration, your marked block would display as shown.

A marked block remains marked until a new block is marked, replacing it. A marked block is "displayed" when highlighted.

Your block can be several pages long; it isn't limited to the short segments we're working with now. If you mark a block that's too long for the computer to handle, a corresponding error message will appear when you try to execute a command, and you can divide the block into smaller parts.

Once your block is marked, experiment with some of WordStar's most powerful commands.

HIDE/REDISPLAY A BLOCK

^KH "hides" and "redisplays" the marked block, which means that it switches the block back and forth between highlighted (displayed) and regular (undisplayed or hidden) screen characters. This command is easy to remember because of the H in Hide. Your first ^KH will make the marked block look like the rest of the screen, hiding it in the process. Enter ^KH again and the highlighted section will reappear.

	xxxxxxxxxx		xxxxxxxxxx
	xxxxxxxxxx		xxxxxxxxxx
Displayed:	xxxxxxxxxx	Hidden:	xxxxxxxxxx
	xxxxxxxxxx		xxxxxxxxxx

Why hide and redisplay a block? Instructions that might be entered by accident can do considerable damage, like the "block erase" command. Once you've marked a block, if you aren't going to do something with it right away or if you've completed your maneuver and are ready to go on to other tasks, use ^KH to hide the block.

WHAT IF YOU MAKE A MISTAKE?

In regular WordStar use (using a computer other than the IBM PC), if you enter the block beginning command after or below the block end code, you receive an error message. However, on the 64K IBM PC, this error message does not appear. Instead, the block beginning marker <B> and the block end marker <K> both display on the screen. No text is highlighted. The ^KH command for hiding a block makes the markers disappear, but you have not really marked a block and the markers remain ineffective until you enter F8 (block end) with the cursor below the <B> marker, or until you enter F7 (block beginning) with the cursor above the <K> marker.

If you mark the block's beginning and forget to mark its end, or vice versa, your block command will generate an error message calling your attention to the problem. Correct it by marking the block's other side. If you hide a block and then enter a block command, you will receive an error message. Redisplay the block and try again.

If you mark the wrong block, use ^KH to hide or remove the displayed section, reposition the cursor, and mark the correct block.

If the block you have marked is too long for the computer to move (a frequent problem on the 64K IBM PC), an error message will appear when you enter the block-move or copy-block command. To complete the maneuver, break the block into smaller segments and move them separately, or move the marked block into a temporary storage file. The "read" and "write" sections that follow explain how to do this.

MOVE A BLOCK

For the next command, select a sentence that has several lines preceding or following it from your practice file. Mark this sentence with F7 and F8 so that it appears highlighted. Now move the cursor a good distance away from the marked block in either direction. Position the cursor in the line you would like your marked block to begin at and press ^KV, the block move command. This is easy to remember because of the V in "mo*V*e."

If your block is not displayed, ^KV will not work.

Your displayed block should disappear from its original place and reappear (in highlighted letters) at the new location. Press ^KH to hide this block.

Your revised paragraphs may need reforming after this move, especially if you positioned the cursor within a line of text before entering ^KV. Use ^B, the paragraph reform command, to correct the text's position.

MOVING BLOCKS WITH THE 64K IBM PC

As mentioned earlier, the 64K IBM Personal Computer generates error messages rather frequently with the ^KV block move command.

How large is the largest block this computer will move with ^KV? Only 900 characters, which is about 150 to 180 words, or about 13 lines of 65-character-wide text. If your block is longer than 900 characters, you'll see this error message:

```
*** ERROR E9:  BLOCK TOO LONG --
               MOVE OR COPY IN TWO SMALLER BLOCKS ***
```

Use the ^KV command for very short blocks. When moving more than 13-15 lines of text, work around this limitation by using the ^KW block write command, described on page 190.

COPY A BLOCK

If you want to duplicate a block without erasing it from its original position, follow the same procedure but use ^KC ("block*C*opy") instead of ^KV. Try this with any sentence.

Mark the block with F7 and F8, then move the cursor to a new location and press ^KC. The marked block will be highlighted at the new position and appear in regular screen characters at the original location.

Get in the habit of hiding blocks as soon as you move them by typing ^KH. As soon as you enter ^KH, both blocks revert to regular screen letters.

^KV and ^KC will move a block in exactly the format it has on the screen. You might move a single-spaced block into a double-spaced report, or the block you relocate may have different margins from those you're now using. Reform any moved block with the ^B command.

COPYING BLOCKS WITH THE 64K IBM PC

WordStar will not copy with ^KC any block larger than the previously described 900 characters (about 13 to 15 average lines of text).

Work around this size limitation by using the ^KW block write command described in the next section whenever you want to copy a block of text longer than what the system will copy with ^KC.

WRITE A BLOCK

^KW is the write block command, easy to remember because of the W in *W*rite.

The difference between WordStar's "read a file" and "write a block" commands is your place at the time of the move —- or, phrased another way, the destination of the block being moved.

Both are block-moving procedures, but one moves material from the file you're using to a different file, and the other moves text from a different file to the one you're now in.

^KW, the write command, moves material from your present file to another one. Its purpose is to store the marked block in that file. You can retrieve it later for a variety of purposes.

Before using the ^KW writing command, you should understand that before it will work, you must have a marked, displayed block and a proposed destination file. Your destination file can be on the same or another disk, and it can be a file that WordStar creates just for the file's storage or one that exists already — the catch being that WordStar will erase everything already stored in that file as it writes your marked block.

Before entering ^KW, you can use ^KF to display the disk's file directory. After entering ^KW (or any WordStar command that generates a screen message requesting a file name or other input), ^F does the same. ^KF and ^F always display the logged disk's directory; to see the other disk's directory you will have to change the logged disk drive with ^KL. ^KF and ^KL commands are reviewed in Chapter 37.

EXERCISE: BLOCK COMMANDS

To work a simple example, start a new file by returning to WordStar's No-File Menu. (Use ^KD or ^KQ.) Call your new file PLACE.B.

Type this paragraph:

Beginning in 1978, the Bureau of Labor Statistics introduced a revised consumer price index for urban wage earners and clerical workers, who make up about 40% of the United States population. This revised index is based on a new, larger market basket of goods priced in 85 areas across the country. The new market basket includes television and sound equipment and repairs, additional children's clothing, luggage, auto body work, medical supplies and a variety of other goods not previously included.

Mark the last sentence of this paragraph with F7 and F8. It will appear in highlighted form. Now enter ^KW. the block write command. The message line at the top of the screen will ask where you want the material copied:

```
NAME OF FILE TO WRITE MARKED TEXT ON? ■
```

Answer by typing: PLACE.A@

Because the file PLACE.A does not already exist, the computer writes your marked, displayed block into a new file labeled PLACE.A. If this file existed already, you would see a verification message:

```
FILE [name] EXISTS -- OVERWRITE? (Y/N) ■
```

You would respond with Y for Yes if you want to erase the destination file's previous contents, or enter N for No. If you answer N, WordStar waits for you to name another destination file.

You'll know when the write command has finished because the message line disappears and your regular status line redisplays.

If there is not sufficient space on the specified disk for your block, an error message appears:

```
*** ERROR E12: DISK FULL ***
```

You have not lost your marked block, only its incomplete copy. In Chapter 37 you will learn more about ^KJ, the command for erasing one file while editing another. Use this command to delete the incomplete destination file. If you have space on the other disk (dual drive unit), try the command again. Alternately, you can display the disk's file directory with ^KF and use ^KJ again to delete unnecessary files. To view the file directory of the other disk drive, use ^KL to change the logged drive. You may want to read Chapter 37 for more information about ^KL, ^KF, and ^KJ, which are File and Disk Operations.

ERASE A BLOCK

Meanwhile, the sentence is still highlighted in your file, PLACE.B. You can use ^KH to hide this block, or you can leave it displayed and do something else. For our exercise, erase this block from the file you're still working in by entering ^KY, the delete block command. (Y is WordStar's main erase code, helping you remember the command.)

Now the marked block will disappear. Move the cursor down a line or two and try WordStar's "read" command.

READ A FILE

The read file command is ^KR (R for *R*ead), and its procedure is similar to that explored above except that now you're moving material from a separate file into your document. What will be moved? Everything that is stored in the "read from" file. Where will it go? It will be inserted at the cursor's position.

Enter ^KR. The message line will say:

```
NAME OF FILE TO READ? ■
```

If you need to refresh your memory at this point, you can use ^F to display the disk's file directory. Before entering the ^KR command, you can display the directory with ^KF. Note that this command causes the logged disk's directory to display.

For this exercise, answer the screen question with: PLACE.A@. Now the contents of file PLACE.A will be read into your document file (PLACE.B), beginning at the cursor's position.

The read file and write block commands are especially handy for form letters or any material you use repeatedly. Make a list of your different storage files and their contents so you'll remember what is where without having to look in each location. After a storage file serves its purpose, you can erase it from the No-File Menu with Y (erase file). Or you can leave the file for future storage; the ^KW command will erase its contents when you store something else.

USING ^KW AND ^KR TO REPLACE ^KV and ^KC COMMANDS

Even if you have more than 64K to work with, you may want to use ^KW and ^KR to move very long blocks of text or to move blocks of any size long distances. Even a block of ten words can generate a DISK FULL message if you move it from the end of a long file to its beginning.

The 64K IBM PC limits the amount of text you can move with the ^KV (move block) and ^KC (copy block) commands to 900 characters, or about 13 to 15 lines of text. When you try to move or copy something longer, the BLOCK TOO LONG error message appears.

To avoid this problem, use ^KV and ^KC only when you know the block is short enough and the total distance short enough to move or copy with those commands.

When the block is longer or the distance greater, use this procedure.

- Mark the block you want to copy or reposition.
- Use ^KW (the write block command) to move displayed material to a storage file. The storage file need not exist already. If you name an already-existing file, WordStar verifies your intentions before erasing its contents. If the storage file is on another disk, preface the file name with its drive, such as A: or B:.
- If desired, erase the original displayed block with ^KY at any time after ^KW. This procedure duplicates the ^KV block move function. To duplicate the ^KC block copy function, hide the marked block with ^KH so it remains undisturbed.
- Move the cursor to the new or "move to" position.
- Use ^KR (the read file command) to insert the storage file's contents at the cursor's position. Enter the file name as you did for ^KW, or use the ^R (restore entry) shortcut. ^R duplicates the last-entered file name given in response to a ^KW or ^KR screen message.
- You do not have to use a save command with ^KW. Whatever material you move into another file will be permanently stored there. You should store with ^KS after using the read file command (^KR).

CHANGING DISKS WHILE USING ^KR

What if the file you want to read into your current file is on another disk?

The ^KR read file command offers an exception to WordStar's rule against changing disks unless the No-File Menu is on-screen.

WordStar allows you to change disks only if the file entered in the command is to be read. You cannot change disks while the computer is getting ready to write something on a disk, or to execute a command that moves the cursor, for example. But if the other disk's file is to be read and that's all, you can change disks during editing.

First, find the section in which you want to insert a file stored on another disk. Position the cursor. Enter ^KR and the "read from" file's name, but do not press RETURN to execute the command.

Now you can remove the disk holding your document file and replace it with the disk holding the file named in your command. Press RETURN. All of that file's contents will be read into your document file, and you will see the first lines of that text on your screen, beginning at the cursor location.

As soon as the status line returns to its normal display, remove the "read from" disk and replace it with your document file's disk.

Save the insertion with ^KS and continue editing.

If the file being read is very long, or if your file has already generated DISK FULL warning messages during storing or other maneuvers, store with ^KS before using ^KR; then store again immediately after using ^KR. That way you'll preserve previous editing changes and, if the file doesn't fit, you won't lose additional editing efforts, too. Your "read from" file remains intact and you can use it again later.

If your document file's disk was not in the logged drive, be sure to enter the ^KR command with the appropriate drive prefix. Unless you specify another drive, WordStar will assume that the file to be read is in the logged disk drive.

TO REVIEW BLOCK COMMANDS ON-SCREEN

WordStar provides two convenient means for reviewing block commands on-screen.

The first is the Block Menu's straightforward listing of commands, which appears at help levels 2 and 3 whenever you enter ^K by itself. The IBM PC keys F7 and F8 are not mentioned in the Block Menu.

The second review is a more complete description of text-moving operations. It appears regardless of help level when you enter ^JV.

Here is WordStar's Block Menu:

```
                      < < <        B L O C K    M E N U        > > >
-Saving Files-    | -Block Operations- | -File Operations-   |  -Other Menus-
D Save & resume   | B Begin     K End  | R  Read   P  Print  | (from Main only)
D Save--done      | H  Hide /  Display | O Copy    E  Rename | ^J Help   ^K Block
X Save & exit     | C Copy     Y Delete| J Delete            | ^Q Quick  ^P Print
Q Abandon file    | V Move     W Write | -Disk Operations-   | ^O Onscreen
-Place Markers-   | N Column on(OFF)   |L Change logged disk| Space Bar returns
0-9 set/hide 0-9|                      |F Directory on (OFF)| you to Main Menu.
```

Not all of these commands have to do with the block maneuvers you've just encountered. At left are WordStar's save commands and place marker entry codes.

Beneath the block operations is a column mode notation, which you will see again in Chapter 27. And at right are file and disk operations, features explained in Chapter 37.

Here is the text of WordStar's ^JV help menu:

```
            *****  TO MOVE A BLOCK OF TEXT  *****
  1.  Put cursor on first character, type ^KB to mark start.
  2.  Put cursor after last character, type ^KK to mark end
      (for end line, use start next line to include RETURN).
  3.  Put cursor at destination, type ^KV to move the text,
      or ^KC to make a duplicate copy.
To undisplay markers afterwards, use ^KH.
^KB and ^KK may be entered in either order, with or without
     other intervening commands.
All above commands are on ^K menu.              press space bar:
```

REVIEW: BLOCK COMMANDS

- A block is marked with F7 or ^KB at its beginning and F8 or ^KK at its end. Either command may be entered first, but the F7 position must be above the F8 placement. If you enter F7 first, <B> appears on the screen at that point; if you enter F8 first, <K> appears on-screen. As soon as you enter the second or completing command, the <B> or <K> notation disappears and the marked block displays in highlighted letters.
- A hidden block appears in normal screen intensity; a displayed block is highlighted.
- ^KH hides and redisplays a marked block.
- ^KV moves a displayed block from its original position to the cursor's location.
- ^KC copies a displayed block at the cursor's position while leaving the original block undisturbed.
- ^KR is the read file command, which inserts all the material stored in another file into your document at the cursor's place.
- ^KW is the write block command, which copies a displayed block into another file, creating the file (if it does not yet exist) or erasing its previous contents (if it does exist), and leaving the displayed block undisturbed.
- ^KY erases a displayed block.
- Error messages appear if you try to move an undisplayed block, if there is not sufficient disk space to write the displayed block, or if you try to move or copy a block that's too long for the system.
- A block can be hidden and redisplayed throughout an editing session. The ^KS storage command will not disturb a marked block, and the block will remain marked until you replace it with another marked block or until you erase it with ^KY or with the ^KD or ^KX save command.

QUIZ

1. What is a marked block?
2. What is a displayed block?
3. What is a hidden block?

4. What can you do with a displayed block?
5. Translate these block commands:
   a. ^KC
   b. ^KV
   c. ^KW
   d. ^KR
   e. ^KY
   f. ^KH
6. What command should you use if you want to move a section of text to another part of the document, but you don't want to erase it from its original location?
7. What is the difference between the read file and write block commands?
8. How can these commands help you edit a long document or move long sections of text?
9. What command can you use to move the cursor to the beginning of a marked block? Does the marked block have to be displayed for this command to work?

QUIZ ANSWERS

1. A marked block has been labeled with F7 or ^KB at its beginning and F8 or ^KK at its end.
2. A displayed block appears in highlighted letters.
3. A hidden block is a marked and formerly highlighted block now appearing in letters of regular screen intensity.
4. You can move, copy, or delete a displayed block; you can store it in another file; you can hide and redisplay it.
5. a. Copy the displayed block in the same file.
   b. Move the displayed block to another position in the same file.
   c. Write the displayed block into another file, retaining the original.
   d. Read contents of another file into current file at cursor position.
   e. Erase displayed block.
   f. Hide (or redisplay) marked block.
6. ^KC
7. "Block write" copies your displayed block into another file. "Read file" enters the contents of another file at cursor position.
8. Use a separate file for storing large blocks or blocks that must be moved long distances; then reposition the cursor and use ^KR to re-enter material without generating a DISK FULL or BLOCK TOO LONG error message.

26

Finding and Restoring Blocks

A hidden block is still a marked block, and WordStar remembers where the original <B> and <K> markers went. Remember that a marked block remains marked until you mark a new block, thus replacing it.

Block markers survive ^KS save commands, so even after numerous editing commands, additions of new material, and other revisions, your most recently marked block remains marked.

FIND BLOCK BEGINNING/END

Whenever you want to move the cursor to the beginning of a marked block, use ^QB. You can remember this code by thinking, *Q*uickly move to the *B*eginning of the marked block.

^QK will position the cursor at the end of a marked block. You have already associated K with the end of bloc*K*, making this command easy to recall.

These commands work whether the block is hidden or displayed.

Entering ^QB when a block is displayed simply moves the cursor to the block's beginning. Entering ^QB when a block is hidden moves the cursor to the block's beginning and adds a highlighted <B> to the screen at that point.

Entering ^QK when a block is hidden moves the cursor to the block's end and adds a highlighted <K> unless you have already used ^QB. In that case, entering ^QK moves the cursor to the end of the marked block and displays the block in highlighted letters.

Similarly, entering ^QB when there is a highlighted <K> on the screen from the ^QK command puts the cursor at the beginning of the block and redisplays the block.

After relocating (moving or copying) a block to another part of the file, you can return to your previous cursor position by using ^QP. ^QP moves to the cursor's position before the last command was entered. (*Q*uickly return to *P*revious cursor position.)

MOVE TO BLOCK SOURCE

^QV moves you to the position a marked block occupied before the most recent block-moving maneuver, that is, to the original setting of <B> prior to that block's move, copy, delete, or write command's execution. Use ^QV to go back and inspect the place you moved the text from.

As noted in the find and find-and-replace command chapters, ^QV can also move the cursor to the place it occupied before the last find or find-and-replace search was executed. Therefore, this command's destination depends on what has been entered most recently.

It's convenient to enter ^QV immediately after a block move, block write, block delete, or block copy command; however, the command can be entered at any time during editing. ^QV will move you to a marked block's position prior to the last block write/block delete/ block copy/ block move or to the cursor's position prior to the last find/find-and-replace command, whichever was most recent.

RESTORING A BLOCK

What if you accidentally erase a block you meant to keep?

If the block is new material that you never stored with a ^KS, ^KD, or ^KX save command, and which you didn't move to another file for safekeeping by using ^KW, it's lost for good and you'll have to retype it.

But if you've been saving your text all along and the material you marked was preserved in this fashion, you can bring it back by interrupting with ^KQ, the abandon edit command. This will sacrifice all unsaved editing changes but it will bring back your erased block.

^KQ takes you back to WordStar's No-File Menu. By entering D and your document file, you can return to the text and find your block intact. As mentioned, unsaved editing changes made before the block erasure will be lost. You've gotten plenty of "store often" reminders, and here's another!

EXERCISE: BLOCK COMMANDS

1. Create two new files. Call one STORAGE (use ^KD to save this empty file) and name the other FABLE.
2. In FABLE, set single spacing. Word wrap and justification should be on. Use margins of 1 and 65 with a tab stop at column 6.
3. Type these stories from Aesop's Fables, centering the titles as shown.

The Hen and the Golden Eggs

A cottager and his wife had a Hen that laid a golden egg every day. They supposed that the Hen must contain a great lump of gold in its inside, and in order to get the gold they killed it. Having done so, they found to their surprise that the Hen differed in no respect from the other hens. The foolish pair, thus hoping to become rich all at once, deprived themselves of the gain of which they were assured day by day.

The Fox and the Lion

When a Fox who had never yet seen a Lion, fell in with him by chance for the first time in the forest, he was so frightened that he nearly died with fear. On meeting him for the second time, he was still much alarmed, but not to the same extent as at first. On seeing him the third time, he so increased in boldness that he went up to him and commenced a familiar conversation with him.

Acquaintance softens prejudice.

4. Place the cursor before "The Fox and the Lion" and enter ^KB. Move to the end of the story and enter ^KK. The fable should be highlighted. Move it into STORAGE with ^KW, the write command.
5. Leave the fable highlighted and enter ^KY to erase it in your present file.
6. With the cursor two lines below the first paragraph, type this story:

The Lioness

A controversy prevailed among the beasts of the field as to which of the animals deserved the most credit for producing the greatest number of whelps at a birth. They rushed clamorously into the presence of the Lioness and demanded of her the settlement of the dispute. "And you," they said, "how many sons have you at a birth?" The Lioness laughed at them, and said: "Why! I have only one; but that one is altogether a thoroughbred Lion."

The value is in the worth, not in the number.

7. Mark this story as a block and move it, with ^KV, to the top of the file.
8. Leaving the block displayed, move the cursor to the end of the file and enter ^KC to copy the block. "The Lioness" will appear twice.
9. Hide the displayed block (the last paragraph) with ^KH.
10. Use ^QB to locate the marked but hidden block's beginning. Use ^QK to find its end.
11. Erase the last paragraph and its title by redisplaying it with ^KH and then entering ^KY.
12. Move to line 1 with ^QR. Now use ^QV, which will take you to the most recent block source (your block's position before the ^KY entry).
13. Move to line 1 with ^QR and enter ^KR, the read command. In response to the screen message, enter STORAGE, or use ^R, which will restore your last file entry (STORAGE). "The Fox and the Lion" will return.
14. Your screen should look like this as you scroll:

```
                    The Fox and the Lion

     When  a Fox who had never yet seen a Lion,   fell in with him
by chance for the first time in the forest,   he was so frightened
that  he nearly died with fear.   On meeting him for  the  second
time, he was still much alarmed, but not to the same extent as at
first.  On seeing him the third time, he so increased in boldness
that he went up to him and commenced a familiar conversation with
him.
     Acquaintance softens prejudice.
                         The Lioness

     A  controversy prevailed among the beasts of the field as to
which  of the animals deserved the most credit for producing  the
greatest  number of whelps at a birth.  They rushed  clamorously
into  the  presence  of  the Lioness  and  demanded  of  her  the
settlement of the dispute.   "And you," they said,  "how many sons
have  you  at a birth?"  The Lioness laughed at them,  and  said:
"Why!  I have only one; but that one is altogether a thoroughbred
Lion."
     The value is in the worth, not in the number.

                 The Hen and the Golden Eggs

     A  cottager  and his wife had a Hen that laid a  golden  egg
every day.   They supposed that the Hen must contain a great lump
of gold in its inside,  and in order to get the gold they  killed
it.   Having  done so,  they found to their surprise that the Hen
differed in no respect from their other hens.   The foolish pair,
thus  hoping to become rich all at once,  deprived themselves  of
the gain of which they were assured day by day.
```

REVIEW: FINDING AND RESTORING BLOCKS

- ^QB moves the cursor to a marked block's beginning. The block does not have to be displayed.
- ^QK moves the cursor to a marked block's end. The block does not have to be displayed.
- ^QP moves the cursor to the position it occupied before the last command was entered.
- ^QV moves the cursor to a block's <B> marker or source position prior to the last block move, block erase, block copy, or block write command was executed, or to the cursor's place before the last find or find-and-replace command was executed, whichever was most recent.
- To restore an accidentally erased block, use the ^KQ abandon edit command, enter D from WordStar's No-File Menu, and return to the file. If the erased block is very short, simply retype it.

QUIZ

1. What does ^QB do?
2. What does ^QK do?
3. If you enter ^QV immediately after repositioning a block, where will the cursor go?
4. What is ^QP?
5. ^KQ can restore an accidentally erased block by abandoning the edit, but what editing practice makes this a practical solution?

QUIZ ANSWERS

1. ^QB moves the cursor to the beginning of a marked block. The block does not have to be displayed.
2. ^QK moves to the end of a marked block.
3. ^QV returns the cursor to the position a displayed block occupied prior to the last block move, block erase, block copy, or block write command's execution. This location is called the block's "source." However, if a find or find-and-replace command was entered more recently than the block command, the cursor will return to the position it occupied just before that command was executed.
4. ^QP returns the cursor to the position it occupied before the last command was entered.
5. For this to be a practical way of restoring accidentally erased blocks, editing changes must be stored or saved frequently. ^KQ will erase all unsaved changes.

SOME EDITING TRICKS

When editing a long file, you will get DISK FULL warnings as you move blocks of text long distances. To avoid this problem, mark a block and use ^KW to store it in another file and ^KY to erase the original block from your document file. After you've moved the cursor to the place you want the block to appear, use ^KR to read the block back into your file. This is the same procedure to use if your system issues BLOCK TOO LONG error messages when you enter ^KV or ^KC.

^QR is the command that moves you to the beginning of a file, but ^KS (the save command) will move you to the beginning of a long file faster than ^QR will, and it has the added advantage of preserving your editing changes at the same time.

Boiler plate is the term used for standard paragraphs used over and over. When you plan to prepare several "original" letters using common material, or whenever you need the same paragraphs in different documents, store the boiler plate information in a special file or several files and rely on the ^KR read file command to insert it where appropriate.

When you're working on a long file, disk space is a crucial concern. If you try to store material and get a WARNING: DISK FULL message, you can make more room on your disk by erasing unnecessary files. The fastest way to do this is with ^KJ, the DELETE FILE command.

When you enter ^KJ, the message line will say: NAME OF FILE TO DELETE? Enter the name of any file you can live without and you'll have more room for your current document. If you can't remember all the files on your disk, display them at the top of the screen with ^KF, which turns the disk file directory on and off. To see what files are stored on the other disk, change the logged disk drive with ^KL. You will meet these commands again in Chapter 37.

27

Working with Columns

REGULAR TEXT COLUMN ENTRY

When creating columns of text or number, you can proceed in three different ways.

1. Set the text horizontally, using tabular formatting. You did this in Chapter 21 when you created tables using regular and decimal tab stops.

- Column 1 Heading —— tab→Column 2 Heading @
- Column 1 text ———— tab→Column 2 text @
- More column 1 text—— tab→More column 2 text, etc.

2. Set text vertically using tab stops with insertion turned off. This mode of entry does not allow you to use word wrap or to justify the right margin, but it permits the construction of one entire column followed by the second column, etc.

   When insertion is turned off, neither the RETURN key nor TAB key disturbs already-entered text; each moves the cursor "through" or "over" text instead. Because each line ends with a hard return, this column has a ragged or unjustified right margin.

```
L-------------------------!-------------------------!----------R
Here is a column@      ——► Here is a second@       ——► etc.
set by using@           ▲  Column set by using@     ▲
the RETURN key@         |  the TAB bar to reach@    |
at the end of each@     |  the left margin. The@    |
line, with insertion@   |  cursor "jumps over"@     |
turned off.————————————►|   text at left.——————————►|
```

3. Thanks to WordStar's column mode, you can take advantage of word wrap and margin justification while creating adjacent columns. Here, in miniature, is such a procedure.

```
a a a a a a a
a a a a a a a
a a a a .
b b b b b b b
b b b b b b b
b b b b .
c c c c c c c
c c c c c c c
c c c c .
```

The column at left stays in its original position, but the other two blocks are moved up, one at a time, to adjacent locations.

The result is:

```
a a a a a a a        b b b b b b b        c c c c c c c
a a a a a a a        b b b b b b b        c c c c c c c
a a a a .            b b b b .            c c c c .
```

In regular WordStar use, you can't move a column from one place to another if there is other text on the source lines; you cannot move a narrow column into lines of text without disrupting the document.

But with a special COLUMN MODE command, you can mark, move, copy, or delete a column without disturbing adjacent columns or other text.

COLUMN MODE

Column mode is a convenience in preparing newsletters, columns of figures, and special tables for insertion in a report.

WordStar defines a column as a rectangle, beginning at a specified line and column/space and ending at a specified line and column/space. If you begin a column block on line 5 at space 1 and end it on line 10 at space 9, it covers this area:

Space/column:	123456789
line 5	xxxxxxxxx
line 6	xxxxxxxxx
line 7	xxxxxxxxx
line 8	xxxxxxxxx
line 9	xxxxxxxxx
line 10	xxxxxxxxx

WordStar will not define this area as a column block until you do two things:

1. Turn column mode on (^KN).
2. Mark the block with F7 and F8.

When you enter the block beginning code, your entry in the above example will look like this:

```
<B>xxxxxxxxx
xxxxxxxxx
xxxxxxxxx
xxxxxxxxx
xxxxxxxxx
xxxxxxxxx
```

As soon as you enter the block-ending code one space after the last entry on the last line, your block will move back into alignment and appear highlighted. This is a marked and displayed column block.

This is different from the block created in regular block mode. In regular block mode, the block begins at beginning marker's position and includes everything on the cursor's line to the right of that position, and everything on every line until the block end marker's line, and everything on that line to the left of the block end marker.

In column block mode, you mark a rectangle as a block and the block will not include any text on the same line as the block text unless it's part of the block's rectangle.

In regular block mode, the markers shown will generate this marked block, pretending that the x characters are highlighted and the o characters are regular screen letters.

```
ooooooooooooooooooooooooooooooooooooooooooooooooooooooo
ooooooooooooooooooooooooooooooooooooooooooooooooooooooo
ooooooooooooooooooooooooooooooooooooooooooooooooooooooo
ooooooooooooooooooooooooooooooooooooooooooooooooooooooo
ooooooooooooooooooooooooooooooooooooooooooooooooooooooo
ooooooooooooooooooooooooooooooooooooooooooooooooooooooo
```

Set the block beginning marker at the first underline and the block end marker at the second underline.

In regular block mode, the section marked x will display highlighted:

```
ooooooooooooooooooooooooooooooooooooooooooooooooooo
oooooxxxxxxxxxxxxxxxxxxxxxxxxxxxxxxxxxxxxxxxxxxxxxx
xxxxxxxxxxxxxxxxxxxxxxxxxxxxxxxxxxxxxxxxxxxxxxxxxxx
xxxxxxxxxxxxxxxxxxxxxxxxxxxxxxxxxxxxxxxxxxxxxxxxxxx
xxxxxxxxxxxxxxxxxxxxxxxxxxxxxxxxxxxxxxxxxxxxxxxxxxx
xxxxxxxxxxxxxxxxxxxxxxxxxoooooooooooooooooooooooooo
```

In column block mode, x marks the displayed block:

```
ooooooooooooooooooooooooooooooooooooooooooooooooooo
oooooxxxxxxxxxxxxxxxxxxxxoooooooooooooooooooooooooo
oooooxxxxxxxxxxxxxxxxxxxxoooooooooooooooooooooooooo
oooooxxxxxxxxxxxxxxxxxxxxoooooooooooooooooooooooooo
oooooxxxxxxxxxxxxxxxxxxxxoooooooooooooooooooooooooo
oooooxxxxxxxxxxxxxxxxxxxxoooooooooooooooooooooooooo
```

After marking a block, try switching back and forth between column mode and regular block mode by pressing ^KN several times. The highlighted section will change, as in the example above.

COLUMN BLOCK COMMANDS

To hide the column block, use ^KH.

Once you have marked and displayed a column block, you can

1. Move it with ^KV,
2. Copy it with ^KC, or
3. Delete it with ^KY.

In column block mode, you *cannot*

1. Write a block with ^KW or
2. Read a block with ^KR.

Column block mode does not affect hard or soft returns the way regular block mode does.

When you move text in regular block mode, the line returns go along with the rest of the block. In column mode, line returns stay in the original location, leaving an empty gap marked with hard returns (<) at the screen's right.

The original block markers, <B> and <K>, may stay on the screen, depending on your computer, in which case they continue to show the position or source of the block you have just moved or erased. (Block markers usually display this way on the 64K IBM PC.)

In normal block mode you can erase a page of empty lines by marking it as a block and using ^KY. In column block mode, ^KY will not remove hard or soft returns, so this procedure doesn't work. You can remove blank lines one at a time by using ^Y, or return to regular (noncolumn) block mode and use ^KY.

The <B> and <K> markers may stay on-screen at the block source position after a block has disappeared, again depending on your computer. You can use ^QB (find block beginning) or ^QK (find block end) to relocate the different ends of the empty zone, regardless of whether the markers display.

^QV, which finds the block source, will move the cursor to your original <B> marker's location.

CHECKING COLUMN MODE'S STATUS ON-SCREEN

To tell whether you are in block column mode, use F1 2 or F1 3 to return WordStar's Main Menu to the top of the screen, then press ^K by itself. The screen will show column mode as (ON) or (OFF). To complete the command entry after checking the screen, enter the second part of a ^K command or void the command by pressing ESC, RETURN, ^U, or the space bar.

MOVING COLUMN BLOCKS WITH THE 64K IBM PC

Unfortunately, you cannot move blocks with the ^KW write and ^KR read commands in column mode. And even more unfortunately, WordStar defines the 900-character block move/block copy limit as the source area's size, not the marked block's size.

This means if you're trying to move a skinny column (25 or 30 words) that comes from a zone of solid text measuring 15 or more lines, the screen will display an error message and you'll gnash your teeth.

What's the solution? You can do what the screen suggests and move your block in tiny segments. Or you can use regular block mode to move not just your column but the whole section of text in which it resides; then, after reading the block into its new location, erase all the noncolumn material.

If your column-block-to-be-moved is alone on the screen and not contained within or adjacent to other text, you'll have an easier time using ^KV and ^KC. If a BLOCK TOO LONG message appears, you can move back and forth between the marked block and the new location with ^QV and ^QP commands, or you can set place markers.

You may also find that you can move text up (toward the beginning of your file) without generating an error message when the same block moved down (toward the end of your file) produces one.

MAINTAINING COLUMN ALIGNMENT

When in block column mode, you will not be able to add words to your column with insertion on or use delete commands without disturbing text already positioned to the right on the same line.

If you move a column to an already-occupied area, WordStar will set the column as instructed, shifting the already-entered text to the right.

Columns of numbers can be changed, assuming the revisions are minor, with insertion turned off. Turning insertion off allows you to enter new material over the old, replacing it a character at a time, without disturbing the rest of the line.

If your column is made up of words rather than numbers, and you want to edit it with the help of word wrap and justification, you won't be able to leave it where it is. Neither will you want to move it into a blank zone marked with carriage return flags, because word wrap will consider each line a self-contained unit terminated by a hard return.

If you can move the column block to the end of the file, you won't have hard returns on the right and you can set margins, add material, use word wrap, and revise the column extensively. If your system limits the amount of text you can move with ^KV, you can make the chore easier by using a separate file for the creation of your column project and, when it's perfect, moving the whole thing into your document with the read command (^KR in regular block mode). Necessity is the mother of invention, and if you want to create the perfect document, you'll figure out a clever way of doing so. The spirit of adventure, time, practice, and experience will make you a column-moving expert.

If you have left room in a document for a typewritten figure or table of text, you can prepare the table separately and move it into the empty space with ^KV. In planning this kind of block move, leave empty space along the page's right side as you enter the original text. Column blocks moved to the left of already-entered text shift that text to the right. This means your table can be inserted at right or left.

For example:

```
xxxxxxxxxx   becomes   xxxxxxxxxx    or    xxxxxxxxxx
xxxxxxxxxx             xxxxxxxxxx          xxxxxxxxxx
xxxxx                  oooooxxxxx          xxxxxooooo
xxxxx                  ooooooxxxx          xxxxxooooo
xxxxx                  ooooooxxxx          xxxxxooooo
xxxxxxxxxx             xxxxxxxxxx          xxxxxxxxxx
```

depending on whether you insert the new block to the left or right of previously entered text.

PRINT CONTROLS IN COLUMN MODE

When entering print control commands, such as for underlining or boldface type, put the control at the beginning and end of each line you want so featured. Then, no matter where the column appears, it will not underline text in adjacent columns.

When the screen shows:

```
^Soooooooooo^S    oooooooooo
^Soooooooooo^S    oooooooooo
^Soooooooooo^S    ^Boooooooooo^B
ooooooooo        ^Boooooooooo^B
ooooooooo        oooooooooo
```

This will print:

```
oooooooooo        oooooooooo
oooooooooo        oooooooooo
oooooooooo        oooooooooo
oooooooooo        oooooooooo
oooooooooo        oooooooooo
```

By entering F5 or^PS (^S on the screen) at the beginning and end of each featured line in the left column, you avoid underlining the first three lines of the second column. F6 (^B on the screen) at the beginning and end of each featured line in the second column prevents lines in the first column from being set in boldface type.

COLUMN MODE AND THE SOFT HYPHEN

Column mode can be convenient for setting adjacent columns of text, such as for a newsletter or table. But if you have used word wrap and hyphen-help to arrange the text, be sure to check the position of soft hyphens. A soft hyphen will print only if positioned at the end of a line. Soft hyphens at the end of the left column (or at any position other than the far right of a line) will not appear. Change soft hyphens to hard hyphens with a replacement command (turn soft hyphen entry mode on with ^OE, then enter ^QA - @ ^P- ESC) or by turning insertion off and over-typing each soft hyphen with a regular hyphen.

COLUMN MODE AND LINE RETURNS

After setting columns of text with word wrap, you may turn insertion off and use the RETURN key to move down the screen without rearranging text. But this procedure replaces each soft return with a hard return. Future reforming with ^B will be interrupted by each hard return flag (>). You're probably safer moving the cursor with the down-arrow key when editing columns of text set by word wrap.

WHAT IF YOU MAKE A MISTAKE?

The answer to that question is, Don't be discouraged. Column blocks take a bit of practice.

If you mark a column block positioned with other text and everything, including the text not in your block, gets highlighted, it's because you're still in regular block mode. Enter ^KN and the highlighting will shift automatically.

If you move a block with the cursor positioned in space/column 1 and the block arrives safely but indented several spaces from column 1, it's because some empty spaces are part of the block. If the cursor is three spaces to the left of your column's left edge when you enter F7, WordStar will consider those three spaces part of your block. Wherever you move it, the spaces will comc, too.

Prevent this problem by marking the <B> in the first space of the first line of your column if you plan to set it at the far left or if precision is important. ^KY will not erase carriage returns in column mode, but it will erase blank spaces. To shift a column to the left, mark the indentation as though it were a block of text, with F7 and F8. It's hard to tell whether a block of blank spaces is highlighted or not, but the disappearance of your <B> marker is a good sign. Enter ^KY and the column should shift left.

If you mark a block and not all of it displays higlighted, it's because your F7 block beginning marker was too far to the right or your F8 block end marker was too far to the left. Reset the marker by entering F7 or F8 at the right position.

If material you didn't intend to underline has been underlined, it's because you neglected to place a ^PS or F5 underline control at the end of the column's line. Print controls that apply to one column only have to be placed at the beginning and end of each line in the column.

CORRECTING MISTAKES IN COLUMNS

If you produce a perfect set of columns and then notice a mistake in the middle of one, turn insertion off and think carefully about the repair job. Insertion off prevents any new entry from disturbing text on the screen; it allows you to replace characters one at a time by "overprinting" them. As a backup, you may want to make a copy of the complete table before attempting its repair; turn column mode off (^KN) and use the block write or block copy command to make a duplicate.

If you create a perfect set of columns and then absentmindedly press the tab key or erase a word or enter a letter where you didn't intend to, you have a problem. It's a good idea to set up special storage files as you create complicated tables; that way you have a copy in reserve. Before trying to repair a set of columns, analyze your problem. The spontaneous approach may not be the best one. Perhaps you can re-enter the erased word or remove the accidentally created spaces and bring everything back into alignment. If you erased a whole line, perhaps you can reconstruct it all across the table. If only one column is in chaos, consider moving it to the end of the file for repair and then moving it back.

If you enter F7, then move down to enter F8 and the block doesn't shift into highlighted letters, check to see if a <K> appears where you ended the block. If so, the block is marked but not displaying. Use ^QB to find the block beginning <B> and this should cause the block to display.

EXERCISE

Set up a new file and call it RECIPE. Use single spacing; set the left margin at 1 and the right margin at 36. Type these instructions exactly as shown, inserting the ^PH overprint command and ^PT for the superscript. (If you use the IBM Matrix Printer, the superscript will not print in single spacing, so substitute the letter F for Fahrenheit (350 F) instead. Use a hyphen in "care-fully" to conserve space.

```
Simmer  chicken breasts in beer  and
sufficient  water  to  cover,  15-20
minutes  or  until  tender.   Drain,
saving liquid.   Trim chicken  care-
fully.  Slice into 18 narrow strips
and set aside.
    Saute ^PH` onion and garlic  in
oil  until  tender.  Add  tomatoes,
tomato  sauce,  water,  pan  liquid,
chilies,  cumin and herbs.  Bring to
a boil, then reduce heat and simmer
30 minutes.  Stir occasionally.
    Meanwhile,  heat  oven to 350^PTo^PT
and soften tortillas by heating in a
lightly  oiled  skillet,  one  at  a
time.
    Lightly  grease two  10 X 6-inch
baking dishes or one large dish.
    Add  sour  cream to  sauce  and
stir well.  On each tortilla, place
1  slice  chicken,  1  Tablespoon
sauce,  and  2 Tablespoons  shredded
cheese.  Roll up and place seam side
down in dish.  Pour remaining  sauce
over  tortillas;   sprinkle   with
remaining cheese.
    Cover;  bake for 35-40 minutes.
Serve  with  rice and refried beans.
Serves 8.
```

Now move down two lines and set the right margin at space/column 25. Use single spacing. Turn justification off (^OJ). Set a tab stop at space/column 5 (^OI 5). Use F6 to set boldface type where shown. Type this list, using the TAB key to position text. In recipe writing, teaspoon is usually spelled with a lower case t, Tablespoon with a capital T.

```
[F6]Chicken Enchiladas[F6 @@]
3    large chicken breasts
1    12-oz. bottle beer
     water
2    Tablespoons oil
1    onion, chopped
1    clove garlic, minced
6    large ripe  tomatoes,
     chopped
1    cup water
1    8-oz. can tomato
     sauce
1    4-oz. can green
     chilies, seeded,
     rinsed and chopped
2    teaspoons ground
     cumin
1    teaspoon dried
     oregano
1    Tablespoon fresh
     minced basil, or 1
     teaspoon dried basil,
     crushed
18   corn tortillas
4    cups shredded jack
     cheese (approximately
     1 lb.)
1    cup sour cream
```

You will now move the ingredients column up to the directions column, placing them side by side, using column block mode.

Enter ^KN to activate column mode.

Set the block beginning marker (F7) in column 1 of the first line of the title line.

Move the cursor down to the last line and then move it over to space/column 29. Enter the block ending marker (F8) at that position.

Your column block measures 28 lines down and 29 column/spaces across. Unfortunately, if yours is the 64K system, you may not be able to move the entire block in one command. Try it, and if you get an error message, reset the block end marker (F8) in the column's 15th line at space/column 29.

The entire marked block, whatever its size, should display in highlighted letters. If any letters display in bright light, you may have typed text to the right of column/space 29, or you may have set the block end marker to the left of that column. Correct the display by moving the block end marker; move the cursor to the right as many spaces as necessary and press F8 again.

Be sure that you are in column mode before moving the block. Return to help level 2 or 3 with F1. Now press ^K by itself. Column mode will display (ON) or (OFF), depending on its present status. If off, turn it on by entering N (the second part of your ^KN command). If it's on, press the space bar. Remove the on-screen menus with F1 and 0 or 1.

Move the cursor to the first line of text by using F10 (return to file beginning) or by saving with ^KS.

With the cursor positioned in space/column 1 of the first line of text, enter ^KV (block move).

If you have to break the block into smaller segments, move the first 15 lines; then return for the remaining segment.

Your ingredients block should begin at the cursor location and cover 28 lines, extending to column 29. Everything already on the screen bumps right to compensate. Because the block being moved is a rectangle, the previously entered text remains aligned.

Now store with ^KD, print the file, and invite friends for dinner. (The recipe was printed with a daisy wheel printer.)

Chicken Enchiladas

3 large chicken breasts
1 12-oz. bottle beer
  water
2 Tablespoons oil
1 onion, chopped
1 clove garlic, minced
6 large ripe tomatoes, chopped
1 cup water
1 8-oz. can tomato sauce
1 4-oz. can green chilies, seeded, rinsed and chopped
2 teaspoons ground cumin
1 teaspoon dried oregano
1 Tablespoon fresh minced basil, or 1 teaspoon dried basil, crushed
18 corn tortillas
4 cups shredded jack cheese (approximately 1 lb.)
1 cup sour cream

Simmer chicken breasts in beer and sufficient water to cover, 15-20 minutes or until tender. Drain, saving liquid. Trim chicken carefully. Slice into 18 narrow strips and set aside.

Sautè onion and garlic in oil until tender. Add tomatoes, tomato sauce, water, pan liquid, chilies, cumin and herbs. Bring to a boil, then reduce heat and simmer 30 minutes. Stir occasionally.

Meanwhile, heat oven to 350° and soften tortillas by heating in a lightly oiled skillet, one at a time.

Lightly greese two 10x6-inch baking dishes or one large dish.

Add sour cream to sauce and stir well. On each tortilla, place 1 slice chicken, 1 Tablespoon sauce, and 2 Tablespoons shredded cheese. Roll up and place seam side down in dish. Pour remaining sauce over tortillas; sprinkle with remaining cheese.

Cover; bake for 35-40 minutes. Serve with rice and refried beans. Serves 8.

REVIEW: COLUMN MODE

- ^KN turns column mode on and off. Column mode is off by default.
- To determine whether you are in column mode, return to help level 2 or 3 (F1 2 or F1 3) and press ^K by itself. A screen notation shows column mode (ON) or (OFF).
- In column mode you can:
  - Mark a column block with F7 and F8.
  - move a displayed column block with ^KV,
  - Copy a displayed column block with ^KC, or
  - Delete a displayed column block with ^KY.

- The block's beginning point is defined as the cursor's position when you enter F7. WordStar will match this point to the cursor's position when you enter a block move (^KV) or block copy (^KC) command. Position the cursor carefully when you mark a column block and when you move it.
- Material added to a column when insertion is on will disturb text at right on the same line; you cannot edit adjacent columns using word wrap and justification.
- In column mode, you cannot use ^KR or ^KW.
- A print control character, if used on more than one line of a column, should be entered at the beginning and end of each line featured.
- When you remove a column block from a section of text, columns, or text to the right of the removed block will shift left.
- When moving a column into an already-entered section, the block will go exactly where you position the cursor. Anything in the destination space or to its right will be shifted right.

REVIEW: COLUMN BLOCK COMMANDS ON-SCREEN

The Block Menu, produced when you enter ^K at help level 2 or 3, reviews block commands. ^JV, which displays regardless of the help level, reviews the instructions for marking and moving a block. Although ^JP is called the "Place Marker Help" Menu, it too reviews the commands for marking and maneuvering blocks of text.

QUIZ

1. What is column mode? What does it allow you to do?
2. What does column mode not permit?
3. What is the column mode entry command? How can you tell whether you are in column mode?
4. How do you mark a column block?
5. How should you enter print control commands in a column?

QUIZ ANSWERS

1. Column mode is a special function that allows you to mark columns of text or numbers and to move, copy, or erase those columns without disturbing the rest of the text. This is different from regular block mode, which considers everything between the first and last line of a block to be part of that block.
2. Column mode does not allow ^KR (block read) or ^KW (block write) entries, or the use of word wrap or margin justification.
3. ^KN. To check current status, enter ^JH3 to restore help menus, then enter ^K by itself.
4. Mark a column block by positioning cursor above or in the column's first line and to the left or at the left edge of the column before entering F7 for the beginning marker <B>. Position cursor on or below the column's last line and to the right of its right edge before entering F8 for block end <K>.
5. Print control commands should be entered at the beginning and end of each line individually.

28

Introduction to Dot Commands

You don't like the three-line margin at the top of each printed page. Or you're using legal-sized paper, which measures 14 inches long instead of the standard 11. You'd rather have page numbers print at the top, not the bottom, and it would be nice if they appeared in the outside corner of each page. You want to use chapter headings on every manuscript page, and the computer could save you a lot of work by printing them automatically. Your report is stored in five separate files on two different disks and you want appropriate page numbers to print in the right places. You don't like the way your printer spaces the lines on a page; you'd like more white showing between the lines of your single-spaced document. Every time you edit a paragraph it throws off your careful arrangement of headings and titles; sometimes a title shows up at the bottom of the page before the one it belongs on. You want to use letters that are smaller than the standard characters and you want to reduce the amount of space between characters, or you want to spread characters across the page for a special effect. You don't like the way the computer spreads a word during microjustification and you want letters to print exactly as they appear on the screen. You're preparing the final camera-ready copy of an important sales brochure and you want every letter to print perfectly, so it's important to improve the quality of your output. You want to insert an editing reminder into your file, but you don't want that notation to print.

What to do? Dot commands to the rescue!

WHAT ARE DOT COMMANDS?

Dot commands get their name from the dot (.) that precedes them. Each command in this category consists of two letters and, in several cases, a number. In the case of chapter headings and footings, the dot command consists of a dot, two letters, and an entire line of text.

Even if you don't use dot commands right away, it helps to understand how they're entered.

Every dot command has to begin in the far left column (space or column 1) in order to work. This means that any period entered in column 1 will be interpreted as the first part of a dot command, so be careful when entering decimal points, dots, ellipses, and periods at the beginning of a line.

If your line has to begin with a dot, indent one space before typing it, and make the space a non-break space (^PO) so that future editing and paragraph reform will not move it left.

WordStar never prints a line that has a period in column 1 unless it is a properly entered heading or footing.

THE RULES OF ENTRY

To enter any dot command:

- Position the dot in space (column) 1.
- Enter the two-letter code in spaces 2 and 3.
- Press the space bar once and enter whatever number or text is appropriate, if any.
- Press the RETURN key.

You will notice a special flag at the far right of the screen when you enter the dot: a question mark (?) appears. This question mark disappears as soon as you enter a valid dot command.

If you enter letters that are not recognized by the computer, the question mark will remain at far right and the computer will ignore the command. However, the text in that line, if any, will not print.

```
      "Is it true," he asked, "that you shot her with a
.38 caliber revolver?"
```

Unless indented from column 1, the second line of this sentence will not print. .38 is an invalid dot command. A ? flag remains at right, signaling an unrecognized code.

Be careful even when the screen doesn't show a ? flag. Dot commands can be entered in upper- or lowercase letters, and the computer will recognize a dot followed by the two letters of any authorized dot command not requiring a number. We'll come back to this discussion after you meet the two-letter codes, but note this example:

```
"Absolute  truth is indestructible...vast and deep
...transcendental and intelligent."  -- Confucius
```

The code ".." (two periods) is a valid dot command; it means, Do not print this line. Unless indented from column 1, the quotation's second line will not print.

DOT COMMANDS AND THE REVISED LEFT MARGIN

Even if you indent the left margin with ^OL, the cursor moves to space or column 1 every time you enter a hard return. This makes it easy to position dot commands when using a revised margin setting.

PAGE BREAK LINE

.PA is one of the easiest dot commands to use and remember. As P and A are the first letters in *PA*ge, this command is appropriate for marking the beginning of a new page. If you finish one section and want the next chapter to begin on a new page, enter .PA@ and watch the page break line appear:

```
.PA
---------------------------------------------------------------P
```

This command ensures that the title you put at the top of a page will always appear at the top of the page, no matter how the document might be rearranged by future editing. Nothing is more frustrating than completing a long report and watching a title print on the last line of the page preceding its text—- unless it's a dozen titles that print at the bottom of a dozen pages.

You can enter this dot command as you type original material, creating new pages as you go, or you can revise a typed document and enter this command where appropriate.

Although .PA stays on the screen, neither it nor the page break line will print. Both notations remain in your document until you remove the dot command.

Note

If you enter .PA at the end of your file (after all text, where the screen flags at far right are dots representing un-entered space below the file). .PA by itself will not create a page break line. You must complete the command by pressing the RETURN key.

If you enter .PA within already-entered text, .PA by itself creates the page break line.

ERASE A DOT COMMAND

To eliminate a dot command, use the DELETE key or any delete command, such as ^Y. Sometimes a page break line created by .PA will be so close to a natural page break line that you find a blank page in between. You can prevent this problem by using the conditional page break, described next, or by removing the .PA command.

CONDITIONAL PAGE BREAK

The conditional page break is handy when you want to keep blocks of text or tables from being interrupted. The *C*onditional *P*age break command is .CP, followed by a number. This number represents the minimum number of uninterrupted lines you need, such as the number of lines in a table you've just prepared. Enter the command one line above the table, section, or text.

Example: .CP 16 means that if the edited page doesn't have 16 uninterrupted lines following the dot command, WordStar will set a new page. If 16 lines (or more) follow the .CP command's position, no new page is necessary.

Be careful not to set this dot command in a line of text, because the text won't print. Also, when you set it a line above the text you want to protect, be sure to compensate for the line this command erases. In a double-spaced document, .CP entered between two lines will erase the blank line separating them.

EXERCISE

To experiment with our first two dot commands, type a few lines of text in a new file. Return the cursor to the beginning of your entry. Now type .PA (positioning the cursor in column 1 as you do so) and watch the screen's far right. First, when you enter the period, a question mark flag will appear. This goes away as soon as you complete the two-letter code, and a page break line will cross the screen in the cursor's line.

Now move the cursor to the end of your entry, which is also the end of the file. Position the cursor below the last line; the screen flag at far right will be a dot, showing that this part of the file has not yet been entered.

Type the .PA command again. Once more, the ? flag will appear and then disappear at far right. But until you press the RETURN key, no page break line will cross the screen. When entering this dot command at the end of a file, you have to press the RETURN key to complete it.

Remove the dot command with any delete code, and the page break line will disappear.

Before using .CP, the conditional page break command, skip down the screen using the RETURN key until you reach the naturally occurring page break line.

Move the cursor five lines up from the page break and enter the command .CP 4@. This instructs the computer to begin a new page if there are not four uninterrupted lines available immediately below the dot command. Because you have five available lines, nothing should happen. The command remains on-screen, but no new page break line appears.

Now change the .CP 4 command to .CP 14. You do not have 14 available lines immediately below the code, so WordStar will draw a new page break line at the command's position. If you place the .CP 14 command above a table or graph measuring 14 lines in length, the code ensures that no matter how the document is edited or rearranged, your 14-line table will not be interrupted by a naturally occurring page break line.

Change the .CP code back to .CP 4 and the page break line will disappear.

Remember that the line occupied by a dot command will not print. Move the cursor up one line from the dot command and check the status line. Now move down to the dot command's line with ↓ (2), and down another line with ↓ (2), still watching the status line. If you begin this part of the exercise on line 11, the status line will show line 12 after the first ↓ (2), and it will show line 12 again after the second ↓ (2). This is because the dot command line doesn't count; it's an "invisible" line.

REVIEW: DOT COMMANDS ON-SCREEN

You have not yet met all the dot commands in this on-screen summary, but you should know that the command ^JD will display this explanation, regardless of the help level in use.

Here is the text of WordStar's ^JD help command:

```
                  ***** Print Directives *****
PRINT CONTROL CHARACTERS may be entered anywhere in a line
     to invoke underlining, boldface, subscripts, pauses,
     etc.  They are entered by typing ^P and a letter.  A
     directory of most print controls is given on the ^P
     PREFIX MENU; see manual for more.
DOT COMMANDS are special lines beginning with a period and a
     two-letter code.  They control page breaks, headings,
     page numbering, page layout, etc.  Dot commands are
     typed in like other text.
Space bar for DOT COMMAND SUMMARY, ^u to return to editing.
```

```
                   ***** Dot Commands *****
  PUT EACH DOT COMMAND ON SEPARATE LINE, WITH . IN COL 1
.PA       new PAge
.CP n     new page if less than n lines left on this page
.OP       Omit Page numbers when printing, starting this page
.PN       print Page Numbers, starting this page      (default)
.PC n     Page number Column (default 33 (30 if 64-col screen))
.PO n     Page Offset; extra indent when printed      (default 8)
.. text   comment, not printed
                                   press space bar for next frame:
```

```
.HE text     HEading used until next .HE           (default blank)
.FO text     FOoting (replaces page number)                (blank)
.PL n    Paper Length: total number of lines        (default 66)
.MT n    Margin at Top: # lines, top paper to text              (3)
.MB n    Margin at Bottom: # lines, end text to end paper    (8)
      # lines text on page is PL - MT - MB     (defaults to 55)
.HM n    Heading Margin: blank lines between head and text  (2)
.FM n    Footing Margin: blank lines, text to footing          (2)
       FOR PAGE BREAKS TO DISPLAY AS THEY WILL PRINT, USE
.PL, .MT, .MT, AND .LH (next frame) AT FILE BEGINNING ONLY.
                              Depress space bar for next frame:
```

```
       THE FOLLOWING WORK ONLY WITH INCREMENTAL PRINTERS:
.LH n   Line Height in 48ths of an inch           (default 8)
.CW n   Character Width in 120ths of an inch, for standard or
        alternate pitch, whichever is in use (see ^P menu).
              (default 12 for standard, 10 for alternate)
.SR n   Subscript / Superscript Roll in 48ths of an inch   (3)
.UJ OFF/ON   "MicroJustification" off/on          (default ON)
        Use insure that printed column alignment exactly
        matches screen, e.g. for tabular material:
        Put .UJ OFF before table, put .UJ ON after table.
             Space for next frame, ^U to return to editing:
```

```
SPECIAL CHARACTERS in HEADINGS (.HE) and FOOTINGS (.FO):
  #     prints as current page number
  \     do not interpret next character as a special character
  ^K    do not print following spaces if on even-numbered page
PAGE NUMBER POSITIONING: If a footing text is specified (.FO
 dot command), the default bottom center page number is not
 printed.  Use a # in heading or footing to position page
 number where desired.  ^K followed by spaces followed by #
 may be used to produce alternating left/right page numbers.
             Space for next frame, ^U to return to editing:
```

[Final frame describes Merge-Print Dot Commands, not discussed in this manual.]

REVIEW: INTRODUCTION TO DOT COMMANDS

- Dot commands are two-letter codes preceded by a period. They are used to alter a document's format.
- In order to work, a dot command must be entered with the dot or period in column 1, and with the two-letter code immediately following. If the code requires a number, you must enter a hard space after the two-letter code and then the number. Press RETURN after completing the dot command's entry.
- When you enter a dot or period in column 1, a ? flag appears at the screen's far right. This flag disappears as soon as you enter the two-letter code (or code plus number) of a valid dot command. The ? flag remains on-screen if you enter an invalid or unauthorized dot command.
- WordStar will not print any line containing a period in column 1.
- The dot command .PA creates a page break line. This is a fixed or permanent page break, which will remain effective until you erase it.
- The dot command .CP is a conditional page break code; it is entered with a number (.CP n), n representing the number of uninterrupted lines required for a table or section of text immediately following the command. If a naturally occurring page break line interrupts this area, WordStar sets a new page beginning at the dot

command's position. If no page break line interrupts the designated area, WordStar does not begin a new page at that point.

- Dot commands can be erased with any delete command.

QUIZ

1. Where must a dot command be placed in order to work?
2. What happens when you enter an invalid dot command?
3. How can you erase a dot command?
4. What is the difference between .PA and .PC?
5. What is the main purpose of dot commands?
6. It is important to press RETURN after entering a conditional page break command. Why is this?
7. When must you press RETURN with the .PA command?

QUIZ ANSWERS

1. The dot must be in column 1.
2. A ? flag stays on-screen at right and the line does not print.
3. Use any delete command.
4. .PA sets a permanent page break at the command position; .CP sets a page break only when the command's number (.CP n) requires more interrupted lines than are available below the command point.
5. Dot commands revise a document's basic format or configuration.
6. Because WordStar never prints a line containing a dot command, each conditional page break code removes a line from your text. Pressing return separates the command from any text or blank line it would otherwise erase. In a double-spaced document, the .CP command inserted between two lines of text erases the empty line on which it appears and creates, when the file is printed, single spacing between those two lines.
7. The .PA command will not work without the RETURN key if you are at the end of a file when entering the code.

29

Headings and Footings

WordStar normally sets a three-line margin at the top of a page. The text heading dot command lets you create an automatically repeating line of text at the top of that margin. Your heading appears at the top of the page and a two-line space separates the heading from your text.

WordStar allows you to use any of its special effects in a heading, including boldface type, underlining, subscripts and superscripts, a different colored ribbon, and so on. The same is true for WordStar's footing command, which you'll meet shortly.

Any print control command entered in a heading or footing will influence only that line's text. Even if you neglect to enter a second command terminating the special effect (such as boldface type or underlining), it will not continue into your document.

THE HEADING DOT COMMAND

The text *HE*ading dot command, .HE, is easy to remember.

Let's look at a simple chapter heading. You're working on a mystery novel and you want each page to include the chapter's title. "Mrs. Peacock Finds the Knife" is this chapter's theme. To enter it, put .HE in the far left columns, press the space bar once, then type the chapter's title. The dot command .HE will not appear in your hard copy, so the heading actually prints four spaces to the left of where it appears on the screen. Every heading dot command consists of four nonprinting spaces: the dot, the two-letter code, and the blank space following. If you forget to leave a blank space between .HE and your text, the heading will not print.

Enter this command once, at the beginning of the chapter about Mrs. Peacock and her discovery, and the heading will print on every page until you replace it with another heading command.

You can enter a heading at any time and on any page, but in order to have it print on page 1, it must be entered at the beginning of the file, above any text.

TEXT HEADING OPTIONS

WordStar provides several options that expand the usefulness of headings. As you'll see shortly, the same options can be used in footing commands.

PAGE NUMBERS

WordStar normally prints page numbers at the bottom of each page. But with a heading command, you can use "#" to position page numbers at the top of the page. Wherever you place # in the heading line, the appropriate page number will print.

Most manuscripts and reports require page numbers in the upper-right corner, so to make your numbers print to the right of the right margin (in column 66 or 67) after entering the .HE, move with the space bar to column 70 or 71 and enter #. The dot command and the space after it occupy four columns, but the heading text will shift four spaces to the left when printed.

If you want to position the page number slightly to the left of the text's right margin, position it accordingly.

There is no "right margin" in a heading command; you can type all the way to column 250, or farther. Of course, that won't do you much good if your paper isn't 250 columns wide, but it's nice to know that you needn't worry about the right margin and word wrap as you enter a heading and approach column 65 or the R notation on your ruler line.

PAGE NUMBERS IN THE HEADING

In our mystery novel, here's how to set the chapter heading so that page numbers print at the upper right corner:

```
.HE Where is Colonel Mustard?                                          #
↑                                                                      ↑
column 1                                                       column 71
```

To print page numbers in the upper-left corner, put the # symbol immediately after the dot command:

```
.HE# Professor Plum Meets Miss Scarlet
```

This is one of two exceptions to the "enter a space after the code" rule. (You'll meet the second exception in a moment.) Type .HE#, then a space, and then the heading.

You can even make page numbers print in both corners at once, or in three places. Wherever you enter a # in the heading line, the page number will print.

TEXT PLUS PAGE NUMBER

If you enter the command typing "Page #" instead of the # symbol by itself, numbers will print like this: Page 1, Page 2, Page 3, etc.

If you're preparing a manuscript whose pages should be numbered according to chapter or section, use the appropriate notation before #. Example: "Section A-#" causes page numbers to print like this: Section A-1, Section A-2, Section A-3, etc. "Chapter 21-#" will create page numbers like this: Chapter 21–1, Chapter 21–2, Chapter 21–3, etc.

ALTERNATE-CORNER PAGE NUMBERS

When preparing camera-ready copy for a brochure, book or booklet that will be printed on both sides of the paper, you can enter a special print control command in the heading line that instructs the printer to print odd-numbered page numbers in the upper-right corner and even-numbered page numbers at upper left. Most books and magazines use this outside corner format.

^PK is the special print control command. It instructs the printer to alternate the position of # with the position of ^K (^PK appears on-screen as ^K).

To enter the command for printing page numbers in alternating outside corners, type .HE^PK at the far left and # at far right. This is the second exception to the "space after code" rule.

If you enter ^PK in the center of the line instead of at the left edge, page numbers will alternate between the # symbol's position on odd-numbered pages and the top center of even-numbered pages.

If you want page numbers in the inside corners, close to the binding, enter the command with # next to the dot command instead of at the right margin. In that case, place ^PK at the end of the line: the dot command .HE# goes at the far left and ^K appears at the right. Odd-numbered pages will be numbered at left, even-numbered pages at right.

CENTERING A HEADING

To center a heading, enter the text first, using ^OC to center it, then insert .HE and a space at far left. With ^QD, move to the end of this line and press the RETURN key.

To position numbers at the center of the top line when you're not using a text heading, enter the # first, use ^OC to center it, then add the .HE dot command. Move the cursor to the end of the the line and press RETURN.

SPECIAL CHARACTERS

Two symbols will not normally print in a heading. These are # and \. If you want to use either of these characters, the way to make them print is with the \ key. Enter it in the space before the symbol you're using. This key instructs the computer to print the symbol immediately following. Example: .HE \#\\ will print as #\.

WordStar will acknowledge only one .HE command. If you enter more than one, it will recognize the last one it reads.

SAMPLE HEADING COMMANDS

Note: Notations at right are entered in column 70 or 71 for the standard or default page; where text appears at right, the rightmost letter occupies column 70 or 71.

1. `.HE                                                                 #`

   (Prints page number only, positioning number at right.)

2. `.HE#`

   (Prints page number only, positioning number at left.)

3. `.HE A Candlestick in the Conservatory                                #`

   (Prints chapter title at left and page number at right.)

4. `.HE#                          A Candlestick in the Conservatory`

   (Prints page number at left and chapter title at right.)

5. `.HE^PK                                                               #`

(Prints page numbers in outside corners, alternating odd numbers at right with even numbers at left.)

6. `.HE#                                              ^PK`

(Prints page numbers in inside corners, alternating odd numbers at left with even numbers at right.)

7. `. HE            Professor Plum Makes an Accusation`

(Prints chapter title centered at top of page with no page number.)

8. `. HE                         #`

(Prints page number only, centered at top of page.)

9. `.HE                                         The Fatal Clue`

(Prints title at upper-right corner with no page number.)

10. `.HE The Fatal Clue`

(Prints title at upper-left corner with no page number.)

11. `.He`

(This command cancels the previously entered heading; nothing will print at the top of the page until a new heading command replaces it.)

FOOTINGS

Just as .HE is the heading command, .FO instructs the computer to print a *FO*oting. Default page numbers are centered on the footing line. You can keep the page numbers there and add text, or you can eliminate the page number and substitute a line of text.

The same options listed for the .HE command operate here. The entry

```
.FO Mr. Green Takes the Secret Passage
```

will print this chapter's title at the lower-left corner of each page while eliminating the default page number (the .FO line contains no # symbol).

If you are using the .FO command, no page number will print at the bottom of the page unless you include a # in your footing line.

The command .FO by itself, with no text and no # symbol, will suppress the default page number until you replace it with a footing command that includes the # symbol.

REVIEW: HEADINGS AND FOOTINGS

- .HE is the heading dot command.
- .FO is the footing dot command.
- To enter either, position the dot in column 1, the code in columns 2 and 3, and a hard space in column 4. Begin heading text in column 5.

- Exceptions: When printing numbers at far left or using the print control command ^PK, enter the page number # or print control command in column 4 and a hard space in column 5.
- # prints as the current page number.
- # may be positioned anywhere on the line and the page number will appear in that space.
- # may be entered more than once and the page number will print at each location.
- ^PK entered just after the dot command with a # at the end of the line causes page numbers to appear in the outside corner, away from the normal binding edge (right corner of odd- numbered pages, left corner of even-numbered pages).
- ^PK entered at the end of the heading/footing line with a # in column 4 causes page numbers to print in the inside corner, close to the normal binding edge (left corner of odd-numbered pages, right corner of even-numbered pages).
- The symbols # and \ do not print in a heading or footing. To cause either symbol to print, precede it with a \.
- Once entered, a heading or footing will print on every page until replaced. To cancel a heading command, enter .HE by itself. To reinstate a heading, enter .HE and the appropriate text. Do the same with .FO in the footing line.
- The dot commands .HE and .FO have no page-numbering capability without a # in the same line. To continue page numbering after removing a text heading, be sure to supply a # in the new .HE/.FO line. To resume page number printing after generating several unnumbered pages, enter .HE with # on the appropriate page.
- Because a dot command does not print, all heading or footing text will appear in hard copy four spaces to the left of its screen position.

QUIZ

1. What is the heading dot command?
2. If you enter a text heading, where will it normally print?
3. How much space separates the normal heading from the first line of regular text?
4. What must be included for the current page number to print in a heading or footing?
5. How can you cause the symbol # to print in a heading?
6. What is the footing dot command?
7. What does ^PK do?
8. How can you cancel a heading so that it will not print on certain pages? How do you reinstate it?

QUIZ ANSWERS

1. .HE
2. Four spaces to the left of its screen position.

3. Two empty lines.
4. The # symbol.
5. Precede it with \, as \#.
6. .FO
7. ^PK places the print control character ^K on-screen at the cursor position; it causes the page number # to alternate its printing position with the ^K placement on adjacent pages. If ^K appears at screen left, odd numbers will print at right and even numbers at left; if ^K appears at screen right, odd numbers will print at left and even numbers at right.
8. Enter .HE by itself. To reinstate, enter .HE with appropriate text.

30

Dot Commands and Page Numbers

PAGE NUMBERS IN HEADINGS AND FOOTINGS

As described in the preceding chapter, you can enter page numbers using the # symbol in a heading or footing command.

```
[column 1]                                                      [column 71]

↓                                                                   ↓
.HE#
(Page number at upper left)

.HE                                                                 #
(Page number at upper right)

.HE                         #
(Page number at top center)

.FO
(Page number at lower left)

.FO                                                                   #
(Page number at lower right)
```

WordStar's preset or default format includes the current page number printed at the center bottom of each page. This number will print even if you set a heading command; that is, using the .HE dot command with a # symbol does not cancel the default bottom-of-page number.

OMIT DEFAULT PAGE NUMBER

One way to prevent the printing of the page number that normally appears at the bottom of each page is to use .FO, the footing command, with nothing added after the code. This cancels the printing of the footing page number.

However, WordStar offers a command whose only purpose is to suppress the default number. This dot command is .OP, which stands for *O*mit *P*age numbers. This command code applies only to the default page number usually appearing at the center bottom of each page.

REINSTATE DEFAULT PAGE NUMBER

To reinstate the bottom page number after suppressing it with .OP, enter .PN (*P*age *N*umber) to reinstate it. This command can be entered at any point in the text; it becomes effective immediately following the next page break line.

CHANGE POSITION OF DEFAULT PAGE NUMBER

To change the column number at which the preset or default page number will print, use .PC and a column number.

Think of *P*age number *C*olumn.

.PC 12@ places the page number at space or column 12. To print in the lower-left corner, enter .PC 1@; to print at lower right, enter .PC 65@ or .PC 67@.

CHANGE PAGE NUMBER

WordStar numbers pages from the beginning of your file. If you're working on a long document, such as our hypothetical mystery novel, you'll want to rearrange the page numbers.

.PN n (n stands for page number) instructs the computer to shift from its own numbering, which it displays on the status line, to your selection. The first page of Chapter 8 in our mystery novel is page 164 of the total manuscript. The command to use on page 1 of the Chapter 8 file is .PN 164.

The screen will continue to show PAGE 1 on the status line, so make a reference note on paper whenever you revise page numbers.

When you print this file, the P print command will recognize your revised page numbers. To initiate the printing of Chapter 8 at page 179 of the manuscript (page 16 of the Chapter 8 file), enter 179 at the START AT PAGE NUMBER print option.

SUPPRESS HEADING PAGE NUMBER

The .HE dot command entered without a # page number symbol cancels the previously entered heading and its page number command.

REINSTATE HEADING PAGE NUMBER

To resume the printing of page numbers at the top of each page after an interruption, enter .HE with the appropriately positioned # command.

NOTES ON ENTERING MORE THAN ONE DOT COMMAND

You can enter as many dot commands as you like, one below the other. WordStar reads the commands in order; if two contradict each other, it accepts the second code. If a dot command doesn't work the way it's supposed to, try removing it and entering the command again, and check to be sure nothing contradicts it. Each command must be positioned correctly.

This sequence of commands, if positioned in column 1 at the top of a document, instructs the computer to set page numbers in the upper-left corner, to begin numbering with page 87, and to suppress the default page number at the bottom.

```
.HE#
.PN 87
.OP
```

.OP was placed below .PN 87 so that the default page number would not be printed at the bottom. Remember that .PN reinstates printing of the default page number if entered after an .OP command. When arranged as shown, .PN 87 labels the heading correctly without reversing .OP, which suppresses the footing page number.

You can position the cursor under 10 different dot commands and the status line will continue to read LINE 1. This is because dot commands don't print and they don't take up room in your document, so their lines are "invisible."

EXERCISE

Practice setting the different page-numbering dot commands, reminding yourself how each one works.

Now try this sequence. Be sure the cursor is positioned in column 1 of line 1 at the beginning of your file. First, enter a heading with page numbers, as follows:

```
.HE Chapter 14                                    #
```

This command causes the title, "Chapter 14," to print at the upper-left corner of every page, with the current page number at upper right.

To label the first page of Chapter 14 as page number 124, enter this command next:

```
.PN 124
```

To suppress or cancel the default page number, type the command:

```
.OP
```

Even though you have entered three lines of dot commands, your status line should continue to show the cursor on line 1.

Skip down a few lines and begin a new dot command sequence. This time, reinstate the default page number by typing:

```
.PN
```

Change the position of this page number, so that instead of printing at the center bottom of the page, it prints at far left, in column 1:

```
.PC 1
```

Suppress the heading command, so that "Chapter 12" and the current page number no longer print at the top of the page:

```
.HE
```

(This command entered by itself, with no text and no page number symbol #, cancels the previously entered heading.)

In every case, a ? flag will appear at far right when you enter the dot and first letter of a command; it will remain on-screen until you complete the command. In the case of the .PC entry, the ? will not disappear until you enter the column number that completes this code.

To see your dot commands in action, make up a few different headings and footings, combining them with other dot commands as described here. Use .PA to position each set of commands on a separate page. Now print your file and compare the hard copy with the dot commands that created the printout.

REVIEW: DOT COMMANDS AND PAGE NUMBERS

- Page numbers can be entered in headings and footings, using the # symbol as described in the preceding chapter.
- WordStar provides a default or preset page number location at the bottom center of each page. To suppress the printing of this page number, use the command .OP.
- Suppress the printing of page numbers in an already-entered heading or footing by typing a new .HE or .FO command, omitting the # symbol.
- Reinstate the default page numbering after an .OP command by entering .PN.
- Reinstate page numbering in a heading or footing by typing a new .HE or .FO command which includes the # symbol.
- Change the position of the default page number with the command code .PC n, in which n is the appropriate column number.
- Change the page number itself by entering .PN n, with n the revised number.
- WordStar interprets dot commands in order. If two commands cancel or reverse each other, WordStar obeys the last-entered command. Because the command .PN can be used both to set a new page number and to reinstate the default number, it should not be listed after or below the .OP command.

QUIZ

1. How many ways can you think of to cause page numbers to print at the center bottom of each page?
2. What is the command for suppressing the printing of the default page number?
3. What is another way to cancel the default page number?
4. What does .PN 45 mean?
5. What does this sequence mean?

```
.HE Summer Verses
.PC 65
.PN 28
```

QUIZ ANSWERS

1. a. Leave the default page numbering undisturbed.
   b. Enter .FO #, with # centered on the line.
   c. Enter .PC 32, which positions the default number at column 32, in the center of a 65-column line.
2. .OP
3. Enter .FO without a # symbol.
4. Begin numbering the pages from page 45 at this point.
5. "Summer Verses" appears at the upper-left corner of each page; the page number prints at lower right; pages are numbered from page 28, beginning at the dot command's page.

31

Formatting Text with Dot Commands

Daisy wheel or incremental printers provide an almost infinite number of formatting possibilities, because they offer, in addition to different type styles, fractional readjustments of line height, character width, subscripts, and superscripts. An accomplished WordStar user can reset a document in so many different ways that the results look like dozens of unrelated originals.

While those using dot matrix or nonincremental printers have fewer variations to work with, text formatting dot commands still create a variety of shapes, sizes, and configurations in a document's final printing.

WORDSTAR'S PRESET OR DEFAULT PAGE

Before studying the individual dot commands for changing the position and format of text on a page, become familiar with the default values WordStar provides.

On the preset or default page:

- The LINE HEIGHT is set for 1/6 inch, so that 6 lines = 1 vertical inch.
- The PAPER LENGTH is set for 66 lines. Combined with the preset line height described above, this means that the preset page is 11 inches long, or standard stationery size. Paper length is measured in lines, not inches, but you can convert lines to inches by dividing the number of lines by the number of lines per inch.
- The TOP MARGIN, the empty space allowed between the top of the page and the first line of text, is three lines. If a heading is entered, it appears on the top margin's first line.
- The BOTTOM MARGIN is the blank area at the bottom of the page between the last line of text and the end of the paper. The preset bottom margin is eight lines. In standard or default use, the page number appears on the third line of that margin, with two lines separating text from the page number.
- The HEADING MARGIN is the amount of top margin left between heading and text when a heading is entered with .HE. The normal heading margin is two lines. The heading margin is contained within the top margin.
- The FOOTING MARGIN is the amount of space between the last line of text and the footing or the default page number. The normal footing margin is two lines. The footing margin is contained within the bottom margin.
- The PAGE OFFSET COLUMN is the column to which the left margin is indented before printing. WordStar presets the left margin eight columns or spaces from the left edge of the paper.
- The preset right margin is at column 65, which is normally 12 columns or spaces from the paper's right edge. You don't need a dot command to change the position of this margin because you have^OR, the right margin setting command. However, the right margin's printed position depends on the left margin's printed location, and the left margin's printed position can be changed with a dot command. Note that this revised left margin is not the left margin on the screen; rather, it's the position of the left margin during printing.
- The preset or default character width is 10 characters per inch (10 cpi). Your daisy wheel may print 12 or 15 cpi instead. You can change character width with dot

commands, and narrow characters give correspondingly more characters to the line. Similarly, you can use a dot command to set very wide spaces between letters; this creates fewer characters or spaces per line.

CHANGING LINE HEIGHT

Line height can be changed on a daisy wheel or incremental printer. The IBM Matrix Printer cannot change line height. WordStar's *L*ine *H*eight command is .LH n.

Line height is measured in 48ths of an inch, meaning that your dot command for changing the line height is entered as a number representing 48ths of an inch. The default value is 8, or 8/48 inch (1/6 inch).

For example, the default line height would be set as .LH 8. The default value (1/6 inch) is adequate for normal 10-pitch and 12-pitch typing, especially if you use double spacing.

However, if you have a 15-pitch printwheel, whose characters are very small, you'll want the lines closer together. A line height setting of .LH 6 positions the lines 6/48 or 1/8 inch apart.

You may prepare a single-spaced document in which you want extra white showing between the lines. For example, some technical societies require that authors of papers accepted for publication prepare their own camera-ready copy on special mats. When a single-spaced document is photo-reduced, it can be hard to read unless extra space is allowed between lines. A line height setting of .LH 9 provides an extra 1/48 inch, which may be all that's needed.

Be sure to enter the .LH command at the beginning of your file. If you change line height in the middle of a document, page break lines will be inaccurate. But enter .LH last of all the dot commands, for reasons you'll see in a moment.

If you're used to a typewriter that offers half-line spacing, so that you can set the machine for single spacing, 1 1/2 line spacing, double spacing, 2 1/2 line spacing, etc., you can achieve the same effect with a line height adjustment. Set the line height at .LH 4, which is half the normal setting. Set the line spacing at ^OS2 (double spacing) for what will now be single spacing. Because your lines are twice as close together as usual, you have to double the space between them to get normal single spacing. To create 1 1/2 line spacing, set ^OS 3, the command for triple spacing. Your double-space command is now ^OS4, etc. If you use ^OS1, the single space command, your lines will be very close together. Experiment with your different daisy wheels to find the line spacing you prefer.

Here is a table showing the number of lines per inch created by different line height settings:

Dot Command	Lines per Inch
.LH 1	48.0
.LH 2	24.0
.LH 3	16.0
.LH 4	12.0
.LH 5	9.6

Dot Command	Lines per Inch
.LH 6	8.0
.LH 7	6.8
.LH 8	6.0
.LH 9	5.3
.LH 10	4.8

Line height commands can be entered in any size, but the settings you're most likely to need are those between 4 and 10.

ENTER LINE HEIGHT REVISION LAST

WordStar doesn't measure length in inches; it measures length in lines. The handy rule of thumb that says six lines equal 1 inch is true only if the line setting is the default or preset value at the time of an entry. If you change the line height afterward, the 6 lines = 1 inch equation will remain true for all dot commands entered above or before the .LH line height revision.

For example, the top margin heading will be measured differently, depending on whether its dot command comes before or after the line height dot command. If you enter a top margin heading of six lines, it would normally measure one inch. If you change the line height *after* entering the top margin, it will still measure 1 inch. But if you enter the line height change first and *then* the top margin command, WordStar will interpret this margin in the new line size, and it won't be one inch.

Thus, if you want to measure top and bottom margins, paper length and heading/footing positions in inches, while taking advantage of the simple 1 inch = 6 lines equation, set any line height adjustment last.

Line height commands are ignored by nonincremental printers, but if you're using a matrix printer to prepare the draft of a document which will be printed in final form on a daisy wheel printer, enter the line height commands to set correct page break lines.

CHANGING PAPER LENGTH

WordStar's paper length command is set in lines. The dot command is .PL n (*P*aper *L*ength), with n representing the number of lines on the page or form in use.

The default or preset command is .PL 66, which is 11 inches long. (6 lines = 1 inch, so 66 lines = 11 inches.)

If you set a .PL command ahead of any line height command, continue to use the 6 lines = 1 inch equation. Note that the page length is described in the total number of lines from top to bottom, not the number that actually print or that are available for text entry.

If you're using legal-size paper, which is 14 inches long, set your paper length at .PL 84.

If you're using a form of some other length, compute the proper dot command by multiplying the number of inches by 6. Remember that as long as you set the line height command last, your paper length command can be computed by this equation (1 inch = 6 lines), regardless of the line height change you make later.

However, if you prefer, you can always set the line height command first and then compute the paper length by multiplying the length of your form (number of inches) by the number of lines per inch you are going to print. While this procedure is simple enough, especially if you use a pocket calculator, most WordStar users will find the consistent 1 inch = 6 lines equation convenient. If you are using the IBM Matrix Printer, you will have to use the 1 inch = 6 lines equation because you cannot change line height.

If you're using an incremental printer, the equation you use depends on where you place the line height dot command relative to the page length dot command. Use the 1 inch = 6 lines equation if .PL preceeds .LH; if you enter .LH before .PL, you must multiply the length of your page (in inches) by the number of lines per inch in order to determine the proper .PL dot command.

The table below shows page length dot commands based on the preset or default line height of six lines per inch:

Paper Length	Page Length Command
3 inches	.PL 18
4 inches	.PL 24
5 inches	.PL 30
6 inches	.PL 36
7 inches	.PL 42
8 inches	.PL 48
9 inches	.PL 54
11 inches	.PL 66
12 inches	.PL 72
13 inches	.PL 78
14 inches	.PL 84
15 inches	.PL 90
16 inches	.PL 96
17 inches	.PL 102
18 inches	.PL 108
19 inches	.PL 114
20 inches	.PL 120

If you plan to vary the line height, place your line height command after, not before, the page length command. If you remember to do this, the table above will be accurate. If you enter the line height command first, the conversions will change accordingly.

Some non-daisy printers use a permanent line spacing of eight lines to the inch instead of six lines to the inch. If this is your situation, set the dot command .PL 88 at the beginning of your file when you use 11-inch paper. You won't be able to use the table above. Instead, multiply the number of inches (page length) by 8 to get the proper .PL setting for different forms and paper lengths. The IBM Matrix Printer uses the previously described line height of six lines to the inch.

CHANGING THE TOP MARGIN

WordStar presets a top margin of three empty lines. If you enter a heading, the heading appears on the first of these three lines. You can create a larger or smaller top margin with .MT, the top margin (*M*argin at *T*op) dot command. The default or preset margin is three lines, which would be entered .MT 3 if you were setting it yourself.

The number of lines available for text on any page is the number of lines on the page less the number of lines allowed for the top margin and the number of lines allowed for the bottom margin. The default or preset page is 66 lines long, three of which are occupied by the top margin and eight of which are occupied by the bottom margin. This leaves 55 lines for text.

To eliminate the top margin completely, enter .MT 0; to make it two lines deeper than usual, use .MT 5.

CHANGING THE HEADING MARGIN

The heading margin is the amount of space left between the heading and the first line of text. WordStar's *H*eading *M*argin command is .HM, followed by a number.

In preset or default use, the top margin is three lines deep, the heading (if any) is printed on the first of those lines, and two lines remain as the heading margin. Note that the heading margin is contained within the top margin.

The default heading margin is, as mentioned, two lines. You can increase this value, but you can't decrease it by much. Its upper limit is defined by the top margin. If you enter a heading margin larger than the top margin, WordStar will leave a heading margin of one line less than the top margin.

If you want your heading set down a bit from the top of the page, set a larger than normal top margin.

CHANGING THE BOTTOM MARGIN

In default or standard use, WordStar prints your page number at the bottom of the page, two lines below the last line of text. The bottom margin normally extends eight lines below the last line of text, and the page number or footing line is within this margin. The dot command for setting the bottom margin is .MB (*M*argin at *B*ottom), followed by the number of margin lines you wish to have. If you were to set the default margin yourself, the command would be .MB 8. To eliminate the bottom margin, enter .MB 0. To make it deeper, enter a number larger than the standard 8 lines, such as 10 or 12.

CHANGING THE FOOTING MARGIN

The footing margin is the amount of space between the last line of text and the page number/footing line. This area is contained within the bottom margin. In preset or default use, WordStar sets a bottom margin of eight lines in which the page number or footing is printed on the third line below the last line of text; two empty lines separate this footing from the last line of text, so the default footing margin is two lines.

WordStar's *F*ooting *M*argin command is .FM, followed by a number.

If you were setting these default values yourself, you would enter .MB 8 for the bottom margin and .FM 2 for the footing margin. As in the heading margin described above, you cannot have a larger footing margin than bottom margin.

REVISING THE LEFT MARGIN'S PRINTING POSITION

When printing, WordStar normally indents the left margin (column 1) a total of eight spaces from the left edge of the paper. If you're working with a special form that has different margins, or if you want to set a wide document and stay on the paper, you can adjust this allowance. The dot command is .PO, for *P*age *O*ffset, followed by a number. To set the text as far left as possible, use zero: .PO 0. The default value, as mentioned, is eight spaces. To indent farther to the right than usual, use a larger number, such as .PO 10, .PO 12, etc. If you're using the default or preset character width, as for a 10-pitch printing element, every 10 spaces equals 1 inch. Note that if you change the character width before entering this command, horizontal measurements change accordingly.

Example: Your IBM Matrix Printer accommodates paper and forms up to 8 1/2 inches in width. If you set a line of text that is 75 to 80 columns wide, the printer brings overrun letters down to the next line in a choppy, unsatisfactory arrangement. Where does the printer deposit these extra letters? In the left margin area. In order to print an 80-wide document, you can enter .PO 0, which eliminates those eight unused spaces, and text begins close to the paper's left edge. Now the printer will accommodate a line up to 80 characters wide, so you can set the right margin at 80 and type knowing your text will fit on the paper without unsightly printer adjustments.

CHANGING CHARACTER WIDTH

If yours is an incremental printer, you can alter the amount of space allowed for each character on the line by using dot commands. As mentioned in the chapter on print controls, one way to shift between the two most frequently used print sizes (10-pitch and 12-pitch) is to use the print controls ^PA and ^PN. (These commands do not work for the IBM Matrix Printer.)

The *C*haracter *W*idth dot command, .CW n, gives a larger variety of settings, ranging from very tiny (30 characters per inch) to very large (5 cpi).

As most daisy wheels come in three sizes, these are the commands you may need most often:

.CW 10 12 cpi (can also be set with ^PA)
.CW 12 10 cip (the default value)
.CW 8 15 cpi (very small type)

Where did these numbers come from?

WordStar defines character width in increments of 1/120 inch. Thus, if you want 12 characters per inch, each character should measure 1/12 inch in width, or 10/120. That's why the command for 12 characters per inch is .CW 10.

This chart gives five character width commands and the right margins you would normally use on a page 8 1/2 inches wide.

Dot Command	Pitch (cpi)	Set Right Margin
.CW 8	15	99
.CW 10	12	79
.CW 12	10	65
.CW 15	8	53
.CW 20	6	40

You don't have to change print wheels to make use of character width dot commands. A slightly wider-than-normal spacing leaves a bit more space showing; a slightly closer arrangement of letters creates a different effect.

REVIEW: FORMATTING WITH DOT COMMANDS

- A document's line height can be varied on incremental printers with the use of .LH n, in which n gives the actual height of each line in 48ths of an inch. The default value is 8, or 8/48 inch (1/6 inch). Higher numbers generate more white space between lines; lower numbers place lines closer together.
- Line height revision commands should be entered last so that WordStar's standard 6 lines = 1 inch equation remains correct for dot commands entered above the line height revision.
- Paper length is measured in lines. WordStar's preset page is 11 inches long (66 lines). To change the form length, enter .PL n, with n representing the number of lines.
- The top margin is the area separating the top of your page/form from the first line of text. WordStar's default margin is three lines. The top margin command is .MT n, with n the number of blank lines measured from top.
- The top margin contains the heading margin, which is the number of blank lines separating the heading from the first line of text. This value is usually 2, but it can be changed with the dot command .HM n.
- The heading margin is contained within the top margin.
- WordStar's bottom margin (the blank area separating the last line of text from the bottom of the page/form) is normally eight lines. This can be changed with .MB n, with n representing the number of blank lines.
- The footing margin separates the last line of text from the footing, which normally consists of the current page number. In standard use, this footing margin is two empty lines. To change the footing margin, enter .FM n, with n the number of blank lines.
- The footing margin is contained within the bottom margin.
- Unless you change this condition with a dot command, WordStar causes the printer to indent eight spaces from the left edge of paper before printing the left margin. To change this value, use .PO n, the page offset command, with n representing the number of blank spaces separating the left edge from printing margin.
- WordStar's normal character width is 10 cpi (characters per inch). You can change character width on incremental printers. The character width is measured in 120ths of an inch; the command .CW n changes character width, with n representing the number of 120ths of an inch needed for each character. The default value is .CW 12 because 12/120 inch = 10 characters per inch.

QUIZ

1. How is line height measured?
2. What is the line height dot command?

3. Why should this command be entered last?
4. How is page length measured?
5. What is the page length dot command, and how would you set WordStar's default page length using it?
6. How would you set the commands for a page measuring 14 inches in length on which lines should appear 1/8 inch apart?
7. What are the top and heading margins?
8. How would you set the commands for a heading margin of four lines in a top margin of 10 lines?
9. What are the bottom and footing margins? Set the commands for a footing margin of three lines in a bottom margin of nine lines.
10. What is the command for printing the text's left margin five lines from the paper's left edge?
11. What is the default character width? How would you set it with a dot command?
12. What command would you use for a 15-pitch printwheel?

QUIZ ANSWERS

1. Line height is measured in 48ths of an inch, with the preset or default value 8/48 (1/6) inch.
2. .LH n, with n the number of 48ths of an inch.
3. If entered last, the .LH command does not interfere with the equation 6 lines = 1 inch, which is convenient for computing other dot commands.
4. Page length is measured in lines, usually six per inch (using WordStar's default or preset line height).
5. The page length command is .PL n, with n the number of lines on a page. The default value, 11 inches, would be set .PL 66 (based on 11 inches × 6 lines per inch).
6. .PL 84
   .LH 6
7. The top margin consists of blank space between the top of a page and the first line of text; it contains the heading margin, which separates the heading from the first line of text. Both are measured in lines.
8. .MT 10
   .HM 4
9. The bottom margin separates the last line of text from the bottom of the page; it contains the footing margin, which separates the last line of text from the footing. Both are measured in lines. To set a footing margin of three lines in a bottom margin of nines lines, enter:

   ```
   .MB 9
   .FM 3
   ```

10. .PO 5

11. WordStar's default character width is 10 cpi (characters per inch). The dot command .CW n measures character width in 120ths of an inch, so the default value is 12/120 (10 characters per inch means that each character occupies 1/10 inch; 1/10 = 12/120), or .CW 12.
12. .CW 8

32

Miscellaneous Dot Commands and Dot Command Review

If you do not have an incremental printer, you will not be able to use some of the dot commands introduced here, but you should at least read their descriptions so you will understand WordStar's capabilities. This chapter also reviews the dot commands you have already worked with.

MICROJUSTIFICATION ON/OFF

As word wrap spreads words across a line, microjustification makes the distribution of letters and spaces as even as possible. Letters are not microjustified on your screen, which is why screen spacing is often uneven. Not all printers microjustify, but if yours does, you can turn this feature on and off with dot commands. The IBM Matrix Printer does not microjustify; it disregards this command.

Microjustification is on by default. To turn it off, enter the dot command .UJ 0; to turn it back on, enter .UJ 1. Alternately, enter .UJ OFF and .UJ ON. These commands will be easier to remember if you think of the J in *J*ustification.

Microjustification OFF causes words to print exactly as they appear on the screen. If you are entering a column or table and want to prevent the accidental addition of soft spaces during future editing, use this dot command.

Microjustification applies only to incremental (daisy wheel-type) printers. The command has no effect if entered at a nonincremental printer.

BIDIRECTIONAL PRINTING ON/OFF

Your printer prints from left to right and from right to left, making it fast as well as efficient. In some cases, turning *B*idirectional *P*rinting off produces a better quality output. This is especially true whenever vertical lines are being printed.

To print only from left to right, enter .BP 0 (or .BP OFF). To reinstate both-direction printing, use .BP 1 (or .BP ON).

The IBM Matrix Printer disregards the .BP dot command. It always prints in both directions: from left to right and from right to left.

CHANGING THE SUBSCRIPT/SUPERSCRIPT ROLL

Daisy wheel printers roll the carriage a fraction of an inch up or down before printing subscripts and superscripts. Nonincremental printers, such as the IBM Matrix Printer, set the subscript a full line down and the superscript a full line up, which is a good reason for double spacing or even triple spacing a report featuring such notations.

Daisy wheels create a more polished document, and if the preset line shift on your incremental printer isn't to your liking, you can make your printout even more refined. WordStar measures its subscript/superscript roll in 48ths of an inch. The default value is 3 (3/48 inch). To change the carriage roll, enter any number after the dot command .SR, which stands for *S*ubscript (or *S*uperscript) *R*oll. .SR 3 would set the default value; .SR 4 would move the subscripts and superscripts a bit farther from the line of text; .SR 2 would print them closer, etc.

ENTERING A NONPRINTING SCREEN REMINDER OR NOTATION

To place in the file an on-screen reminder which will not print should you forget to remove it, use two dots. The command ".." will not print, nor will anything in its line. That's why you used this dot command when entering mid-text ruler lines in the section on tabular formatting.

WordStar will interpret any "unofficial" or undefined dot command the same way, but when WordStar encounters a dot command with no meaning, the ? flag stays on-screen at the far right. "Official" or recognized dot commands, including .., remove the question mark at far right.

The WordStar manual lists an alternate dot command for entering a nonprinting comment: .IG. for "*IG*nore this line."

ACCIDENTAL ERRORS

This brings us back to the business of accidental errors. Question mark flags (?) at the right warn of unauthorized dot commands, but none of the following column 1 entries will generate a ? warning:

.Pardon me.
.Help!
.Follow us.
.Open the door.
.Pneumonia isn't fun.
.Ignorance is bliss.

These are WordStar's commands for setting a new page, setting a heading, setting a footing, omitting default page numbers, reinstating default page numbers, and inserting a non-printing screen comment, neatly hidden in a few dot-preceded sentences.

None of the lines will print. WordStar never prints a line containing a dot in column 1.

To make sure you don't have an accidentally entered dot lurking in the first space of any line, use the special find character you met on page 175 after ^QF, the find command. With the cursor at the beginning of your file, enter:

^QF ^PN.ESC

This means: Find any dot immediately following a hard or soft return.

The cursor will stop at every authorized dot command, and it will find the unexpected ones, too. Use ^L to repeat the command until you reach the end of the file.

PROOFREADING DOT COMMANDS

Because properly set dot commands will not normally print, their proofreading can be inconvenient. But there is a way to print the exact contents of your file, including all its dot commands. The printer will not interpret these commands; that is, it will not set the conditions described by the dot commands. Instead, it lists each one as entered.

The option to use when printing your file is a "Y" or Yes response to the SUPPRESS PAGE FORMATTING question offered by the P Print command.

The SUPPRESS PAGE FORMATTING option has no top or bottom margins, no page offsets, no headings or footings, no page numbers, and no separation between pages. However, this option does not usually interfere with the interpretation of print control characters, so underlined words will be underlined, boldface words darkened, etc.

ORDER OF DOT COMMANDS

For best results, use a checklist as you prepare dot commands to enter them in an effective order.

If you are using the IBM Matrix Printer, see Chapter Thirty-Three, which reviews only those dot commands you can use. The following list assumes yours is an incremental printer.

While parts of the sequence can be rearranged, here is a good general order for dot command entry:

	.PL n	Page Length
	.MT n	Top Margin
If using heading	.HM n	Heading Margin
	.HE	Heading
	.MB n	Bottom Margin
If using footing	.FM n	Footing Margin
	.FO	Footing
	.CW n	Character Width
	.PC n	Default Page Number Position
	.SR n	Subscript Roll
	.PO n	Page Offset at Left
	.UJ	Justification
	.BP	Bidirectional Print
	.PN n	Revised Page Number
	.OP	Omit Default Page Number
	.LH	Line Height

Note: The commands for changing page length, top margin, bottom margin, and line height should go at the beginning of your file. Any of these commands entered after text will produce this warning message:

```
PUT AT FILE BEGINNING FOR CORRECT PAGE BREAK DISPLAY        ?
```

DOT COMMAND SUMMARY

Note: n represents number entered after command; column at right shows units.

Command	Function	Default Value	Measured In
.PA	PAGE BREAK		
.CP n	CONDITIONAL PAGE BREAK		LINES
.LH n	LINE HEIGHT	6 PER INCH (8/48)	1/48 INCH
.CW n	CHARACTER WIDTH	10 CHAR PER INCH (12/120)	1/120 INCH
.PL n	PAGE LENGTH	11 INCHES (66 LINES)	LINES
.MT n	TOP MARGIN	3	LINES
.MB n	BOTTOM MARGIN	8	LINES
.HM n	HEADING MARGIN	2	LINES
.FM n	FOOTING MARGIN	2	LINES
.PO n	PAGE OFFSET/LEFT	8	COLUMNS
.PC n	PAGE # POSITION	CENTERED	COLUMNS
.HE	HEADING	(BLANK)	
.FO	FOOTING	(PAGE NUMBER)	
.OP	OMIT BOTTOM PAGE NUMBER		
.PN	REINSTATE BOTTOM PAGE NUMBER		
.PN n	SET NEW PAGE NUMBER		
.SR n	SUBSCRIPT ROLL	3/48 INCH	1/48 INCH
.UJ	MICROJUSTIFY	ON	0 (OFF) 1 (ON)
.BP	BIDIRECTIONAL PRINT	ON	0 (OFF) 1 (ON)
..	IGNORE COMMENT/NO PRINT		
.IG	IGNORE COMMENT/NO PRINT		

REVIEW: DOT COMMANDS ON-SCREEN

One of the help commands listed in WordStar's Help Menu is ^JD, which brings a screen message regardless of the help level in use. This entry generates a six-part review of both dot commands and print control characters.

See page 309 for the text of WordStar's ^JD screen message.

QUIZ

1. What is the proper way to enter a dot command?
2. What happens at the screen's far right when you enter the first dot?
3. What commands can you enter for starting a new page at the cursor's position? What is the difference between these two commands?

4. How is the length of a page defined by WordStar?
5. How is the amount of space available for text determined?
6. List the commands for changing:
   a. Line height
   b. Paper Length
   c. Top margin
   d. Bottom margin
   e. Heading margin
   f. Footing margin
7. What is the difference between the top margin and the heading margin? Between the bottom margin and the footing margin?
8. What normally prints on the footing line?
9. How do you set a heading? What can go in a heading? What are the heading options?
10. How do you set a footing? List the footing options.
11. How do you turn off and then reinstate the automatic numbering of pages at the bottom of the page?
12. How can you reposition the page number at the bottom of the page?
13. What dot command changes the character width? What is the default or preset character width?
14. How can you change the amount of space shifted for subscripts and superscripts?
15. What is microjustification? How do you turn it on and off? What is the default position?
16. What is bidirectional printing? What happens when you turn it off? Give the commands for on and off.
17. Why is it important to enter the line height command last if you are changing line height?
18. Describe what will happen if these commands are entered at far left at the top of a file:

```
.PL 84
.MT 5
.HM 3
.HE Recipes From Old Virginia
.MB 6
.FM 4
.FO^K                                          #
.PO 10
.BP 0
```

19. Describe what will happen if these commands are entered in the middle of a document:

```
.PA
.PN 47
```

20. What characters will not normally print in a heading or footing? How can you make these characters print?

QUIZ ANSWERS

1. Enter the dot in column 1, the two-letter code in columns 2 and 3, then skip a space before entering the number or text.
2. A question mark flag (?) appears. It vanishes as soon as you complete an authorized or recognized dot command.
3. .PA begins a new page unconditionally; .CP n begins a new line if the number of lines needed (n) exceeds the number remaining on the page.
4. Page length is defined by lines, not inches. If the page length command is entered before a line height change, the default conversion is 1 inch = 6 lines. The standard 11-inch page is therefore 66 lines long; this is the default value.
5. Space available for text depends on the top margin, bottom margin, offset left margin, and right margin.
6. a. .LH n b. .PL n c. .MT n d. .MB n e. .HM n f. .FM n
7. The top margin is the distance from top of the page to the first line of text. The heading margin is the distance from the heading line to the first line of text. The heading margin is contained within the top margin. The bottom margin is the distance from the last line of text to the bottom of the page; the footing margin is the distance from the last line of text to the footing line. The footing margin is contained within the bottom margin.
8. The default page number usually prints in the center of the footing line.
9. Set a heading with .HE . Text or page number or both can go on the heading line. Options include #. to mark page number; ^PK, a print control command, to alternate the page number position between # and the print control character; and \, to make the symbols \ and # print in a heading.
10. The footing command is .FO. Options are the same as for heading commands.
11. Turn off the default page numbering with .OP; reinstate with .PN .
12. Use .PC n, with n representing the desired column number.
13. .CW changes the character width. Character width is measured in units of 1/120 inch. The default or preset character width is 10 characters per inch, or 12/120 (.CW 12).
14. Use .SR, the subscript roll command. Enter a number representing the superscript/subscript printing position above/below the text line, measured in 48ths of an inch. The default position is 3/48 inch, or .SR 3 .
15. Microjustification spreads words evenly across the page. Use .UJ 0 or .UJ OFF to turn off; .UJ 1 or .UJ ON turns it on. This function is on by default.
16. The printer normally prints from right to left and from left to right. Turning bidirectional printing off slows the printer and may improve its output, especially the printing of vertical lines. .BP 0 or .BP OFF turns this function off; .BP 1 or .BP ON turns it back on.
17. If line height is entered last, the 1 inch = 6 lines rule makes it easy to compute other dot command settings. If the line height is entered first, the equation must be recomputed.
18. On a legal-sized (14-inch) page, the heading ("Recipes From Old Virginia") appears on the second line of the page, three lines above the first line of text.

(The heading itself occupies the second line, and three blank lines separate it from the text.) The page number appears in the lower-right corner of odd-numbered pages and the lower-left corner of even-numbered pages, or away from the binding. Page numbers are printed on the fifth line below the last line of text, beneath a four-line margin, or one line above the bottom of the page. The left margin begins 10 spaces from the left edge of the paper. The printer will print in one direction only.

19. A new page will begin at the cursor's line and the new page will be page 47, regardless of its position in the file.

20. # and \ do not normally print in a heading or footing. The command \ means "print next character," so \\ prints one \ and \# prints one #.

33

Dot Command and Print Control Review for the IBM Matrix Printer

As several chapters have called to your attention, WordStar offers a number of features that cannot be used with the IBM Matrix Printer.

This is because the matrix printer is a nonincremental printer. Its carriage cannot shift up or down a fraction of an inch to position subscripts and superscripts; nor can the carriage accommodate changes in line height or character width; nor are letters "micro-justified" or spread evenly across the page. The printout you receive from your IBM Matrix Printer matches your screen text's distribution of words and spaces across a line.

Should you acquire a daisy wheel or thimble printer to use with your IBM Personal Computer, the previous chapter reviews the dot commands you will then find convenient.

For now, you should concentrate on the commands your printer will accommodate. This chapter reviews not only the dot commands you can use but the print control commands as well.

PRINT CONTROL COMMANDS AND THE IBM MATRIX PRINTER

In Chapters 15 and 16 you met the ^P-prefix commands, called print controls because they control the action of your printer.

Here are the print controls you can use with the IBM Matrix Printer.

Controls Placed Before and After Featured Text

F5 Underline
^PS Alternate Underline Command
F6 Boldface
^PD Doublestrike
^PX Strikeout or Crossout
^PV Subscript
^PT Superscript

Text in which subscripts or superscripts appear must be set with double spacing or triple spacing. If you use single spacing with ^PV or ^PT, the printer will ignore your command.

Controls Placed Between Characters/Lines to Overprint

^PH Overprint Next Character
^PM Overprint Next Line
^P@ Overprint Next Line (Alternate)

Additional Print Controls

^PO Non-Break Space (Non-Expanding)
^PK Alternates with # Position in Heading or Footing Dot Command
^PC Printer Pause (Causes Printer to Stop Before Printing Line Containing ^PC Command)

The IBM Matrix Printer will interpret ^PB, the regular WordStar boldface command, as triple-strike. It will not respond to the print controls ^PF (phantom space), ^PG (phantom rubout), ^PA (alternate pitch), ^PN (resume standard pitch), or ^PY (change ribbon color).

DOT COMMANDS

Command	Function	Default Value	Measured In
.PA	PAGE BREAK		
.CP n	CONDITIONAL PAGE BREAK		LINES
.PL n	PAGE (FORM) LENGTH	66	LINES
.MT n	TOP MARGIN	3	LINES
.MB n	BOTTOM MARGIN	8	LINES
.HM n	HEADING MARGIN	2	LINES
.FM n	FOOTING MARGIN	2	LINES
.HE	HEADING		
.FO	FOOTING	(PAGE NUMBER)	
.PO n	PAGE OFFSET AT LEFT	8	COLUMNS
.PC n	PAGE # POSITION	BOTTOM CENTER	COLUMNS
.OP	OMIT BOTTOM PAGE NUMBER		
.PN	REINSTATE BOTTOM PAGE NUMBER		
.PN n	SET NEW PAGE NUMBER (DEFAULT, HEADING OR FOOTING)		
..	IGNORE SCREEN COMMENT/NO PRINT		
.IG	IGNORE SCREEN COMMENT/NO PRINT		

The IBM Matrix Printer will not obey dot commands for changing line height, character width, or subscript roll. The dot commands for turning microjustification and bidirectional print on and off will not work, either.

With the .PO (page offset) dot command, you can shift the left margin's printing position to the paper's far left edge; this allows you to set the right margin to column 80 without having text lines broken by the printer. .PO 0 sets the left margin as far left as possible; .PO 8 is the default position. This means that in default or standard use, your text is indented eight spaces before printing.

See Chapter 35 for a Dot Command Worksheet designed for your printer.

34

A Dot Command Worksheet: Incremental Printer

No matter how much WordStar experience you may have, setting the dot commands for an unusual form or strangely shaped page can be a time-consuming project.

The section that follows can be photocopied for your convenience.

Go through the worksheet, completing those categories which apply. When finished, fill out the Dot Command Checklist, then enter dot commands in order at the beginning of your file.

The preset or default page has this configuration:

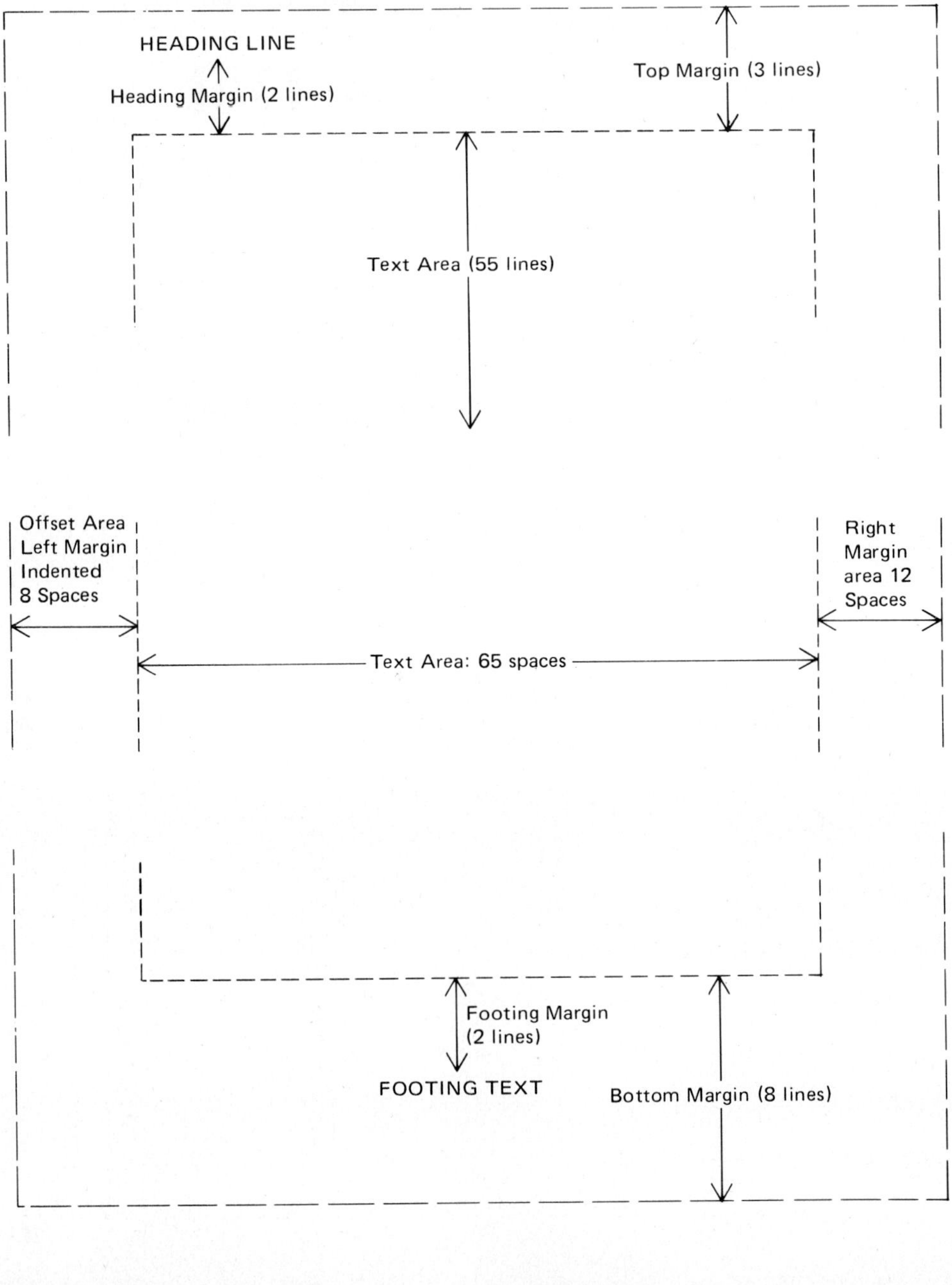

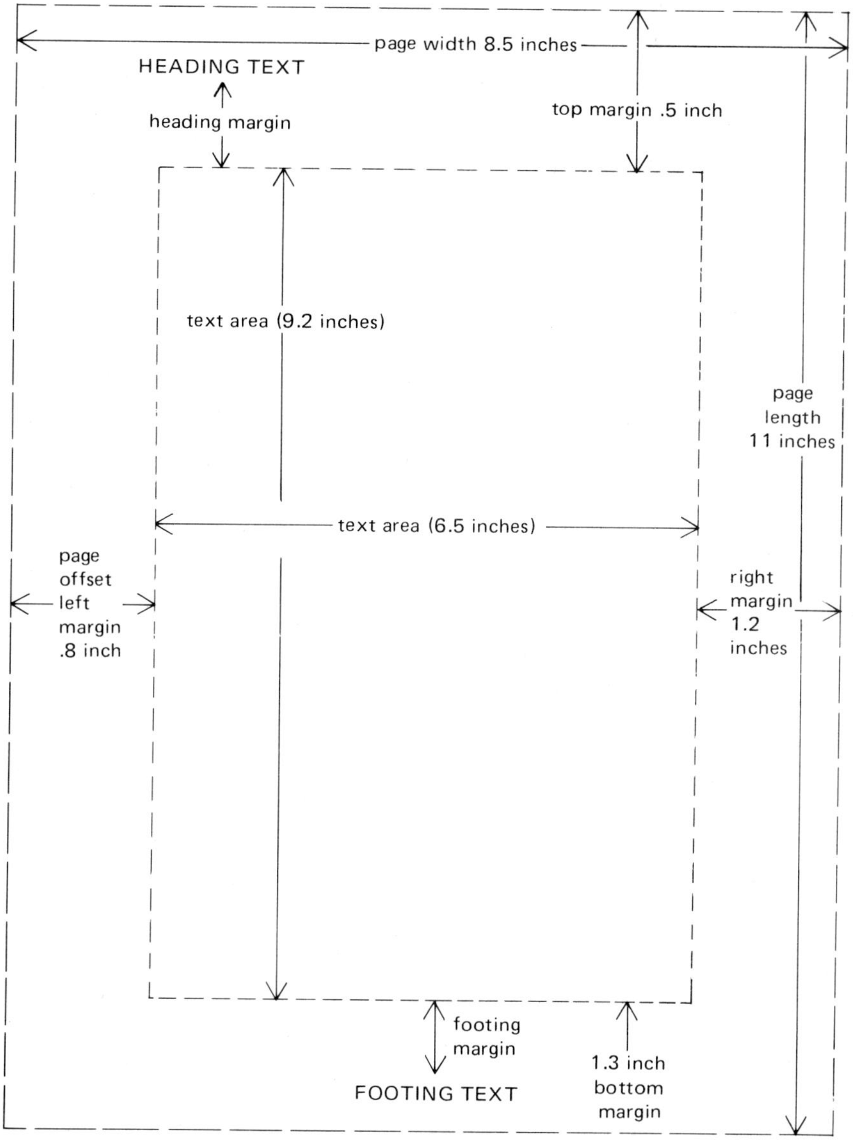

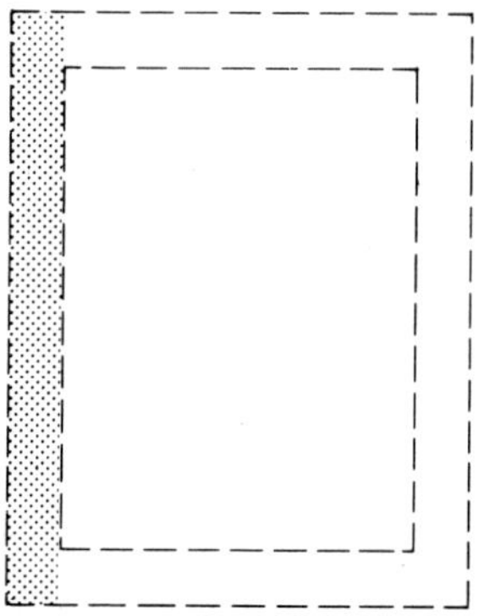

PART ONE: LENGTH OF FORM

A. How long is your page/form?

___ inches × 6 lines per inch = ___ lines

Page length dot command: .PL ___

B. How long is the text portion of your page/form, not counting any heading or footing? (If your text area depends on fixed top and bottom margins, subtract the needed margins from the paper length to determine the area available for text entry.)

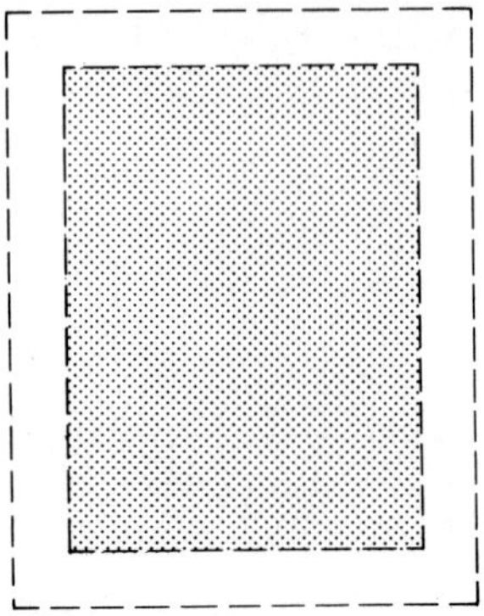

____ inches × 6 lines per inch = ____ lines for text.

C. Subtract (B) from (A) to determine space available for top/bottom margins.

(A) ____ lines
– (B) ____ lines

Total margin space: ____ lines

D. How much space do you want separating the top of your page/form from the first line of regular text?

- 1 inch = 6 lines
- 2/3 inch = 4 lines
- 1/2 inch = 3 lines
- 1/3 inch = 2 lines

Top margin dot command: .MT ____

E. How much space do you want separating the bottom of your page/form from the last line of regular text?

Bottom margin dot command: .MB ___

Note: (D) + (E) should = (C).

F. If using a heading, how many lines do you want separating the heading from your first line of regular text?

Heading margin dot command: .HM ___

Note: The heading margin is contained within the top margin.

Top Margin	.MT ___
(minus) Heading Margin	– .HM ___
	– 1 (line occupied by heading)
Lines between heading and top of page →	_______

G. Heading dot command: .HE ______________________________

Note: If you do not enter .HM and/or .MT, WordStar will use these default values: .HM 2 and .MT 3.

H. If using a footing, how many lines do you want separating the footing from your last line of regular text?

Footing margin dot command: .FM ___

Note: The footing margin is contained within the bottom margin.

Bottom Margin	.MB ___
(minus) Footing Margin	– .FM ___
	– 1 (line occupied by footing)
Lines between footing and bottom of page →	_______

I. Footing dot command: .FO ______________________________

Note: The default footing consists of the current page number, printed at the bottom center of each page. This page number normally appears two lines below the last line of regular text. If you use the default page number or enter a new footing without using .FM, WordStar uses the default value .FM 2. The default bottom margin is .MB 8.

J. To determine the number of lines available for text entry after a line height revision, multiply the number of text inches by n, the number of lines per inch.

___ inches × n ___ = ___ lines available for text.

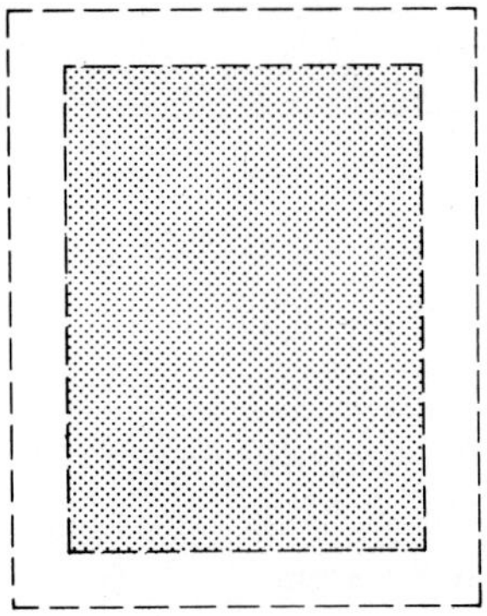

.LH 10 = 4.8 lines per inch
.LH 8 = 6 lines per inch
.LH 6 = 8 lines per inch
.LH 4 = 12 lines per inch

Line height dot command: .LH ___

PART TWO: WIDTH OF FORM

A. How wide is your form/page?

___ inches

Will you use regular 10-pitch type?

___ 10 cpi (.CW 12)

Or will you use an alternate character width?

___ 12 cpi (.CW 10)
___ 15 cpi (.CW 8)
(other) ___ cpi (.CW n)

Character width dot command: .CW ___

B. How much space do you want the printer to indent from the left edge of your paper/form before printing the left margin of your text?

___ inches indentation × ___ cpi = ___ columns/spaces

Note: The default indentation is 8 columns/spaces.
Page offset dot command: .PO ___

C. How wide is your text?

___ inches × ___ cpi = ___ columns/spaces.

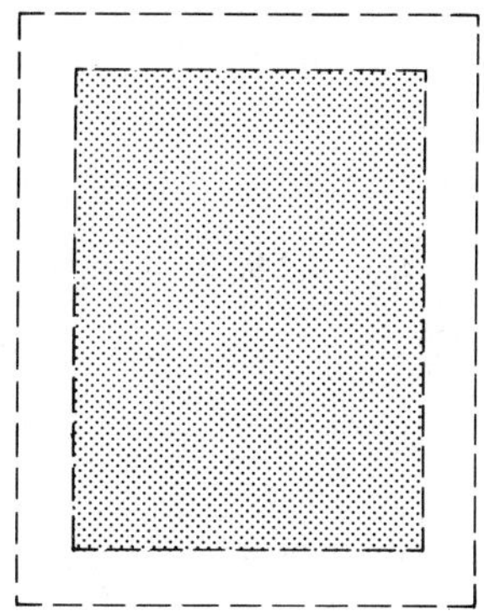

This answer is your ^OR right margin setting: ^OR ___

D. The resulting right margin (empty space to the right of your text) is

(C) - (B), or ___ columns/spaces

(For the values C and B, use the answers you obtained in questions C and B above.)

When using the margin release or changing the right margin, note the paper's right edge and stay to its left.

Right edge = (C) + (D) = ___ columns/spaces

(For the values C and D, use the answers you obtained in questions C and D above.)

E. For tabular formatting, indentation, or tab stops, measure on your actual printing form from the printer-indented left margin (the answer you obtained in question B, above). Note the corresponding column number of each tab stop or convert from inches:

Tab Stop	Setting
1. Indent ___ inches from left margin × ___ cpi	= ___ column/space
2. Indent ___ inches	= ___ column/space
3. Indent ___ inches	= ___ column/space
4. Indent ___ inches	= ___ column/space
5. Indent ___ inches	= ___ column/space
6. Indent ___ inches	= ___ column/space
7. Indent ___ inches	= ___ column/space
8. Indent ___ inches	= ___ column/space

List column numbers of consecutive tab stops:
1.___ 2.___ 3.___ 4.___ 5.___ 6.___ 7.___ 8.___
Enter ^ON A@ to remove all stops. Enter OI and the column numbers above to set revised stops.

PART THREE: MISCELLANEOUS COMMANDS

A. To reposition the default (bottom-of-page) page numbering, enter a revised column number: .PC ___ To suppress default page numbering, enter .OP. To reinstate default page numbering, enter .PN.

B. To change the page number, enter .PN ___, using a revised number. If the page number is printed at the top of page (.HE #), enter .OP after the .PN command to continue suppressing default page numbering.

C. To adjust subscript/superscript roll (normally 3/48 inch), enter a new number (n/48 inch): .SR ___

D. To turn microjustification off or to reinstate it, use:

- (off) .UJ 0 or .UJ OFF
- (on) .UJ 1 or .UJ ON

E. To turn bidirectional printing off or to reinstate it, use:

- (off) .BP 0 or .BP OFF
- (on) .BP 1 or .BP ON

DOT COMMAND CHECKLIST

Enter dot commands in this order. Default values appear in brackets.

.PL ___	(paper length) [66]
.MT ___	(top margin) [3]

.HM ___	(heading margin) [2]
.HE ______________________________	(heading)
.MB ___	(bottom margin) [8]
.FM ___	(footing margin) [2]
.FO ______________________________	(footing)
.CW ___	(character width) [12]
.PC ___	(default page number position) [center]
.SR ___	(subscript roll) [3]
.PO ___	(page offset at left) [8]
.UJ ___	(microjustification) [on]
.BP ___	(bidirectional printing) [on]
.OP ___	(omit default page numbering)
.LH ___	(line height) [8]

Change dot commands within the file as necessary, but do not change line height, page length, top margin, or bottom margin. To maintain correct page break lines, these commands must be in line 1.

35

A Dot Command Worksheet: IBM Matrix Printer

The section that follows can be photocopied for your convenience.

Go through the worksheet, completing those categories which apply. When finished, fill out the Dot Command Checklist, then enter dot commands in order at the beginning of your file.

PART ONE: LENGTH OF FORM

A. How long is your page/form?

___ inches × 6 lines per inch = ___ lines

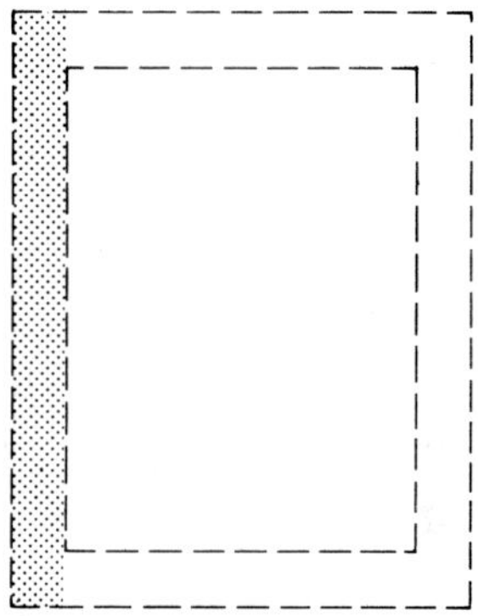

Page length dot command: .PL ___

B. How long is the text portion of your page/form, not counting any heading or footing? (If your text area depends on fixed top and bottom margins, subtract the needed margins from the paper length to determine the area available for text entry.)

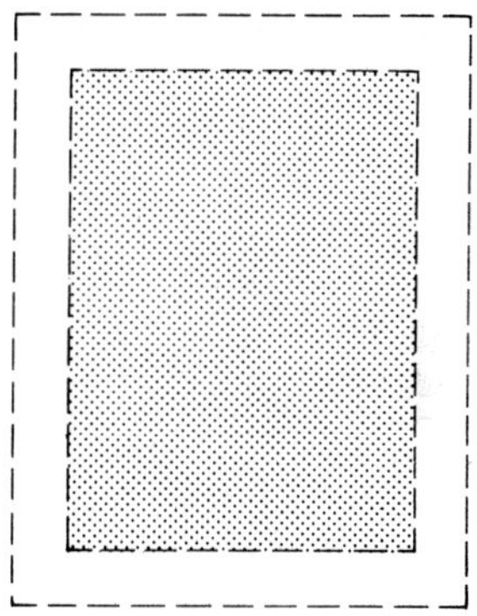

___ inches × 6 lines per inch = ___ lines for text.

C. Subtract (B) from (A) to determine space available for top/bottom margins.

(A) ___ lines
– (B) ___ lines

Total margin space: ___ lines

D. How much space do you want separating the top of your page/form from the first line of regular text?

- 1 inch = 6 lines
- 2/3 inch = 4 lines
- 1/2 inch = 3 lines
- 1/3 inch = 2 lines

Top margin dot command: .MT ___

E. How much space do you want separating the bottom of your page/form from the last line of regular text?

Bottom margin dot command: .MB ___
Note: (D) + (E) should = (C).

F. If using a heading, how many lines do you want separating the heading from your first line of regular text?
Heading margin dot command: .HM ___

Note: The heading margin is contained within the top margin.

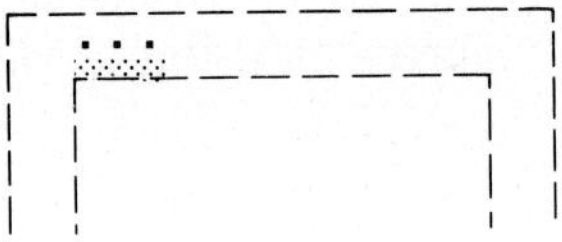

Top Margin	.MT ___
(minus) Heading Margin	− .HM ___
	− 1 (line occupied by heading)
Lines between heading and top of page →	___

G. Heading dot command: .HE ______________________________
Note: If you do not enter .HM and/or .MT, WordStar will use these default values: .HM 2 and .MT 3.

H. If using a footing, how many lines do you want separating the footing from your last line of regular text?

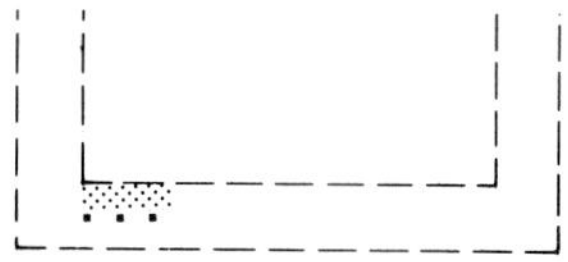

Footing margin dot command: .FM ___
Note: The footing margin is contained within the bottom margin.

Bottom Margin	.MB ___
(minus) Footing Margin	− .FM ___
	− 1 (line occupied by footing)
Lines between footing and bottom of page →	______

I. Footing dot command: .FO ______________________________
Note: The default footing consists of the current page number, printed at the bottom center of each page. This page number normally appears two lines below the last line of regular text. If you use the default page number or enter a new footing without using .FM, WordStar uses the default value .FM 2. The default bottom margin is .MB 8.

PART TWO: WIDTH OF FORM

A. How wide is your form/page? ___ inches

Note that the IBM Matrix Printer will not accomodate any form wider than 8 1/2 inches.

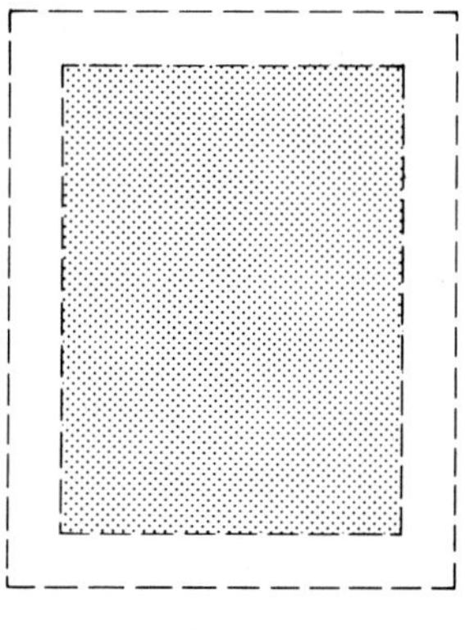

B. How much space do you want the printer to indent from the left edge of your paper/form before printing the left margin of your text?

___ inches indentation × 10 characters per inch = ___ columns/spaces

Note: The default indentation is 8 columns/spaces, or 8/10 inch. To set the printed left margin as far left as possible, use .PO 0. Page offset dot command: .PO ___

C. How wide is your text?

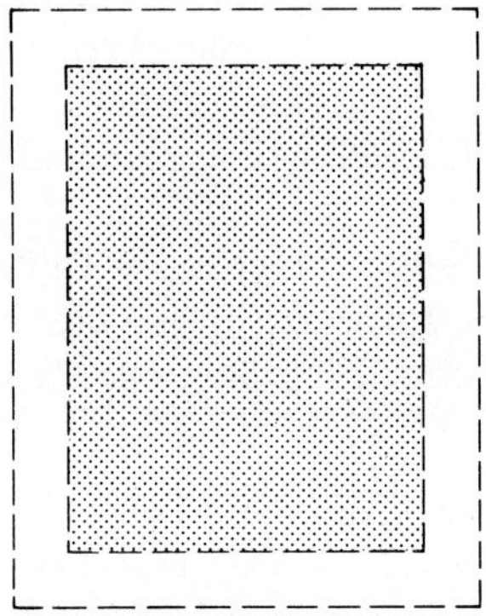

___ inches × 10 cpi = ___ columns/spaces.

Measure from the left margin's print position.

The printer cannot print a line wider than 80 characters.

This answer to (C) above is your ^OR right margin setting: ^OR ___

D. The resulting right margin (empty space to the right of your text) is

(C) - (B), or ___ columns/spaces

(For the values C and B, use the answers you obtained in questions C and B above.)

When using the margin release or changing the right margin, note the paper's right edge and stay to its left.

Right edge = (C) + (D) = ___ columns/spaces

(For the values C and D, use the answers you obtained in questions C and D above.)

Remember that if you use a line wider than 72 spaces without changing the .PO page offset number, or if you use a line wider than 80 column/spaces after using .PO 0, the printer will "carry over" any characters that do not fit on the printed line and print them on the next line.

E. For tabular formatting, indentation, or tab stops, measure on your actual printing form from the printer-indented left margin (the answer you obtained in question B, above). Note the corresponding column number of each tab stop or convert from inches:

Tab Stop	Setting
1. Indent ___ inches from left margin × ___ cpi	= ___ column/space
2. Indent ___ inches	= ___ column/space
3. Indent ___ inches	= ___ column/space
4. Indent ___ inches	= ___ column/space
5. Indent ___ inches	= ___ column/space
6. Indent ___ inches	= ___ column/space
7. Indent ___ inches	= ___ column/space
8. Indent ___ inches	= ___ column/space

List column numbers of consecutive tab stops:
1. ___ 2. ___ 3. ___ 4. ___ 5. ___ 6. ___ 7. ___ 8. ___
Enter ^ON A@ to remove all stops. Enter OI and the column numbers above to set revised stops.

PART THREE: MISCELLANEOUS COMMANDS

A. To reposition the default (bottom-of-page) page numbering, enter a revised column number: .PC ___

To suppress default page numbering, enter .OP.
To reinstate default page numbering, enter .PN.

B. To change the page number, enter .PN ___, using a revised number. If the page number is printed at the top of page (.HE #), enter .OP after the .PN command to continue suppressing default page numbering.

DOT COMMAND CHECKLIST: IBM MATRIX PRINTER

Enter dot commands in this order. Default values appear in brackets.

.PL __	(paper length) [66]
.MT __	(top margin) [3]
.HM __	(heading margin) [2]
.HE ________________________________	(heading)

.MB ___ (bottom margin) [8]
.FM ___ (footing margin) [2]
.FO____ (footing)
.PC ___ (default page number position) [center]
.PN ___ (set new page number) [default begins with 1]
.PO ___ (page offset at left) [8]
.OP ___ (omit default page numbering)

If beginning a file with the dot commands above, they should go in column 1, line 1. Enter the commands in order.

Change commands as necessary throughout the doucment, but do not change top margin, bottom margin, or page length. These must be in line 1 for correct page break lines.

A new heading or footing can be entered at any time, and the new version will print beginning with the next page. Headings and footings continue until replaced, or until you reach the end of the file.

36

Printing Options

Chapter 13 introduced WordStar's print function, and page 276 reviews ^KP, the alternate printing command. If your system has sufficient memory to support the command, ^KP lets you print one file while editing another. The 64K IBM PC does not have sufficient memory for ^KP to work.

Using either P from the No-File Menu or ^KP from within a file, WordStar offers six printing options.

DISK FILE OUTPUT (Y/N):
START AT PAGE NUMBER (RETURN for beginning)?
STOP AFTER PAGE NUMBER (RETURN for end)?
USE FORM FEEDS (Y/N):
SUPPRESS PAGE FORMATTING (Y/N):
PAUSE FOR PAPER CHANGE BETWEEN PAGES (Y/N):
Ready printer, press RETURN:

Each question has a default answer, which can be given by pressing the RETURN key. In all four Yes/No questions, the default response is "No." The default page numbers are 1 (the beginning of a file) and its last page (the end).

What happens if you answer Yes instead of No to the Y/N questions?

DISK FILE OUTPUT

"Disk file output" means that the file will be printed not on paper but on a disk. The screen message OUTPUT FILE NAME? requests a destination for this printing operation. What arrives on the disk isn't an exact copy of the file being printed; it's what WordStar calls an "expanded" version. All dot commands are interpreted rather than listed, so if you changed the page numbers, provided headings and footings, altered the top and bottom margins, or made other revisions, you can see how they'll look without having to print the file on paper. You may print this new file later, or you can use it for editing purposes.

If you select an already-existing file as the print destination, that file's previous contents will be erased.

START/STOP PAGES

"Start at page number" and "Stop after page number" are self-explanatory options. If you revised pagination with the dot command .PN n, WordStar will recognize your new numbers when you specify a page number in either command.

USE FORM FEEDS

The form feeds question is usually answered No because WordStar provides the right number of line feeds to move paper correctly. In addition, the printer has to be equipped to carry out this option, and it must be supplied with continuous, perforated, accordian-fold forms. A Yes response activates the printer's form feeds, eliminating the need for the .PL (paper length) dot command if you are not using 11-inch pages. Once the first form has been positioned, subsequent forms emerge correctly.

SUPPRESS PAGE FORMATTING

Suppressing the page formatting does away with page break lines, top and bottom margins, page offsets, headings, footings, and page numbers. In addition, it causes all dot commands to print rather than be interpreted. This option prints the exact contents of a file rather than its final form. Because dot commands don't normally print, suppressing the page formatting can be valuable for providing hard copy of those directions.

The same option can be used to print disk files created with the disk file output option (in which case the dot commands do not print because they have already been "expanded"), and to print already-paginated files created by programs other than WordStar.

PAUSE FOR PAPER CHANGE

To pause for paper changes, use Y with that option question; otherwise, the printer will assume you have continuous-feed paper. When you use this option, the printer stops after each page, waiting until you enter P (or ^KP if you're printing one file while editing another) before resuming.

If you are using the IBM Matrix Printer, you'll hear a raucous, beeping siren when you run out of paper. This is because when paper is correctly fed into the printer it depresses a small metal prong. As long as this metal part is depressed, the printer assumes paper has been installed correctly. When your long accordian sheet runs out, releasing this metal part, the printer signals that it has run out of paper and printing stops.

To use single sheets of paper, you can "trick" this metal tab by inserting a 3×5 card so the tab remains depressed. Now the printer accepts individual pages because it "thinks" it has been loaded with a long paper form.

CHECK PRINTER

Check your printer carefully before pressing the final RETURN.

If your printer has a wide carriage, paper should be positioned correctly, and not so far left that you print on the platen. Remember that WordStar normally indents the left margin eight column/spaces from its starting point. Position the top of the page to allow for the top margin, normally three blank lines. If you have used dot commands to vary the configuration, be precise as you align paper vertically and horizontally. Your printer must be turned on, and if it has a separate "on-line" key, that must be activated also. When everything's ready, press RETURN and printing begins.

INTERRUPT PRINTING

To interrupt the printing operation, enter P (or ^KP, depending on how you initiated print). As soon as the screen message TYPE "Y" TO ABANDON PRINT, "N" TO RESUME, ^U TO HOLD appears, press the appropriate key. Your printer may strike a few keys after you enter the command and again when you enter the option.

Note that the 64K IBM PC does not have sufficient memory for the ^U option to work.

If you want to abandon print while the printer waits between pages or in response to a ^PC command, enter P (or ^KP) twice. Pressing the print command twice should bring the above message before printing resumes.

THE ^KP COMMAND

Systems with sufficient memory and disk space allow you to print one file while editing another. ^KP entered from within a file generates the same screen responses as P entered from the No-File Menu. Interrupt printing-while-editing by pressing ^KP again. If you stop to change paper between pages, use ^KP to restart the printing. This command is described again in Chapter 37.

PRINT FUNCTION SCREEN MESSAGES

In addition to the printing options you have already met, the following messages may appear as you use WordStar's print commands.

```
FILE [name] NOT FOUND or
INVALID FILE NAME: [name]
```

These messages are self-explanatory. Check the directory; make sure your spelling is correct. If using ^KP, enter ^F to display file directory. (This command works if you have already entered ^KP and WordStar's message is on the screen.) Otherwise, display the file directory with ^KF. If the file is on another disk, check that didk's directory by changing the logged disk drive.

```
WARNING: You are printing the same file as you are editing.
The last saved version will be printed, not reflecting unsaved
changes. Furthermore, WordStar will not allow you to save the
edited version while the print is in progress.
```

On systems that allow simultaneous editing and printing, this message warns that the file name entered after ^KP (print command) is that of the same file being edited. WordStar does not permit saving while the same file is being printed; only the previously saved version will be printed. The ^KP print command should be used to print a different file from the one being edited.

```
END EDIT (^KD) BEFORE STARTING PRINT.
YOUR SYSTEM DOES NOT HAVE ENOUGH MEMORY TO
PERMIT SIMULTANEOUS EDITING AND PRINTING.
```

Because the 64K IBM PC does not have sufficient memory to support simultaneous printing and editing, this message appears when you enter ^KP.

```
ALLOW PRINT TO FINISH BEFORE EDITING A FILE.
YOUR SYSTEM DOES NOT HAVE ENOUGH MEMORY TO
PERMIT SIMULTANEOUS EDITING AND PRINTING.
```

The 64K IBM PC does not support the ^U option after interrupting the print function.

```
*** PRINT OUTPUT DISK FULL.  PRINT PAUSED ***
```

When using the "disk file output" option, the destination disk may become full, causing print to pause. Make additional space available by deleting files, then resume printing; or abandon print and delete the disk output file.

```
FINISH PRINT BEFORE EXIT
(Type ^U to cancel exit command)...
```

If your system supports simultaneous editing and printing, this message appears should you try to store a file with ^KX (which exits from WordStar and returns to the disk operating system) before the print function has finished.

```
FINISH PRINT OF SAME FILE BEFORE SAVING
(Type ^U to cancel Save command)...
```

If you are editing the same file you are printing, WordStar (as mentioned earlier) will print the previously saved version of that file, and it will not save any editing changes you are now making (^KS or ^KD) until the printing function has finished. Don't try to edit and print the same file simultaneously. If the file is long, its printing can take a long time and none of your editing changes can be saved until printing has stopped. If the file is short, why print an earlier and inaccurate version when you can edit, store and print the improved edition in a few minutes? And if printing has paused, the WordStar manual cautions that unless you use ^U to cancel the save command, "WordStar will wait forever."

```
FINISH PRINT OF .BAK FILE BEFORE SAVING
(Type ^U to cancel Save command) ...
```

You can print a backup file, but if you are editing a document file and printing its backup file simultaneously, this message appears when you try to save your editing changes.

37

More About Disks and Files

WORDSTAR'S FILES

WordStar consists of three program files: WS.COM, the main program; WSMSGS.OVR, which contains all the menus and messages; and WSOVLY1.OVR, the overlay file.

All three files should be on your master disk.

Your working file is the document file being edited. No changes will be made in this file until you enter a save command. Entries not saved will be lost should you be interrupted.

When you save a file, WordStar records your editing changes on the disk. At the same time, it preserves your previous version in a backup file, usually labeled with the file's name and .BAK.

In addition, WordStar may create a third file for temporary storage should the system's memory capacity be reached. In that case, some text from the beginning of material stored in RAM (random access memory) will be placed in that file. When moving backward and approaching the RAM capacity, material from the end of text stored in the computer's memory may be placed in a second temporary file.

You cannot edit a backup file, but in an emergency (i.e., you accidentally erase your working file) you can rename it; then WordStar will allow you to edit the file.

In the file directory, a document file (such as TEXT) is listed before its backup file (TEXT.BAK). Temporary files appear at the end of the directory (TEXT.$$$).

If your system has more than 64K, files appear in alphabetical order in your file directory.

CHANGING DISKS

Never change disks while saving or printing. Don't remove a disk when a red indicator light is on. In general, wait until WordStar's No-File Menu is on-screen before changing disks.

There are two exceptions to the rule stated above.

If you want to read a file (^KR) from another disk into your document file, you can change files just before pressing RETURN to execute the command. Enter ^KR, type the "read from" file's name, change disks, press RETURN, and exchange disks back again as soon as the status line redisplays.

Another "read only" feature is the print function. While using P from the No-File Menu or ^KP from within a file, you can enter the command and file name, then exchange disks, inserting the disk containing the file to be read/printed. If you have a single disk drive unit, you will use this procedure for printing files from the No-File Menu.

FILE SIZE

Because file capacity varies from system to system, it's impossible to say how large your files can be. But with experience, you'll be able to define "large" and "small."

Your file can be held entirely in random access memory if the cursor moves from the end to its beginning (F10) in a few seconds. This means the file is still small. When it takes up to a minute or more, your file is growing large.

The status line reports file size in characters when you turn the page break display off (^OP). Check the size of your longest successful files and note their FC numbers for future reference.

For example, a 5 1/4-inch single-sided, double-density disk storing a single working file on a 64K IBM PC may generate warning messages during storage or when moving the cursor (or text) long distances after reaching 45,000 or 50,000 file characters in length. As the total disk space is 160,256 bytes, this may seem an unnecessarily conservative screen message, but size is a function of memory as well as disk space. Someone using inefficient editing techniques can receive a DISK FULL message in a file of 50,000 or 60,000 bytes using single-sided disks. Of course, double-sided disks accommodate longer files and so do systems with more than 64K memory. And after you have stored a file, you can copy it onto another disk for storage only (not editing) and fill the entire disk with finished files.

When the message line warns that a backup file is being deleted to make space, take that as a warning: Your disk is filling up.

When editing long documents, be ready to delete other files, as appropriate, to create more room, or use a files-only disk, or divide the file in half and make it two files. See Chapter 39, the WordStar Clinic, for more first aid for full disks.

FILE OPERATIONS

The Block Menu, which appears at help levels 2 and 3 when you enter ^K, lists five file operations, all of which pertain to files other than the one you're editing.

^KR, the "read file" command, was introduced in Chapter 25. It transfers material from a specified file into your working file beginning at the cursor position.

^KJ deletes a file. To erase unnecessary files while you edit a growing document, use this command. The screen will ask for a file name; when entered, that file will be erased.

^KO copies a file. Again, the screen will ask for names, first the source file and then its destination. If the destination is an already-existing file, WordStar's copy commands (O from the No-File Menu and ^KO from within a file) erase the destination file's previous contents.

^KE renames a file, just as the command E does when entered from the No-File Menu. The screen will ask for the file's current name and then its revised name.

Note that after you enter the command (^KO, ^KE, ^KJ, or ^KR), you can display the disk's file directory by pressing ^F by itself. Whenever the screen asks for a file name or other information, ^R restores the response last entered for that command and ^F displays the file directory.

^KP allows you to print one file while you edit another, assuming that your system supports this function. (The 64K IBM PC generates an error message.) ^KP elicits the same screen responses as P from the No-File Menu.

To interrupt printing initiated by ^KP, enter that command again. To resume printing after pausing to change paper, use the same command (^KP).

Your keyboard will respond more slowly when another file is printing, so the simultaneous edit is best confined to minor corrections and text review rather than the rapid typing of new material.

DISK OPERATIONS

While editing a file, you can change the logged disk drive (^KL) or display the file directory (^KF). The first command generates the same screen responses as L entered from the no-file menu. ^KF displays the current directory at the top of the screen. If this list is too long to display completely, scroll with ^W or ^Z.

REVIEW: DISK AND FILE OPERATIONS ON-SCREEN

To review file and disk operations on-screen, enter ^K at help level 2 or 3. This brings WordStar's Block Menu to the screen.

REVIEW: DISKS AND FILES

- WordStar's three programs are WS.COM, WSMSGS.OVR, and WSOVLY.OVR. These three files should be on your main program disk.
- A working file is any file in use for document or nondocument preparation and editing.
- Backup files are usually labeled .BAK; a document file's backup file stores the most recent previous version of that file.
- Temporary files, usually labeled .$$$, may be created by WordStar as it edits long documents.
- In general, the safest time to change disks is when WordStar's No-File Menu is on the screen.
- Maximum file size is determined by your system's memory and available disk space; file size varies from one system to another. Check the FC (file character) number at the end of your longest files for future reference. When approaching a previous maximum, take steps to avoid disk full error messages.
- WordStar's file operations allow you to use one file while editing another. These operations are:

  ^KR (read from another file)
  ^KJ (erase a file)
  ^KO (copy a file)
  ^KE (rename a file)
  ^KP (print a file)

- WordStar's disk operations permit these actions while editing:

  ^KL (change logged drive)
  ^KF (display file directory)

- The command ^KP generates an error message on the 64K IBM PC. This configuration does not support simultaneous editing and printing.

QUIZ

Match the function to its command code:

1. ^KJ	a.	Copy a file while editing
2. ^KE	b.	Display current disk's contents
3. ^KF	c.	Erase a file while editing
4. ^KR	d.	Insert contents of another file
5. ^KL	e.	Print another file while editing
6. ^KO	f.	Change logged drive while editing
7. ^KP	g.	Rename a file while editing

8. If a working file's name is AUDIT, what will its backup disk be named? What will its temporary storage file, if any, be named?

9. It is safe to change disks:
   a. while the printer is running.
   b. while saving a file.
   c. while using the ^KW command.
   d. when the drive's red indicator light is on.
   e. when WordStar's No-File Menu is on the screen.
   f. All of the above.

10. How can you review WordStar's file and disk operations on-screen?

QUIZ ANSWERS

1. c
2. g
3. b
4. d
5. f
6. a
7. e
8. AUDIT.BAK and AUDIT.$$$
9. e
10. Enter the prefix ^K at help level 2 or 3.

38

Editing Review

Successful editing depends on organization: understanding your computer and WordStar, planning the stages of each document, recognizing pitfalls that trap the unwary, and knowing how to solve problems as they develop.

Before you open a document file, think ahead. Will this be one of many small files on a single disk? Is it the first part of an ambitious manuscript? How can you arrange the material for best results?

LONG DOCUMENTS

While your first long document may simply grow that way when you aren't looking, you'll soon be able to plan around the limitations (if any) of your system.

Short files are those the cursor can traverse from back to front (F10 or^QR) in a few seconds. Long files take a minute or more, and how long your longest file can be depends on available disk space and memory.

Keep track of your longest successful files and their FC (file character) numbers. This information appears when you turn the page break display off with ^OP; position the cursor on your last page before entering the command. Or use the disk operating system DIR directory listing command. Your file and its length in bytes will appear on the screen. Then, as you edit future files, compare their length with your benchmark. As your editing techniques improve, you can revise this figure upward, but take extra care whenever you approach a previous maximum.

Because backward-moving commands generate DISK FULL errors faster than forward-moving commands, organize your work to move from the beginning of the file toward its end.

Instead of using a backward-moving command such as F10, ^QF/^QA with the B option, or a block move that transfers material toward the front of the file, save with ^KS first. This preserves your editing changes and returns you to the beginning of the file. Block markers, place markers, and the previous find/replace command survive this save.

Don't start a global replacement (G option with ^QA) without first returning to the front of the file with ^KS.

If your project consists of one long document, such as a book manuscript, thesis, or report, arrange your files accordingly. Depending on your system's memory and available disk space, consider putting only one or two chapters or major sections on a disk. It's better to have spare disk space than a full disk.

When you plan to move blocks of text long distances, ^KV and ^KC are unwieldy commands. Instead, create storage files before going into your working file, and use them with ^KW and ^KR. You may want to create such files even if you don't plan a block move, just for convenience.

If disk Drive B contains an all-file disk, create one or more ^KW storage files on your WordStar (Drive A) disk. Call for these files when B is the logged drive by prefacing the file name with A: .

MOVING LONG BLOCKS, MOVING BLOCKS LONG DISTANCES

Use this technique to move blocks that are large enough to generate error messages and to move blocks of any size long distances.

1. Mark the block you plan to move or copy.
2. Use ^KW to write it into your storage file.
3. If moving the block (equivalent to ^KV), erase the displayed section with ^KY. If copying the block (equivalent to ^KC), hide it with ^KH.
4. On paper, note the storage file and its contents.
5. Continue editing as you move toward the end of the file (going the other way may create a full disk).
6. When you reach the block's destination, enter ^KR to read the storage file's contents into your document at that point.
7. If the block's destination comes before its source, use ^KS to return to the file's beginning, then locate the destination and use ^KR.

COLUMN MODE BLOCK MOVES

Unfortunately, you cannot use the read file and write block commands while in column mode, but you can achieve the same effect another way.

To move large column blocks, or to move column blocks of any size long distances:

1. Return to regular block mode.
2. Mark the beginning and end of the entire section containing your target column.
3. Use ^KW to store this block in another file.
4. If desired, erase the displayed (source) block with ^KY. To retain it, hide the block with ^KH.
5. With the cursor at your destination, use ^KR to read the entire block.
6. Return to column mode (^KN). To remove any noncolumn material from the section you have moved, mark it as a column block and erase it with ^KY.
7. To combine columns, setting one adjacent to another, ^KV works well so long as the source and destination are close together. If your system accepts only short blocks for transportation via ^KV and ^KC, divide the column and move it in sections.

When moving directly from a ^KW write block command to a ^KR read file command involving the same file, save keystrokes by using ^R for the file name. ^R means "restore this entry" when the screen asks for a file name.

WIDE DOCUMENTS

Although WordStar's version 3.2 features horizontal scrolling, wide documents are sometimes easier to set in regular 65-column lines. That way you can see all your text on the screen at one time. After setting text, reform it using a new (wide) right margin and ^B.

To set a wide table, especially one using print controls, remove all tab stops with ^ON A@. Set new stops as needed for horizontal text entry. Set the text or numbers first, inspect the screen, then insert print controls. Be sure insertion is turned on when you add print controls to already-entered text.

To reduce the printer's left margin (usually indented eight columns from left edge), enter the dot command .PO (page offset) and the number 4 or 2 or 0, depending on how much additional printing space you want at left. On the IBM Matrix Printer, you must use the .PO dot command on lines wider than 72 characters, and the printer (even with .PO 0) will not be able to print a line wider than 80 characters without bringing "over-run" letters down to the next line.

How wide can your lines be? Word wrap and other functions operate effectively if the right margin is set at column 240 or less. The left margin should never be set to the right of column 240. For most word processing projects, these are generous limits.

MULTIPLE FILES

If your project will involve many files of "boilerplate," common material inserted into individual letters or separate reports, keep an eye on your file directory. Each working file creates at least one backup file, so your maximum file allowance may be smaller than you realize.

If, while editing, you need additional disk space and want to remove a file or two, display the file directory with ^KF. Change the logged drive (^KL) to view the other disk's directory. If you can't find a file to erase, perhaps you can move a file from one disk to the other with ^KO, creating more space on your file's disk. Delete any unnecessary file(s) with ^KJ.

PARAGRAPH REFORM

When making numerous corrections and revisions to consecutive paragraphs and pages, take advantage of place markers and their portable nature.

Place marker <1> will move whenever you enter ^K1. You can simplify paragraph reform by following this procedure:

1. Enter marker <1> in the first line of a paragraph to be altered, or in the first line you rearrange.
2. Continue through the paragraph, adding, deleting, and revising as necessary.
3. After completing the corrections, enter ^Q1, which returns the cursor to marker <1>.
4. Press ^B, the paragraph reform code.
5. Move to the next paragraph scheduled for revision and take marker <1> with you. Enter ^K1, complete the edit, return to the marker with ^Q1, enter ^B for paragraph reform, and so on.

The fastest way to reform a document after revising its right margin or changing from a justified to ragged margin is to use ^QQB. ^QQ causes the next-entered command to repeat automatically until interrupted. (Hyphen-help, if on, interrupts ^QQB; the space bar or any other key can be used to stop this function.)

This works best with short documents containing straightforward text or with a file whose every paragraph will conform to the same format conditions. It may not work well if you change the line spacing because ^B does not add a line between a hard return and the next line of text (a handicap when changing from single to double spacing), nor does it remove the blank line between two hard returns (which may be inconvenient when changing from double to single spacing, unless you prefer a blank line separating paragraphs.)

FIND/REPLACE ENTRIES

When requesting the same word match in multiple files, save time by using ^L in the new file. WordStar remembers the last find or find-and-replace command, even after ^KD. If you plan to change option codes, use ^R to restore the target and/or replacement word.

In some but not all cases, you can enter print control commands as target or replacement characters in find/replace commands. Experiment with your system. On the 64K IBM PC you can enter ^PD, ^PX, ^PT, or ^PV in your ^QA or ^QF command. (For example, you could replace a subscript with a superscript, or replace a phrase containing doublestrike.) You can use ^PO as part of the replacement entry in a ^QA command (don't try to use it as part of the target or "find" entry in either ^QF or ^QA). The commands F5 (for underlining) and F6 (for boldface) do not work in find/replacement commands on the 64K IBM PC.

If word wrap has upset a neatly typed chart by inserting soft spaces after letters or numbers in a list of items, eliminate the soft (added) spaces by using ^PO, the non-break space, with ^QA.

For example, let's say you typed a chart using this format:

1. [Text]
2. [Text], etc., in which text begins after a two-space separation. Word wrap often adds a soft space after a period, but you can return to the beginning of the section and erase those soft spaces with this sequence:

   ^QA FIND? .*space space space@* REPLACE WITH? .^PO^PO*ESC*

   Make the replacement, then use ^B to reform the line. If there is still an extra soft space, press ^T to remove it before using ^B. Repeat the replacement command with ^L.

When using ^QA to make a series of identical replacements in text requiring editing along the way, use ^L as both a command and "No" response. Instead of using three keys to enter and respond to the replacement command, you use two. ^L means both "Repeat this command" and "No, don't make this replacement." WordStar recognizes any letter but Y as a No response.

If you don't plan to edit between replacements, but you know that not every word matching the target word needs replacing, use the G (global) option and respond to WordStar's confirming "yes/no" question with these two keys: Y for Yes and U for No. These letters are adjacent to one another on the keyboard, making it easy to respond quickly when the screen offers a replacement.

RETAINING EMPTY LINES

To remove a line of text without removing the line itself (lower lines move up when you use ^Y), try ^QY with the cursor positioned in column 1. Lower text is not disturbed and you retain the empty line. ^Q DEL does the same from the opposite end of the line.

SETTING A PERMANENT PLACE MARKER

Although normal place markers do not survive the ^KD save command, you can set place markers that will. Select as your marker an unusual word or combination of letters or symbols, then enter it after the dot command .. (two periods) or .IG, another dot command designed for nonprinting comments, or even after a single dot.

A find request like ^QF ..xxxxx or ^QF ..&&& will return you to the permanent but "invisible" marker without delay. You don't have to include the dot(s) that precede your marker because ^QF stops at the first matching string it encounters, regardless of adjacent text. Your marker can stay in the file forever, and it will not print.

A SOLID UNDERLINE

WordStar does not underline between words when you use the print control F5.

To create an uninterrupted underline, use F5 but type a _ ("capital" underline) between words, or use the line overprint command (^PM or ^P@) and enter a separate underline with the _ key.

The underline created by the IBM Matrix Printer isn't a solid underline because it consists of individual dashes. But most incremental (daisy wheel-type) printers do create a solid underline.

PARAGRAPH TABBING

When using the F2 command for paragraph tabbing, keep an eye on your ruler line. The indented area should display in bright light. If you haven't indented enough, enter F2 again. If you indented too far, return to the beginning of the line with ^QS to cancel the command, and begin again.

HYPHEN-HELP

To condense a document through hyphenation, use ^B and hyphen-help. But before you embark on the project, consider hyphenating certain key words, especially those used often, with the help of ^OE (soft hyphen entry) and ^QA (find-and-replace). Enter the target word and its soft hyphen-separated replacement. Because soft hyphens print only at the end of a line, mid-text hyphens will disappear. Using ^B and text that has been "prehyphenated" speeds the condensing process.

Hyphen-help follows the laws of probability when it selects break points, but English can be an improbable language. Don't accept a hyphen just because a computer offers it. Check the dictionary if you aren't sure.

DOT COMMANDS

Because no line with a dot or period in column 1 will print, decimal points and ellipses require extra care.

To check for accidental dot commands, use the find command ^QF with the special character ^PN (line return) and a period: ^PN . ESC. This means, find a period immediately following a hard or soft return, and skip all the options. The cursor will stop at authorized dot commands, but it will find the accidental ones, too. Use ^L to repeat the search.

While you inspect dot commands, watch for .CP (conditional page) entries and other dot commands that may be placed between two double-spaced lines. As the dotted line will not print, it creates single spacing when it disappears. To retain the line spacing in use, insert a hard return (^N) after every mid-text dot command.

Before entering dot commands at the beginning of a file, make a checklist, following the recommendations in Chapter 34 or 35. It is important to keep dot commands from contradicting each other. To change the page number in a heading (.PN n) while suppressing the default (bottom-of-page) page numbering, enter .PN n first, then .OP. If you type them the other way around, .PN will do two things: revise the page number as you requested, and reinstate the default numbering at the bottom of the page.

An alternate and more permanent way to suppress the default page numbering is with .FO, the footing command, entered by itself. It needs the # signal to print page numbers, so omitting the # means that no number will print. This command overrides or replaces the default (page number) footing.

Whenever you change page numbers with .PN n, make a note on paper. The status line will continue to measure pages from the beginning of your file.

INTERRUPTING

If you enter the prefix of most two-letter commands and change your mind, WordStar is very accommodating. Press the space bar, RETURN key, ESCAPE key, or ^U and the command cancels, returning you to the document file's edit. This works nicely with^Q, ^O, ^J, and ^K commands. However, the rule with ^P commands is *space bar only*. Pressing RETURN, ESCAPE, or ^U after the ^P prefix inserts a character on-screen at the cursor position.

If you enter both letters of a two-part command and change your mind after the screen requests information (^QF, ^QA, ^KR, ^KW, ^OL, ^OR, etc.), use ^U to interrupt.

If you enter all the parts of a command and realize you made a mistake, use ^U to interrupt. Exception: If you enter a save command by mistake, let it continue.

FILE COPIES

Your best backup is the copy you make of your disk at the end of an editing session. The more important the project, the more important the copy. Use WordStar to copy one file at a time or the operating system to copy a file at a time or the entire disk.

39

The WordStar Clinic

When your computer does the unexpected, it's probably following your instructions to the letter —- but it may take a moment to reconstruct the letter you entered to bring an unanticipated result.

This chapter reviews some common symptoms and offers a prescription or two. You'll encounter other problems from time to time, and it's a good idea to keep track of them. When you can't explain why something didn't work, or why the unexpected did, take notes. Review this guide and the regular WordStar manual, and experiment with your file. In most cases, you'll find a logical explanation, or at least an easy solution.

FULL DISK

- Help! My disk is full!

```
*** ERROR E12: DISK FULL *** press ESCAPE Key ■
```

- Error message E12 may appear as you move the cursor backward in a long file. If this is what happened, press ESC to remove the message, then enter ^KS. If ^KS (save and re-edit) works, it will store your latest changes and you may be able to add more, moving toward the end of the file instead of toward the beginning.

If you were moving toward the end of the file, or if the message appeared while saving, put your disk's directory on-screen (^KF) and hope you can erase something with ^KJ. If you can't erase a file on your disk, perhaps you can move it with ^KO and then erase the original. This will provide extra space for storage and editing.

In an emergency, you can erase WS.COM or WSMSGS.OVR, replacing these WordStar files from another disk after your rescue operation.

After deleting a file or two, try again. If successful, and if you want to add more material to the document, copy the disk and make two files out of your too-large file. On one disk, mark the first half of the file as a block and erase it; on the other, erase the second half. Change the file names accordingly: for example, what was Chapter.1 can now be Chapter.1A on the first disk and Chapter.1B on the second.

If erasing files doesn't leave enough room, consider these drastic actions. Abandon the edit, divide the file into two files, and start over.

If the other disk drive has space, mark the changed and unsaved sections as a block, then store them on the other disk with ^KW.

Alternately, erase the unchanged sections and replace them later from your duplicate disk or your .BAK file. While you cannot enter a .BAK file from the No-File Menu, you can rename it or copy it into an appropriately titled file and then proceed.

Should the DISK FULL message result from a block write (^KW command), the problem is far less dramatic. You can erase the destination file (^KJ) without losing anything from your working file. Use ^KS to protect recent changes, then delete other files, or use a file on the other disk as your destination.

What's the worst possibility? Another DISK FULL error message when you press the escape key as instructed in the first message. Or the message FATAL ERROR F27: DISK FULL. Although the WordStar manual refers to F27 as a "disk directory full" problem, the IBM PC generates the above version of F27 and returns you to the disk operating system. You can't rescue the file's unsaved contents. Take a break at that point and resolve to prevent full disks in the future.

Whenever you successfully edit a file that's longer than your others, turn the page break display off (^OP) with the cursor at the end of your document. Write down the FC (file character) number and keep this as a reference. When you contemplate additions to a long file in the future, check the FC number. If it's close to your "healthy maximum," proceed with care. Save with ^KS more frequently, be sure to work forward rather than backward, take advantage of space on the other disk for temporary storage, look for a logical place to divide the file, make a duplicate when you finish an editing session, and don't try to work when you're tired. These are the same procedures you should use when editing short files on a disk already storing other material.

- I erased three files on my storage disk, and now I keep getting fatal DISK FULL messages when I try to copy files onto that disk.
- Use the CHKDSK command to check the disk you erased files from. You should see a screen message like this:

```
[number] bytes disk space freed
```

It means that disk space (no doubt the space formerly occupied by your erased files) was mistakenly marked as allocated. The space was freed as the CHKDSK command executed, and it is now available.

TAB PROBLEMS

- When I press TAB, the cursor moves down instead of across the screen.
- You probably removed all the tab stops with ^ON A@ and the cursor can't find any. Check the ruler line.
- My tab stops aren't working right.
- You may have entered ^OV (variable tabbing on/off) by mistake. Check the ^O menu to see if this function is off. The fixed tabbing mode has stops at columns 9, 17, 25, 33, 41, etc.

If the TAB key is "skipping over" text and stopping at the correct column without moving text along with it, insertion is off. Check the status line; if the INSERT ON message has disappeared, turn insertion it back on.

SUBSCRIPT ERRORS

- My subscripts and superscripts don't print correctly. They stay on the text line.
- You may be using single spacing with a nonincremental printer (such as the IBM Matrix Printer). Instead, double or triple space your document; a nonincremental printer places subscripts a full line below and superscripts a full line above the text, but only if space is available. If that isn't the problem, could you have entered the dot command .SR 0? This reduces the subscript roll to 0/48 inch, or zero for short. Finally, your printer may not be capable of responding to the WordStar commands ^PT and ^PV.

THE ^R RESTORE ENTRY COMMAND

- I'm confused by the command ^R, which is supposed to restore or re-enter the file name most recently used in response to a screen question. Why can't I open a file and then save it and print it using ^R to repeat the original file name?
- WordStar remembers the file names (and other information) entered in response to screen messages in categories. Its memory of these file names lasts through an editing session, and if no file name has yet been entered in a category, ^R will not produce a word or name.

D (open a document file) and N (open a non-document file) belong to the same category. Throughout an editing session (beginning when you call up WordStar and ending when you return to the operating system), ^R entered after D or N at the No-File Menu will repeat whatever was last used for either D or N.

The No-File Menu commands O (copy a file), Y (erase a file), and E (rename a file), and the file operations ^KO (copy a file), ^KE (rename a file), and ^KJ (erase a file) belong to the same category. Once you have entered a file name (or a pair of file names) in response to any of these commands, ^R will restore the file name(s) when you enter the next same-category command. If the command asks for only one file name (^KY, for example), the screen displays only the first name of a pair, if a pair of names was the last-used response to any command in the category.

The commands ^KR (read a file) and ^KW (write a block) belong to the same category. You can save keystrokes when using these commands for storage and retrieval by storing first with ^KW and then retrieving with ^KR and the ^R (restore file name) command.

^QF (find) and ^QA (find-and-replace) belong to the same category. ^R will restore the last "find" word in response to either ^QF or ^QA; if using ^QA, it will also restore the "replacement" word last entered in response to ^QA's second screen question. If using options, ^R will restore the last-used options, too.

The print commands P and ^KP belong to the same category.

The margin and tab commands ^OL, ^OR, ^OI, and ^ON constitute individual categories. In each case, ^R will restore the last-entered response. ^R entered after ^OL will restore the last ^OL response; ^R entered after ^OR will restore the last ^OR response, etc.

DISAPPEARING TEXT

- My hard copy is missing a line.
- Look for a period in column 1. WordStar won't print a line with a dot in column 1, even if it isn't part of a recognized dot command.
- The cursor is erasing my text.
- When insertion is off, the space bar will "erase" previously entered text, moving the cursor over those letters and leaving blank spaces behind. Letters and symbols will "overprint" previous text, literally replacing a character at a time. Because the insertion key is close to the right shift key, close to the shift key, you may hit it by

accident. This is an on/off toggle key. Check the screen: INSERT ON appears on the status line when insertion is on, and the message disappears when the function is off.

- A whole section of text disappeared from the screen as I scrolled with PgDn(3). The status line shows line 21 above line 48 and nothing inbetween.
- If moving the cursor doesn't restore the missing section, move into the last "correct" line and press the space bar or any letter key. Although you'll insert a space/character into your file, it should cause the screen to redisplay correctly and you can remove it with the delete key. If this doesn't work, move down into an "incorrect" line and do the same. The 64K IBM PC sometimes "skips" lines and even whole pages during scrolling, especially in long files.

MALFUNCTIONING DOT COMMANDS

- One of my dot commands isn't working.
- Check their order of entry. Any command contradicted by a later command will be ignored. Follow the checklist and suggestions in Chapters 32 through 35.
- Even though I'm at the beginning of my file, the top margin (.MT) dot command keeps generating a question mark flag and the warning, "PUT AT FILE BEGINNING FOR CORRECT PAGE BREAK DISPLAY."
- Check the status line for your cursor's line number location. You may have placed the code in line 2. Unless it's in line 1, the top margin dot command will generate this warning. So will the commands for changing line height, bottom margin, and page length.

FIND COMMAND PROBLEMS

- After ^QF or ^QA, the cursor refused to stop at a phrase that was in the file.
- It happens. Redefine the target, using a single word. If you can, include a punctuation mark. If the file is short, try again going backward. Or try the options U and W.

It helps to understand why this problem is so common. First, WordStar cannot distinguish between hard and soft spaces when responding to your ^QF or ^QA command. This means that if word wrap has added an extra space between two of the words in your target phrase, the cursor won't stop. If word wrap has separated two words, putting them on adjacent lines with a soft return between them, the same thing happens because WordStar cannot distinguish between hard and soft spaces when responding to your ^QF or ^QA command.

If you have printed the file and can refer to hard copy before entering the find or find-and-replace command, you can take these factors into consideration. Also, refer to page 183 for instructions on using WordStar's special character ^PN (line return) in your ^QF or ^QA response.

DISAPPEARING PRINT CONTROL CHARACTERS

- When I enter a print control command, the character flashes on-screen for a fraction of a second and disappears.
- The print control display (^OD) may be off. Enter ^OD to turn it back on. Erase any extra control characters you entered in your attempt to get one on the screen.

RIGHT MARGIN PROBLEMS

- Words aren't aligning properly at the end of the line.
- ^OJ, the margin justification, may be turned off. Check the ^O menu, or enter ^OJ and try again. If that isn't the problem, check your right margin on the ruler line; it may have been moved accidentally to a new column.
- Words don't stop when I reach the right margin.
- Check the status line for the notation MAR REL, which means the margin is released. If so, enter ^OX to turn it off. Otherwise, check the ^O menu to see if word wrap is off. If so, turn it back on with ^OW. Reform the paragraph with ^B. If you're in a new file, you might have created a non-document file by pressing N instead of D from the No-File Menu. Word wrap is off by default in a non-document file.

PARAGRAPH REFORM PROBLEM

- After moving some text, I can't get ^B to work. The cursor keeps stopping.
- Are there hard return flags (<) at right? There may be if you moved text using column mode (^KN), or if you used the RETURN key with insertion off. Remove hard returns by placing the cursor at the end of the paragraph's first line and using ^T to bring words up; continue until you have a single long line. Now ^B should work

If the cursor stops at the end of a line in the middle of a word, hyphen-help is offering a hyphen at that point. Accept it with the - key or continue by pressing ^B again.

THE PRINTER WON'T STOP

- I used P to interrupt the printer, but when I entered Y (the abandon print option), the printer kept running and the screen asked what file I wanted to delete.
- Be sure to wait for a message to appear on-screen before responding with an option. Your computer interpreted Y as a No-File Menu code. Respond to this command with ^U (interrupt command); then try P again. Wait for the screen message and then enter Y.
- The printer goes right off the paper and types on the platen.
- Unless you change WordStar's default specifications with dot commands, the printer will move three lines down before beginning the page and eight spaces to

the right before printing your leftmost text. Reposition your paper accordingly, or use dot commands to reconfigure the page.

CONFUSION

- Help! I don't know what I did, but I'm not where I wanted to go and I'm not sure where I am.
- It's easy to press the wrong command keys as you're getting used to the computer —- and even after you know what you're doing. ^QP will return you to your previous position.

In fairness to users of the 64K IBM PC, it should be noted that some commands don't always work the way they should. For example, whenever you re-enter an unusually long file, the command PgDn(3), which should scroll down a screenful, may take you to the end of the file. Your first editing command in a long file may generate a frightening amount of noise from the disk drives and a WAIT message on the status line. If something happens that you didn't command, especially if the cursor's action or screen text isn't what it should be, use ^KQ to abandon the edit and enter the file again.

STRANGE STATUS LINE

- The status line has disappeared and some strange numbers are at the top of the screen.
- You probably turned the page break display off with ^OP; the new status line shows your position by character number, line number, and column. Type ^OP to turn the page break display back on; your regular status line should reappear. If this is a new, unused file, you entered N (non-document file) instead of D (document file) from the No-File Menu. If that happened, use ^KQ to abandon the edit, return to the No-File Menu, and enter D and your file name.

STRANGE HYPHENS

- My hyphens and dashes look funny.
- If they're highlighted (in faint light or inverse video), they were positioned by hyphen-help, or you entered ^OE, the soft hyphen entry command. None of these hyphens will print unless at the end of a line. If you need hard hyphens, the kind that print regardless of their position, turn soft hyphen entry off with ^OE and replace them. Alternately, before leaving soft hyphen entry, use this sequence to replace soft hyphens with their printing counterparts: ^QA FIND? - @ REPLACE WITH? ^P- ESC .

KEEPING TRACK OF TOGGLE COMMANDS

- I've lost track of my toggle commands.
- The status line will tell you whether insertion and the margin release are on (INSERT ON and MAR REL). To check word wrap, hyphen-help, soft hyphen

entry, margin justification, and other on/off commands, reinstate help level 2 or 3, and enter the prefix ^O by itself. This produces the On-screen Menu; bright light, parentheses, and capital letters show whether a toggle function is (OFF) or (ON). To check the status of column mode, put the Block Menu on-screen with ^K at help level 2 or 3.

STRANGE PRINTWHEEL

- I bought a special print wheel with elegant type, and it produces nonsense.
- It may be a proportional spacing wheel, one which requires supporting software in order to work. Proportional spacing daisy wheels usually carry warnings to this effect.

READING ERRORS

- I keep getting disk reading error messages.
- Your disk drives may need cleaning (use a cleaning kit regularly); your disk may have encountered electromagnetic disturbances; environmental conditions may be creating problems; or your system may have malfunctioned.

Computer rooms don't have to be the isolation units of 20 years ago, but the machines, though sturdier, are still delicate, temperamental, and easily disturbed. Review your physical setup and disk-handling routines to improve them if possible. Try another disk; consider buying a better quality disk. When all else fails, call your IBM dealer.

A BLANK FILE DISK

- My file disk seems to be completely blank.
- When this happened at a college computer center one day, a "computer detective" came to investigate the mysterious erasures. After interviewing everyone, he discovered that a temporary secretary had neatly stacked several disks under a pair of scissors before leaving for the night. Her choice of paperweight was unfortunate; the scissor tips were magnetized.

Exposure to a magnetic field can erase any disk. Don't rest disks against a magnetized copy holder, or store them near memo magnets, calculators, or tape recorders, or wear magnetic jewelry while handling disks. If a disk's contents disappear and you can't find the reason, you need a "computer detective," too.

COLUMN MODE PROBLEMS

- Column mode doesn't work.
- If you're trying to type adjacent columns using word wrap and margin justification, the problem is that even column mode won't accommodate these features. Study Chapter 27 before trying again.

- After moving a narrow column to the right of another column, several + flags show at the right. When I move to the end of any line showing the + flag, the screen shifts to display a lot of empty space.
- Some hard spaces were stored to the right of your first column; when you moved the second column, these were bumped to the far right. Each line of hard spaces extending beyond column 79 is marked with a +, and if you use ^QD, the cursor will go all the way to the end of the empty line.

To remove the empty spaces, position the cursor at the end of each "real" line by pressing ^D when you reach the last word. As soon as the cursor is one space to the right of the last word, enter ^T. This removes the space at right, however wide it might be. Now ^QD should take you to the end of the last word on each line, and the + flags should disappear.

MARKED BLOCK DOESN'T DISPLAY

- I entered F7 and, several lines below it, F8. Instead of displaying, the block remains invisible but the <B> and <K> markers are on the screen.
- If you positioned both block markers in the same column/space (column 1, for example), the block won't display if you are in column mode. Press ^KN and the block should display.
- I entered F7 and the <B> marker displayed. Then I entered F8 and the <B> marker disappeared, the <K> marker displayed, and my marked block remained unhighlighted.
- Leave <K> where it is and use ^QB to find the original <B> marker. This should cause the marked block to display.

Reference Manual

The following appendices form a REFERENCE SECTION reviewing WordStar's commands, screen messages, and functions.

Appendix A presents WordStar's startup procedure and basic commands in a logical sequence for those new to WordStar but already familiar with computers.

Appendix B lists WordStars screen messages, including error messages and information lines.

Appendix C is a glossary of WordStar terms.

Appendix D describes WordStar version 3.3, noting commands and procedures that are different from those of WordStar 3.2.

APPENDIX A

Summary of WordStar Commands

NOTE ON ABBREVIATIONS

Note: Two abbreviations are used throughout this guide:

^ represents the CONTROL key. When this symbol appears, depress the CONTROL key as you enter the letter code(s) that follow. Do not depress the CONTROL key when entering a number that follows the letter code.

@ represents the RETURN key. In commands requiring the entry of text or numbers, this signals the end or completion of the entry.

CALLING UP WORDSTAR

Boot up or restart the computer. You may want to use a single disk containing both DOS and WordStar files, or you can remove the DOS disk and replace it with WordStar.

With WordStar's files in drive A, respond to the A> screen prompt:

```
WS@
```

The entry can be made in upper- or lowercase letters.

WordStar's No-File Menu will appear:

```
                < < < N O - F I L E   M E N U > > >

--Preliminatry Commands--   |  --File Commands--  |  --System Commands--
L Change logged disk drive  |                     |    R Run a program
F File directory off (ON)   |   P  Print a file   |    X EXIT to system
H Set help level            |                     |
--Commands to open a file-- |   E RENAME a file   |  -WordStar Options-
 D Open a document file     |   O COPY a file     |    M Run MailMerge
 N Open a non-document file |   Y DELETE a file   |    S Run SpellStar

DIRECTORY of disk A:
  PRACTICE    PRACTICE.BAK   STORAGE    STORAGE.BAK   TEMP.A    TEMP.B
  TEMP.BAK
```

NO-FILE MENU COMMANDS

Following are the preliminary commands one may enter from the No-File Menu:

L Change Logged Disk

Screen message will note current logged drive and request entry of new logged drive.

F File Directory On/off

File directory (such as the list of files above) is on by default. After changing disks or changing the logged disk drive, press this key twice to display current file's contents.

H Set Help Level

Help level 3 (maximum on-screen command review) is set by default.Enter new help level (0, 1, 2, or 3) with this command. Entering H with the help level set at level 1, 2, or 3 displays an explanation of WordStar's help levels.

Help Level 3: All menus and explanations displayed
Help Level 2: Main editing menu (one-letter commands) suppressed
Help Level 1: Prefix menus (two-letter commands) suppressed
Help Level 0: All command explanations suppressed

D Open a Document File

Enter D when the No-File Menu is displayed. The screen will ask for a file name.

A file name consists of one to eight letters or digits, followed by (optional) a period and (optional) one to three additional characters. Do not use an asterisk (*), question mark (?), or the CONTROL key in your file name. Do not begin the file name with a period (.). Do not use a colon (:) in the file name unless indicating an unlogged disk drive. Do not use the extensions .BAK or .$$$ or the file names CON, AUX, COM1, LPT1. PRN, or NUL.

Press the RETURN key to signal completion of the file name.

You can preface the file name with another disk drive, such as B:, showing that the file will be stored on the disk in Drive B.

When entering a file name, correct spelling errors by using these delete/restore commands:

^S = delete character   ^Y = delete entry
^D = restore character   ^R = restore entry

^S removes one letter at a time, right to left; ^D restores erased letters. If entered by itself, ^D spells the most recently entered file's name, one letter at a time. ^Y removes or erases the file name; ^R restores it. If entered alone, ^R displays the last file name entered in response to the D command. (Note that ^D and ^R restore whatever name, word, or other response was most recently given, in the current editing session, to the command now featured.)

The DELETE and BACKSPACE keys also removes single characters, right to left, during file name entry.

Two additional commands can be used while opening a document file:

^F = file directory   ^U = cancel command

^F displays the file directory if this is not already on-screen.

To view all the files in a long directory, scroll with ^Z to see lower lines; scroll with ^W to review upper lines.

^U interrupts the document file opening; pressing the ESCAPE key after this command returns the No-File Menu.

A document file is so named because it arranges text into numbered pages, sets the right margin and wraps text, justifies text at the right margin, sets variable tab stops at five-space intervals beginning in column 6, displays a formatting ruler line, and offers automatic hyphenation during paragraph reform.

N To Open a Non-Document File

A non-document file does not employ word wrap, margin justification, or hyphen-help. The page break display feature is inoperative in this mode, so individual pages are not created. Fixed rather than variable tab stops appear at eight-space intervals beginning in column 9. The cursor "pops" across tab stops; you cannot place the cursor in the same column. A tab deletes as a single character, and a single character will overtype a tab. No ruler line is displayed. See the headings "Non-Document Files" and "Fixed Tabbing Mode" in the regular WordStar Manual.

To open a non-document file, enter N while the No-File Menu is displayed. Follow the same procedure for naming the file as described above.

S Spellstar and Mailmerge

The No-File Menu displays the WordStar options M (run MailMerge) and S (run SpellStar). These are optional programs manufactured by MicroPro International Corporation; one creates mailing lists and form letters, the other is a dictionary proofreading program. Neither is explained in this manual, which deals only with WordStar. The entry of M or S from the No-File Menu will operate only if the requested program has been installed.

WORDSTAR'S YES/NO RESPONSES

Several screen messages require a Yes or No response, indicated to the right of a message line by the notation (Y/N).

WordStar interprets any depression of the Y key as a Yes response: ^Y, Y, ^y, or y. Every other key is interpreted as a No or negative answer.

OTHER ENTRIES FROM THE NO-FILE MENU

P Print a File

P entered from the No-File Menu initiates the printing of a file. See the review of WordStar's print commands on page 323.

E Rename a File

To rename a file, enter E from the No-File Menu. The screen will ask for the file's current name, then its revised name.

O Copy a File

Duplicate a specified file without leaving WordStar by entering O from the No-File Menu. You may copy only one file at a time. To copy from or to another disk, both disks must be on-line and the unlogged disk drive entered where appropriate. Example:

```
NAME OF FILE TO COPY FROM?   LETTERS@
NAME OF FILE TO COPY TO?  B:TEXT.1@
```

This instructs the computer to copy the contents of a file called Letters (in Drive A) into a file (which may or may not exist already) named Text.1 (in Drive B). For this command to work, you must have an existing source file and sufficient disk space to accommodate its duplication.

If the destination file exists already, the entry described above generates a verification message:

```
FILE B:TEXT.1 EXISTS -- OVERWRITE? (Y/N):
```

Entering Y for Yes will destroy the current contents of file Text.1 in Drive B, replacing them with the contents of Letters, a file in Drive A. WordStar will recognize Y, y, ^Y, or ^y as "Yes" responses to this question. Pressing N or any other key means "No." In that case, the question will be reasked.

If the destination file does not already exist, no message appears and WordStar copies the source file, labeling the duplicate file as instructed.

Press the RETURN key, ESCAPE key, or ^U to abort the copy command.

Y Delete a File

To delete a file, enter Y from the No-File Menu. The screen will ask for the file's name; press the RETURN key after entering the name and the file will disappear. To erase a file on another disk, enter the drive name first. To interrupt this command if you change your mind, press the RETURN key or ^U. Do not use the ESCAPE key in this situation as it will erase the file.

SYSTEM COMMANDS: RUN A PROGRAM, EXIT TO SYSTEM

The command R entered from the No-File Menu lets you run an executable (.COM) program without leaving WordStar. When finished, the screen message says, "Hit any key to return to WordStar."

To exit from WordStar and return to the computer's operating system, enter X from the No-File Menu. The operating system prompt, usually A>, appears on the screen.

INSIDE THE DOCUMENT FILE

After entering a document file with the D command, you'll see two lines in faint light at the top of the screen.

The STATUS LINE shows your current disk drive, file name, cursor position (page number, line, and column number), and the "insert on" notation. If you change the line spacing, a corresponding message will appear at far right. As you enter WordStar commands, particularly two-letter codes, a corresponding notation appears at far left.

The RULER LINE shows the position of left and right margins (L and R), regular column spaces(- - - -)and preset tab stops (!). As you alter the margins and tab stops, the ruler line will change accordingly. If you set decimal tab stops for convenience in entering numerical tables, the symbol # will appear on the ruler line at each decimal tab stop.

THE DEFAULT PAGE

The preset or default document page, created in WordStar's document (D) file, has these conditions:

- Single spacing.
- Left margin at column 1, right margin at column 65.
- 55 lines are available for text entry.
- A top margin of three lines and a bottom margin of eight lines appear on the printed page.
- Tab stops are preset at five-space intervals, beginning at space or column 6 and ending at column 56.
- Tab stops are "variable" stops and can be changed.
- Character width is 10 cpi (characters per inch).
- Line height is 1/6 inch (6 lines = 1 inch).
- Word wrap is on.
- Justification is on.
- Ruler display is on.
- Page break display is on.
- Soft hyphen entry is off.
- Hyphen-help is on.
- Current page number prints at bottom center of page. Pages are numbered from the beginning of each file.
- During printing, the left margin is indented eight spaces from the paper's left edge.

WORDSTAR'S MENUS

WordStar's Main Menu appears on the screen when help level 3 is in use. This menu reviews the basic cursor-moving, scrolling, and delete commands (see page 304.)

The Quick Menu, reviewing those commands whose prefix is Q, appears when the help level is 2 or 3 and the prefix ^Q is entered (see page 305.)

The Block Menu reviews WordStar's block-marking, block- moving, saving and storing, file operations and disk operation commands. This menu appears (at help levels 2 and 3) whenever the ^K prefix is entered (see page 305.)

WordStar's On-Screen Menu appears (at help levels 2 and 3) when the ^O prefix is entered. It reviews format commands and indicates the current status of eight toggle codes (see page 305.)

The Print Menu appears whenever the prefix ^P is entered (help levels 2 and 3), reviewing WordStar's print controls which create special effects (see page 306.)

The Help Menu appears (help levels 2 and 3) when the prefix ^J is entered. This menu summarizes the 10 help commands. Help commands bring onscreen explanations, regardless of the help level in use, reviewing various codes and procedures (see page 305.)

All of WordStar's menus are illustrated in the section's that follow.

HELP COMMANDS

Screen menus (lists of commands organized by function) appear when the help level is set at 2 or 3 and you type the prefixes ^P, ^O, ^Q, or ^K. In each case, letters shown on the screen require the appropriate prefix (^P, ^O, ^Q, or ^K) when entered.

In addition, ^J brings the following summary to the screen, noting the on-screen explanations available. Although the menus listed above do not appear at help levels 0 or 1, the following summaries appear at all help levels.

^JH	Set/display help level (Use F1 key as alternate)
^JB	Explain paragraph reform
^JP	Explain place markers
^JD	Explain dot commands
^JM	Explain margins and tabs
^JR	Explain ruler line
^JS	Explain status line
^JF	Explain flags
^JV	Explain moving text
^JI	Command index

Illustrations of WordStar's menus begin on this page. Illustrations of the help commands listed above begin on page 306.

```
                    < < <      M A I N   M E N U      > > >
  --Cursor Movement --       | -Delete-  |  -Miscellaneous-    |  -Other  Menus-
^S char left ^D char right |^G char     | ^I Tab    ^B Reform | (from Main only)
^A word left ^F word right |DEL chr lf  | ^V INSERT ON/OFF    |^J Help   ^K Block
^E line up   ^X line down  |^T word rt  |^L Find/Replce again|^Q Quick  ^P Print
   --Scrolling--           |^Y line     |RETURN End paragraph|^O Onscreen
^Z line up   ^W line down  |            | ^N Insert a RETURN |
^C screen up ^R screen down|            | ^U Stop a command  |
```

WordStar's Main Menu displays only at help level 3. The Help Menu, Quick Menu, On-Screen Menu, Block Menu, and Print Menu display at help levels 2 and 3 when the appropriate prefix is entered (^J, ^Q, ^O, ^K, or ^P). As noted in each case, pressing the space bar returns you to the Main Menu (at help level 3); pressing the space bar removes the featured menu at help level 2. None of these menus will display at help level 1 or help level 0.

```
              < < <     H E L P     M E N U      > > >
                                  :                     :  -- Other Menus --
H  Display & set the help level   : S Status line       :  (from Main only)
B  Paragraph reform (CONTROL-B)   : R Ruler line        :  ^J Help   ^K Block
F  Flags in right-most column     : M Margins & Tabs    :  ^Q Quick  ^P Print
D  Dot commands, print controls   : P Place markers     :  ^O Onscreen
I  Index of commands              : V Moving text       :  Space Bar returns
                                  :                     :   you to Main Menu.
```

The command summaries listed above appear on pages 306–310. Enter the prefix ^J before each command code shown in the Help Menu. The IBM PC offers an alternate entry for the ^JH "set help level" command: the F1 key at the keyboard's left side. Help Menu commands display regardless of help level in use.

```
              < < <    Q U I C K   M E N U    > > >
  ---Cursor Movement---       : -Delete- : --Miscellaneous-- : --Other Menus--
S left side  D right side :Y line rt :F Find text in file: (from Main only)
E top scrn   X bottom scrn:DEL lin lf:A Find & Replace   :^J Help   ^K Block
R top file   C end file              :L find Misspelling :^Q Quick  ^P Print
B top block  K end block             :Q Repeat command or:^O Onscreen
0-9 marker   Z up    W down          :  key until space  :Space Bar returns
P previous   V last Find or Block    :  bar or other key :you to Main Menu.
```

Enter the prefix ^Q before each command code shown.

The IBM PC keyboard offers alternate entry commands for the following: ^QR (cursor to top of file) = F10; ^QC (cursor to end of file) = F9; ^QX (cursor to bottom of screen) = End(1) key on numeric pad keyboard; ^QE (cursor to top of screen) = Home(7) key on numeric pad; ^Q DEL (delete from cursor to beginning of line) = ^Q BACKSPACE.

Note that the Quick Menu lists a command (^QL) which does not operate without SpellStar, an optional program. If you do not have SpellStar's supportive software, ^QL will generate appropriate screen messages but the command won't work.

```
            < < <    O N S C R E E N   M E N U       > > >
 -Margins & Tabs-  : -Line Functions- :  --More Toggles--   : -Other Menus-
L Set left margin  :C Center text     :J Justify    off (ON):(from Main only)
R Set right margin :S Set line spacing:V Vari-Tabs off (ON):^J Help   ^K Block
X Release margins  :                  :H Hyph-Help off (ON):^Q Quick  ^P Print
I Set  N Clear tab :  -- Toggles--    :E Soft hyph on (OFF):^O Onscreen
G Paragraph tab    :W Wrd wrap off(ON):D Prnt disp off (ON):Space Bar returns
F Ruler from line  :T Rlr line off(ON):P Pge break off (ON): to Main Menu.
```

Enter the prefix ^O before each command code shown in the On-Screen Menu. Entering a toggle command code reverses the function's current status, which is shown in bright light, capital letters, and parentheses.

The IBM PC keyboard offers these additional codes: F3 sets the left margin at the cursor location; F4 sets the right margin at cursor. F2 is the indent to paragraph tab command (^OG).

```
              < < <      B L O C K   M E N U     > > >
-Saving Files-  : -Block Operations- : -File Operations-  :  -Other Menus-
D Save & resume : B Begin    K End   : R  Read   P  Print  : (from Main only)
D Save--done    : H  Hide / Display  : O Copy   E  Rename  : ^J Help   ^K Block
X Save & exit   : C Copy     Y Delete: J Delete            : ^Q Quick  ^P Print
Q Abandon file  : V Move     W Write : -Disk Operations-   : ^O Onscreen
-Place Markers- : N Column on(OFF)   :L Change logged disk: Space Bar returns
0-9 set/hide 0-9:                    :F Directory on (OFF): you to Main Menu.
```

Enter the prefix ^K before each command code shown in the Block Menu. The current status of two toggle commands (column mode and file directory) appears in bright light, parentheses, and capital letters.

The IBM PC keyboard offers these altnerate entries: F7 marks the beginning of a block (same as ^KB) and F8 marks the end of a block (same as ^KK).

```
                  < < <      P R I N T     M E N U       > > >
------ Special  Effects  ------  : -Printing Changes-  :   -Other Menus-
(begin and end) :  (one time each)  : A Alternate pitch   : (from Main only)
B Bold D Double : H Overprint char  : N Standard pitch    : ^J Help   ^K Block
  S Underscore  : O Non-break space : C Printing pause    : ^Q Quick  ^P Print
  X Strikeout   : F Phantom space   : Y Other ribbon color: ^O Onscreen
  V Subscript   : G Phantom rubout  : --User Patches--    : Space Bar returns
  T Superscript : RET Overprint line: Q(1) W(2) E(3) R(4) : you to Main Menu.
```

Enter the prefix ^P before each command shown in the Print Menu.

If you are using the IBM Matrix Printer, use F6 instead of ^PB for boldface type. F5 is an alternate entry for the ^PS underline command.

Those commands marked Printer Changes are not supported by the IBM Matrix Printer, nor are the phantom space and phantom rubout codes. To use WordStar's subscript and superscript commands, text must be double or triple spaced.

Note that the Print Menu lists four user patches (^PQ, ^PW, ^PE, and ^PR) which operate only if your system has been modified during installation to accommodate these special commands.

HELP COMMAND MENUS

Each of the Help Command Menus shown below will appear at the top of your screen regardless of the help level in use. Whereas the previously illustrated menus appear only at help levels 2 and 3, the following menus appear at levels 0, 1, 2, and 3.

Several of the menus are arranged in segments. Pressing the space bar causes the next segment to display; pressing ^U interrupts the display and returns you to the document file.

COMMAND: ^JH MENU: DISPLAY AND SET HELP LEVEL

```
HELP LEVELS
  3  all menus and explanations displayed
  2  main editing menu (1-control-char commands) suppressed
  1  prefix menus (2-character commands) also suppressed
  0  command explanations (including this) also suppressed

CURRENT HELP LEVEL IS 3

ENTER Space OR NEW HELP LEVEL (0, 1, 2 OR 3)
```

COMMAND: ^JI MENU: INDEX OF COMMANDS

```
COMMANDS TO --                       ARE --
move cursor                         on main and ^Q menus
scroll file up or down              on main menu; also find (^QF)
delete text                         on main and ^Q menus; also ^KY
move or copy text                   on ^K menu
end edit / save file                ^KD; see ^K menu
print (while editing)               ^KP
set tabs and margins                on ^O menu
reformat text                       ^B; ^JB gives info
find a string; replace              ^QF; ^QA; ^L repeats last
                      space bar for "entering text":
```

```
                  ***** ENTERING TEXT *****
To enter text at cursor position, just type the text.
Use RETURN key for paragraph end or other fixed line break;
     let word wrap form lines within paragraph.
Type ^V to turn insertion off (to overtype) or back on.
^N may be used to create blank lines ahead of cursor,
     as before inserting a paragraph.
Use ^B to realign margins after corrections.
^JM shows info on margins, tabs, table entry, outline entry.
                              press space bar after reading:
```

COMMAND: ^JF MENU: FLAGS IN RIGHT-MOST COLUMN

```
   ***** FLAG CHARACTERS (rightmost column of screen) *****
   <     line ends in "hard" carriage return, entered by user
 space   this line break arose from word wrap or paragraph
            reform, and may be moved on subsequent reform
   +     this line of document continues on next screen line
   -     next line will overprint this line
   ?     unrecognized or incomplete dot command
   M     Merge-Print (optional feature) dot command
   P     page break
   :     this screen line is before beginning of document
   .     after end of document                press space bar:
```

This menu's + flag notation applies to earlier versions of WordStar. A + flag now signals that text continues off-screen and may be viewed with a horizontal scroll command. When you set the right margin to the right of column 79, a + appears on the ruler line at far right, indicating that the right margin (R) is not visible.

COMMAND: ^JS MENU: STATUS LINE

```
              ***** STATUS LINE (top line of screen) *****
^JS              at left end of line is command now executing
A:NAME.TYP       is name of file you are now editing
PAGE n           is page number of cursor (disregards .PN's)
LINE n           is printout line on page of cursor position
COL n            is printout column of line of cursor position
INSERT ON        shows if character insertion is on (^V command)
MAR REL          shows if margins are released (^OX command)
decimal          shows during decimal tabbing
LINE SPACING n      shows if line spacing is not 1 (^OS command)
when WAIT appears, stop typing.               Press space bar:

        If page break display is OFF (^OP command) or edit
        was started with N command, then Status Line shows
        FC = nnnn FL = nnnn    in place of    PAGE n  LINE n.

  FC=nnnn    cursor position in characters (bytes) from
             beginning of file
  FL=nnnn    cursor position in file lines from beginning
             of file, including dot command lines

                                             space bar:
```

COMMAND: ^JR MENU: RULER LINE

```
                      ****  RULER LINE  ****

   L----!----!----!----!----!----!----!----!---------R

   L   Left margin (set with ^OL)
   R   Right margin (set with ^OR)
   !   regular tab stop (set with ^OI, clear with ^ON)
   #   decimal tab stop (set with ^OI, clear with ^ON)
   -   other positions between margins

                          press space bar after reading:
```

COMMAND: ^JM MENU: MARGINS & TABS

```
                   *****  MARGINS *****
To set left margin: Type ^OL.  WordStar will ask for column.
     Type desired column number 1-240 and press RETURN.
     Or, to use column of cursor in file, just press ESCAPE.
To set right margin: type ^OR, proceed as above.
To set both margins to match text in a line already entered:
     place cursor in that line, type ^OF.
To temporarily set left margin to next tab stop: type ^OG.
Margins apply to text subsequently entered.  To remarginate
     text already entered: set margins and use ^B.
                          press space bar after reading:

        *****  LINE SPACING AND JUSTIFICATION  *****

To set line spacing: type ^OS.  WordStar will ask for line
     spacing.  Enter a digit 1 thru 9.
To turn justification off (for ragged right format),
     or to turn justification back on: type ^OJ.
Line spacing and justification settings apply to text
     subsequently entered; they may be applied to previously
     entered text with the paragraph reform command (^B).
                           press space bar for "Tab Stops":

                  *****  TAB STOPS  *****

To set a tab: type ^OI.  WordStar will ask for column number.
     Type column number and press RETURN.  Or, to use cursor
     column press the ESCAPE key.  To set a decimal tab stop,
     type "#" before typing column number or pressing ESCAPE.
To clear a tab stop or all tab stops: type ^ON.
To tab: type ^I or press TAB key if present.  Tabbing
     inserts spaces to next tab stop if insertion (^V) is on.
     Tabbing advances cursor over text if insertion is off.
                                  press space bar:

     ENTERING A COLUMNAR TABLE -- We Suggest:

Set a tab stop for each column of table.
Clear all other tab stops.
If not at end of file, turn on insertion (^V),
     or use ^N to make blank lines.
Tab (^I) after entering each table item.  After last column
     on a line, tabbing will move to first item on next line.
                                            space bar:

     OUTLINE FORMAT TEXT ENTRY -- We Suggest:
Set tab stops at desired indentations.
Set right margin as desired.
For each item:
          Type ^OG's as required for item number indentation.
          Type item number.
          Type ^OG.
          Type text of item, without using RETURN.
          At end of item, press RETURN.  Left margin resets.
          Press RETURN again if blank line desired.
                                        press space bar:
```

COMMAND: ^JP MENU: PLACE MARKERS

```
               *****  PLACE MARKERS  *****

Up to 10 place markers, identified by numbers (n) 0-9,
     may be set in a file while the file is being edited.
To set place marker n at the cursor position: type ^Kn.
     <n> will display to indicate the marker position.
To return the cursor to place marker n: type ^Qn any
     time during the same edit.
To remove the <n> from the display: type ^Kn when the
     cursor is already at the marker position.
                                        press space bar:
```

```
              ****  OTHER MARKER & RELATED COMMANDS  ****

   The block beginning marker, <B>, and the block end marker,
        <K>, are set and moved to in a similar manner; the
        text between these markers can be moved (^KV), copied
        (^KC), deleted (^KY), or written to a file (^KW).

   ^QP moves cursor to its position before preceding command.

   ^QV moves cursor to start of last find/replace, or to
              source of text for last block move or copy.
                                                 press space bar:
```

COMMAND: ^JB MENU: PARAGRAPH REFORM

```
                    ***** PARAGRAPH REFORM (^B) *****
 To realign margins of a paragraph after corrections, place
      cursor at beginning of paragraph and type ^B.
 To change margins of paragraph already entered, set margins
      (^OL, ^OR), place cursor at paragraph beginning, type ^B.
 To change between justified and ragged right, or change line
      spacing, set desired justification (^OJ) & line spacing
      (^OS), place cursor at paragraph beginning, and type ^B.
 To obtain WordStar's help in hyphenating long words, place cursor
      at beginning of paragraph and type ^B.
                              press space bar for more:

 ^B reforms lines to end of paragraph as indicated by "hard"
      carriage return (< in rightmost column).
 Thus, it is important not to use RETURN between lines within a
      paragraph when entering text.
 ^B may be used to form hanging indents, change margins in mid-
      paragraph, etc.  The exact rule is:
      "^B starts on the cursor line, at the left margin col-
      umn, or at the cursor position, whichever is farther
      left, and proceeds to the next 'hard' carriage return".
                                            press space bar:

                         ***** Hyphen-Help *****
 ^B will occasionally stop before the end of the paragraph
      and ask you whether you wish a word hyphenated.
 Following the instructions that appear on the screen, move
      the cursor if desired to adjust the hyphen position,
      then press "-" to hyphenate, or ^B to not hyphenate.
 To turn off "hyphen'help", type ^OH.
                                         press space bar:
```

COMMAND: ^JV MENU: MOVING TEXT

```
                 *****  TO MOVE A BLOCK OF TEXT  *****
   1.  Put cursor on first character, type ^KB to mark start.
   2.  Put cursor after last character, type ^KK to mark end
      (for end line, use start next line to include RETURN).
   3.  Put cursor at destination, type ^KV to move the text,
      or ^KC to make a duplicate copy.
 To undisplay markers afterwards, use ^KH.
 ^KB and ^KK may be entered in either order, with or without
      other intervening commands.
 All above commands are on ^K menu.          press space bar:
```

COMMAND: ^JD MENU: DOT COMMANDS, PRINT CONTROLS

```
                    ***** Print Directives *****
 PRINT CONTROL CHARACTERS may be entered anywhere in a line
      to invoke underlining, boldface, subscripts, pauses,
      etc.  They are entered by typing ^P and a letter.  A
      directory of most print controls is given on the ^P
      PREFIX MENU; see manual for more.
 DOT COMMANDS are special lines beginning with a period and a
      two-letter code.  They control page breaks, headings,
      page numbering, page layout, etc.  Dot commands are
      typed in like other text.
 Space bar for DOT COMMAND SUMMARY, ^u to return to editing.
```

```
                    ***** Dot Commands *****
  PUT EACH DOT COMMAND ON SEPARATE LINE, WITH . IN COL 1
.PA        new PAge
.CP n      new page if less than n lines left on this page
.OP        Omit Page numbers when printing, starting this page
.PN        print Page Numbers, starting this page     (default)
.PC n      Page number Column (default 33 (30 if 64-col screen))
.PO n      Page Offset; extra indent when printed    (default 8)
.. text    comment, not printed
                                   press space bar for next frame:
```

```
.HE text    HEading used until next .HE        (default blank)
.FO text    FOoting (replaces page number)              (blank)
.PL n    Paper Length: total number of lines      (default 66)
.MT n    Margin at Top: # lines, top paper to text          (3)
.MB n    Margin at Bottom: # lines, end text to end paper   (8)
      # lines text on page is PL - MT - MB      (defaults to 55)
.HM n    Heading Margin: blank lines between head and text (2)
.FM n    Footing Margin: blank lines, text to footing       (2)
      FOR PAGE BREAKS TO DISPLAY AS THEY WILL PRINT, USE
.PL, .MT, .MT, AND .LH (next frame) AT FILE BEGINNING ONLY.
                                  Depress space bar for next frame:
```

```
      THE FOLLOWING WORK ONLY WITH INCREMENTAL PRINTERS:
.LH n   Line Height in 48ths of an inch            (default 8)
.CW n   Character Width in 120ths of an inch, for standard or
        alternate pitch, whichever is in use (see ^P menu).
                (default 12 for standard, 10 for alternate)
.SR n   Subscript / Superscript Roll in 48ths of an inch   (3)
.UJ OFF/ON   "MicroJustification" off/on          (default ON)
        Use insure that printed column alignment exactly
        matches screen, e.g. for tabular material:
        Put .UJ OFF before table, put .UJ ON after table.
                Space for next frame, ^U to return to editing:
```

```
SPECIAL CHARACTERS in HEADINGS (.HE) and FOOTINGS (.FO):
   #     prints as current page number
   \     do not interpret next character as a special character
   ^K    do not print following spaces if on even-numbered page
PAGE NUMBER POSITIONING: If a footing text is specified (.FO
 dot command), the default bottom center page number is not
 printed.  Use a # in heading or footing to position page
 number where desired.  ^K followed by spaces followed by #
 may be used to produce alternating left/right page numbers.
                Space for next frame, ^U to return to editing:
```

```
[Final frame describes Merge-Print Dot Commands, not discussed in
this manual.]
```

SAVING AND STORING

WordStar uses three different save commands, ^KS, ^KD, and ^KX.

^KS saves all entered material and editing changes, then returns you to page 1, line 1, column 1 of your file. This is the "save and re-edit" command.

^KD saves all entered material and editing changes, then returns you to WordStar's No-File Menu. Use this save command when you finish editing a file.

^KX saves all entered material and editing changes, then exits from WordStar and returns to the computer's operating system. This command usually generates the A> prompt.

ABANDON EDIT

If you enter a file and change your mind about working there, or if you make editorial changes you decide not to keep, enter ^KQ, the abandon edit command. If changes have been made or new material entered, a verification message appears. If not, WordStar returns you to the No-File Menu.

COMMANDS FOR MOVING THE CURSOR

The cursor is a flashing underline dash represented in this manual as ■. It shows your current position and the space that will be occupied by the next character you enter. In regular (default) WordStar use, if you enter a blank space in the middle of a line, it will bump text at the cursor's right a space to the right. If you add letters in the middle of a line of text, letters to the cursor's left will remain where they are; the new letters will take the cursor's place; and text to the cursor's right will be bumped to the right a corresponding number of spaces.

MOVE THE CURSOR

↑ (8) or ^E	Up one line
↓ (2) or ^X	Down one line
←(4) or ^S	Left one character (^H and BACKSPACE perform the same function)
→(6) or ^D	Right one character
^A	Left one word
^F	Right one word

Note: To move from one part of the screen to another, move up or down first. Then, after cursor lands on correct line, move left or right.

Home(7) or ^QE	Top of screen
End(1) or ^QX	Bottom of screen

Note: As the cursor cannot move out of a file, Home(7) will not move higher than beginning of a file and End(1) will not move lower than the end of a file. File size is determined by text entry, including blank spaces entered with the tab key and space bar, and empty lines entered with the RETURN key.

^QS	To beginning of line
^QD	To end of line

Note: the length of a line is determined by the cursor's previous path across that line, through text entry or because of hard spaces entered with the tab key or space bar. ^QS will move as far left as the cursor has been on a line, ^QD as far right as the cursor has been. If a line is wider than the screen, ^QD will scan to the right in segments; ^QS returns in one step to the line's beginning.

^QP	To position before last command was entered.
^QB	To beginning of marked block.

^QK To end of marked block. (Note: The block does not have to be displayed.)

^QV To block source (beginning of block) before last block move, block copy, block write, or block erase command was executed, or to cursor position before last find/replace command was entered, whichever was most recent.

^Q0–^Q9 To place marker <0>through<9>. Enter appropriate number after ^Q.

F10 or ^QR To beginning of file. [^Q PgUp(9) does the same.]

F9 or ^QC To end of file. [^Q PgDn(3) does the same.]

SCROLL COMMANDS

To view different parts of your text on-screen, you can use scroll commands.

It's easy to become confused over scroll commands because there are two ways of defining scrolling. You can think of scrolling as an action that "pulls" your document through the screen so that you can examine an extra line, an extra screenful, the right side of a wide document, or several pages in a continuous flow. In that definition, you imagine the screen to be stationary and the file to move. Alternately, you can think of the screen as a portable viewing unit, like a hand-held magnifying glass, one that moves up, down, right, or left as you examine a fixed or stationary file. The latter definition is used throughout this book.

All scroll command definitions are measured from the cursor's position. Note that the definitions below (up, down, right, left) do not match those of the WordStar manual or on-screen menus. However, they are consistent with WordStar's use of upper-keyboard letter codes representing "up" and lower-keyboard letter codes representing "down."

Think of the direction your eyes naturally move toward as you wait for new material to appear, or think of the location of the off-screen text you are waiting to view relative to the current screen position. If what you want to see is above (or comes before) what is now on the screen, scroll "up" to view it. If what you want to see is below (or comes after) what is now on the screen, scroll "down" to view it.

^W Reveal additional upper line (scroll up; screen moves up)

^Z Reveal additional lower line (scroll down; screen moves down)

PgUp(9) or ^R Reveal upper screenful (scroll up; screen moves up)

PgDn(3) or ^C Reveal lower screenful (scroll down; screen moves down)

^QW Continuous scroll revealing upper lines (scroll up; screen moves up)

^QZ Continuous scroll revealing lower lines (scroll down; screen moves down)

Note: Enter 1 to 9 at any time during continuous scroll to change speed from fastest (1) to slowest (9). Default speed is 3. Stop continuous scroll by pressing space bar or other key.

^QQR Continuous upper screenful scroll (scroll up; screen moves up)
[^QQR PgUp(9) does the same]

^QQC Continuous lower screenful scroll (scroll down; screen moves down)
[^QQPgDn(3) does the same]

Note: The same 1 to 9 speed options given for ^QZ and ^QW apply here. The default speed is 3. Stop continuous scroll by pressing space bar or other key.

^QD Horizontal scroll right (wide document; screen moves right)

^QS Horizontal scroll left (wide document; screen moves left)

DELETE COMMANDS

^G Remove character over cursor (in cursor's column), remove letters left to right

DEL Remove character at left, remove letters right to left

^T Remove word at right

Note: To remove unwanted space to the right of the cursor, enter ^T. If necessary, this command can bring text up from the following line to "rejoin" text at the cursor position.

^Y Remove entire line

Note: To remove unwanted space between lines, enter ^Y. This command "erases" empty lines.

^Q DEL Delete from one space left of cursor to beginning of line
(^Q BACKSPACE does the same)

^QY Delete from and including cursor column to end of line

Note: ^Y removes entire line and moves lower lines up accordingly. ^QY, ^Q DEL, and ^T remove words from a line without removing the line itself; that is, you can erase the contents of a line and retain the empty space by using these commands.

^KY Erase displayed block

PRINT CONTROL COMMANDS

WordStar's print control characters make it possible to set boldface type, subscripts and superscripts, underlining, and other special effects. All but the special F-function key commands begin with the prefix ^P. The prefix does not appear on-screen, but the second letter of each command will appear with a caret mark or arrow to show entry point.

To interrupt any print control command after entering the ^P prefix but before entering the second letter code, press the space bar. Do not use the ESCAPE or RETURN keys or ^U. Remove any undesired print control with the DELETE key or any delete command.

Note: The control characters listed below must be entered both before and after the word/phrase/paragraph/text to be featured.

F5 Underline (alternate entry code: ^PS)
F6 Boldface (alternate entry code, incremental printers: ^PB; ^PB creates triple strike on the IBM Matrix Printer)
^PD Doublestrike
^PV Subscript
^PT Superscript
^PY Change ribbon color

Note: On the IBM Matrix Printer, subscripts and superscripts work only if text is not single spaced. Subscripts and superscripts print a full line up or down from text. The IBM Matrix Printer does not support ^PY.

Note: The control characters below are entered once.

^PH Overprint next character (prints in same space as preceding character)
^PM Overprint next line (prints on same line as preceding text)
^PG Phantom Rubout
^PF Phantom Space
^PG and ^PF are special characters on daisy wheel printers and some others; these commands are not interpreted by the IBM Matrix Printer.
^PO Non-break space (nonexpanding blank space)
^PK Alternate page position (enter in heading/footing line)
^PA Shift to 12-pitch character width
^PN Resume normal 10-pitch character width
^PC Stop printer at this column/space

Note: The IBM Matrix Printer does not support these commands. ^PC will cause the printer to stop, but not at the column/space indicated; it stops before printing anything on the ^PC line.

ON-SCREEN FORMAT AND TEXT ENTRY COMMANDS

On-screen format commands, most of which begin with ^O, set your document's basic configuration. Tab stops, margins, line spacing, and other factors that determine the position of text on the page can be changed from WordStar's default values.

Setting the Margins

^OL Set left margin
^OR Set right margin

Note: A screen message will ask for desired column number; press RETURN after entering number, or press ESC key to use cursor's position as new margin.

F3 Set left margin at cursor position
F4 Set right margin at cursor position
^OF Set margins/tab stops from cursor line

Note: Left margin will be set at first character on line, right margin at last character. Tab stops from ruler line remain if between the new margins. This command can be used to activate a mid-text ruler line prepared by typing dashes (- - - -) where spaces are desired and exclamation marks (!) where tab stops are desired.

Insertion on/off

Ins Insertion key at right of Caps Lock key. This is an on/off toggle key. ^V is the alternate command.

Note: Insertion is on by default and status line shows INSERT ON message so indicating. When insertion is on, new characters or spaces entered in a line of already-entered text will be inserted between the cursor's position and text coming after. This is true for blank spaces as well as characters. Everything to the right of the cursor is "bumped" farther right to accommodate the new entry. When insertion is off (no message appears on the status line in this condition), new spaces and letters literally replace the old. When insertion is on, the TAB key, RETURN key, and space bar insert new spaces, bumping previously entered text to the right and/or down. When insertion is off, the TAB key and RETURN key move the cursor without disturbing text. Nothing is inserted. In this situation, the space bar erases letters, replacing already-entered characters with blank spaces.

Hard and Soft Spaces, Returns, Hyphens

In WordStar's nomenclature, a hard return is entered by the user (with the RETURN key or ^M or ^N) to note the end of a paragraph or the skipping of a line.

Each line return includes a line feed command so that when the printer reaches the end of a line, it moves the paper accordingly.

When you enter a hard return, the screen flag < appears at far right. A soft return is entered by word wrap during the setting of the right margin and the "wrapping" of text down to the beginning of the next line. No flag or screen notation appears at the far right when a word is wrapped; a blank space at right indicates the entry of a soft return.

The computer remembers hard returns; they are not rearranged in future editing or paragraph reforming. Soft returns are temporary; in future editing or paragraph reforming, soft returns will be rearranged.

A hard space is entered with the space bar or the ^PO nonbreak space command. Use of the TAB key also generates hard spaces. A hard space is permanent; the computer will retain hard spaces. A hard space is permanent; the computer will retain hard spaces no matter how the document may be edited in the future. A soft space is entered by the computer during margin justification, to spread words evenly across the line and make the right margin straight in the process. Soft spaces are temporary; they will be rearranged during future editing of the document.

A hard hyphen is entered, in regular WordStar use, by pressing the hyphen key. This hyphen always prints; it appears on the screen in bright light or regular characters. A soft hyphen is entered by hyphen-help, or by you if you switch to soft hyphen entry mode. A soft hyphen appears highlighted on the screen (in dim light or reverse video). It will not print unless positioned at the end of a line.

Entering Returns

^N	Enter hard return
RETURN	Enter hard return
^M	Enter hard return

Note: ^M and the RETURN key operate identically. Both commands enter the carriage return/line feed in agreement with current line spacing, and the cursor moves down the appropriate number of lines.

^N enters a hard return in single spacing, regardless of line spacing in use, and it leaves the cursor where it was. ^N is usually used to divide an already-existing paragraph or to edit within a document.

Using Tab Stops

TAB	Indent to next tab stop (TAB key)
^I	Indent (identical to TAB key)
^ON	Remove tab stop

Note: Screen message asks for desired column; enter number and press RETURN key, or remove tab stop at cursor's position by pressing ESCAPE key; or remove all tab stops by entering A and RETURN.

^OI Set tab stop

Note: Screen message asks for desired column; enter number and press RETURN key, or set tab stop at cursor's position by pressing ESCAPE key. On the ruler line, ! represents a regular text tab stop; # represents a decimal tab. Set decimal tabs by typing # before the column number or before pressing ESC.

F2 Paragraph tab (^OG is the alternate command)

Note: This command sets subsequent lines with the left margin indented one tab space for each F2 entered. Use for hanging indentation, bibliography entries, and other indented text. Indenting of left margin stops when you enter next hard return. Indented area displays in bright light on the ruler line. Cancel command with ^QS or by moving cursor back to column 1.

Paragraph Reform

Whenever you add words, delete words, rearrange margins, or make other formatting changes, you can make on-screen text conform by using a simple command:

^B Reform paragraph

Note: Position cursor in first line of paragraph or on first line of unconforming text and press ^B. Reforming begins at the cursor position unless the cursor is left of the revised left margin. If the cursor is left of the new left margin, the cursor line is indented, if appropriate, corresponding to indentation of the line before reforming.

In normal use, hyphen-help will offer a hyphen in words that might be hyphenated at the end of a line. To hyphenate where shown, press the - key; to refuse hyphen and continue reforming, press ^B again. To reposition the hyphen, use ←(4) or →(6) to move the cursor; then press -. ^B will reset text between cursor point and next hard return according to line spacing, margins, toggle commands, and tab stops (if using F2) currently in use. Hyphen-help can be turned off with ^OH, below.

Entering Hyphens

^OH Hyphen-help on/off

Note: Hyphen-help is on by default. This function works in conjunction with ^B (paragraph reform) to hyphenate words at the end of a line. To reform a paragraph without having the computer stop to offer a hyphen, turn hyphen-help off. To reinstate hyphen-help, press ^OH to turn back on.

^OE Soft hyphen entry on/off

Note: In normal use, WordStar sets hard hyphens whenever you press the - key. If you turn soft hyphen entry on (^OE), you will enter soft hyphens by pressing the -. To enter a hard hyphen when in soft hyphen mode, type ^P-. Turn function off by pressing ^OE again.

Change Line Spacing

WordStar presets single spacing. You can change to double spacing, triple spacing, or anything up to every-nine-line spacing.

^OS Set line spacing

Note: Screen message will ask for desired spacing; enter number between 1 and 9. If you enter any key other than 1 through 9, line spacing remains as is. The status line shows line spacing if other than default (single) spacing.

Center a Line

^OC Center this line

Note: Enter text first, then press ^OC with the cursor still in the text line. Text will be centered between current margins. To re-center after changing margins, use ^OC again. The cursor may be anywhere in the line when you enter this command.

Margin Release

^OX Release margins

Note: This command cancels automatically when you press RETURN. Left margin will not release unless indented from column 1. To release indented left margin, enter ^OX before entering text; to release right margin, enter command before reaching right margin. If left margin is indented, ^OX causes ruler line to change, displaying tab stop markers (!) in bright light left of the revised left margin. Status line shows the message MAR REL when the margin is released. To turn off manually, enter ^OX again.

Additional Toggle Commands

^OW Word wrap on/off
^OJ Right margin justification on/off
^OV Variable tab stops on/off

Note: When word wrap is off, text does not stop at right margin but continues until you enter a hard return. When ^OJ is off, WordStar creates a ragged rather than justified right margin and spaces are not added to spread words across the line. When variable tab mode is off, tab stops are fixed at eight-space intervals, beginning at column 9. All three toggles are on by default in a document file; in word processing you will not usually change ^OV or ^OW.

Display Toggles

^OT Ruler line display on/off
^OP Page break display on/off
^OD Print control display on/off

Note: ^OT removes and reinstates the ruler line at the top of your screen. ^OP removes all page break lines and pagination, showing cursor location in file characters (bytes) and lines rather than page/line/column position. ^OD removes print control symbols (such as ^B for boldface type) from the screen.

Changing Print Size, Changing Printwheels

These commands work only on incremental (daisy wheel-type) printers and are not supported by the IBM Matrix Printer:

^PA Shift to alternate (12-pitch) character width
^PN Resume normal (10-pitch) character width
(Note: Pitch refers to characters per inch.)
^PC Stop printer here

Note: This command makes it easy to change printwheels or ribbons at a specified point.

PLACE MARKERS

^KO–9 Set place marker
^QO–9 Find place marker

Note: Place markers survive the ^KS save command but not ^KD or ^KX.

Place markers can be moved; to relocate a marker, enter ^K and the number at new location.

To hide a marker, enter ^K and the number with cursor at the marker location. A marker need not be displayed to be located with the appropriate ^Q command. ^Qn finds a hidden marker and redisplays it.

FIND, FIND-AND-REPLACE COMMANDS

To locate a word in the file, use WordStar's find command. To find a word and correct, revise, or replace it with another word, use the find-and-replace command. Several options can be used with both of these entries, and two options are for the replacement command only. Although WordStar will accept any entry up to 30 characters in length, the commands work best with short entries, preferably a single word. The WordStar manual refers to entries of this category as "strings." A string can consist of letters, numbers, spaces and/or symbols. In some but not all cases, it may include print control characters.

^QF Find
^QA Find-and-Replace
^QV Return cursor to position before last ^QA or ^QF
^L Repeat last ^QA or ^QF command

Note: ^QF and ^QA generate screen message requesting input. Use the RETURN key to signal end of entry unless no options are to be entered; if using no options, the ESCAPE key will expedite your search. The find/replace command entered without the use of options will locate the first appearance of the target word, even if it appears within another word (the command ^QF "tar" would stop in the word "s*tar*ring," if that appeared in your file). The no-option command searches from the cursor position to the end of the file. If the target word is not located, an error message appears. In a replacement entry, a verification message appears; answer Y for yes if replacement desired at that position. N or any key but Y is interpreted as a No response. ^L will repeat the most recent find/replace command, including options, if any. ^R will restore (repeat) the last-entered target word, replacement word, or set of options. ^L and ^R can be used throughout an editing session, going from one file to another.

Find Options

[n] Find nth appearance of target word
U Ignore upper/lowercase distinctions
W Match whole words only
B Search backward in file, beginning at cursor position

Find-and-Replace Options

[n] Make replacement n times
U Ignore upper/lowercase distinctions

W Match whole words only
B Search backward in file, beginning at cursor position
G Global (whole file) search/replace, from front to back of file
N No delay (automatic replacement, no verification message)

Special Find Characters

Special find characters may be entered as part of a ^QA or ^QF response. See pages 175, 176, and 183 for complete descriptions.

^PA Match any character
^PN Match carriage return
^Ox Match any character other than x, where x is any character entered immediately after the ^O
^PS Match any character not a letter or digit

BLOCK COMMANDS

A block is any section of text marked by you for a special purpose. Although there are some limits on the size of blocks, most systems accommodate several pages at a time. Any command your system cannot handle will generate an error message; the accompanying screen explanation will suggest breaking the block into smaller segments.

F7 or ^KB Mark block beginning
F8 or ^KK Mark block end

Note: In regular block mode, WordStar defines a block as everything following F7 on the F7 line to and including everything preceding F8 on the F8 line.

^KH Hide, redisplay block

Note: A marked block has been defined with ^KB and ^KK. When first marked, a block is highlighted; this is called a displayed block. The next four commands operate only if the block is displayed. The hidden block is still marked, but it appears on-screen in bright or regular letters, matching the rest of your text.

^KV Move displayed block to cursor position
^KC Copy displayed block at cursor position

Note: The 64K IBM PC limits the size of blocks being moved or copied to 900 characters, or about 13 to 15 average lines.

^KY Erase displayed block
^KW Write displayed block into another file for storage

Note: Destinction file can be on either disk (dual drive unit); if the file exists already, ^KW erases that file's other contents after screen verification message asks for Yes/No response. Original file remains on-screen.

^KR Read file

Note: Screen message asks for source file. Entire contents of source file are then inserted in current file at the cursor position.

^KN Enter column mode/Leave column mode (toggle command)

Note: Column mode does not alter the way in which you create columns, but it allows you to move, copy, and delete columns of text or numbers without moving, copying, or deleting adjacent material. In column mode, WordStar defines a block as a rectangle beginning at the line and column number of F7 and ending at the line and column number of F8. The commands ^KV, ^KC, and ^KY operate in column mode. The commands ^KW and ^KR are inoperative in column mode.

Note: The 64K IBM PC limits ^KV and ^KC in column mode to an average 13 to 15 lines, regardless of the column's actual size. Column mode is best used for transferring short columns over short distances when using the 64K system.

^QB Move to block beginning
^QK Move to block end (Note: Block does not have to be displayed.)
^QV Move to block source <B> before last ^KV, ^KC, ^KY, or ^KW command was executed

Note: ^QV is also used to return cursor to its position prior to last ^QF or ^QA find/replace entry. The cursor's destination depends on which command was most recent.

FILE OPERATIONS AND DISK OPERATIONS

File operations allow you to remain in one file while making use of another. ^KR, the read file command described above, is such a function. Others are:

^KO Copy a file
^KE Rename a file

Note: These commands are identical to O and E entered from the No-File Menu.

^KJ Delete a file

Note: Use this to erase an unnecessary file when a disk full error message appears. Screen will ask for file to delete.

^KF Display file directory

Note: This command displays current files at top of screen. Use in conjunction with ^KJ above to select file for deletion.

^KP Print a file

Note: If you have more than 64K, you will be able to print one file while editing another. Follow the same procedure as for regular print command using ^KP instead of the No-File Menu P command. On the 64K IBM PC, this command generates an error message.

^KL Change logged disk

Note: This command is identical to the command L entered from the No-File Menu.

MISCELLANEOUS COMMANDS

^QQ Repeat next command

Note: ^QQ repeats whatever command you next enter until you interrupt. Depress the CONTROL key while entering the entire command. ^QQR or ^QQ PgUp(9) scans upper screenfuls of text continuously, moving toward the beginning of the file. ^QQC or ^QQ PgDn(3) scans to end of file a screenful at a time. ^QQB reforms one paragraph after another continuously. Interrupt continuous execution with space bar or other key.

^U Interrupt command

Note: Use ^U when you wish to cancel any partly entered command or interrupt a command already being executed. Although ^U interrupts most two-letter codes if you enter the prefix and then change your mind, it is not recommended for ^P commands. Use the space bar to interrupt a ^P command if you have not yet entered the second letter.

DOT COMMANDS

Dot commands can be used to reformat a document's page length, printing position, margins, character width, line height, and other configurations. They provide for the setting of headings and footings, the repositioning and changing of page numbers, and several additional functions. See Chapters 28 through 35 for a detailed explanation. For a dot command to work, it must be positioned at the far left of the screen with the dot (.) in column 1 and a space between the two-letter command and any accompanying number or text.

Note that the commands for changing line height, character width, subscript roll, and microjustificaton require an incremental printer. Not all printers support the bidirectional print on/off command. Not all printers respond to WordStar's subscript and superscript dot commands. The IBM Matrix Printer cannot change character width, line height, or subscript roll; it does not support the bidirectional print off command; it does not microjustify text; and for subscripts and superscripts to work, text cannot be set in single spacing.

SUMMARY OF DOT COMMANDS

.PA Page break
.CP n Conditional page break (n = lines)
.LH n Line height (n = 1/48 inch)
.CW n Character width (n = 1/120 inch)
.PL n Page length (n = lines)
.MT n Top margin (n = lines)
.MB n Bottom margin (n = lines)
.HM n Heading margin (n = lines)
.FM n Footing margin (n = lines)
.PO n Page offset at left (n = lines)
.PC n Page number position (n = column)
.HE Heading

.FO	Footing
.OP	Omit bottom (default) page numbering
.PN	Reinstate bottom page numbering
.PN n	Set new page number (n = number)
.SR n	Subscript roll (n = 1/48 inch)
.UJ	Microjustification on/off (.UJ 1, .UJ 0)
.BP	Bidirectional print on/off (.BP 1, .BP 2)
..	Ignore line; do not print

Note: The commands .LH, .CW, .UJ, and .SR operate only on incremental (daisy wheel-type) printers.

PRINTING A FILE

The command P entered from the No-File Menu, or the command ^KP entered within a file, brings a screen message asking for the name of the file you wish to print. The 64K IBM PC does not support simultaneous editing and printing; ^KP generates an error message. If you have more than 64K, ^KP allows you to edit one file while you print another. WordStar does not permit the simultaneous editing and printing of a single file without delaying the storage of editing changes and without printing only the original (previously saved) version.

So long as the computer has sufficient memory, no printing is in progress when the command is entered, and no printing has been suspended, ^KP produces this message, which is the same that appears when you enter P from the No-File Menu:,

```
NAME OF FILE TO PRINT? ■
```

Enter file name and RETURN key to use the following options:

DISK FILE OUTPUT (Y/N):
START AT PAGE NUMBER (RETURN for beginning)?
STOP AFTER PAGE NUMBER (RETURN for end)?
USE FORM FEEDS (Y/N):
SUPPRESS PAGE FORMATTING (Y/N):
PAUSE FOR PAPER CHANGE BETWEEN PAGES (Y/N):
Ready printer, press RETURN:

The Yes/No questions can be answered with letter keys or the RETURN key. WordStar will recognize any ^Y, Y, ^y, or y response as Yes, and any other letter/number key as No. The Return key also provides the default response; No is the default answer to all Yes/No questions above.2Printing Options

Printing Options

```
DISK FILE OUTPUT (Y/N): ■
```

The default answer (press RETURN key or any letter but Y) causes the print output to go to the printer, producing hard copy. This is normally desired.

Answering Yes to this question prints the file not onto paper but onto another file. This does not make an exact copy of the file because all dot commands are "expanded" or interpreted, so that if you set headings and footings, change the page number's position, and make other dot command alterations, you can see their effect on-screen. Note: dot commands will not be interpreted if a Yes response is given to the SUPPRESS PAGE FORMATTING option.

```
START AT PAGE NUMBER (RETURN for beginning)? ■
```

If you press the RETURN key, WordStar will initiate print with page 1 of your file. To begin on another page, enter the number and press RETURN. If you have changed page numbers with the .PN n command, use the revised number, even though the file's status line continues to number pages from the beginning of the file. Entering characters other than numbers will cause the question to be repeated.

```
STOP AFTER PAGE NUMBER (RETURN for end)? ■
```

Press RETURN to print to the end of the file. To stop print before the end, enter desired page number and press RETURN.

```
USE FORM FEEDS (Y/N): ■
```

A default or No response to this question usually produces the correct number of line feeds to advance from one page to the top of the next when using perforated, accordian-folded long sheets. On some non-daisy wheel printers the use of form feeds is faster: Answering Yes to this question sends a special form feed command between pages and before the first page, eliminating the need for a .PL paper length command and vertical positioning of the paper before printing.

```
SUPPRESS PAGE FORMATTING (Y/N): ■
```

Pressing the RETURN key enters the default answer No, which causes your file to print with all its dot commands interpreted and pagination executed as shown on-screen in your file.

Answering Y for Yes causes the page formatting to disappear (there are no top and bottom margins, but rather an uninterrupted single "page" of the file's exact contents), and dot commands are printed rather than interpreted. This is the only way to print correctly entered dot commands for proofreading. Print control characters, such as ^B (boldface) and ^S (underline), should be interpreted normally when using this option.

Already-paginated files produced by programs other than WordStar and disk files created with the DISK FILE OUTPUT option can be printed using the Yes response.

```
PAUSE FOR PAPER CHANGE BETWEEN PAGES (Y/N): ■
```

The RETURN key produces the default answer, No, which should be used when printing on continuous forms. The computer will not pause between pages but print without interruption.

When using single sheets, letterheads, or other stationery, enter Y for Yes. Print will pause until you're ready to resume. Then enter P (or ^KP if you are editing another file while printing) to resume print.

```
Ready printer, press RETURN: ■
```

Be sure that your printer is ready before pressing the RETURN key. On some printers, all that's necessary is the power switch; on others, the printer must be on-line as well as turned on. Unless you're using the form feeds option, paper must be positioned correctly.

Press the RETURN key or any other key and print begins. If you used P to initiate print, the No-File Menu returns; if you used ^KP, your current editing file returns.

STOP PRINT

To stop the printer, enter P from the No-File Menu or ^KP from your file. Print will stop with this message:

```
"Y" to ABANDON PRINT, "N" TO RESUME, ^U TO HOLD: ■
```

Y (or ^Y, y, or ^y) abandons printing and if you used the P command, it returns the No-File Menu.

N (or any key other than Y or ^U) resumes print as soon as the command is entered. If your paper is crooked or needs adjusting, use this command to continue when ready.

^U suspends but does not abort print. The next P or ^KP command entered will cause this file to complete its printing. Other commands of every description may be entered before resuming. ^U returns you to the No-File Menu if you used the P print command; it returns you to the edit function if you initiated print with ^KP.

Note: The 64K IBM PC does not accommodate the ^U option. ^U generates an error message.

To stop print before printing begins (such as when changing paper between pages), enter P twice (or ^KP twice). The screen message above should appear so that you can abandon, resume, or suspend printing.

To continue printing after changing paper between pages, after changing ribbon or print wheel after a ^PC pause, or to resume print interrupted with ^U above, press P (or ^KP).

APPENDIX B
Screen Messages

In addition to the screen messages you have met already, such as WordStar's requests for additional information, you should become familiar with the following notations.

ERROR MESSAGES

Most of WordStar's error messages explain themselves: they describe a problem and tell you how to resume editing (usually by pressing the ESCAPE key). But one is so dramatic that you should read this carefully — otherwise, if it shows up, you'll think you broke the computer.

Here's what happens:

```
!!!!!!!!!!!!!!!!!!!!!!!!!!!!!!!!!!!!!!!!!!!!!!!!!!!!!!!!!!!!!!!!
!!!!!!!!!!!!!!!!!!!!!!!!!!!!!!!!!!!!!!!!!!!!!!!!!!!!!!!!!!!!!!!!
!!!!!!!!!!!!!!!!!!!!!!!!!!!!!!!!!!!!!!!!!!!!!!!!!!!!!!!!!!!!!!!!
!!!!!!!!!!! The screen fills with exclamation marks !!!!!!!!!!!
!!!!!!!!!!!!!!!!!!!!!!!!!!!!!!!!!!!!!!!!!!!!!!!!!!!!!!!!!!!!!!!!
!!!!!!!!!!!!!!!!!!!!!!!!!!!!!!!!!!!!!!!!!!!!!!!!!!!!!!!!!!!!!!!!
!!!!!!!!!!!!!!!!!!!!!!!!!!!!!!!!!!!!!!!!!!!!!!!!!!!!!!!!!!!!!!!!
```

And that's not all. The terminal beeps.

This happens when the computer receives commands faster than it can process them, usually because you're holding a command key too long and it's repeating automatically. This message means STOP! and WAIT!! As soon as the screen catches up, the exclamation marks disappear and you can continue.

EDIT ERRORS

Most edit function error messages are self-explanatory. They describe a problem so you can correct it, and you can resume editing by pressing the ESCAPE key.

```
*** INTERRUPTED ***   Press ESCAPE Key
```

This message appears when you use ^U, the interrupt command code. It calls your attention to the command's termination and returns you to the document file.

```
*** NOT FOUND: [target word] *** Press ESCAPE Key
```

^QF (find), ^QA (find-and-replace), and ^L (repeat last find/replace entry) generate this message. In normal use, you'll be at the end of the file, although the B option presents it at the file's beginning.

```
*** ERROR E5: THAT PLACE MARKER NOT SET *** Press ESCAPE Key
```

^Q and a number will generate this command if the requested place marker has not been set. <B> and <K> (block begin and block end) markers belong in this category; ^QP and ^QK will being Error E5 to the screen if no block has been marked in the file.

```
*** ERROR E6: BLOCK BEGINNING NOT MARKED
        (OR MARKER IS UNDISPLAYED) *** Press ESCAPE Key
```

The commands ^KV (move a block), ^KY (erase a block), ^KC (copy a block), and ^KW (write a block) generate this message if the block hasn't been marked with F7, or if the block has been hidden with ^KH.

```
*** ERROR E7: BLOCK END NOT MARKED
        (OR MARKER IS UNDISPLAYED) *** Press ESCAPE Key
```

This message is identical to E6 above, except the block end (F8) has not been entered.

```
*** ERROR E9: BLOCK TOO LONG
   MOVE OR COPY IN TWO SMALLER BLOCKS *** Press ESCAPE Key:
```

Computers with little available memory generate message E9 frequently; larger systems rarely see it. The 64K IBM PC limits block moves to 900 characters and column block moves to columns taken from an area storing 900 characters (13 to 15 average screen lines). In regular block (but not column block) mode, you can solve the problem with ^KW and ^KR storage and retrieval as well as by following the screen's suggestion.

```
*** ERROR E12: DISK FULL *** Press ESCAPE Key
```

Here is the message you don't want.

If you're moving the cursor toward the beginning of a file when it occurs, you may be able to save your work; if not, it may be lost forever.

See page 287 in the WordStar Clinic for solutions to the full disk problem.

One DISK FULL error message will convince you to save everything you type, to make copies of your work, and to keep a close eye on your file space.

```
*** ERROR E13:  COLUMN READ/WRITE NOT ALLOWED *** Press  ESC  Ke
```

Message E13 appears when you enter ^KW or ^KR in column mode (^KN). Use regular block mode to use these commands.

```
FILE [name] NOT FOUND
```

Check the spelling of the file name you entered; check the disk directory (enter ^KF if you're editing a file) to be sure it's on this disk.

```
INVALID FILE NAME: [name]
```

A file name containing an asterisk (*), question mark (?), or colon (:) may generate this message; so may files beginning with a period (.) or exclamation mark (!), or any document file containing .BAK or .$$$, the codes for WordStar's backup and temporary storage files. The IBM Personal Computer also reserves these file names: CON, AUX, COM1, LPT1, PRN, and NUL.

MISCELLANEOUS ERROR MESSAGES

```
FILE [name] ALREADY EXITS
```

If you attempt to rename a file (using E at the No-File Menu or ^KE while editing) and select as the revised name a title already on the disk, this message appears. Select a new name.

```
FILE [name] NOT ON SAME DRIVE
```

When changing file names, you cannot move a file from one drive to another.

WARNING MESSAGES

Warning messages don't interrupt your command, but they call attention to potential problems.

```
CAN'T DISPLAY PAGE BREAKS IN A NON-DOCUMENT FILE
```

This warning won't appear if you work with document files, but in a non-document file, the ^OP command (reinstate page break display) produces the message.

```
*** WARNING: WORD TOO LONG TO FIT MARGINS
```

You may accidentally create a margin line that is five columns wide. Or you might enter a row of symbols (- - - - - - or ******) and go past the right margin. WordStar will leave your overlapping word where it is if you go just a few spaces beyond the right margin, or it will look for a logical break point within 10 spaces of the margin, or it will break the word at the right margin.

```
*** WARNING: DISK FULL,
     DELETING OLD .BAK FILE TO MAKE SPACE
     (NORMALLY, THE PREVIOUS BACKUP FILE IS DELETED
     ONLY AFTER EDIT IS SUCCESSFULLY COMPLETED).
```

This is the warning to watch for as you fill your disk. Protect your present file by breaking it into smaller segments for storage on more than one disk or delete other files on the disk to provide more room.

DOT COMMAND MESSAGES

? is the flag that appears at right when you enter a dot in column 1. When you complete the entry of an authorized dot command, this notation disappears; but it remains if the command is unrecognized or invalid. Because WordStar never prints a line containing a dot in column 1, check any ? flag carefully.

```
PUT AT FILE BEGINNING FOR CORRECT PAGE BREAK DISPLAY
```

Certain dot commands should be entered at the beginning of a file; changing the page length, top margin, bottom margin, or line height in the middle of a document interferes with proper page break display. To be sure of accurate pagination, start a new file for the revised section.

INTERNAL ERRORS

None of the following screen messages should appear as you work with WordStar, but if one does, use ^KX immediately to store the file and exit to the operating system. Then make a copy of the backup file (.BAK) because the internal error may have disturbed your document. Call up WordStar and check the file. If you can make the error happen again, MicroPro wants to hear from you.

```
*** INTERNAL ERROR 115: INVALID COPY LENGTH ***
*** INTERNAL ERROR 116: INVALID ADDRESS ***
*** INTERNAL ERROR 117: MEMORY FULL ***
*** INTERNAL ERROR 118: MEMORY SHORTAGE ***
*** INTERNAL ERROR 119: POINTER > 64K FROM CURSOR ***
*** INTERNAL ERROR 136: BAD OVLY # ***
```

WORDSTAR FILE MESSAGES

```
File WSMSGS.OVR not found.  Menus &
messages will display as @@@@ only.
```

This occurs at the No-File Menu should the WordStar file WSMSGS.OVR file not be found in Drive A or the logged drive.

```
@@@@
```

Disk file WSMSGS.OVR is not present; this message displays during editing. Menus are unavailable and some error messages display only in part or not at all.

FATAL ERRORS

These are just as drastic as they sound: WordStar returns you to the operating system. Because this manual assumes you are running a properly installed version of WordStar, not all messages are listed here. See the regular WordStar manual for additional information.

```
*** FATAL ERROR F27: DISKETTE DIRECTORY FULL
```

If you use many small files, this message may appear. The maximum number of files varies from system to system, but it is often 64. WordStar generates one and sometimes two working files in addition to each file entered.

```
*** FATAL ERROR F27: DISKETTE FULL
```

WordStar on the 64K IBM PC may generate this message and return you to the disk operating system while you're still editing. If it happens once, take extra care with long files and disks containing many files. Use the CHKDSK command to release incorrectly allocated disk space.

```
*** FATAL ERROR F28: CLOSE FAILURE
                     SYSTEM FAILURE, OR YOU CHANGED DISKETTES
*** FATAL ERROR F29: RENAME FAILURE
                     SYSTEM FAILURE, OR YOU CHANGED DISKETTES
```

Don't change disks during an edit, and don't delete the working file with ^KJ.

```
*** FATAL ERROR F46: Overlay file WSOVLY1.OVR Not found
```

This file must be in Drive A or the logged drive when WordStar is called up.

APPENDIX C
Glossary of WordStar Terms

ABANDON EDIT: ^KQ, used to erase all recently entered and unsaved text and commands, returns user to the No-File Menu. Previously saved entries are not erased.

ALTERNATE PITCH: WordStar uses the preset character width of 10 cpi (characters per inch), the size of letters on most pica typewriters. To use smaller type, such as 12-pitch (12 cpi) or 15-pitch (cpi) printwheels, the character width should be adjusted accordingly. ^PA shifts to the most common alternate size, 12 characters per inch. To resume normal 10-pitch characters, enter ^PA.

BACKUP FILE: After every edit, WordStar retains a copy of the file's previous version. Most backup files are named with the file name and .BAK (TEXT and TEXT.BAK, for example). The backup file may not be edited but it can be renamed and then edited should the original file be lost. Backup files can be printed.

BIDIRECTIONAL PRINTING: Most printers print from left to right and from right to left for maximum speed. To slow the printer for more perfect output, use the dot command .BP 0 or .BP OFF. The dot command .BP 1 or .BP ON reinstates bidirectional printing. Bidirectional printing is on by default. This command is ignored by some printers.

BLOCK: A section of text marked for a specified purpose. To mark a block, enter F7 at its beginning and F8 at its end. A marked block displays in highlighted letters. Displayed blocks can be hidden (^KH), moved to the cursor location (^KV), copied at the cursor location while retaining the original (^KC), erased (^KY), or written into another file for storage (^KW). In column mode (^KN), blocks are defined horizontally as well as vertically.

BOLDFACE TYPE: Type that is struck twice, slightly offset in the second printing, for dark contrast. The command (F6) must be entered before and after the featured text. See also Doublestrike.

BOOTING UP: Turning the computer on, going from a "cold start" to operating condition. This usually means turning on the power switch after inserting the computer's operating system disk. Respond to the date/time requests with appropriate numbers or press RETURN. The prompt A> appears on-screen when the computer is ready.

BOTTOM MARGIN: The area allowed between the last line of text and the bottom of a page. WordStar's default bottom margin is eight lines. The current page number usually appears in the center of the margin's third line.

CAPS LOCK: The IBM PC's lock shift key, which capitalizes letters but does not provide the "uppercase" symbols on number and symbol keys. When engaged (this is an on/off toggle key), it reverses the shift key's effect.

CARRIAGE RETURN: Word wrap sets text by bringing words down from the end of the preceding line to column 1, automatically arranging the right margin. Line returns created by word wrap are called "soft returns" because they are not permanent; future editing may rearrange them. "Hard returns" are entered by the RETURN key, the command ^M, and the command ^N. These commands create permanent line breaks which will not be rearranged by future editing.

CENTER TEXT: To center a line of text or a title, type the material first. With the cursor anywhere on the text line, enter ^OC. This command centers the line between whatever margins are in effect.

CHANGE DISK: To remove one disk and insert another, wait until the red indicator lights are off and, in most cases, until the No-File Menu is on-screen.

CHANGE LOGGED DISK DRIVE: From WordStar's No-File Menu, enter L; the screen will ask for the new logged drive. While editing a file, enter ^KL for the same result.

CHARACTER WIDTH: The amount of horizontal space allowed for each letter, number, or symbol. WordStar's default character width is 10 characters per inch (10 cpi).

CHARACTER WIDTH, CHANGE: The space allowed for individual characters can be changed from the preset 10 characters per inch or 10-pitch width. The print control ^PA shifts to 12-pitch width, or you can enter the .CW n dot command, in which n represents the width measured in 120ths of an inch. .CW 12 sets the default width. ^PN returns to 10-pitch characters after a ^PA shift.

COLUMN: (1) A single space. The status line indicates cursor position by line and column number; the default margins are set at columns 1 and 65. (2) A block or rectangle, usually of text or numbers. WordStar's column mode allows you to move, copy, and delete column blocks as narrow as one or two spaces and many lines long.

COLUMN MODE: The function that moves, copies, or deletes rectangular blocks of text, setting them adjacent to or removing them from other sections of text. This mode is off by default; its on/off command is ^KN.

CONDITIONAL PAGE BREAK: The dot command (.CP n) in which n stands for the number of lines needed for a following table, text, or figure. During editing, the conditional page break command will set new pages where needed; if sufficient space remains on a page, it will not start a new page at the dot command.

CONTINUOUS COMMAND: (1) Any cursor-moving command can be made a repeating command with the prefix ^QQ. (2) Most keyboards feature repeating keys: Any key depressed for more than a second repeats automatically. By depressing a command entry key, you enter that command several times and the command repeats until the computer "catches up." (3) The scroll commands ^W and ^Z are made continuous scroll entries by the addition of ^Q: , ^QW, ^QZ.

CONTROL KEY: The key abbreviated Ctrl, which is depressed with various letter keys to create WordStar's commands. Its use is abbreviated as ^ in this book and in the WordStar manual.

COPY A DISK: Duplicate the contents of a disk, creating a backup or spare. The IBM DOS command is DISKCOPY. WordStar allows you to copy individual files, one at a time, but not an entire disk in one operation.

COPY A FILE: WordStar's file copy command from the No-File Menu is O; while editing a text it is ^KO. The message line asks for the file to copy from and the file to copy to. If the destination file exists already, this command erases its previous contents. To copy an entire disk in one operation, use the DISKCOPY command. You can also copy one file at a time using the COPY command when not in WordStar mode.

CP/M: Control Program for Microprocessors, the operating system used most often with WordStar. The IBM PC disk operating system is called DOS.

CURSOR: The flashing underline dash (_) that indicates your place in a file. The cursor occupies the column that will be taken by the next letter, number, symbol, or space entered.

CURSOR-MOVE COMMANDS: Those codes that direct the cursor up, down, right, left, to the beginning or end of a file, to a block or place marker, or to the previous position.

DAISY WHEEL: Daisy wheel printers use replaceable daisy-shaped printing elements containing letters, numbers, and symbols on the "petals." Daisy wheel printers accommodate commands changing line height, character width, and other format revisions. They produce letter-quality type.

DECIMAL TAB: A tab stop inserted for the creation of decimal tab columns, in which # marks the tab stop and decimals align beneath it. To enter a decimal tab, use the ^OI command for creating a new tab stop, then enter #, the desired column number, and RETURN.

DEFAULT: "By default." Preset conditions arranging the page, its margins, character width, text entry, and other factors. WordStar's default page is 65 columns wide, 55 lines long, with an indented left margin of eight columns, a top margin of three lines, and a bottom margin of eight lines, in which the current page number is printed three lines below text. Character width and line height are set so that 10 horizontal spaces equal 1 inch and 6 vertical lines equal 1 inch. Tab stops appear at five-space intervals, beginning at column 6 and ending at column 56. The page break display feature is on, so text is arranged in numbered pages with break lines indicating the separation between one page and the next. The status line reports logged disk; file name; cursor position measured in pages, lines and columns; line spacing; insertion; and commands as they are entered. Word wrap, margin justification, hyphen-help, ruler line display, print control display, variable tab entry, and insertion are on. Soft hyphen entry is off. WordStar's bidirectional printing mode and microjustification are on. Default values can be changed with editing commands and dot commands.

DELETE A FILE: From WordStar's No-File Menu, you can erase any file on the logged disk by entering Y and the file's name. While editing a file, enter ^KJ to do the same. Files no longer needed can be erased to accommodate other files.

DELETE COMMANDS: (1) While entering a file name or word(s) requested by a screen message, ^S will erase one letter at a time from right to left and ^Y will remove the entire entry. (2) While editing text, ^G removes one letter at a time left to right, the DELETE key removes one letter at a time right to left, ^Y erases the entire line, ^QY deletes from the cursor to the end of the line, ^Q DEL removes from one space left of the cursor to the beginning of the line, and ^KY erases the displayed block.

DELETE KEY: The key marked Del, which removes one character at a time, right to left. In combination with ^Q, it removes from the cursor to the beginning of a line.

DELETE PAGE NUMBER: WordStar's default page numbers are printed at the bottom center of each page. The dot command .OP suppresses this page numbering.

DISK: Black plastic magnetic "records," measuring 5 1/4 inches or 8 inches, disks record and preserve programs and files. They are manufactured in different combinations of sides and sectors. The IBM PC uses 5 1/4-inch double-sided or single-sided, double-density disks. Disks are usually sold in boxes of 10.

DISK, COPY: See Copy Disk.

DISK DRIVES: The compartments that hold disks during use. Drives are equipped with doors and indicator lights.

DISK, FORMAT: See Format a Disk.

DOCUMENT FILE: A WordStar file designed for word processing, the document file creates pages and margins; it uses variable tabbing, word wrap, margin justification, ruler display, page break display, print control display, and hyphen-help.

DOT COMMANDS: Consisting of a dot (.) in column 1, followed by a two-letter code, and, if applicable, a single hard space and a number or text, dot commands can be used to change the dimensions of a page, revise its text entry, change page numbers, set headings and footings, and create page break lines. Dot commands do not print. They are interpreted by WordStar in the order presented.

DOUBLESTRIKE: One of two dark-type print control commands, ^PD instructs the printer to strike every character twice without offsetting the second striking. The command must be entered before and after the featured text; it is an on/off commmand. See also Boldface.

EDIT COMMANDS: WordStar's commands for moving the cursor, adding new material, deleting text, and revising a document.

ERROR MESSAGE: A screen notation calling attention to a problem, usually following the interruption of a command.

EXIT FROM WORDSTAR: Return to the operating system. X from the No-File Menu and ^KX from within a file leave the WordStar program.

EXIT TO SYSTEM: Same as above.

FC= : See File Character.

FILE: A portion of disk space reserved for the entry of characters (letters, numbers, symbols, spaces) following a specified format. See Document File and Non-Document File.

FILE CHARACTER: The cursor position reported in character numbers ("bytes") instead of page/line/column. The file character appears as FC=(number) when the page break display (^OP) is turned off.

FILE DIRECTORY: A list of files on the logged disk. This normally appears below the No-File Menu. The command F (entered at the No-File Menu) turns the directory display on and off; ^KF, entered from within a file, displays the logged disk's inventory at the top of the screen.

FILE LINE: The notation FL=(number) appears with the cursor's file character position on the status line when page break display (^OP) is turned off. FL shows the cursor's position measured in lines from the beginning of the file.

FILES-ONLY DISK: A disk reserved for document or non-document files only, one which does not also contain WordStar, DOS files, or other programs.

FIND COMMANDS: WordStar's word-matching function which locates "target words" within a document. The command for a simple find is ^QF; to find one word and replace it with another, use ^QA.

FIND COMMAND OPTIONS: After entering a target word with ^QF, you can type B (search backward), U (ignore upper/lowercase distinctions), W (match whole words only), or a number (find the nth appearance of the target word).

FIND/REPLACE OPTIONS: After entering a target word and replacement word with ^QA, you can use B, U, and W, as described above, or a number (make the replacement n times), G (search entire document from beginning to end), or N (make replacements automatically, without stopping for individual verification).

FL= : See File Line.

FLAGS: Flags are signals at the screen's right edge indicating (:) no-entry lines above the file, (.) unentered lines below the file, (<) hard returns entered with the return key, ^M or ^N (blank space) soft returns created by Word Wrap, (+) text continuing off-screen, (-) the overprinting of two lines, and (?) a questionable or unrecognized dot command.

FORMAT A DISK: Prepare the disk to receive and record information. The DOS format command is FORMAT.

FORMAT A DOCUMENT: Set the physical dimensions and arrangement of text and margins according to page size, type size, and entry commands.

FOOTING: A line of text, such as a title, repeated at the bottom of every page.

FOOTING MARGIN: The space allowed between the last line of text and the footing line.

HANGING INDENTATION: Indentation of the left margin by one, two, three, or more tab stops. Hanging indentation is used in bibliographies, charts, and outlines. ^OG is the paragraph tab command, used to create this format.

HARD HYPHEN: A hyphen entered "by hand" (using the - key) as part of a word or name, which will always print. Hard hyphens appear in regular screen light. See Soft Hyphen.

HARD RETURN: A line return entered "by hand" (using the return key, ^M or ^N) that will be retained through future editing and paragraph reform. Hard returns are marked with the < flag. See Soft Return.

HARD SPACE: A space entered "by hand" (using the space bar), which will be preserved during future editing and paragraph reform. See Soft Space.

HEADING: A line of text and/or number and/or title printed automatically at the top of each page.

HEADING MARGIN: The space allowed between the heading and the first line of text.

HELP LEVELS: WordStar displays lists of commands and instructions at the top of the screen for reference. Help level 3 (set by default) displays maximum information; help level 2 suppresses one-letter commands; help level 1 offers occasional instruction; help level 0 removes all help messages. The help level can be changed at the No-File Menu or within a document with F1 and the appropriate number.

HELP MENUS: Lists of commands displayed at the top of the screen for reference. At help level 3, all menus display. At help level 2, one-letter commands are suppressed, but these menus display: the ^Q (Quick) Menu: the ^P (Print Control) Menu; the ^K (Block Command) Menu; the ^J (Help Command) Menu; and the ^O (On-Screen Format) Menu. ^J gives the Help Command Menu, and ^J commands (two-letter codes) can be entered at any time, regardless of current help level, for on-screen reviews of different WordStar functions.

HIGHLIGHTING: The status, ruler, and message lines, place markers, block markers, soft hyphens, and displayed blocks appear in dimmed light or reverse video.

HORIZONTAL SCROLL: The screen shifts right to display off-screen text on wide lines. Use ^QD to display text at right in segments; return to the beginning of a line with ^QS.

HYPHENS, HARD/SOFT: See Hard Hyphens and Soft Hyphens.

HYPHEN-HELP: WordStar's automatic hyphenation function, this feature works in conjunction with the paragraph reform command, ^B. Hyphen-help is on by default; its on/off toggle command is ^OH.

INTERRUPT THIS COMMAND: To interrupt most commands during execution, enter ^U. To interrupt the entry of a two-letter code after pressing its first letter, use the space bar, RETURN key, ESCAPE key, or ^U. (Exception: interrupt ^P commands with the space bar.) To interrupt the setting of margins, the setting of tab stops, the removing of tab stops, any find/replace, block command, or other procedure after entering both letters of its code, use ^U.

INSERTION: Insertion is on by default, meaning that letters or spaces inserted into already-entered text will bump that text to the right; hard spaces and tabbing move text to the right; and the RETURN key moves text down as it creates blank lines. When insertion is off, new letters and spaces literally replace the old by "overprinting" them; the space bar replaces letters with blank spaces; the TAB key moves "over" or "through" text without disturbing it; and the return key moves down the screen without disturbing text. When insertion is on, INSERT ON appears at the right of the status line. The insertion key is labeled Ins.

JUSTIFICATION: A justified margin is straight; an uneven margin is ragged. WordStar normally sets a straight or justified right margin by spreading words and letters across the line. To turn justification off, enter ^OJ; this is an on/off toggle command. In most cases, justified margins are preferred for reports and proposals while ragged margins are preferred for business correspondence.

LEFT MARGIN: (1) The screen's left edge, or the column marked by L in the ruler line, marking the text's left side. (2) The space allowed by the printer between the paper's left edge and the first column of text. You can move the left margin to the right with ^OL or F3, the left margin setting commands. The printing margin can be moved left as many as eight columns with .PO, the page offset dot command.

LINE BREAK: See Carriage Return.

LINE HEIGHT: The vertical distance allowed for each line of characters. WordStar's line height is measured in 48ths of an inch; the default value is 8/48, or 1/6 inch.

LINE HEIGHT CHANGE: WordStar permits line height adjustments (incremental printers) in 48ths of an inch with the dot command. On the default page, 6 lines = 1 inch.

LOGGED DISK DRIVE: The drive in use.

MARGINS: (1) The white or blank space separating text from the top, bottom, left edge, and right edge of the paper when printed. (2) The ruler columns at which the left edge of text and the right edge of text are set.

MARGIN, BOTTOM: The distance between the last line of text and the bottom of the paper. In default use, this margin is eight lines. It contains the footing margin. This value can be changed with the dot command .MB n, in which n is the number of lines desired.

MARGIN, FOOTING: The distance between the last line of text and the footing or default page number, usually two lines. This margin can be changed with the dot command .FM n, with n being the number of lines desired.

MARGIN, HEADING: The space between the first line of text and the heading. This margin is contained within the top margin and can be changed with the dot command .HM n, with n the desired number of lines.

MARGIN RELEASE: The command ^OX releases the ruler line's right margin and, if indented, left margin. Use of the return key usually turns this function off automatically, though ^OX is an on/off toggle command.

MARGIN, TOP: The distance between the top of the page and the first line of text. If included, the heading appears within this margin.

MARKING A BLOCK: Position the cursor at the block's beginning point and enter F7; move it to the block's end and enter F8. The block should change to highlighted characters, called a displayed block.

MARKERS, BLOCK: When entering F7 before F8 has been typed, a <B> signal marks the block's beginning. When entering F8 before F7 has been typed, a <K> signal marks the block's end. Although these signals disappear once the block is displayed, they remain in the computer's memory so that the command ^QB will relocate the beginning of a marked block and ^QK will locate its end. Blocks need not be displayed for the find commands to work.

MARKERS, PLACE: The command ^K and any one-digit number create a place marker, shown on-screen as <0>, <1>, <2>, etc. Markers can be relocated with ^Q and the corresponding number.

MATRIX PRINTER: A high-speed printer which forms letters by hitting tiny rods or sharp wires against ribbon and paper; the resulting dots form letters, numbers, and symbols. The IBM Matrix Printer belongs to this category.

MENUS: Lists of commands. WordStar's No-File Menu appears when calling up WordStar, after saving a file with ^KD, and after executing any command entered from that menu. The Main Menu, a list of cursor-moving commands, appears at the top of the screen by default. Other menus are shown when the prefix of a two-letter code is entered. (Help levels 0 and 1 suppress menu displays.)

MESSAGE LINES: Questions, instructions, and requests for information appear at the top of the screen when appropriate.

MICROSPACE JUSTIFICATION: As it sets the right margin, WordStar spreads words and letters evenly across the line. The screen image, which is not microjustified, looks far less even than the printed product of daisy wheel and other incremental printers. To cause the printed page to match the screen, microjustification can be turned off with a dot command (.UJ 0 or .UJ OFF). This function can be reinstated with .UJ 1 or .UJ ON.

NO-FILE COMMANDS: The No-File Menu offers several letter codes that can be entered to initiate a procedure: opening a document or non-document file, copying a file, renaming a file, displaying the file directory, changing logged disk drive, etc. The corresponding letter codes operate as described only when the No-File Menu appears.

NON-BREAK SPACE: During the setting of a justified right margin, WordStar causes extra spaces ("soft" spaces) to be entered between words. In some cases, soft spaces are not desired. The print control ^PO enters single hard spaces which will not be expanded during editing, word wrap, or paragraph reform.

NON-DOCUMENT FILE: The command N opens a non-document file from the No-File Menu. Non-document files do not create pages, so the status line reports cursor position in file characters and file lines. Unlike the default values in a document file, the non-document file begins with word wrap off, margin justification off, ruler display off, and hyphen-help off. While a document file uses variable tabbing, non-document files use fixed tab stops set at eight-column intervals beginning at column 9. Tabbing operates differently here; the cursor cannot be placed within a tab space but "pops" across it; a tab deletes as a single character; and a single character will overtype a tab. Dot commands are not verified, so no ? flags or dot command screen messages appear. While word wrap, justification, and paragraph reform can be used in this mode, they may cause incompatibility with external programs.

NONPRINTING LINE: WordStar will not print any line containing a dot or period in column 1. If a recognized dot command, the entry will cause a corresponding change; if an unrecognized command, the ? flag appears at right and the line will not print. WordStar features two recognized or authorized dot commands which do not generate the ? flag and which do not cause a formatting change; these are recommended for any on-screen notations not meant to be printed in the document. One consists of two dots (..), the other is .IG, which stands for "Ignore this line."

ON-SCREEN FORMATTING MENU: At help levels 2 and 3, the prefix ^O causes WordStar's On-screen Menu to appear. This is a list of format commands and it displays the current status of ^O toggle codes.

OPEN A DOCUMENT FILE: See Document File.

OPEN A NON-DOCUMENT FILE: See Non-Document File.

OPERATING SYSTEM: The operating system consists of programs that control the flow of information between the computer's disk drives and its central processing unit and memory. The IBM PC's disk operating system is called DOS.

OVERPRINT A CHARACTER: Cause two characters (letters, symbols, or numbers) to print in the same space. The overprint-next-character command is ^PH. It can be used to insert accent marks and other special effects.

OVERPRINT A LINE: Cause the following line to print on top of this line. The command, ^PM, generates a - flag at right. (^P@ is an alternate command.)

PAGE BREAK DISPLAY: This function arranges text into pages according to the configuration set by default or with dot commands; page break lines appear onscreen, indicating the separation between pages, and the status line reports cursor position by page number. The on/off toggle command is ^OP. Turning page break display off causes all page break lines to disappear, and the status line reports cursor position by file character and file line.

PAGE FORMATTING: Format conditions can be set with dot commands, by default, or with the use of different ^O commands. Format commands set the upper, lower, right, and left margins, the tab stops, line spacing, character width, line height, headings, footings, etc.

PAGE NUMBER: WordStar numbers pages from the beginning of each file. Page numbers appear by default at the bottom of each printed page.

PAGE NUMBER, CHANGE: To set a new page number, enter .PN n, n representing the new number. Your revised numbers print on paper, and are recognized by WordStar when you enter the command to print a file, but the status line continues to show page numbers measured from the beginning of the file.

PAGE NUMBER, REPOSITION: To cause page numbers to print at the top rather than bottom of each page, enter a heading command with # positioned at the desired printing location. To suppress the default (bottom of page) numbering, use .OP. To reposition the bottom number, enter .PC n, n being the desired column number. To set the page number in a footing (text) line, use .FO with #.

PAGE NUMBER, REMOVE: To prevent the default page number from printing, use the dot command .OP, or enter a footing without the # symbol. To reinstate page numbering after using .OP, enter .PN.

PAPER LENGTH/PAGE LENGTH: WordStar's preset paper length is 11 inches, the standard typing paper size. Page length is measured in lines, so using the default line height, 11 inches = 66 lines. To set a legal-sized page, use 84 lines. The dot command is .PL n, n being the desired number of lines.

PARAGRAPH REFORM: During editing, a neatly justified paragraph can become several unconnected-looking lines, some only a word in length and others extending beyond the right margin or not matching the line spacing in use. ^B entered in any line of text (usually the first line of a paragraph) will reform everything between the cursor and the next hard return (<) to match the line spacing, margins, and other format commands in use. If hyphen-help is turned on, hyphens will be offered where appropriate.

PARAGRAPH TABS: Tab stops appear as exclamation marks (!) on the ruler line. Pressing the TAB key moves the cursor to the next stop. If insertion is on, it moves any text at the cursor's right a corresponding distance; if insertion is off, it moves the cursor "through" or "over" already-entered text. The command F2 can be entered in any line to indent the left margin of subsequent lines to the next tab stop. Tab stops can be removed with ^ON and entered with ^OI.

PHANTOM RUBOUT and PHANTOM SPACE: Two additional symbols on daisy wheels, entered with the print control commands ^PG and ^PF, respectively.

PITCH: Characters per inch. The default character width is 10 characters per inch (cpi), or the space needed for letters on a 10-pitch print wheel.

PLACE MARKERS: Ten numbered markers can be entered in a file, <0> through <9>. They are set with ^K and the appropriate number and relocated with ^Q and the number.

PREFIXES: (1) WordStar uses several two-letter commands, divided into five categories: codes beginning with ^P set print controls, ^O sets on-screen format configurations, ^Q accelerates or expands a command, ^J provides help commands, and ^K deals with blocks of text. At help levels 2 and 3, entering a prefix displays its entire command menu. Two-letter codes can be interrupted after the prefix by pressing the space bar, return key, escape key, or ^U. (Interrupt ^P with the space bar only.) To interrupt a two-letter command already executing, enter ^U. (2) When referring to a file on the unlogged disk, preface its name with the appropriate disk drive, A: or B:.

PRINT CONTROL CHARACTERS: The print control commands are entered with ^P and a second letter code or with the function keys F5 (underline) and F6 (boldface). The prefix does not appear on-screen, so the surviving notations are ^B for boldface, ^D for doublestrike, ^V for subscripts, ^T for superscripts, ^Y for ribbon color change, ^X for crossing out, ^S for underlining, etc.

PRINT CONTROL DISPLAY: When a print control character appears on-screen, it occupies two columns. As the control characters do not print, WordStar compensates by providing extra spaces on the line for text. The result, if many control commands are used, can be confusing. To remove print control characters from the screen, enter ^OD, which turns the print control display off. Use the same command to reinstate it.

PRINT MENU: The list of print controls that appears at help levels 2 and 3 when the prefix ^P is entered.

QUICK MENU: The list of commands that appears at help levels 2 and 3 when the prefix ^Q is entered.

RENAME A FILE: To rename a file, enter E from the No-File Menu or ^KE from within a file.

RESTORE ENTRY: When the message line requests a file name or target word, ^R will restore the command's most recently entered response. ^R can return a deleted entry to the screen, or it can be entered as a shortcut, repeating whatever was last entered with the featured command.

RETURNS, HARD/SOFT: See Hard Returns and Soft Returns.

RETURN KEY: The key marked ←, which creates hard returns marked with the < flag when insertion is on. When insertion is off, the RETURN key moves the cursor down, "through" or "over" already-entered text without moving or disturbing it. In this guide, the abbreviation @ indicates use of the RETURN key.

RULER LINE: When displayed, a ruler line appears at the top of the screen, showing left and right margins and tab stops. To suppress the ruler line, enter ^OT. This is an on/off command.

RUN A PROGRAM: Without leaving WordStar, run a separate program by entering R from the No-File Menu.

SAVE: Store or preserve; record permanently. WordStar uses three save commands, ^KS (which stores material while remaining in the file), ^KD (which stores material and returns to the No-File Menu), and ^KX (which stores material and exits from WordStar to the operating system).

SHIFT LOCK KEY: See Caps Lock.

SOFT HYPHEN: A hyphen entered in dim light or highlighted, which does not print unless at the end of a line. Hyphen-help enters soft hyphens, and the command ^OE is the soft hyphen entry toggle. Soft hyphen entry mode is off by default. To enter a hard (always printing) hyphen when in soft hyphen mode, use ^P-.

SOFT RETURN: A line break set by word wrap as it adjusts the right margin and brings a word down to the next line. Soft returns are temporary; they may be rearranged during editing and paragraph reform. A blank space at right is the soft return flag.

SOFT SPACE: Hard spaces are entered by pressing the space bar; soft spaces are created by WordStar's margin justification feature, which adds additional spaces to spread words across the line as it sets a straight right margin. Soft spaces are temporary; future editing and paragraph reform may rearrange them.

SPACE, HARD/SOFT: See Hard Space and Soft Space.

STATUS LINE: The screen's top line indicates disk drive, file name, current position (page, line, and column), whether insertion is on, line spacing if other than single spacing, margin release if on, and two-letter commands as entered.

STOP PRINT HERE: To instruct the printer to stop at a specified location so that ribbon or print wheel may be changed, enter ^PC.

STOP PRINT WHILE PRINTING: If printing from the No-File Menu with the command P, enter P again to stop printing. Three options appear on-screen: Y, which abandons print; N, which resumes at once; and ^U, which (if you have more than 64K) allows you to edit a different file and resume printing later. If you have more than 64K, WordStar lets you print a file while editing another file. Initiate print with ^KP and use the same command to interrupt the print function.

STORE: See Save.

SUBSCRIPT: On incremental printers, subscripts position featured text a fraction of an inch (3/48 inch) below the line of text. On nonincremental printers, such as the IBM Matrix Printer, the subscript appears one line below the text but only if double or triple spacing is in use. ^PV is the subscript print control code, and it must be entered before and after the subscripted text. Not all printers support WordStar's subscript command.

SUBSCRIPT ROLL: WordStar presets the subscript adjustment for incremental printers at 3/48 inch below (and, for superscripts, 3/48 inch above) the line of text. The dot command .SR n, with n the 48th-inch units, changes the adjustment by printing subscripts/superscripts higher or lower than the default value.

SUPERSCRIPT: A number or other text printed slightly above the text line. WordStar's superscript command is ^PT. Like ^PV, the subscript entry, this is an on/off code. See Subscript.

TAB STOPS, REMOVE: Enter ^ON.

TAB STOPS, RESET: Enter ^OI.

TOGGLE COMMANDS: On/off commands; a single command code that reverses a function's status. WordStar's toggle commands include the codes for insertion, word wrap, margin justification, hyphen-help, ruler line display, page break display, margin release, and such print controls as those for boldface, doublestrike, underlining, subscripts, superscripts, and ribbon color change.

TOP MARGIN: The space between the top of the page and the first line of text, usually three lines or ½ inch. A heading, if any, appears in the top margin area. To change from the default three-line margin, enter .MT n, n representing the number of lines desired.

UNDERLINE: To underline, position the print control ^PS before and after the featured text. This is an on/off command.

WORDSTAR: The word processing software program you're using, consisting of these files: WS.COM (the main program), WSMSGS.OVR (the message file), and WSOVLY1.OVR (the overlay file). WordStar is a registered trademark; the program is produced by MicroPro International Corporation, San Rafael, California.

WORD WRAP: As the computer sets the right margin, it adjusts text to fit and brings the last word down to the beginning of the next line. This automatic carriage return feature is called word wrap. It can be turned off with the toggle command ^OW.

APPENDIX D:

WordStar Version 3.3

Users of previous editions of WordStar will notice dramatic changes in the new program's documentation: the WordStar 3.3 manual is better organized, more attractive, and easier to understand than any previous version's manual.

In addition, you're now provided with an installation program that's so easy to use, you can customize WordStar to your own requirements without having to know anything about programming.

PROGRAM CHANGES

One of the standard menus described in this book has a new name: the No-File Menu is now called the Opening Menu.

The commands for WordStar 3.3 are identical to those described in this book, with one exception: WordStar documentation for previous editions of version 3 described the **F9** key as moving the cursor to the beginning of a file and the **F10** key as moving the cursor to the end of the file. As noted, that correlation was incorrect: F9 took you to the end of a file and F10 took you to its beginning.

In version 3.3, the keys work as MicroPro intended: **F9** takes you to the **beginning** of your file, and **F10** takes you to the **end** of your file.

Previously, the current position of toggle commands was shown by the word ON or OFF in bright light and parentheses on the Onscreen Menu and Block Menu. Now each toggle command's current position is shown with the simple notation "now ON" or "now OFF."

The only change in the screen's appearance is the addition of a new reference line at the bottom, showing F-Function key commands:

```
1HELP 2INDENT 3SETLM 4SETRM 5UNDLIN 6BLDFCE 7BEGBLK 8ENDBLK 9BEGFIL 10ENDFIL
```

These are the familiar commands for changing the help level (F1 is the same as ^JH), paragraph tabbing for hanging indentation (F2 is the same as ^OG), setting the left margin at the cursor location (F3), setting the right margin at the cursor location (F4), beginning and ending underlining (F5) and boldface (F6) type, beginning (F7) and ending (F8) a block, and moving to the beginning (F9) and end (F10) of a file.

Users of earlier versions of WordStar will appreciate improvements in the program's execution. The addition of new material with insertion on works faster and more efficiently than it did before, and scrolling by line and by screen is faster and less confusing. In general, the program's speed and efficiency have changed for the better. WordStar 3.3 is harder to "crash" than its predecessor, especially on the 64K machine. The maximum block-move and block-copy size on the 64K IBM PC has increased slightly, to approximately 1000 characters.

WORDSTAR FILES

WordStar version 3.3 features more program files than earlier editions. You should have received the following program files on two separate disks:

```
WSU.COM
WSINSTALL.COM
WINSTALL.OVR
WS.INS
PRINT.TST
WSOVLY1.OVR
WSMSGS.OVR
```

INSTALL WORDSTAR

To install WordStar, place the disk containing the WINSTALL program in Drive A and the disk containing the program WSU.COM in Drive B. Answer the A> screen prompt with the command WINSTALL WS@. (Type WINSTALL, a space, the letters WS, and then the RETURN key).

Now simply answer the screen's questions as they appear. The first time you use the installation program, press the RETURN key when you see this question:

Name of file to install, or <RETURN> for B:WSU.COM and again when you see this item:

Enter name of file for installed WordStar, or <RETURN> for B:WS.COM

Installation Menu

A: Menu of Terminals
B: Custom Installation of Terminals
C: Menu of Printers
D: Custom Installation of Printers
E: Menu of WordStar Features
F: Operating System Considerations

When the Installation Menu appears, you can select a specific terminal, printer, or operating system. Users of WordStar on the IBM PC using IBM DOS and the IBM Matrix Printer won't have to use Menus A, B, C, D, or F.

Should you be using a different printer, use option C (Menu of Printers) when the Installation Menu appears on the screen. If your printer isn't one of those listed on the printer menu, use option D (Custom Installation of Printers), which generates a longer questionnaire.

Unfortunately, not all marriages of WordStar and Printer are bug-free. If your printer doesn't act the way it should, review your responses to the installation program to be sure you answered each item correctly. Then, if the printer still doesn't work, call your IBM dealer or MicroPro. Problems with the NEC Spinwriter are especially common, and MicroPro provides a checklist of necessary printer switch changes and other directions.

CHANGING WORDSTAR'S DEFAULT CONFIGURATION

Thanks to the 3.3 installation program, it's easy to revise any or all of WordStar's default values.

It's a good idea to wait until you understand all of WordStar's functions before making changes. Another good idea is renaming the WordStar command file at each revision; you can set up as many "customized" configurations as you like, providing each with a different name.

For example, let's call our hypothetical revision WS1. The screen message below has a different meaning, depending on whether you have already reinstalled WordStar as described here:

```
The uninstalled WordStar program is normally contained in
WSU.COM.   If  you  are  reinstalling  WordStar  or  have
previously  renamed  the  file, enter the new name below;
otherwise press <RETURN>.
```

If you are reinstalling WordStar for the first time, using your new file name (WS1) for the first time, press the RETURN key at this message. If you type the new file's name, the screen will tell you that the file doesn't exist. Pressing RETURN brings a verification message regarding WSU.COM. Press RETURN again, and this message will appear:

```
When you are finished running this program, you will have an
installed  version of  WordStar  in a new file on the logged
disk  drive.  It  will  be  called  B:WS.COM. If you wish to
name  the  file  something  else,  enter  the  name  below.
Otherwise  press  <RETURN>.  To change the name, enter up to
eight   letters   or   numbers.   The   extension   .COM  will
automatically be added to any name.
```

Now is the time to type your new file's name (WS1). When you finish making and saving the changes you want, your new installation program will appear on the screen as WS1.COM. To use it, don't call up WordStar with the familiar WS command; instead, type WS1. WordStar doesn't care what you name the file.

WordStar Features Menu

To change any or all of WordStar's default values, use option E (Menu of WordStar Features) at the Installation Menu.

A: Initial Help Level (Default: Level 3)
B: Decimal Point Character (Default: Period)
C: Non-Document Mode (Default: Document Mode)
D: Initial Directory Display (Default: Directory On)
E: Initial Insertion Toggle (Default: Insertion On)
F: Justification Toggle (Default: Justification On)
G: Hyphen-Help Toggle (Default: Hyphen-Help On)
H: Omit-Page-Numbering (Default: Automatic Numbering On)
I: Top Margin (Default: 3-Line Top Margin)
J: Bottom Margin (Default: 8-Line Bottom Margin)

K: Left Margin (Default: Column 1)
L: Right Margin (Default: Column 65)
M: Lines Per Page (Default: 66 Lines for 11 Inches)
N: Page Offset (Default: 8-Column Indentation of Left Margin)
O: Form Feeds Toggle (Default: Form Feeds Off)
P: Data Field Separator (MailMerge Option)
Q: Variable Name Symbol (MailMerge Option)
R: System Disk Drive (Default: WordStar looks for .OVR files on logged disk and then on system drive.)
X: Return to Installation Menu

The installation manual does a good job of describing each function, and the screen's directions are clear and easy to follow. You may want to change the following conditions.

A (Initial Help Level). The Main Menu is inconvenient and distracting once you've learned WordStar's basic commands. Use this menu option to reset the default help level to 0, 1, or 2, depending on how much on-screen assistance you need.

E (Initial Insertion Toggle). If you prefer typing with insertion turned off, use this option to change the default configuration to "Insert Off."

F (Justification Toggle) and G (Hyphen-help Toggle). Normally, the screen shifts text to create a straight right margin. If you prefer a ragged margin, use item F to change the default value from Justification On to Justification Off. During paragraph reforming, hyphen-help presents possible hyphenations, whether you want them or not. If you turn justification off, the delay is especially irksome. Item G turns hyphen-help off when you call up WordStar.

WordStar prints the page number at the bottom of each page by default. The WordStar Features Menu provides an Omit-Page-Numbering toggle, menu item H. To suppress the default page number without having to use the dot command .OP, use this menu option.

I (Top Margin) and J (Bottom Margin) are controlled by dot commands. The default margins are top 3 lines and bottom 8 lines. Use these menu options to set a different configuration.

You will probably leave the left margin set at column 1, but the right margin (item L) and page offset (item N) may not be to your liking. WordStar's default right margin is set for column 65, and the page offset value (the left margin's printing position on paper) is indented 8 spaces.

REDEFINING F-FUNCTION KEYS

The F-function keys at left are preset to provide these commands:

A. F1 = Set Help Level (^JH)
B. F2 = Hanging Indentation (^OG)
C. F3 = Set Left Margin at Cursor Location (^OL ESC)
D. F4 = Set Right Margin at Cursor Location (^OR ESC)
E. F5 = Start/Stop Underline (^PS)

F. F6 = Start/Stop Boldface (^PB)
G. F7 = Mark Block Beginning (^KB)
H. F8 = Mark Block End (^KK)
I. F9 = Move to Beginning of File (^QR)
J. F10 = Move to End of File (^QC)

Perhaps you'd rather have F1 enter a save command (^KS). Or maybe you'd like F3 to set the left margin, but not at the cursor position.

Item S on the WordStar Features Menu brings a menu of F-Function keys, as shown above. As in all the installation program menus, each item is indexed by letter (A to J). To change any item, press the appropriate letter.

The screen provides a verification message, confirming the key whose definition you want to change. Then a more lengthy message appears, telling you that you can enter a value in ASCII, Hexadecimal, or Decimal codes.

- ASCII : (:^A enters ASCII ^A, a single value)
- Hexadecimal , (,41 enters hexadecimal 41)
- Decimal # (#61 enters decimal 61)

In addition, the screen tells you to enter each character in the sequence separately, following each entry with the RETURN key. To leave a value unchanged, press RETURN. To end the definition, type a period and press RETURN.

Should your command include a line return, period, or backspace, use these hexadecimal codes:

- LINE RETURN ,OD (zero, not the letter O)
- PERIOD ,2E
- BACKSPACE ,08 (zero, not the letter 0)

The F-Function key's definition cannot be longer than 6 characters. You can also change the key's on-screen definition, and the definition cannot be longer than 6 characters.

Example Revision

For example, to define F1 as the simple save command ^KS, enter the code like this. Select A as the F-Function Key Menu item to change, and answer the screen's verification message with "C" for "Change." The message regarding ASCII codes will appear, and at the bottom of the screen you'll see this message:

```
Current    New
Value      Value
^J
```

The F1 key's current value is ^JH, so the screen message pertains to the command's first character.

Type a colon (:), then Control+K, then RETURN.

The screen will show the command's new value as ^K. A second line will appear, showing the current value of the command's second character as H.

To set its new value, type a colon (:), the letter S, and RETURN.

The screen will show the old command's third character as an asterisk (*), which means that the old definition ended here. To end the new definition, type a period and press RETURN.

Correcting Mistakes

If you make a mistake, use the left-arrow or backspace key to erase the incorrect character. If you make a mistake but don't realize it until you go to the next line, end the definition by typing a period and pressing RETURN. The screen will ask if your input is correct. Answer N for No, and you can begin the definition again.

Change Part of a Command

To change only part of a command, press RETURN when the screen shows the character you don't want to change; then type a new character or end the definition where appropriate.

For example, to change the "Set Left Margin" command, F3, so that it asks for a column number instead of setting the left margin at the cursor location, use item C on the F-Function Key Menu. When the screen shows you the first character of the old definition (^O), keep it by pressing RETURN. Do the same when the screen displays L, the command's second character.

It's the third character you want to remove, so when the screen displays ^[, which represents the ESC key and which sets the left margin at the cursor location, end the definition by typing a period and pressing RETURN.

F3 will produce a screen message asking where you want the left margin set. To do the same with the right margin command, use menu item D, which redefines the F4 key.

Change Edit Screen's Information Line

Once you define the command correctly, the screen will ask if you want to change the command's message on the information line at the bottom of the screen. In our ^KS example, an appropriate notation would be "Save." However you type the word (in upper or lower case letters) is how it will appear on the screen.

To change the information lines' abbreviation without changing the command, use the appropriate menu letter, but don't change the F-function key's definition. Instead, wait for the message regarding its onscreen abbreviation, and change only that. If you don't type anything when the screen asks for your new message but press the RETURN key by itself, an empty rectangle will appear on your edit screen's information line.

Additional Examples

Before leaving the F-Function keys' definitions, here is an example using the hexadecimal RETURN key command.

^ON erases tab stops, and one of the command's options is the "A" key, which removes all stops. To erase all of the tab stops on your ruler line, enter ^ON, then the letter A, and then the RETURN key.

To define an F-Function key so that it enters the entire command, type:

:^O	(Control+O)
:N	
:A	
:0D	(Zero, not the letter O)
.	(Period ends the definition)

Another example saves time when using mid-text ruler lines. If our hypothetical configuration were designed for the easy construction of charts, one F-Function key could erase all the preset tab stops, another could set new tab stops (^OI), and the last could set the nonprinting line command for convenience when typing mid-text ruler lines. You would use the command after typing the ruler line and pressing RETURN with Insertion off.

:^E	(move up one line, to mid-text ruler)
:^E	(move up another line, just above mid-text ruler)
,2E	(period)
,2E	(period; this creates the dot command "..")
:^P	(print control prefix)
,0D	(second part of print control ^PM, or line overprint command)

The definition ends here because we've used all six available characters. When entered, this F-key command moves the cursor to the beginning of the line above the mid-text ruler line, types two periods (the "don't print this line" dot command) and enters the line-overprint command, as described on page 159.

F-Function Key Definitions

Define your F-Function keys according to the commands you use most often. You might define keys F1, F2, and F3 as ^KS (simple save), ^KD (done editing save), and ^KQ (quit edit). Another convenient definition is ^B, the paragraph reform command. ^QF and ^QA, the find and find/replace commands, are easier to use as F-Function keys, and another time-saver is ^QP, which returns you to your previous position when you press a command accidentally.

Leave the Installation Program

To leave the F-Function Key Menu, press X, which returns you to the WordStar Features Menu. Another X command takes you back to the Installation Menu, and a third X command produces this message:

```
The changes made during this session of  INSTALL  are stored
in a temporary file.  You may now save these changes in your
installed file WS1.COM.
```

A review of computer terminal, printer, communications protocol and driver will appear, and then you'll see the Exit Options Menu:

```
A  Save the changes made during this INSTALL session
B  Quit this session of INSTALL without saving changes
C  Change any of your choices / Remain in INSTALL
```

To save your revised default values and F-Function key definitions, use option A. When you return to the operating system, remove the installation program disk from Drive A and store it in a safe place. Your WordStar program disk now contains two command files that will call up WordStar: the original WS.COM, whose "load WordStar" command is WS, and your new file, named WS1.COM, whose command is WS1.

Additional Revision

To make further revisions in your WS1 file, run the WINSTALL program again, and this time answer both questions regarding the name of your installation file with the file's name (WS1.) Or, if you want to keep the WS1 file and create a slightly revised version of it as a third file, answer WS1 to the first filename question and provide a new name (WS2, for example) when the second filename question appears.

As you create different configurations with the installation program, keep track of their file names and contents. The command WS will always call up WordStar according to the WS.COM file, retaining all of the default conditions described in this book.

Alphabetical Index of WordStar Commands

Command	*Function, Page*
^KS	Save and remain in file 96
^KV	Move displayed block to cursor position 189
^KW	Write displayed block to another file 190
^KX	Save and exit from WordStar 96
^KY	Erase displayed block 191
L	Change logged disk drive 53
^L	Repeat last Find/Replace command (including options, if any) 171
.LH	Set line height 234
M	MailMerge (optional program) 54
^M	Same as Return key 139
.MB	Set bottom margin 236
.MT	Set top margin 236
N	Edit Non-Document File 53
N	Automatic replacement (Find/Replace option) 181
N	Resume print (Print option) 101
N	Answers NO to screen question
^N	Insert hard return 139
NumLock	Use to activate directional keys at right
O	Copy a file 53
^O	On-screen format command prefix
^OC	Center a line 87
^OD	Print control display on/off 113, 146
^OE	Soft hyphen entry on/off 113, 146
^OF	Set margins/tabs from cursor line 88
^OG	Paragraph tab, indent margin (same as F2) 127
^OH	Hyphen-help on/off 136, 146
^OI	Set new tab stop 91
^OJ	Justification on/off
^OL	Set left margin 87
^ON	Clear tab stop 91
^OP	Page break display on/off 145
.OP	Omit page number 228
^OR	Set right margin 87
^OS	Set line spacing 87
^OT	Ruler line on/off 145
^OV	Variable tabs on/off 146
^OW	Word wrap on/off 145
^OX	Margin release on/off 144
^Ox	Enter special find character 176
P	Print 53, 100
^P	Print control prefix
^P-	Enter hard return (soft hyphen mode)
.PA	Page break 215
^PA	Set alternate (12-pitch) type size 120
^PA	Enter special find character 175
^PB	Set boldface or triplestrike type (depends on system and printer; use F6) 112
^PC	Stop print here 120
.PC	Reposition page number 228

Command	*Function,*	*Page*
^QW	Continuous scroll showing upper lines	75
^QX	Move cursor to bottom of screen (same as End)	66
^QY	Delete to end of line	81
^QZ	Continuous scroll showing lower lines	75
R	Run a program	54
^R	Scroll screenful upper text (same as PgUp)	75
^R	Restore entry (entering file name)	55
^R	Restore entry (entering file name while editing)	289
Return	Return/Enter (down left arrow key)	
S	SpellStar (optional program)	54
^S	Move cursor one character left (same as ← key)	61
^S	Delete one character (entering file name)	55
.SR	Set subscript roll	243
^T	Delete word at right	80
U	Ignore upper/lowercase (Find/Replace option)	171
^U	Interrupt command	55
^U	Edit and resume print (Print option)	101
.UJ	Microjustification on/off	243
^V	Insertion on/off (same as Ins key)	105
W	Match whole words (Find/Replace option)	171
^W	Scroll showing upper line	74
X	Exit to operating system	54
^X	Move cursor down one line (same as ↓ key)	62
Y	Delete file	53
Y	Abandon print (Print option)	101
Y	"Yes" response to question	
^Y	Delete line	81
^Y	Delete entry (entering file name)	55
^Z	Scroll showing lower line	74
#	Set page number location in heading/footing	221
#	Set decimal tab in ^OI command	160
\	Print next character (heading/footing)	223
^	Used here to represent Control key	
@	Used here to represent Return key	
←(4)	Left one character (same as ^H, ^S, Backspace)	
→(6)	Right one character (same as ^D)	
↑(8)	Up one line (same as ^E)	
↓(2)	Down one line (same as ^X)	

Index

CUT HERE FOR CONDENSED INDEX OF WORDSTAR COMMANDS

CONDENSED INDEX OF WORDSTAR COMMANDS

(Numbers in parentheses are key at right; F numbers are keys at left.)

Move the Cursor

↑ (8) or ^E up one line
↓ (2) or ^X down one line
→ (6) or ^D one letter right
←(4) or ^S one letter left
^H or BACKSPACE one letter left
^F one word right
^A one word left
Home (7) or ^QE to top of screen
End (1) or ^QX to bottom of screen
^QS to beginning of line
^QD to end of line
F10 or ^QR to beginning of file
F9 or ^QC to end of file
^Q1 to place marker <1> (^Q0-9)
^QB to Block Beginning
^QK to block end
^QP to Previous position
^QV to block source or last ^QA/^QF entry

Scroll

^W reveal upper line
^Z reveal lower line
^QW continuous upper lines
^QZ continuous lower lines
PgUp (9) or ^R upper screenful
PgDn (3) or ^C lower screenful
^QQ(9) or ^QQR continuous screenful scroll, upper text
^QQ(3) or ^QQC continuous screenful scroll, lower text
^QD horizontal scroll right
^QS horizontal scroll left

Delete/Erase Commands

^G character at cursor column
DEL character at left
^T word at right
^Y entire line
^QY cursor to end of line (including cursor column)
^Q DEL cursor to beginning of line (excluding cursor column)
^KY displayed block

Enter Text

Ins or ^V Insertion on/off
^N insert hard return
^M same as return key
^I same as tab key
^ON remove variable tab
^OI set variable tab
^OF set margins/tabs from cursor line

Format Commands

^OC Center a line
^OL set Left margin F3 at cursor position
^OR set Right margin F4 at cursor position
^OS set line Spacing
F2 or ^OG paragraph tab
^B paragraph reform

Format Toggle Commands

^OW Word wrap on/off
^OT ruler display on/off
^OJ Justification on/off
^OH Hyphen-help on/off
^OE soft hyphen Entry on/off
^OD print control Display on/off
^OP Page break display on/off

Place Markers

^K0-9 set place marker
^Q0-9 find place marker

Save Commands

^KS Save and re-edit
^KD Done edit, return to no-file menu
^KX save, eXit from WordStar
^KQ abandon (Quit) edit

Miscellaneous Commands

^QQ repeat next command
^U interrupt command

Block Commands

F7 or ^KB mark beginning
F8 or ^KK mark end
^KH Hide/redisplay
^KV moVe block
^KC Copy block
^KY delete block
^KW Write displayed block to another file
^KR Read (insert) another file

Print Controls [use before and after]

F5 or ^PS underline
F6 boldface
^PD Doublestrike
^PV subscript
^PT superscript
^PX cross out
^PY change ribbon color

Print Controls

[use once]

^PO non-break space
^PH overprint next character
^PM overprint next line
^P@ overprint next line
^PK page # in heading/footing

[incremental printer]

^PA change to 12-pitch
^PA return to 10-pitch
^PC stop printer
^PF phantom space
^PG phantom rubout

Find/Replace Commands

^QF find
^QA find-and-replace

[Find Options]

N find nth appearance
U ignore upper/lower case
W match whole words only
B search backward from cursor position

[Replacement Options]

n replace n times
G search entire file, front to back
N no delay; automatic replace
plus U, W, B as above

[Special Characters in find/replace commands]

^PA any character
^PN line return
^PS any character not a letter or digit
^Ox any character other than x

While Answering Screen

^S delete character at left
^D restore character
^Y delete entry
^R restore entry
^F display file directory

File/Disk Options

^KR Read (insert) contents of another file
^KP Print another file
^KO cOpy another file
^KF display File directory on/off
^KJ delete another file
^KE rEname a file
^KL changed Logged drive

Help Commands

^JB explain paragraph reform
^JD explain Dot commands
^JI Index of commands
^JF explain screen Flags
^JS explain Status line
^JR explain Ruler line
^JM explain Margins and tabs
^JV explain moVing text
^JP explain place markers
F1 or ^JH set help level

At Help Level 2, 3

^J help menu
^K block menu
^O onscreen menu
^P print menu
^Q quick menu

Dot Commands

.PA page break
.CP conditional break
.OP omit default #
.PN restore default #
.PN change page #
.PC page # column
.PO offset left margin
.MT top margin
.HM heading margin
.MB bottom margin
.FM footing margin
.HE heading
.FO footing
.CW character width*
.LH line height*
.PL set page length
.SR subscript roll*
.UJ microjustification on/off*
.BP bidirectional printing on/off
.. nonprinting note
[*incremental printers only]

F-Function Keys

F1 set help level
F2 paragraph tab indent
F3 left margin at cursor
F4 right margin at cursor
F5 underline
F6 boldface
F7 mark block beginning
F8 mark block end
F9 cursor to end of file
F10 cursor to beginning of file